The Conflict and Culture Reader

The Conflict and Culture Reader

EDITED BY

Pat K. Chew

New York University Press

NEW YORK AND LONDON

NEW YORK UNIVERSITY PRESS
New York and London

Library of Congress Cataloging-in-Publication Data
The conflict and culture reader / Edited by Pat K. Chew.
p. cm.
Includes bibliographical references and index.
ISBN 0-8147-1578-8 (cloth : alk. paper) —
ISBN 0-8147-1579-6 (pbk. : alk. paper)
1. Social conflict. 2. Culture conflict. 3. Ethnic conflict.
4. Conflict management. I. Chew, Pat K., 1950– II. Title.
HM1121 .C66 2000
303.6—dc21   00-011951

New York University Press books are printed on acid-free paper,
and their binding materials are chosen for strength and durability.

Manufactured in the United States of America

10 9 8 7 6 5 4 3 2 1

*This book is dedicated
to Robert, Luke, and Lauren,
to my Chew family and my Kelley family.*

Contents

Acknowledgments   *xi*
To the Reader   *xiii*

PART I: Approaching Conflict and Culture: Inquiries, Assumptions, and Constructs

Introduction   3

1   Conflict Resolution in Intercultural Settings:
    Problems and Prospects   7
    Kevin Avruch and Peter W. Black

2   Culture, Negotiation, and the Eye of the Beholder   15
    Jeffrey Z. Rubin and Frank E. A. Sander

3   Preparing for Peace: Conflict Transformation across Cultures   17
    John Paul Lederach

4   Everyone Agrees to Peace   23
    Heather Forest

5   Practice and Paradox: Deconstructing Neutrality in Mediation   24
    Sara Cobb and Janet Rifkin

6   In a Grove   31
    Ryunosuke Akutagawa

7   Harmony Models and the Construction of Law   38
    Laura Nader

8   Vantage Point   45
    Pat K. Chew

9   Toward a Theory of Conflict and Culture   46
    Stella Ting-Toomey

10 Multimethod Probes of Individualism and Collectivism   52
    Harry C. Triandis, Christopher McCusker, and C. Harry Hui

    Further Comments   56
    Teaching Ideas   58

PART II: Gender and Conflict

    Introduction 63

11 The Necessity of Seeing Gender in Conflict 65
    Anita Taylor and Judi Beinstein Miller

12 In a Different Voice: Psychological Theory and
    Women's Development 74
    Carol Gilligan

13 The Mediation Alternative: Process Dangers for Women 80
    Trina Grillo

14 Role of Ethnic and Gender Differences in Mediated Conflicts 88
    James W. Grosch, Karen G. Duffy, and Paul V. Olczak

15 New Mexico Research Examines Impact of Gender and
    Ethnicity in Mediation 91
    Michele Hermann

16 The Architecture of Bias: Deep Structures in Tort Law 93
    Martha Chamallas

17 Gender and Conflict: What Does Psychological Research
    Tell Us? 95
    Loraleigh Keashly

18 Gender Regulation as a Source of Religious Schism 97
    Phil Zuckerman

19 Anti-Essentialism, Relativism, and Human Rights 109
    Tracy E. Higgins

    Further Comments 120
    Teaching Ideas 124

PART III: Ethnicity, Race, and Conflict

    Introduction 129

20 Conflict Resolution, Cultural Differences, and the Culture
    of Racism 133
    Howard Gadlin

21 "Eyes in the Back of Your Head": Moral Themes in
    African American Narratives of Racial Conflict 141
    Janie Victoria Ward

22 Use and Abuse of Race and Culture: Black-Korean Tension
    in America 152
    Kyeyoung Park

23 Both Edges of the Margin: Blacks and Asians in
Mississippi Masala, Barriers to Coalition-Building   163
Taunya Lovell Banks

24 Not Our Problem   167
Margaret Read MacDonald

25 Immigrants and Ethnics: Conflict and Identity
in Chicago Polonia   169
Mary Patrice Erdmans

26 To Set Right: Ho'oponopono, A Native Hawaiian Way
of Peacemaking   176
Manu Aluli Meyer

27 Individualizing Justice through Multiculturalism:
The Liberals' Dilemma   182
Doriane Lambelet Coleman

Further Comments   191
Teaching Ideas   197

PART IV: Global Perspectives

Introduction   203

28 Conflict Resolution among Peaceful Societies: The Culture
of Peacefulness   207
Bruce D. Bonta

29 A Critique of Western Conflict Resolution from a
Non-Western Perspective   220
Paul E. Salem

30 Conflict Resolution Approaches: Western and Middle Eastern
Lessons and Possibilities   230
Mohammed Abu-Nimer

31 The Relevance of Culture for the Study of Political Psychology
and Ethnic Conflict   236
Marc Howard Ross

32 The Power of Not Understanding: The Meeting of
Conflicting Identities   241
Z. D. Gurevitch

33 The Telltale Heart: Apology, Reparation, and Redress   249
Mari J. Matsuda and Charles R. Lawrence III

34 The Chinese Concepts of "Face"   252
Hsien Chin Hu

35   Pirates, Dragons, and U.S. Intellectual Property Rights in
     China: Problems and Prospects of Chinese Enforcement   261
     Glenn R. Butterton

36   Autonomous Lawmaking: The Case of the "Gypsies"   266
     Walter Otto Weyrauch and Maureen Anne Bell

37   Institutional Non-Marriage in the Finnish Roma Community
     and Its Relationship to Rom Traditional Law   276
     Martti Gronfors

38   Values in Tension: Ethics Away from Home   283
     Thomas Donaldson

39   Nisa: The Life and Words of a !Kung Woman   295
     Marjorie Shostak

40   How War Was Ended   302
     Heather Forest

     Further Comments   304
     Teaching Ideas   306

     Index   309
     About the Editor   313

Acknowledgments

My sincere thanks to the many individuals who offered their ideas and their support for this project. A number suggested specific works or authors to include in the reader. Given the limited space and particular focus of the book, I apologize for not being able to include many excellent pieces.

My thanks to the University of Pittsburgh School of Law and particularly to Dean David Herring and former dean Peter Shane; my secretary Marlene Mullin; and the Document Technology Center staff (LuAnn Driscoll, Karen Knochel, Darleen Mocello, Valerie Pompe, Barbara Salopek). My research assistant Lisa Martinelli helped identify and review potential articles.

Finally, my thanks to Niko Pfund of New York University Press, who believed in this book and is an ongoing source of encouragement and enthusiasm.

To the Reader

This book gathers together some of the most provocative writings on how conflict and culture interrelate. Thanks in part to ideas offered by literally hundreds of colleagues from all over the country, I was able to make a very extensive review of relevant writings from many disciplines. I quickly concluded that the book could not be a comprehensive or even necessarily a representative sampling of works on the topic. It could, however, provide a well-organized selection of pedagogically constructive pieces, offering both theoretical and practical perspectives from a range of disciplines and philosophical approaches. It could be both intellectually intriguing and relevant to today's pressing problems. Having taught various seminars and larger classes on this topic, I knew there was a need for such a book.

The book is organized into four major parts:(1) "Approaching Conflict and Culture: Inquiries, Assumptions, and Constructs", (2) "Gender and Conflict", (3) "Ethnicity, Race, and Conflict", and (4) "Global Perspectives." This organization allows you to mix and match the topics of most interest and relevance to your academic inquiries. Each part begins with some orienting comments, essentially describing the part's contents and my rationale for including these particular pieces. At the end of each part are "Further Comments" that describe other resources, expand on an issue, or juxtapose an idea to those found in the readings in that part. Also included are "Teaching Ideas" for further inquiries and exercises—intended to help the reader relate the issues to current contexts and disputes.

I think of this book as a journey into an important and fun topic, and the journey begins with some basics. Part 1 introduces the reader to some fundamental inquiries: What is culture? What is conflict? Why should we study the relationship between culture and conflict? It encourages the reader to be both cautious about these inquiries (for instance, about the danger of overgeneralizing) and open to varied and perhaps unfamiliar ways of thinking. This part also questions fundamental assumptions we may have about conflict and how these assumptions may be socially constructed. Analyzing different perspectives on culture in the abstract is very difficult, so this part ends with some specific constructs, such as individualism and collectivism, that provide useful reference points for this venture.

Part 2, "Gender and Conflict," considers how gender and conflict are interrelated and the ensuing implications of these interrelationships. It begins with basic inquiries: Why study gender and conflict? In what ways are "sex" and "gender" different? In what ways are power and power imbalances linked to gender and conflict? Included are classic pieces, such as Carol Gilligan's proposal that critical differences exist between girls'/women's and boys'/men's moral reasoning in resolving conflicts. Another is Trina Grillo's proposal that dispute resolution processes, such as mandatory mediation, can pose disproportionate dangers for women. Next is a sampling of cutting-edge research on intersections between conflict and gender. This is followed by a case study of a specific dispute in which issues of gender and religion are at the core. Finally, questions of cultural relativism are raised in the context of international human rights for women.

Part 3, "Ethnicity, Race, and Conflict," surveys the dispute resolution approaches of various racial and ethnic groups in the United States. While acknowledging the distinctive contributions of each group, the readings also explore the complications and challenges of this diversity. There are writings on Black-White conflict, conflict between the minority ethnic groups, and conflict within a single ethnic group. Cultural contexts range from those of Indigenous Americans to immigrant groups. Finally, issues of cultural relativism are revisited in the context of the "cultural defense"—where immigrant defendants argue that their criminal conduct is explainable in part by their immigrant norms and traditions. Should the American judicial system incorporate or reject these alternative value systems?

Part 4 explores global perspectives on culture and conflict, drawing from a range of geographical contexts. All the works, however, share a common purpose. They prompt us to reflect, to question, and at times to reframe our own, Western cultural model of conflict. Myriad issues are raised: What distinguishes peaceful societies from others? How do other countries' premises about conflict affect their approaches to conflict? What are dramatically different ways of thinking about conflict and its resolution? There are foci on Middle East disputes, Asian concepts such as "face," and Gypsy culture, among others. A discussion of cultural relativism offers continuity from Parts 2 and 3, although in this part the context is ethical dilemmas in international business. The part ends with a narrative by an African tribal woman, who describes with dignity and humor an interpersonal dispute and its resolution.

In this reader, some authors discuss a particular dispute resolution process such as negotiation, mediation, or another form of alternative dispute resolution, rather than discussing conflict resolution more generically. While the readings may discuss a particular process, they were selected in part because the issues they raise are applicable to dispute resolution more broadly. Perhaps some brief clarification on terminology would be helpful. "Alternative dispute resolution," sometimes abbreviated "ADR," refers to any process that is an alternative to litigation. There are many variations of ADR, although the most common ones are negotiation, mediation, and arbitration. Though these processes have many variations, each process has core characteristics. "Negotiation" is typically a discussion between opposing parties, with each party presumably acting in its self-interest and arguing on its own behalf. The parties try to reach a mutually acceptable resolution, typically without the help or intervention of a third party. "Mediation" is a process wherein the parties also try to resolve their own dispute but are assisted by a mediator. Mediators intervene in different ways; some assume more evaluative and expert roles, while others merely facilitate the parties' process. They do not, however, impose a binding resolution on the parties. "Arbitration" is typically a private forum where a third party, the arbitrator, listens to the opposing parties' arguments and comes to a binding decision.

Some editing comments: I omitted virtually all the footnotes and endnotes that accompanied the original writings. The citation for each original work, however, is provided on the first page of each chapter so that the interested reader-researcher can locate the notes and references. In many cases, the original text has been abridged for inclusion here. On rare occasions, and when the substance of the writing was not affected, I used a feminine or nongendered subject/pronoun instead of a male subject/pronoun to provide balance. Substantive editing is noted by brackets.

While numerous books on the general topic of culture and conflict exist, none explores these subject categories under one cover. Other books also tend to use writings from a particular discipline, whereas I intentionally sought out interdisciplinary perspectives. Herein are writings by anthropologists, sociologists, psychologists, law scholars, philosophers, historians, and "wise" people—among others. There is also variety in presentation. Some of this variety is explained by the fact that the book draws from many disciplines, and anthropologists, psychologists, and legal scholars do not "talk" alike. In addition, among these classic and cutting-edge pieces you'll find essays, narratives, fables, and, yes, even traditional academic writings. Finally, I looked for writings where the voice of the author was most clearly heard. Sometimes I agreed with what I heard, and sometimes I did not—but I believe that they are all worth listening to. While I admit to the subjectivity of my choices (and hearing), I hope that these writings speak to you as well.

Bon voyage,
Pat Chew

Part I

Approaching Conflict and Culture
Inquiries, Assumptions, and Constructs

Introduction

The pieces in Part 1 are intended to set the stage for the rest of the book. Kevin Avruch and Peter W. Black's article begins by explaining what "culture" and "conflict" are and why the study of their interrelationship is so important. They propose that culture is the lens through which we see conflict and learn to navigate it, and they illustrate a way in which to analyze an unfamiliar culture. But, as Jeffrey Z. Rubin and Frank E. A. Sander remind us in a short excerpt, there are challenges to studying conflict and culture—such as being ever mindful of the dangers of predicting a particular individual's behavior from cultural stereotypes. John Paul Lederach, a Mennonite scholar and cross-cultural trainer of conflict resolution processes, then invites us to contemplate other cultures and their approaches through an "elicitive" approach, where we are engaged as active and nonjudgmental learners. More typically, he observes, our inclination is to be "prescriptive," coming as experts and considering our own culture as the standard by which other cultural approaches should be compared. By being more elictive than ethnocentric, we stay open to the excitement of discovery and creation. Though Lederach's advice is intended for dispute resolution trainers, it is applicable to us as well.

The next set of contributions, by Sara Cobb and Janet Rifkin, Ryunosuke Akutagawa, and Laura Nader, encourage us to question and rethink some fundamental assumptions about conflict and culture. Cobb and Rifkin's article is based on communication theory and posits that the processes used to resolve disputes are not inherently neutral. The parties in a mediation tell their version of what happened. These narratives, depending on how the participants and mediator interpret them, become part of a "political" process in the sense that some become more dominant and some are suppressed. Next, Akutagawa's piece is a literary example of the power of the narrative. We listen to multiple and differing "stories" of the same tragic event in a Japanese bamboo grove, as told from the perspectives of different "witnesses." Consider how the causes of the conflict, the roles and motives of the participants, and the resolution are viewed by each person. Anthropologist Laura Nader then questions whether our positive impression of harmony and our goal of peace always make sense. Using numerous historical examples from various cultures, she illustrates instead that societal pressure or laws—in the pursuit of control and conformity—have been used to suppress and coerce individuals.

As we explore "cultures"—whether they be based on ethnicity, geographical boundaries, gender, religion, or other possibilities—it is useful to have guidelines by which to begin our analysis and to make some comparisons about each culture's approach to conflict. The reading by Stella Ting-Toomey describes one of the most utilized social science constructs for this purpose: "high-context" versus "low-context" conflict approaches that analyze what, when, and how conflict is dealt with in various cultures. Harry Triandis continues with an explanation of "individualism" versus "collectivism." These constructs have been widely researched in a range of cultures and have been directly linked to conflict resolution styles and values. Rather than limiting how we think about different cultures, these constructs are intended to be illustrative. While we should question the relevance of these and other guides, as we continue our journey, we should learn to devise our own evolving and meaningful constructs.

To know yet to think that one does not know is best; Not to know yet to think that one knows will lead to difficulty. It is by being alive to difficulty that one can avoid it.

—Lao Tzu

Chapter 1

Conflict Resolution in Intercultural Settings
Problems and Prospects

Kevin Avruch and Peter W. Black

To be fair, when one examines the concept of culture used by many theorists and practitioners in conflict resolution, one sees why it is so often relegated to a secondary place. In brief, "culture" in this view stands for rather superficial group differences. It is generally associated with descriptions of traditional, stereotypical modes of behavior, characteristic of some group of "others." Hence, such discussions of culture largely focus on questions of etiquette and tolerance. Culture is spoken of as though it were a thing, as if it were evenly distributed across members of the group of which it is an attribute, as though it were synonymous with "custom" and "tradition," and, finally, as if it were impervious to change through time. Such discussions also seem bedeviled by an intractable confusion between statements about cultural matters (those having to do, that is, with features of human consciousness) and statements about the actual behavior of individuals or groups of individuals. The point here is that culture is not reducible to behavior; to "know" a culture is not to be able to predict each and every act of each and every member of a group. In this vein, culture is sometimes treated merely as a label for group differences—as a way of naming the groups. This is especially true in intercultural conflict situations, where "culture" and "ethnicity" (or ethnic identity) are used synonymously. That these terms are unselfconsciously used this way by the parties to the conflict themselves—as well as by analysts or third-party interveners—is what makes the confusion intractable.

In contrast, our perspective on the role of culture in conflict arises from a conception of social life in which culture is seen to be a fundamental feature of human consciousness, the *sine qua non* of being human. It is held to be constitutive of human reality, including such behavioral manifestations of that reality as "conflict." Metaphorically speaking, culture is a perception-shaping lens or (still metaphorically) a grammar for the production and structuring of meaningful action. Therefore, an understanding of the behavior of parties to a conflict depends upon understanding the "grammar" they are using to render that behavior meaningful.

From Dennis J. Sandole and Hugo van der Merwe, *Conflict Resolution Theory and Practice: Integration and Application*, 131–140. Copyright © 1993 by Manchester University and reversion to Kevin Avruch and Peter W. Black.

If one wishes to understand conflict behavior, it is particularly useful to attend to the indigenous understandings of being and action which people use in the production and interpretation of social action. These understandings, like all cultural knowledge acquired through social learning, are organized into sets of propositions and prescriptions of various levels of complexity and generality. Providing one bears in mind their often inchoate, contradictory, and symbolic rather than logical organization, it makes sense to call such understandings "theories." The sets of understandings about conflict held *by the people involved* in a dispute are crucially important. We have called such cultural knowledge "ethnoconflict theories." These theories undergird the techniques or processes of conflict resolution used indigenously, which we have called "ethnopraxis." It is useful to consider theories and practices put forth by academics and practitioners in conflict resolution from the perspective of ethnotheory and ethnopraxis. All theory and practice—be it "scientific" or "folk"—rests on implicit assumptions about such culturally constituted beliefs as the nature of human nature. And, in its turn, every theory of conflict is but a piece of some general theory of action.

When the parties to a conflict come from different cultures—when the conflict is "intercultural"—one cannot presume that all crucial understandings are shared among them. Their respective ethnotheories, the notions of the root causes of conflict, and ethnopraxes, the local acceptable techniques for resolving conflicts, may differ one from another in significant ways. The first task of a third-party intervener in intercultural conflict situations is to pay serious analytical attention to these cultural dimensions. The third party must assay a *cultural analysis* of the situation.

Cultural Analysis

Conflict resolution in intercultural settings requires, perhaps on the part of the parties to the conflict and most certainly on the part of the third-party intervener, an analysis of the conflict that is also a cultural analysis. This cultural analysis is preliminary to other aspects of third-party intervention, although it may well continue throughout the intervention. What does such an analysis consist of, and what are its entailments?

In the terms and analogies we have used, one's own culture provides the "lens" through which we view and bring into focus our world; the "logic" (known as common sense) by which we order it; the "grammar" by which it makes sense. Above all, our culture provides ways of seeing, thinking, and feeling about the world which in essence define normality for us—the way things are and the way things ought to be. In intercultural encounters it is precisely one's sense of normality that may be put at risk. But in most people, a sense of normality is fairly well established and pretty well defended. So rather than question our own normality, we tend to assert the relative abnormality, the strangeness and bizarreness of the other: "the French are arrogant"; "the English are cold"; "Moroccans are untrustworthy." In most intercultural encounters, in fact, moments of noncomprehension and unintelligibility are deflected and dismissed by being glossed over by terms laden with value-judgments. Not only do the French think about this differently than we do, but they are "wrong" (arrogant, rude, etc.) to do so. Thus, intercultural encounters present us with situations (other peoples' behaviors and understandings) that appear strange and bizarre; our common sense labels them as such and our moral sense evaluates them as good or (more likely) bad. To revert to the lens metaphor, our own culture seems to us transparent, and the world seen through it seems to us veridical, simply the way things are. A glimpse of the world *through* another culture (one possible result of an intercultural encounter) presents us with areas of opacity, things we cannot see through clearly. We demarcate these; then we set about dismissing them.

A cultural analysis demands first that one *stops* at moments of noncomprehension and unintelligibility; that one resists deflecting them dismissively (and pleasurably) in moral terms; that one makes them—the seemingly opaque and unintelligible—the objects of scrutiny. In short, the analyst is well advised to remain reflexively attuned to the disconcerting moment. To turn to one's advantage the sensation of surprise is not an easy thing to do, however, because it demands that one resists such dismissive reflexes when being faced with the strange and bizarre. Second, a cultural analysis is a scrutiny with a peculiar sort of goal. "Cultural analysis," writes Raymonde Carroll, in a study of French-American cultural misunderstandings, is "a means of perceiving as 'normal' things which initially seem 'bizarre' or 'strange' among people of a culture different from one's own." It is a way of making transparent that which first appeared as opaque. "To manage this," Carroll continues, "I must imagine a universe in which the 'shocking' act can take place and seem normal, can take on meaning without even being noticed."

The key word here is "meaning," of course. Since our culture provides us with systems of symbols by which meaning is asserted (or, as often as not, negotiated) and established in the world, a cultural analysis at root is the searching out of meaning in these systems of symbols. When directed toward a culture different from our own, such an analysis orients us to different meanings—other lenses, other logics, other grammars. Notice that in principle one can attempt a cultural analysis of one's own culture, and in practice as well, although many anthropologists deem this to be a much harder analysis—because one is usually not "stopped" by moments of noncomprehension and unintelligibility in dealings with one's own culture. This is exactly what one's own culture allows one to avoid. It takes a subtler mind and a more perverse sensibility (not to mention perhaps a case of chronic and clinical alienation) to allow oneself to be struck by, and stop at, the utterly familiar and veridical. And of course, conceptually, one result of a cultural analysis of one's own culture produces an effect opposite to that done on another culture. Aimed at one's own culture, such an analysis can have the eerie effect of rendering the previously "normal" both strange and bizarre. It can make opaque that which was transparent. It is almost always unsettling, very often critical, and so usually taken by others to be subversive—or surreal.

So much for what a cultural analysis is; how does one do it? Carroll uses the word "imagine" as a kind of shorthand answer to this question. Is this a methodology? Clearly any sort of analysis introduced with reference to subtle minds, perverse sensibilities, and clinical alienation—not to mention shameless recourse to metaphors like opacity and its opposite—is likely to seem problematic to social or behavioral scientists used to the comforting rigors of formal techniques for testing operationalized hypotheses. Nevertheless, there is a method for pursuing cultural analysis. Although it may take a certain sensibility to do it easily or well (and what methodology doesn't?), it certainly does not demand a mystical or occult one.

Here we follow (part of the way, at least) the now classic account found in Geertz, and its very lucid précis by Carroll. For Geertz, the essence of a cultural analysis is that it consists of "thick description," an ethnographic presentation of an event (a conversation, a person, a practice, a dispute, a belief, etc.) that stresses the placement of the event, for the social persons who enact it, within deeper and deeper, richer and richer, more and more layered contexts of meaning ("structures of signification," in Geertz's words). Carroll's interest lies in using cultural analysis to explore specific intercultural (French-American) misunderstandings; thus she emphasizes how one would go about describing something "thickly."

First, if one is trying to analyze the culture of another, be on the lookout for the bizarre: recognize the opacities. Be prepared to stop and avoid the social scientist's tendency to immediately explain (and explain *away*) the phenomenon by reference to causal theories—psychodynamic, materialist, ecological, or biological, to name a few. Because culture does not "cause" behavior—neither aggression, nor the business cycle, nor the grand flow of history—cultural analysis is not causal analysis. Precisely where causal analysis and cultural analysis come together, if they do, has been a matter of some considerable intramural debate between those committed to "interpretive" and "explanatory" anthropology. Simplifying the debate, one camp allows cultural analysis in as part of the ethnographic, descriptive stage—as a database-provider for the powerful Science (the theories of underlying causality) to come. The other camp asserts that cultural analysis *is* the science to come. When it comes to the understanding of human social action, these partisans maintain, the inscription and specification of meaning is the terminus (and an asymptotic one, at that) of our enquiry. For the first camp, ethnography serves Science; for the second, the science consists of Ethnography.

Our own position in this debate lies at neither extreme, but is rather more respectful of the search for causes(cybernetically construed, at any rate) than not. In fact, it is our respect for the power of causal theories—which tend to be indiscriminately omnivorous of databases in the hands of the naive or scientistic—that makes us place such a high premium on the avoidance of explaining away before one has the chance to explain. In this more limited sense, then, we agree with Geertz and Carroll that in cultural analysis one is not operating in the same conceptual domain as in causal analysis.

The second thing to be on the lookout for is the glossing of the strange with value-judgments ("the English are cold", "the French are rude," and so forth). These propositions are not so dissimilar in fact to the first set we advised avoiding: value-judgments are, after all, causal explanations put in the modality of a moral discourse; they are the "science" of our own culture's common sense. For most of us most of the time, the value-judgment, the moral accounting, is entirely sufficient as explanation. Too many social scientists, however, use value-judgments as a way-station to a fully causal explanation: "Why did your colleague say that to you at the departmental meeting? He is French, you know; they are rude. . . . And why are they rude, you ask? Didn't you know they are all weaned with vinegar?" (psychodynamic); "The red wine they drink to excess inhibits endorphin production" (biological); and so on.

Next, having been struck (stopped) by the opaque or the strange and having avoided moralizing, psychologizing, biologizing, ecologizing, or economicizing it away, one gets down to its proper, thick, description. This involves recording it ("inscribing" it, in the text-oriented work of these analysts) and, text now before you, contextualizing it. Simply put, this key procedure (or act of imagination, in Carroll's term) requires that like "text" be put into different, deeper, and more widely ramifying frames of meaningful reference. As the frames of reference ramify, the initial strangeness should begin to ease; within the deepening and widening contexts of the cultural analysis, at least, the bizarre should begin to make sense, the opaque reveal the shadow of what lies behind it. One begins to translate. It is during this inscription/contextualization process that the true, the *interpretive*, nature of the enterprise emerges.

To call any analysis "interpretive" immediately raises questions of validity and verification. Such questions are justified. All interpretations—at least in our world—are not equal. An interpretation should be judged by how well it accounts for and explains—in the sense of "makes meaningful"—other aspects of the culture that appear bizarre, or the same aspect as it appears in the culture in other "texts." This is not, of course, "prediction" in the sense promised by covering-law, causal theories. It is closer to the "retrodiction" of a grammatical analysis: tell us the sentence just now uttered; we will tell you if it is grammatically appropriate in that language.

Finally, since one is always and necessarily doing this from the standpoint of one's own cultural presuppositions, the entire process is iterative. One is always in effect tacking back and forth in cultural analysis: between an interpretation that makes sense in the other culture and a translation—for every translation is also an interpretation—that makes sense in your own. (This is a simple gloss on the "hermeneutical circle" formed between interpreter and text.) In this sense we would argue that a cultural analysis is in fact the paradigmatic form of an enlightened intercultural encounter—one that is now ready for problem-solving.

Intercultural Encounters

Consider an American tourist in a foreign land. She does not speak the language (needless to say). She asks an old man, a native of the country, for directions to the train station. The old man does not speak English. He looks at the tourist quizzically. The tourist repeats her question, this time in a louder voice. From the old man another quizzical look, perhaps a nod of the head or shrug of the shoulders. The tourist speaks yet more loudly and, looking around, tries to imitate (pulling an imaginary cord to train whistle: "choo, choo") the sound of a train. Now the quizzical look becomes open amusement, but still without comprehension. The tourist looks around again and sees a young boy approaching them. "Do you speak English?" "A little." "Do you know where the train station is?" "I do not, but I will ask this old man." And he does, and the tourist will make her train.

What makes this little scenario the very model of an opaque intercultural encounter is, of course, the fact that neither party speaks the language of the other. Our tourist tries to get around this first by raising her voice (a reflexive, but not a bad, first option: in a monolingual setting, it probably is the case that noncomprehension is linked to not hearing the message, perhaps because of noise). Then she tries to bypass speech and use an alternative channel of communication: gesture and mimicry. The first option, raising the voice, consists of simply repeating the original message in the original code and medium, but varying physical parameter (amplitude). The second option is of a different order entirely and consists of a transformation of the original message and code. Here, the tourist is attempting a translation of her question into a (gestural) code she believes is more universal than (even) English. Alas, she is wrong, for in this native's land the gesture of pulling on a cord signifies a bad attack of dysentery, while the sound "choo, choo" conventionally signifies a male's appreciation of an attractive female. Not surprisingly (but nevertheless fortunately), the old man is amused. Luckily, a third party comes along—a native himself—who shares enough of the tourist's linguistic code to be able to interpret and translate the question.

A "cultural analysis" of this encounter could be rudimentary, indeed. The opacity, the noncomprehension, was simply the result of mutual nonsharing of linguistic codes, and the third party was an interpreter in the weakest sense of that term. Moreover, the problem that needed solution—directions to the train station—was simple enough and straightforward enough that the third party's admitted limitations as an interpreter (he spoke a "little" English) were not fatal. Moreover, in this scenario the older native was merely amused by the tourist's gestures—rather than offended, angered, insulted, and moved to retaliate in kind. If he had been, then we might imagine the third party as having a more substantial and difficult role to play. Correspondingly, our cultural analysis of the encounter (anger and passion have colored the opacity: why?) grows more complex. The tourist's recourse to a code—gesture and body language—that she thought was generic or universal turned out to be neither, although it was definitely full of meaning. The third party, *even if he understood what the tourist meant*, might find it harder to translate the gestures and placate his countryman. "Translation" implies that the third party attempts a cultural analysis of the tourist's gestures (what Americans *mean* by "choo, choo"), and "placation" implies that he communicates the results of his analysis to his countryman (and that such communication is feasible or likely: can a young boy mollify an old man, appropriately, in this culture? Maybe not, if the old man seems to get angrier and angrier). And now, the third party's limitations—intellectual, temperamental, or social-structural—as an interpreter (a cultural analyst) and problem-solver might well prove fatal.

This scenario—the revised one, in which the older native becomes angry—is a model intercultural encounter in another sense. For here we have an instance of a conflict that we can say with assurance is caused by "culture." To be more precise, the conflict is a result of cultural *differences* in the interpretation of meaning, by the parties, of the same events: the initial noncomprehension (what are you trying to say?) compounded subsequently by misapprehension (just who the hell are you accusing of diarrheal lechery?). Such intercultural conflicts "caused" by culture do occasionally occur, of course, and they are the ones most amenable to thin cultural analysis on the level of explaining to the parties involved the differential etiquettes at play. They are the ones where problem-solving can be reduced to simply correcting "a failure to communicate." But while such conflicts do occur, they should not be taken as representative of most conflictual intercultural encounters, and certainly not of conflicts of the deeply rooted sort.

This is so for two reasons. First, many intercultural encounters take place in shared linguistic settings, for instance nation-state diplomacy (where diplomats use English or French) or intranational interethnic disputes. In these cases, the shared language (the presumed mutual comprehension) can actually mask paralinguistic or other deeper cultural differences. Shared language can fool the parties into thinking much else, or all else, is shared as well. Second, and more profoundly, although it is only sometimes the case that cultural differences can themselves be said to account for *all* of the noncomprehension, and thus *all* of the reasons for the conflict, it is always the case that culture molds the ways in which the parties understand what the conflict is about, how to carry on through it, and what possible resolutions look like. In the rather homely and synthetic scenarios we have been spinning thus far, we can imagine the distinction in this way: If two parties, speaking different languages (cultures), think they are both vying for the same *pie*, but it turns out that one is really after the bottle of *lye*, then the dispute was about their noncomprehension, and a simple translation ought to solve the problem in a positive-sum (win-win) manner. But, if it turns out that both parties really do want the same pie (and each wants all of it), then translation serves only to clarify what the conflict is about (an important step, to be sure), but it does not represent its solution. The conflict is about control of valued resources; it is *about* the pie. Here we have encapsulated of the core of the "realist" position in international relations and much of the "materialist" position in the other social sciences. But the conflict also is very much about why certain resources—things like pies— are valued, about how one ought to fight over them (and how to fight to win), about how fights end, and about the costs, bearable and unbearable, involved. And these parts of the conflict, always present, are culturally constituted; they comprise ethnotheory.

So much for synthetic scenarios. They have the virtue of allowing us to introduce wrinkles and manipulate variables at will—now we have insulted the old man. We can also find the same processes at work in the "real world." At the level of nation-state diplomacy, for example, Raymond Cohen has written extensively of the cultural factors which have complicated recent Egyptian-Israeli relations. Preferring an auditory metaphor to the visual one (lenses and opacity) used here, he has characterized the Egyptian-Israeli case as a sort of "dialogue of the deaf," marked by the "symmetrical autism" of mutual and costly noncomprehension.

Writing about the 1979–1981 Iranian hostage crisis, William Beeman has focused on the key cultural understandings ("beliefs") that marked the Americans' perception of how foreign policy ought to be pursued, and how these perceptions contributed to the American mishandling of the crisis and the new revolutionary regime.

On the intranational interethnic front, where language is shared, Thomas Kochman has written incisively of the many cultural differences that bedevil interactions between African-American and white in the United States. These differences include the differential valences in both cultures between argument and confrontation; the appropriate role that emotionality should play in discussions and negotiations; how male-female interactions ought to play out; how to know when a "fight" has really begun; whether information about a person is akin to private property; what constitutes valid "truths" or evidence, or guilt or responsibility—in other words, matters of fundamental importance. In a real sense, the sharing of a common language serves here only to cover up profound differences in perception, style, and moral evaluations of conflictual behaviors.

Again on the interethnic front, a similar situation is described by Edward Hall (a pioneer in the exploration of intercultural encounters) for Anglo- and Spanish-Americans in New Mexico. We quote at length to give some flavor of the process:

> In Anglo-American disputes, one progresses by steps and stages—from subtle innuendo and coolness (one must be polite) to messages via a third-party, to verbal confrontation, then legal action, and finally force—if nothing has worked and the law is on your side. For the Spanish-American, another system is used. First there is brooding . . . and, since verbal confrontation is to be avoided, the "If I could have found my tongue, I would not have struck him" law is applied. The first inkling that something is wrong is a show of force. Force or action is to the Spanish-American not a step in a chain but a communication in itself. It is designed to get attention. Later, much later in the process, they resort to the courts.[1]

Each of these examples, alluded to briefly here, is much richer—thicker and more complex—than the simple and made-up scenario of the old man, the young man, and the monolingual tourist. Each invites—demands—a cultural analysis as a key component of intercultural conflict resolution or problem-solving.

NOTE

1. This quote by Edward Hall, marked by his characteristic lucidity and sense of prescriptiveness, is a good place to repeat the caution we noted earlier in our discussion of culture and behavior. A cultural model for conflict (or anything else) is not a prediction for a given individual's behavior in a given situation. (One should not mistake the map for the territory.)

Chapter 2

Culture, Negotiation, and the
Eye of the Beholder

Jeffrey Z. Rubin and Frank E. A. Sander

To understand why culture should be so powerful an organizing stimulus, it is first necessary to understand the contributing role of labeling and stereotyping in our interpersonal perceptions. Social psychologists have observed that although we typically dismiss labeling (and the stereotyping to which it leads) as problematic, stereotyping has several apparent "benefits": First, it allows the perceiver to reduce a world of enormous cognitive complexity into terms of black versus white, good versus evil, friend versus enemy—thereby making it easier to code the things and people one sees. Second, armed with stereotypes, it becomes far easier to communicate in shorthand fashion with others who we suspect share our views; "He's such a boy" conveys lots of (stereotypic) information very, very quickly, as does the time-worn phrase "ugly American."

On the other hand, if stereotypes allow us to reduce cognitive complexity to simple terms, and to convey our perceptions in shorthand fashion, then it is also true that stereotypes rob both perceiver and "victim" of a sense of underlying individuality. Instead of understanding other people as highly complex and differentiated individuals, the perceiver trades nuance for simplicity. And sadly, the object of stereotypic judgments is deprived of individuality, and is instead rendered a pigeon-holed occupant of some set of preconceived notions. Once these preconceived notions are set in place, there is little that the object of stereotyping can do to undo or reverse these prejudices.

What, then, are some implications of this brief essay for more effective negotiation across cultural/national boundaries? First, while cultural/national differences clearly do exist, much of what passes for such differences may well be the result of expectations and perceptions which, when acted upon, help to bring about a form of self-fulfilling prophecy. Perhaps the best way to combat such expectations is to go out of one's way to acquire as much information as one can beforehand about the way people in other cultures view the kind of problem under consideration. Thus, if we are negotiating with a German about a health care contract, we should

From *Negotiation Journal* 249 (1991).

try to find out whatever we can about how Germans tend to view health care. Of course, in large countries, there may be regional variations that also need to be taken into account.

Second, it is important to enter into such negotiations with self-conscious awareness of the powerful tendency we share toward stereotyping; this kind of consciousness-raising may, in its own right, help make it a bit less likely that we will slip into a set of perceptual biases that overdetermine what transpires in the negotiations proper.

Third, it is important to enter into negotiations across cultural/national lines by trying to give your counterpart the (cultural) benefit of the doubt. Just as you would not wish others to assume that you are nothing more than an exemplar of people from your culture, try to avoid making the same mistaken assumption about the other person. Few of us, if asked to characterize an American negotiation style, would be able to do so, arguing that the differences between Texans and Bostonians, Hawaiians and Tennesseans, are so vast that it makes no sense whatever to attempt a single characterization. Yet we are often willing to seek information about the Japanese negotiating style, the French way of conducting international business, and so forth. Unless and until proven otherwise, it is wise to begin by assuming that differences within a culture or national group are as profound as the differences between various groups. In short, we should be continually open to treating what we learned about the foreign culture as simply a hypothesis, to be constantly tested against the data that we are in fact continually receiving.

Some of our colleagues, when asked their advice about how best to prepare for negotiations with others from different cultures and nationalities, argue that one simply cannot prepare. Others take the position that there really are no differences of any consequences; the underlying process or negotiation is thus assumed to be generalizable across boundaries of setting and culture/nationality. Still others urge negotiators to read manuals on how foreigners negotiate, thereby attempting to gain some necessary additional leverage. Finally, there are those who recommend that a negotiator hire a counterpart from the culture in which negotiations are about to take place, and have that individual carry out the negotiations in question.

We are of the view that, while the above advice may have its place, and while cultural differences certainly do exist, probably the wisest thing any of us can do to prepare for such negotiations is to: be aware of our biases and predispositions; acquire as much information as possible about our counterpart as an individual; and learn as much as we can about the norms and customs (of all kinds) that are to be found in our counterpart's home country.

One final thought: Although our focus has been primarily on cultural issues, we believe that similar considerations apply to other differences that come into play in negotiation, such as gender, race, and age. Here, too, we can become more effective negotiators acknowledging the possible effects of labeling on the negotiating process, while remaining open to information about our counterpart as an individual.

Chapter 3

Preparing for Peace
Conflict Transformation across Cultures

John Paul Lederach

The dusty road seemed to go on forever. Outside of Panama City the macadam became gravel, and the gravel mostly dust, rivets, and potholes in the middle of dry season as we made our way to Yaviza, the remote town near the Colombian border. There, some six hours out of the capital, the highway ends and travel begins by canoe, horse, or foot.

My heart jumped as we entered the school compound at the edge of Yaviza where I was to give a week-long training seminar on conflict resolution to leaders of the indigenous Wounaan and Embere communities. The participants of the seminar came out to greet the arrival of our pickup, some of them having come from as far away as two days' travel by canoe. Looking back at my journal entry, I remember a feeling of anxiety and challenge paralleled by the words of Father Niall O'Brien in the opening lines of the book on his Asian experience. "I thought again," he wrote, "how presumptuous I had been in coming to the Philippines thinking only to teach. The truth was most of the time I was the one learning."

The purpose of this chapter is to provide a comparison of the prescriptive and elicitive models. In building these models, I have suggested that they represent typifications on extreme ends of a spectrum and not exact descriptions of actual training practice. In real life, any given training inevitably has some elements of both. However, setting up the spectrum and comparing these models help us to identify a number of key aspects about how we approach both training and the complex issue of culture.

Comparing the Models

There are numerous areas where the differences between the two models emerge with clarity. Each of these could well merit a detailed explanation; however, the

From *Preparing for Peace: Conflict Transformation across Cultures*, by John Paul Lederach (Syracuse: Syracuse University Press, 1995), 3, 63–69, 89–92. By permission of the publisher.

purpose here is to provide a summary, highlighting the key distinctions, as laid out in Figure 3.1.

In the prescriptive model, training is conducted on the basis of transfer, of passing on to the participants the approach, strategy, and technique mastered by the trainer. The event itself is built around providing, teaching, and learning a specific model of conflict resolution. The elicitive approach, on the other hand, undertakes training as an opportunity and an encounter for participants in a given setting to discover and create models of conflict resolution in the context of their setting. This fundamental difference in how training is understood and approached creates a number of distinct features in the two models.

The guiding framework for the prescriptive approach lies in the how to's, in other words, in providing recipes suggesting how conflict and its management ought to be pursued. The guiding elicitive framework is constructed around the what do's, in providing a process for people to engage what they know and build from that knowledge.

Thus, in the elicitive model, the participants and the knowledge they bring about conflict in their setting are a significant resource in the training. The prescriptive approach, however, underscores the centrality of the trainer's models and knowledge. In the latter instance, training is content oriented, with the express purpose of having the participants master the approach and techniques. The trainer plays out the role of expert, providing a model for how the technique works and facilitating the event. The elicitive model is process oriented, providing an opportunity for people to participate in model discovery and creation. The trainer constructs a role of catalyst and facilitator.

Both models can create dynamic education to empower people, but do so from a different basis. The prescriptive approach empowers participants inasmuch as they learn and master new ways, techniques, and strategies for facing and handling conflict. The elicitive pursues empowerment as validating and building from resources that are present in the setting.

Training and Culture

Succinctly, the prescriptive approach sees culture as technique. The elicitive understands culture as a seedbed and as a foundation. Both perspectives merit further exploration.

At one level, prescription assumes a certain amount of universality. The model is transfer based: knowledge and experience that has emerged from and has been applied in a particular cultural context is now moving to another. The premise of universality suggests not only that such a transfer can successfully take place across lines of culture, class, and context but further that the techniques are culturally neutral. Participants who learn the basic components and techniques involved in the model can and will adapt them to meet their particular cultural context and needs. At a second level, the prescriptive approach sees culture itself as an

FIGURE 3.1
Prescriptive/Elicitive: A Comparative Summary

Prescriptive and Elicitive

Prescriptive ◄───► Elicitive

Training as transfer	Training as discovery and creation
Resource: Model and knowledge of trainer	Resource: Within-setting knowledge
Training as content oriented: Master approach and technique	Training as process oriented: Participate in model creation
Empowerment as learning new ways and strategies for facing conflict	Empowerment as validating and building from context
Trainer as expert, model, and facilitator	Trainer as catalyst and facilitator
Culture as technique	Culture as foundation and seedbed

area of advanced training. Here, practitioners already trained in the basic model receive advanced levels of skill training related to culture. This training is often reduced to short recipes: how to recognize cultural differences, how to work with a given ethnic group, or how to negotiate effectively across cultures.

In these approaches, culture is understood primarily as a special area of technique, an assumption that makes few if any provisions for two key factors. First, such a transfer can easily sidestep the resources available in a given context by embracing those coming from outside the setting. And second, the working assumption that the incoming model is culturally neutral and applicable across contexts is taken at face value. In fact, the incoming model is embedded with culture but is rarely recognized as such.

For example, if I use a prescriptive approach to teach Hondurans how to do neighborhood mediation, based on my experiences in Virginia, my model will carry implicit cultural assumptions common to a Virginia setting. These assumptions will affect how participants see the role of the third parties and conflictants; the pace, purpose, and style of communication; and the purpose of the resolution process—to name a few. I will likely also make more concrete cultural assumptions in terms of specific conflict-resolution techniques that are fundamental to the implementation of the model we use in Virginia. For example, conflictants may be expected to be autonomous decision-makers, who can openly and directly talk about their problems and negotiate an agreement in a two-hour "session" in my office.

Given a fundamental proclivity toward technique skill development in most trainings, many of the techniques will be based on suggestions evolving around language and communication patterns common to the Virginia setting, for example. In a pure prescriptive approach, I would likely use role plays developed around typical cases I have experienced in Virginia, which are useful for highlighting aspects of the process or practicing the model. Each and every one of these aspects of training includes implicit cultural assumptions, which are often appropriate and helpful to a particular sociolinguistic context and community but are foreign and may even be counterproductive in others.

In sum, prescription suggests universality of technique. Transfer into different cultural contexts is accomplished through model adjustments or minimization of the relative importance of cultural boundedness in the proposed model to be transferred.

On the other side, the elicitive approach does not see culture as an element to be added as a further level of technique or as a challenging complication to which techniques must be adapted. Cultural context and knowledge about conflict-in-setting make up the foundation through which the model development happens. Participants' natural knowledge, their way of being and doing, their immediate situation, their past heritage, and their language are seen as the seedbed in which the training and model building will be rooted. Validating and exciting these cultural elements as resources is the fundamental goal of the training endeavor.

Editor's Note: Lederach later describes his use of the elicitive approach with Central American groups. He poses the following questions to the groups: Whom do you turn to when there is conflict? Why that person? What do you expect from that person? Through various group discussions, the Central Americans and Lederach begin to identify a number of common words, images, and themes that will prove useful in building one piece of their dispute resolution model.

First, key to why certain people are chosen were the ideas of "trustworthiness," that "we know them," that "they know us" and can "keep our confidences." These terms often came together in a single overarching concept: *confianza*, a profoundly cultural term that is inadequately translated as trust or confidence. In several groups, *confianza* became a key to understanding how they work at conflict and how they think about resolution and healing. *Confianza* points to relationship building over time, to a sense of "sincerity" a person has and a feeling of "security" the person "inspires" in us that we will "not be betrayed." *Confianza* is a key for "entry" into the problem and into the person with whom we have the problem. From the eyes of everyday experience in Central America, when I have a problem with someone I do not look for an outside professional. Rather, I look for someone I trust who also knows the other person and is trusted by them. This kind of person can give "orientation" and "advice." Through this person, entry is accomplished.

Second, a number of terms often emerged around the idea of "support," "talk," and "listening." These almost always involved a popular term for an informal chat, *platicar*. This is more than simply "talking." It involves cultural understanding of communicative mechanisms for "sharing," "exchanging" and "checking things out." *Platicar* is fundamentally a way of being with another, of reaffirming the relationship, and in many more delicate situations of preparing the way for "dialogue" that may involve confrontation. Through the *platica* people feel "supported," "heard," "understood," and "accompanied."

Third, people want "help," "advice," and "direction." From others we seek "paths" that can lead us "out of the problem." Often, in working with these words and concepts, two ideas stood out. First, was the concept of looking for or

FIGURE 3.2
The Ins and Outs of Conflict Help in Central America

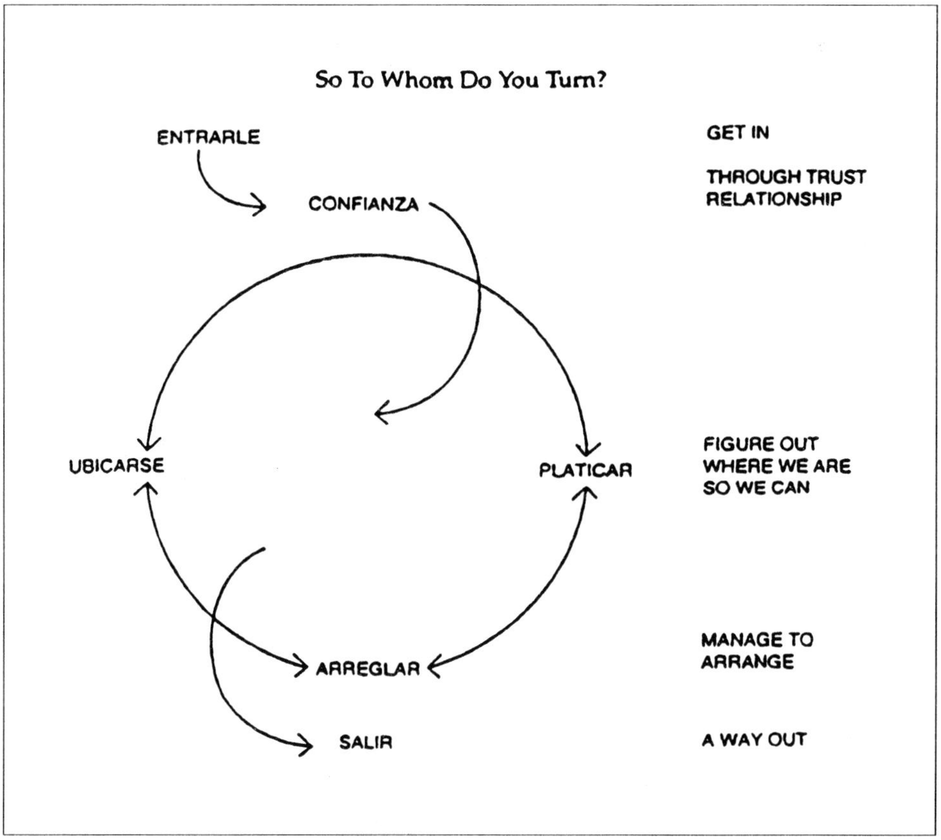

So To Whom Do You Turn?

ENTRARLE

CONFIANZA

GET IN

THROUGH TRUST
RELATIONSHIP

UBICARSE

PLATICAR

FIGURE OUT
WHERE WE ARE
SO WE CAN

ARREGLAR

MANAGE TO
ARRANGE

SALIR

A WAY OUT

giving *consejo*, or advice. At a popular level, conflict resolution thinking is advice driven and sought. But it is not in the sense of giving advice that North American helping professions may advise against. Seeking and giving advice often has more to do with participation in seeking solution—in other words, brainstorming—than in narrowing to choose action or impose solution. Looking for advice is seeking the pool of collective wisdom, seeking support and understanding. Thus, in the course of a conversation, much advice may be batted around, providing the seeker with a sense of solidarity and ideas. Additionally, people often talked about the idea of *ubicarse*, which literally is to "locate oneself," or in our vernacular, "figuring out where I am." Getting advice, "identifying the problems," providing "orientation" are all part of figuring out what's going on, where I am, and where I should go.

Finally, a number of terms emerge around the concern of how I "get out" of this mess. People look for "solutions" most often understood as an *arreglo*, an "arrangement" This term combines a number of ideas, from "fixing things" and "putting things back together" to "getting an agreement" or "understanding."

Key to an *arreglo* is a way of thinking that is holistic in nature, that is, seeing one-self and the problem in the context of a network rather than as isolated from it. Thus, an "arrangement" creates a *salida*, a common term meaning a way out, but a way out that maintains the network and relationship and fosters dignity. In other words, it saves face.

Pulling these ideas together, one group in Costa Rica outlined their understanding of how we get in and out of conflict and provide "help" by building on their terms as guidelines.

It is worth noting that this overall outline resonates with important metaphors and images common to the way people think about conflict in a Central American setting. The language of conflict describes a journey involving the tasks of getting in, figuring out where we are, and getting out. In fact, this set of concepts helps reinforce key cultural premises: a focus on relationship, trust building, restoration of community, and use of people in the network. It focuses on being with others as a mode of restoration rather than applying technique as a mode of resolving problems.

In terms of model building, we are now in a position to take a further step. Each of these words—such as *confianza* or *arreglar*—has rich cultural and practical meaning and represents important organizing categories for model building. These common, everyday terms describing the action of working on the restoration of relationship and the resolution of conflict, renamed, become empowering tools. The model-building exercise rooted these words and processes within the culture and encouraged participants to name them, providing categories for further discovery, for exploration, and for use as the building blocks of a more explicit model.

Important questions can now guide the next steps in understanding more fully the applicability and implementation of the model: What are the approaches to building *confianza*? How does one pursue *la platica*? What are constructive elements for getting situated and arranging a way out?

Chapter 4

Everyone Agrees to Peace

Heather Forest

A sly fox tried to trick a rooster into coming down from [its] perch.

"[Friend] Bird," the fox said, "come down for a chat!"

"No," said the rooster. "I'm sure you'd eat me."

"Oh, I wouldn't," said the crafty fox. "Haven't you heard? Everyone has agreed to live in peace."

"Is that so?" said the rooster, who was just as crafty. Stretching its neck, the rooster pretended to look at something far in the distance.

"What are you looking at?" asked the curious fox.

"Oh, just a pack of hungry fox hounds headed right this way."

On hearing this, the fox trembled in its tracks and ran off.

"Come back!" crowed the rooster. "Why are you running away? I thought you said that everyone had agreed to live in peace."

"Well, perhaps those hungry hounds haven't heard about it yet," said the fox as it bounded away.

—Tale from Ancient Greece

From Heather Forest, *Wisdom Tales from Around The World* (Little Rock: August House, 1996), 48.

Chapter 5

Practice and Paradox
Deconstructing Neutrality in Mediation

Sara Cobb and Janet Rifkin

Political Processes in Mediation

Narrative processes in mediation are the machinery by which one description/explanation becomes dominant, accepted, and used as the "natural" description of a set of events. Alternative stories that contest the dominant story can be either colonized or silenced altogether; some narratives dominate by construing other stories as "crazy" or "bad" and, in doing so, establish themselves as legitimate, appropriate, and "true." The social processes by and through which stories come to dominate the discursive field can be referred to as "hegemonic" processes—those political processes involved in the production of consensus in the discourse.[1]

In mediation, these political processes are visible in cases where one side never tells its own story; it simply refutes or denies the story told by the other.[2] In these cases, one story is colonized by a dominant story; the "silenced" remain delegitimized, frozen inside of negative descriptions that impose moral, legal, and perhaps economic sanctions. And unwittingly, the "silenced" contribute to their own oppression and domination by arguing on the grounds set for them by others.

Political processes are also visible in the domination of a particular plot line: some people chain events together in very linear ways, while others "knit" a set of events together and the logics are more circular. Many times the "linear" plot (more often than not told by males) will predominate over a "circular" plot (more often than not told by women). Still other political moments are visible when a "legal" discourse based on a rhetoric of "rights" is used instead of a discourse of "relationships" to set "the" moral context in place. As discourses provide speakers with moral and political grounds for the elaboration of their stories and contesting others' stories, the domination of one discourse over another has clear implications for disputants' *access* to the rhetorical tools needed to stake the discursive claims that legitimize them and their story. These political processes are a function of (1) mediators' participation in narrative processes within the session; (2) the structure of the mediation session itself; and (3) the psychological nature of the mediators' discourse about mediation.

From 16 *Law and Social Inquiry* 35, 52–62 (1991). University of Chicago Press.

The Politics of Mediator Participation

The mediators we observed participate politically by asking questions and making summaries. Their questions bring the focus to one particular event sequence (plot), one particular story logic (theme), and/or adopt the character positions advanced by one disputant *about* another (character). Examples from a specific case demonstrate the political nature of mediator questions.

One of our cases was audiotaped in a room off the courtroom as part of a show-cause hearing. The situation was a complicated one involving a father and his wife (Mr. and Mrs. Jones) on one side of the dispute and a daughter (Kathy), boyfriend (Steve), and their attorney on the other side. Mr. Jones filed a complaint against Steve, alleging that Steve had threatened him in a parking lot and, in doing so, had caused him to suffer chest pain that he thought was indicative of a heart attack. Mr. Jones was rushed to the hospital where it was discovered that he was suffering from a panic attack, not a heart attack. In the process, he incurred a hospital bill for which he was asking reimbursement from Steve. Mr. Jones also complained that Steve had been dishonorably discharged from the Army, which undermined Mr. Jones's trust and faith in Steve as a potential husband for his daughter.

The session opens with Mr. and Mrs. Jones describing the "threatening incident":

> *Mr. Jones:* I was on my lunch break and Steve drove by and he kind of motioned me to come over and I saw Kathy in front of him, my daughter, driving her car and I says, "Oh good," she probably spoke to him . . . so I went over and he threatened me, he says, "I'm gonna knock you out old man." He said it several times and finally I just walked away.

After establishing the consequences of this threatening incident (loss of work time and a hospital bill), the mediator begins to question Steve:

> *Mediator:* Thanks for being patient, Steve. Maybe you could give me a little background on your perspective on the situation.
> *Steve:* Well, I didn't drive up and tell him I was gonna knock him out. I drove up, waved him over, I asked him what the problem was, 'cause before all this started happening we used to get along pretty good. So I called him over and said, "What's the problem?" And he says, "Just beat it!" and I says, "I don't want to beat it—I want to find out what the problem is." He says then, "Get the hell out of here!" I says, "I ain't going nowhere" I says, "You want me to leave, make me!" He says, "I'll make you leave." I says, "Anytime you think that you are ready." He says, "If I was your age again, I'd tie one hand behind my back and whip you." I says, "Any time."
> *Mediator:* After you threatened him and he walked away, what did you do?
> *Steve:* Well, I don't know because I drove away first.

In this exchange, Steve is clearly being asked a question that is based on the narrative proposed by Mr. Jones. The exchange in the parking lot, labeled as a "threat" by Mr. Jones, is embedded in the question that the mediator puts to Steve, as is the plot sequence Mr. Jones offered: first he was threatened and then he left the parking lot.

Later in the session, the mediator questions Steve about his discharge from the Army; Mr. Jones has complained that the dishonorable discharge, coupled with Steve's lies about it, eroded the trust in the relationship. The mediator again questions Steve, using the story that Mr. Jones has put into place.

> *Mr. Jones:* You know that he kept telling Kathy that he got out on medical. He didn't get out on medical. . . . He got thrown out of the service because he couldn't hack it, thrown out of his own accord . . . and I think that's when things turned, I mean . . . 'cause like I say, I'm military, all my sons and sons-in-laws are military. And in fact, I even gave him a nice pair of shoes that I got, that I got from my father, patent leather shoes. My father died and well, he wore the same size as I do and so I was keeping them as a spare but since he was gonna go in, I says, "Here, you'll look nice in the uniform with these shoes," I give him the shoes to show him my good heartedness . . . and he turned around and pulled something like that. . . .
>
> *Mediator:* Steve, perhaps, since the issue seems to be one of honesty, you could clarify your discharge for us. . . .
>
> *Steve:* I talked to Kathy about it and I didn't think that, ah, in my opinion, I didn't think it was gonna change either her father's or her mother's life so . . .

At this point, Steve refuses to participate in the continuation of Mr. Jones's story, which the mediator is pressing him to do. Not only has the mediator adopted the narrative offered by Mr. Jones, he has adopted the moral framework that Mr. Jones has used to delegitimize Steve—dishonesty. Problematically, Steve refuses to tell any story about his discharge from the Army, so the session participants are forced to use the one constructed by the Joneses. Questions such as these make focal one plot sequence and instantiate one moral order, requiring all speakers to stand on the semantic ground provided by one side of the dispute.

Mediators also participate politically in the story transformation by making summaries that recontextualize important events in the plot. At one point in the session described above, the mediator states: "It sounds as though this initial 'contact' was problematic for both of you." Summaries such as these create symmetry in the dominant story; even though the stories are different in important ways, this summary creates a dimension in which they are similar. The word "contact" also divests the characters of any bad intentions (for "contact" does not imply bad intent on anyone's part). As mediators themselves noted in interviews, summaries provide an important opportunity for mediators to shift the semantic frames and moral orders in disputants' stories. The mediators' questions and summaries are political precisely because they do constrain the development of certain story lines and favor others.

The Politics of the Mediation Structure

In addition to the mediator's participation, the structure of the mediation session itself contributes to allowing one story to set the semantic and moral grounds on which discussion and dialogue can take place. For example, the first speaker, usually the complainant, puts in place a particular plot, the coherence of which is established through a particular causal logic (theme), all of which serve to construct particular roles for persons to play (characters).

The following excerpt is taken from a session in which one woman has lodged a criminal complaint against another woman for "harassment." Rita speaks first, recounting why she lodged the complaint against JoAnn, explaining that JoAnn had her evicted from her apartment. According to Rita, JoAnn had called Rita's landlord with information (about Rita's boyfriend—JoAnn's former boyfriend) that led to Rita's eviction.

> *Mediator:* What happened after you were notified that you had to move out?
>
> *Rita:* I called JoAnn. I was very angry. I screamed and hollered into the phone. She then came over to my house and then she was making threatening phone calls to me. . . . I identified myself when I called her. I told her, "This is Rita. You have nothing to gain by hurting me and my kids." And we both did a lot of hollering and screaming. Neither of us was very nice.
>
> *Mediator:* Was there any other contact between the two of you after that?
>
> *Rita:* No, uh, she has gone up and down my street screaming obscenities. The neighbor upstairs complained that it woke up her children. I've done my best to stay away. I go to work and stay home with my children.
>
> *Mediator:* Has there been any other contact?
>
> *Rita:* No, uh, no.
>
> *Mediator:* Uh, JoAnn, do you want to tell us what brings you here tonight?
>
> *JoAnn:* Yeah, but can I ask a question first? Could you please tell me what time . . . I was driving down the street? I have a time for everywhere that I've been.
>
> *Rita:* My neighbors told, I believe it was Friday or Saturday evening. Maybe 11:15, 11:00.
>
> *JoAnn:* I bowl Saturday nights and I'm at bingo on Friday nights.
>
> *Rita:* I'm just going on what . . . I don't know anyone else that would go up and down the street hollering obscenities like that.
>
> *JoAnn:* Well, I have not been up and down your street. I have no reason to be down on Bliss Street and I have not been down Bliss Street. OK? So you can tell your neighbors to make it clear, it hasn't been me and I have proof.

The adversarial pattern in the above exchange is replicated throughout the session, even *after* the agreement is signed. This is a function of the first speaker's initial accusation. Rita's story identifies some morally inappropriate behavior that is enacted with *intention* by JoAnn. As a speech act, this initial story functions as an "accusation," the complement to which is, of course, "justification." Together this speech act pair functions to reconstruct an adversarial context; the second speaker must refute/deny the discursive position provided by the first speaker, both speakers vying for a legitimate position in the story, in the discourse.

In mediation sessions, positive positions are constructed on the basis of negative positions of/for the other persons—"I am the innocent and he is the guilty." Positive character roles (moral and appropriate behavior) are positive only in *relation* to negative roles established for the other. In the sequence above, Rita claims that she "go[es] to work and stay[s] home with her children." This description is positive in relation to the negative role JoAnn plays in Rita's story—screaming obscenities and harassing Rita. In all thirty taped mediation sessions [that the authors studied—*editor*], the initial speaker attributes negative intent to the other disputant—it is never just the case that the initial story details some inappropriate behavior that could be interpreted as an accident; in all cases, the inappropriate behavior is depicted as willful and full of bad intent. For this reason, it appears that the construction of a positive role for self *necessitates* the attribution of bad intent to the other. Thus the construction of positive and negative "positions" in mediation discourse favors the maintenance of the adversarial context, whether or not an agreement is reached.

Psychological Vocabulary: Obscuring Political Processes

Mediators are trained to reduce adversarial processes; to do so they track *emotions, attitudes, concerns, fears, interests, hopes, needs*, and other psychological processes; they do not attend to discourse or narrative processes. Their vocabulary of psychological terms keeps mediators focused on individuals rather than communication patterns, on intrapsychic rather than interpersonal processes. Nowhere is this more evident than in the caucus, where mediators share assumptions about persons and their processes. The following excerpt is from a mother/daughter dispute; the mother complains that the daughter is out of control; the daughter complains that the mother is unduly rigid and harsh. Both mother and daughter have been physically violent with each other.

> *Mediator 1:* Well, I think that we have here . . .
> *Mediator 2:* She is obviously very lonely, I think she's quite depressed.
> *Mediator 1:* Yeah, like she's saying, "Please pay attention to me."
> *Mediator 2:* The mother's expectations seem way out of proportion to this, to her needs.
> *Mediator 1:* I feel really sad, this is so depressing.
> *Mediator 2:* They are not sad, at least they don't say they are.
> *Mediator 1:* But the mother seems really depressed—I mean, wouldn't you be?
> *Mediator 2:* I wonder if there's some deep dark tragedy in the mother's life, other than this divorce. I mean people get divorced all the time—maybe we don't have the full picture.
> *Mediator 1:* Yeah but I think that at this point, we should, we have to deal with their needs now.

The mediators' focus on intrapsychic processes eclipses the possibility of descriptions about *relationships*; with their vocabulary about psychological processes, they are not able to access information about patterns. Thus they are not able to create descriptions about the interactional interdependence of mother and daughter—they cannot and do not notice how the mother's behavior invokes the daughter's, producing more of the same in the interactional patterns. The mediators' psychological vocabulary favors a focus on individuals and obscures the role of discourse in the session; the mediators cannot witness their own role in the creation of alternative stories, nor can they address the colonization of one story by another. Their psychological (even Freudian) vocabulary allows the ideological processes in discourse to go unchecked and therefore contributes to the marginalization and delegitimization of disputants. Rather than reduce adversarial communication patterns, the mediators' psychological vocabulary contributes to maintain problematic patterns, obscuring the process of the production of consensus in sessions.

Conclusion

Mediation is a highly political process. It is composed of stories, narratives, that seldom call attention to the fact that they provide an interpretive framework for knowing the world; stories masquerade as representing a world that, in fact, they are in the process of constructing. So the discourse itself contributes to obscure its role in the production of any consensus about the world.

Furthermore, some narratives become dominant while others are marginalized, effectively delegitimizing disputants whose stories are colonized. Mediators participate in these political processes by asking questions and making summaries that contribute to the oppression (suppression) of one story, shaping the grounds on which agreement and disagreement can take place.

The structure of the mediation process itself contributes to the marginalization of one disputant (the second disputant to tell the story), setting an accusation/justification sequence in place that perpetuates adversarial interactions and reconstitutes one story as dominant. Agreements are written on the semantic and moral grounds of the dominant story; the material consequences of this marginalization mirror the marginalization in the discourse in the session.

Mediators are not trained to attend to narrative processes; instead, they speak in a vocabulary of psychologized terms that perpetuates a focus on individuals and intrapsychic processes; their disattention to discourse, promoted by their vocabulary, permits unchecked the political processes that constitute and reconstitute one story as dominant in the session, in the agreement, and in the world.

Narrative processes, mediator participation, mediators' psychologized vocabulary, and the structure of the mediation process itself all contribute to the production of consensus (the dominant story) *in ways that are not available for discussion by the mediators or the disputants*. The highly political processes in discourse are neither visible nor accessible, given the current descriptions and understanding about mediation process.

In this sense, mediation functions antithetically to its own ideology: it is not, from this perspective, a communication context where all persons have equal time and equal access to the storytelling process—it is not a communication context insured against ideology: *in twenty-four of thirty cases, the settlements emerge out of the initial narrative!* This means that 80 percent of the time, the second speaker never is able to tell a story that is not colonized by the first or dominant story!

From this perspective, the location for struggle and conflict is not only differences in interests; the location for struggle is also over meaning and is a function of what V. N. Volosinov refers to as "the multi-accentuality" of words: because meaning is never a property of the word but is constructed in *use*, in particular social contexts, as part of particular practices, the social construction and management of meaning is a political activity.

In fact, mediation is a hegemonic process precisely because it generates a dominant ideology (a dominant story) by creating a web of shared meanings, a web created out of the available stories/myths and their engendered forms of practices. The dominant ideology "dominates" not by coercion (mediators do not tell disputants what to say) but by consent (disputants *use* this web of meaning, co-constructed with mediators, as grounds both to affirm *and* to contest).

To adopt such a perspective on mediation requires radical shifts in notions of power, ideology, justice, and neutrality. First, power is no longer just a commodity to be possessed by an individual; power is also an attribute of discourse and manifest in the production and contestation of consensus. Ideology is no longer just a function of hidden interests but is also a function of the way discourse masks the processes by which dominant descriptions of the world come into being and reconstitute themselves. Justice is no longer a condition resulting from either substantive or procedural guidelines and codes; justice is a question of access, of participation in the construction of dominant descriptions and stories. Because of the unity in the discourse of neutrality, changes in the meanings of this interrelated web of justice, ideology, and power reverberate in both the understanding and practice of neutrality in mediation.

Neutrality becomes a practice *in discourse*, specifically, the management of persons' positions in stories, the intervention in the associated interactional patterns between stories, and the construction of alternative stories. These processes require that mediators participate by shaping problems in ways that provide all speakers not only an opportunity to tell their story but a discursive opportunity to tell a story that does not contribute to their own delegitimization or marginalization (as is necessarily the case whenever one party disputes or contests a story in which the person is negatively positioned).

The adoption of a poststructural perspective on neutrality accents the discursive processes through which stories are constructed, contested, and transformed, which is precisely the ideological terrain in which mediation is practiced. Not only is this perspective more pragmatic (it focuses on the actual practices in mediation, i.e., storytelling); it also enables practitioner and researcher alike to avoid the paradoxes and dilemmas that necessarily arise within the current rhetoric of neutrality.

NOTES

1. "Consensus" as we are using it does not mean agreement, as the term might suggest; "consensus" refers to the semantic grounds on which positions in discourse are created, reified, and changed. Applied to mediation, "consensus" does not refer to settlement but to the language and discursive structures in which conflicts are framed and transformed.

2. In our data set, this happens in twenty-four of thirty cases; this means that in about 80 percent of our cases, the second disputant to speak simply refutes or denies the story told by the first speaker. If our data are reliable, it means that much of the time, one speaker in a session is not able to legitimize himself or herself.

Chapter 6

In a Grove

Ryunosuke Akutagawa

Testimony of a Woodcutter before a High Police Commissioner

Yes, sir. Certainly, it was I who found the body. This morning, as usual, I went to cut my daily quota of cedars, when I found the body in a grove in a hollow in the mountains. The exact location? About 150 meters off the Yamashina stage road. It's an out-of-the-way grove of bamboo and cedars.

The body was lying flat on its back dressed in a bluish silk kimono and a wrinkled head-dress of the Kyoto style. A single sword-stroke had pierced the breast. The fallen bamboo-blades around it were stained with bloody blossoms. No, the blood was no longer running. The wound had dried up, I believe. And also, a gadfly was stuck fast there, hardly noticing my footsteps.

You ask me if I saw a sword or any such thing?

No, nothing, sir. I found only a rope at the root of a cedar near by. And . . . well, in addition to a rope, I found a comb. That was all. Apparently he must have made a battle of it before he was murdered, because the grass and fallen bamboo-blades had been trampled down all around.

"A horse was near by?"

No, sir. It's hard enough for a man to enter, let alone a horse.

Testimony of a Traveling Buddhist Priest before the High Police Commissioner

The time? Certainly, it was about noon yesterday, sir. The unfortunate man was on the road from Sekiyama to Yamashina. He was walking toward Sekiyama with a woman accompanying him on horseback, who I have since learned was his wife. A scarf hanging from her head hid her face from view. All I saw was the color of her clothes, a lilac-colored suit. Her horse was a sorrel with a fine mane. The lady's height? Oh, about four feet five inches. Since I am a Buddhist priest, I took

From "In a Grove," from Rashōmon and Other Stories, by Ryunosuke Akutagawa, translated by Takashi Kojima, 19–33. Translation copyright 1952 by Liveright Publishing Corporation. Reprinted by permission of Liveright Publishing.

little notice about her details. Well, the man was armed with a sword as well as a bow and arrows. And I remember that he carried some twenty odd arrows in his quiver.

Little did I expect that he would meet such a fate. Truly human life is as evanescent as the morning dew or a flash of lightning. My words are inadequate to express my sympathy for him.

Testimony of a Policeman before the High Police Commissioner

The man that I arrested? He is a notorious brigand called Tajomaru. When I arrested him, he had fallen off his horse. He was groaning on the bridge at Awataguchi. The time? It was in the early hours of last night. For the record, I might say that the other day I tried to arrest him, but unfortunately he escaped. He was wearing a dark blue silk kimono and a large plain sword. And, as you see, he got a bow and arrows somewhere. You say that this bow and these arrows look like the ones owned by the dead man? Then Tajomaru must be the murderer. The bow wound with leather strips, the black lacquered quiver, the seventeen arrows with hawk feathers—these were all in his possession I believe. Yes, sir, the horse is, as you say, a sorrel with a fine mane. A little beyond the stone bridge I found the horse grazing by the roadside, with his long rein dangling. Surely there is some providence in his having been thrown by the horse.

Of all the robbers prowling around Kyoto, this Tajomaru has given the most grief to the women in town. Last autumn a wife who came to the mountain back of the Pindora of the Toribe Temple, presumably to pay a visit, was murdered, along with a girl. It has been suspected that it was his doing. If this criminal murdered the man, you cannot tell what he may have done with the man's wife. May it please your honor to look into this problem as well.

Testimony of an Old Woman before the High Police Commissioner

Yes, sir, that corpse is the man who married my daughter. He does not come from Kyoto. He was a samurai in the town of Kokufu in the province of Wakasa. His name was Kanazawa no Takehiko, and his age was twenty-six. He was of a gentle disposition, so I am sure he did nothing to provoke the anger of others.

My daughter? Her name is Masago, and her age is nineteen. She is a spirited, fun-loving girl, but I am sure she has never known any man except Takehiko. She has a small, oval, dark-complected face with a mole at the corner of her left eye.

Yesterday Takehiko left for Wakasa with my daughter. What bad luck it is that things should have come to such a sad end! What has become of my daughter? I am resigned to giving up my son-in-law as lost, but the fate of my daughter worries me sick. For heaven's sake leave no stone unturned to find her. I hate that robber Tajomaru, or whatever his name is. Not only my son-in-law, but my daughter . . . (Her later words were drowned in tears.)

Tajomaru's Confession

I killed him, but not her. Where's she gone? I can't tell. Oh, wait a minute. No torture can make me confess what I don't know. Now things have come to such a head, I won't keep anything from you.

Yesterday a little past noon I met that couple. Just then a puff of wind blew, and raised her hanging scarf, so that I caught a glimpse of her face. Instantly it was again covered from my view. That may have been one reason; she looked like a Bodhisattva. At that moment I made up my mind to capture her even if I had to kill her man.

Why? To me killing isn't a matter of such great consequence as you might think. When a woman is captured, her man has to be killed anyway. In killing, I use the sword I wear at my side. Am I the only one who kills people? You, you don't use your swords. You kill people with your power, with your money. Sometimes you kill them on the pretext of working for their good. It's true they don't bleed. They are in the best of health, but all the same you've killed them. It's hard to say who is a greater sinner, you or me. (An ironical smile.)

But it would be good if I could capture a woman without killing her man. So, I made up my mind to capture her, and do my best not to kill him. But it's out of the question on the Yamashina stage road. So I managed to lure the couple into the mountains.

It was quite easy. I became their traveling companion, and I told them there was an old mound in the mountain over there, and that I had dug it open and found many mirrors and swords. I went on to tell them I'd buried the things in a grove behind the mountain, and that I'd like to sell them at a low price to anyone who would care to have them. Then . . . you see, isn't greed terrible? He was beginning to be moved by my talk before he knew it. In less than half an hour they were driving their horse toward the mountain with me.

When he came in front of the grove, I told them that the treasures were buried in it, and I asked them to come and see. The man had no objection—he was blinded by greed. The woman said she would wait on horseback. It was natural for her to say so, at the sight of a thick grove. To tell you the truth, my plan worked just as I wished, so I went into the grove with him, leaving her behind alone.

The grove is only bamboo for some distance. About fifty yards ahead there's a rather open clump of cedars. It was a convenient spot for my purpose. Pushing my way through the grove, I told him a plausible lie that the treasures were buried under the cedars. When I told him this, he pushed his laborious way toward the slender cedar visible through the grove. After a while the bamboo thinned out, and we came to where a number of cedars grew in a row. As soon as we got there, I seized him from behind. Because he was a trained, sword-bearing warrior, he was quite strong, but he was taken by surprise, so there was no help for him. I soon tied him up to the root of a cedar. Where did I get a rope? Thank heaven, being a robber, I had a rope with me, since I might have to scale a wall at any moment. Of course it was easy to stop him from calling out by gagging his mouth with fallen bamboo leaves.

When I disposed of him, I went to his woman and asked her to come and see him, because he seemed to have been suddenly taken sick. It's needless to say that this plan also worked well. The woman, her sedge hat off, came into the depths of the grove, where I led her by the hand. The instant she caught sight of her husband, she drew a small sword. I've never seen a woman of such violent temper. If I'd been off guard, I'd have got a thrust in my side. I dodged, but she kept on slashing at me. She might have wounded me deeply or killed me. But I'm Tajomaru. I managed to strike down her small sword without drawing my own. The most spirited woman is defenseless without a weapon. At last I could satisfy my desire for her without taking her husband's life.

Yes, . . . without taking his life. I had no wish to kill him. I was about to run away from the grove, leaving the woman behind in tears, when she frantically clung to my arm. In broken fragments of words, she asked that either her husband or I die. She said it was more trying than death to have her shame known to two men. She gasped out that she wanted to be the wife of whichever survived. Then a furious desire to kill him seized me. (Gloomy excitement.)

Telling you in this way, no doubt I seem a crueler man than you. But that's because you didn't see her face. Especially her burning eyes at that moment. As I saw her eye to eye, I wanted to make her my wife even if I were to be struck by lightning. I wanted to make her my wife . . . this single desire filled my mind. This was not only lust, as you might think. At that time if I'd had no other desire than lust, I'd surely not have minded knocking her down and running away. Then I wouldn't have stained my sword with his blood. But the moment I gazed at her face in the dark grove, I decided not to leave there without killing him.

But I didn't like to resort to unfair means to kill him. I untied him and told him to cross swords with me. (The rope that was found at the root of the cedar is the rope I dropped at the time.) Furious with anger, he drew his thick sword. And quick as thought, he sprang at me ferociously, without speaking a word. I needn't tell you how our fight turned out. The twenty-third stroke . . . please remember this. I'm impressed with this fact still. Nobody under the sun has ever clashed swords with me twenty strokes. (A cheerful smile.)

When he fell, I turned toward her, lowering my blood-[s]tained sword. But to my great astonishment she was gone. I wondered to where she had run away. I looked for her in the clump of cedars. I listened, but heard only a groaning sound from the throat of the dying man.

As soon as we started to cross swords, she may have run away through the grove to call for help. When I thought of that, I decided it was a matter of life and death to me. So, robbing him of his sword, and bow and arrows, I ran out to the mountain road. There I found her horse still grazing quietly. It would be a mere waste of words to tell you the later details, but before I entered town I had already parted with the sword. That's all my confession. I know that my head will be hung in chains anyway, so put me down for the maximum penalty. (A defiant attitude.)

Confession of a Woman Who Has Come to the Shimizu Temple

That man in the blue silk kimono, after forcing me to yield to him, laughed mockingly as he looked at my bound husband. How horrified my husband must have been! But no matter how hard he struggled in agony, the rope cut into him all the more tightly. In spite of myself I ran stumblingly toward his side. Or rather I tried to run toward him, but the man instantly knocked me down. Just at that moment I saw an indescribable light in my husband's eyes. Something beyond expression . . . his eyes make me shudder even now. That instantaneous look of my husband, who couldn't speak a word, told me all his heart. The flash in his eyes was neither anger nor sorrow . . . only a cold light, a look of loathing. More struck by the look in his eyes than by the blow of the thief, I called out in spite of myself and fell unconscious.

In the course of time I came to, and found that the man in blue silk was gone. I saw only my husband still bound to the root of the cedar. I raised myself from the bamboo-blades with difficulty, and looked into his face; but the expression in his eyes was just the same as before.

Beneath the cold contempt in his eyes, there was hatred. Shame, grief, and anger . . . I don't know how to express my heart at that time. Reeling to my feet, I went up to my husband.

"Takejiro," I said to him, "since things have come to this pass, I cannot live with you. I'm determined to die, . . . but you must die, too. You saw my shame. I can't leave you alive as you are."

This was all I could say. Still he went on gazing at me with loathing and contempt. My heart breaking, I looked for his sword. It must have been taken by the robber. Neither his sword nor his bow and arrows were to be seen in the grove. But fortunately my small sword was lying at my feet. Raising it over head, once more I said, "Now give me your life. I'll follow you right away."

When he heard these words, he moved his lips with difficulty. Since his mouth was stuffed with leaves, of course his voice could not be heard at all. But at a glance I understood his words. Despising me, his look said only, "Kill me." Neither conscious nor unconscious, I stabbed the small sword through the lilac-colored kimono into his breast.

Again at this time I must have fainted. By the time I managed to look up, he had already breathed his last—still in bonds. A streak of sinking sunlight streamed through the clump of cedars and bamboos, and shone on his pale face. Gulping down my sobs, I untied the rope from his dead body. And . . . and what has become of me since I have no more strength to tell you. Anyway I hadn't the strength to die. I stabbed my own throat with the small sword, I threw myself into a pond at the foot of the mountain, and I tried to kill myself in many ways. Unable to end my life, I am still living in dishonor. (A lonely smile.) Worthless as I am, I must have been forsaken even by the most merciful Kwannon. I killed my own husband. I was violated by the robber. Whatever can I do? Whatever can I . . . I . . . (Gradually, violent sobbing.)

Story of the Murdered Man, as Told through a Medium

After violating my wife, the robber, sitting there, began to speak comforting words to her. Of course I couldn't speak. My whole body was tied fast to the root of a cedar. But meanwhile I winked at her many times, as much as to say "Don't believe the robber." I wanted to convey some such meaning to her. But my wife, sitting dejectedly on the bamboo leaves, was looking hard at her lap. To all appearance, she was listening to his words. I was agonized by jealousy. In the meantime the robber went on with his clever talk, from one subject to another. The robber finally made his bold, brazen proposal. "Once your virtue is stained, you won't get along well with your husband, so won't you be my wife instead? It's my love for you that made me be violent toward you."

While the criminal talked, my wife raised her face as if in a trance. She had never looked so beautiful as at that moment. What did my beautiful wife say in answer to him while I was sitting bound there? I am lost in space, but I have never thought of her answer without burning with anger and jealousy. Truly she said, "Then take me away with you wherever you go."

This is not the whole of her sin. If that were all, I would not be tormented so much in the dark. When she was going out of the grove as if in a dream, her hand in the robber's, she suddenly turned pale, and pointed at me tied to the root of the cedar, and said, "Kill him! I cannot marry you as long as he lives." "Kill him!" she cried many times, as if she had gone crazy. Even now these words threaten to blow me headlong into the bottomless abyss of darkness. Has such a hateful thing come out of a human mouth ever before? Have such cursed words ever struck a human ear, even once? Even once such a . . . (A sudden cry of scorn.) At these words the robber himself turned pale. "Kill him," she cried, clinging to his arms. Looking hard at her, he answered neither yes nor no . . . but hardly had I thought about his answer before she had been knocked down into the bamboo leaves. (Again a cry of scorn.) Quietly folding his arms, he looked at me and said, "What will you do with her? Kill her or save her? You have only to nod. Kill her?" For these words alone I would like to pardon his crime.

While I hesitated, she shrieked and ran into the depths of the grove. The robber instantly snatched at her, but he failed even to grasp her sleeve.

After she ran away, he took up my sword, and my bow and arrows. With a single stroke he cut one of my bonds. I remember his mumbling, "My fate is next." Then he disappeared from the grove. All was silent after that. No, I heard someone crying. Untying the rest of my bonds, I listened carefully, and I noticed that it was my own crying. (Long silence.)

I raised my exhausted body from the root of the cedar. In front of me there was shining the small sword which my wife had dropped. I took it up and stabbed it into my breast. A bloody lump rose to my mouth, but I didn't feel any pain. When my breast grew cold, everything was as silent as the dead in their graves. What profound silence! Not a single bird-note was heard in the sky over this grave in the hollow of the mountains. Only a lonely light lingered on the cedars and mountain.

By and by the light gradually grew fainter, till the cedars and bamboo were lost to view. Lying there, I was enveloped in deep silence.

Then someone crept up to me. I tried to see who it was. But darkness had already been gathering round me. Someone . . . that someone drew the small sword softly out of my breast in its invisible hand. At the same time once more blood flowed into my mouth. And once and for all I sank down into the darkness of space.

Chapter 7

Harmony Models and the Construction of Law

Laura Nader

The Spread of Harmony Law Models

Harmony and conflict are not antithetical as previous theories of conflict have suggested. From the outset we need to firmly fix in our minds that there is nothing wrong or right with either conflict or harmony behavior per se. It is the uses and the consequences of behavior that are of interest. The idea of a neutrally valued harmony or conflict is difficult for Westerners to grasp unless we understand from the start that a morality about harmony and conflict is just as much a construction as is the construction of a social organization that mirrors the ideology of either. Harmony may be used to suppress peoples by socializing them toward conformity in colonial contexts, or the idea of harmony may be used to resist external control. In what follows we concentrate on harmony models that operate as control or as pacification in the colonial and missionizing contexts.

In 1963, James Gibbs observed a model of harmony while studying what he thought of as the therapeutic processes of conciliatory dispute settlement used by the Kpelle of Liberia in Africa. Before him others had noted the influence of models of conciliation or reasonableness among the African peoples they had studied. All of these anthropologists make brief mention of the colonial government and missionary influence in passing. For example, Gluckman mentioned that the Lozi had absorbed the beliefs and ideology of Christianity although few were practicing Christians. He notes that "Litigious consensus breaks down when judges and litigants have different norms as where a Catholic husband might deny the kuta's power to divorce his wife." He refers to the break-up of the homogeneity of Lozi society further in "The Case of the Watchtower Pacifists," indicating how Christian sect values enter into the Barotse courts. Nadel paints the broader picture when he writes:

> Christianity—the rigid, orthodox persuasion of missions—is an uncompromisingly alien creed. It cannot be satisfied with underlining the universal moral tenets—the

From Kevin Avruch, Peter W. Black, and Joseph A. Scimeca, eds., *Conflict Resolution: Cross Cultural Perspectives* (Westport, CT: Greenwood, 1991), 41, 44–54. Reproduced with permission of Greenwood Publishing group, Inc., Westport, CT.

evilness of murder, respect for property or marital rights. It ignores traditional marital rights in preaching monogamy; it breaks up the family system; it bans dances as bad, or beer-drinking as immoral, and thus denies vital features of social integration. It aims at changes so radical that they demand themselves the protection of *ad hoc* created laws rather than lend strength to a slowly emerging new morality.

There are differing constellations in the examples from Africa that indicate the double impact of Christian missions and colonial courts on African law and the consequent ubiquitousness of harmony ideology. In a recent analysis of the African documents Martin Chanock draws our attention to the idealization of African dispute processes that has evolved from the colonial situation as "a way of settling personal disputes and conflicts of interest by trying to find a solution acceptable to both parties . . . the antithesis of settlement by compromise is settlement by reference to abstract principles." Chanock goes on to note that legal writers concurred with the view of anthropologists:

> African law was a system of keeping the balance . . . geared . . . not to decisions imposed but to acceptable solutions. In the traditional African community there was no polarization of needs, of taste, or of values, and once the facts were established, "the same solutions will appeal to all and ways to achieve them will seem obvious" . . . the feeling of balance will be something spontaneous and self-evident.

In Chanock's brilliant exposition of the myths and images of African customary law, the processes of reconciliation and the egalitarianism of precolonial societies are contrasted with the stark historical realities. For example, among the Chew it seems clear that the precolonial period was a time of harsh punishment for sorcery, theft, adultery, and the like—a contrast to later notions that Chewa judicial institutions functioned to remove hatred by patient examination and persuasion. Chanock also quotes Canter on the Lenje of Zambia, noting the contradiction in values that the Lenje offer when speaking of reconciliation, that is, harmony with force. Chanock observes that maintaining harmony with force loses its egalitarian warmth.

For our purposes the data that Chanock brings together on the missionary presence in Africa from the 1830s onward is revealing of the original connection between local law, the presence of Christian missions, and the spread of harmony models. Chanock uses the term "missionary justice" to call attention to the fact that from the early 1860s missionaries were heavily involved in the settlement of disputes according to a Victorian interpretation of the biblical law they had brought with them and that they generally fit with English procedures as they knew them. Chanock mentions several early missions that were notorious for their zeal and violent punishments. He notes that these early excesses in punishment led to a change in policies, but that the missions continued to be active as conciliators in disputes. Although there were regional variations and differences among mission groups, mission justice suffered from contradiction. Missionaries found it difficult to respect the separation of religion from law, a separation that is so much a part of the Western system. They found this separation especially difficult to maintain in relation to the law of marriage and divorce, which they saw through the lens of mid-Victorian Christian law. Indeed, some missionaries promulgated the Ten Commandments as the law of God, and according to Chanock, the missionaries were glad to be peacemakers and hand down Christian judgment while the colonial courts evolved the whole into something we call customary law, which emphasized conciliation and compromise operating on the principles of Christian harmony ideology.

Chanock's work is rich on the origin, use, and modern-day consequences of harmony ideology. From the point of view of local law, compromise is the politics of adjustment. But more important, compromise becomes a politics of survival when indigenous communities are trying to restore a lost social solidarity as they learn to cope with threats from more powerful outside societies. In postcolonial time community courts became places where people engaged in discourses that established and reinforced common beliefs and values, discourses that were conscious political strategies for places where indirect rule and relative local autonomy were imposed by the colonials. Groups that support harmony often share the belief that the forces of disorder lie outside of their group. In fact, it is the recognition of external threat that sometimes mobilizes religious-based beliefs. African peoples used harmony at different points in their contact experiences—when war and raiding were being routed, when sophisticated African native courts were dealing with colonization of the governing and missionizing kind, or when agriculturalists sought to protect their communal lands from developers.

Recent fieldwork in Swaziland provides the clearest formulation of the uses of harmony over the politics of land. Takirambudde has described Swaziland as a unique case of the "triumph of indigenous authority and a substantial subordination and/or containment of alien legal norms." In *The Politics of Harmony* Laurel Rose describes how harmony ideology is used at different points in the disputing process, predominantly by the chiefs. Commoners and new elites are challenging old formulations about land, and chiefs' uses of harmony rhetoric are said to be a strategy of indigenous hierarchical control. Harmony rhetoric is found in the speeches made at customary legal proceedings and national meetings and rituals.

Swazi statements about harmony suggest its multidimensional nature: unity, consensus, cooperation, compliance, passivity, and docility. And while all Swazis define harmony as social unity and cultural integrity, the manner of its use in disputing claims differs by class. Rose reports that the traditional elites use harmony ideologies to legitimate their administrative roles and validate the continuance of the traditional land tenure system. The new elites use harmony to legitimate their positions, and while they may create an illusion of unity that accords with their individual land class interests, they often are responsible for internal social conflict. Both traditional and new elites use harmony ideologies to justify control. Swazi commoners strategically respond to harmony ideologies in presenting their case by abiding by the principles of harmony ideologies. Commoners resist harmony rhetoric when they feel that the social good has been violated or when they, as individuals, will suffer severe consequences. Harmony models of law are not benign in Swaziland or elsewhere.

*

The most powerful force in introducing and spreading harmony ideologies need not be the Christian missionaries. Note, for example, the state-sponsored legal informalism in parts of the Indian subcontinent in the nineteenth and twentieth centuries. The "state" in the guise of the Company Raj, Imperial India, or modern India has promoted "arbitration" and "compromise," an ideal most persistently expressed as *panchayat* justice. The history of the rise and spread of the idea of *panchayat* justice is still being written, but it is generally conceded that its political intent is and has been pacification, a quieting of the population. Following the tradition of indirect rule the British East India Company courts in rural south India decentralized the reorganized local self-government using the institutional forms of *panchayats*. A brief summary of state introduction of harmony rhetoric into U.S. legal models is an example that is more recent and closer to home.

Christian Life, Social Harmony, and Legal Culture

In a 1640 case quoted by Jerold S. Auerbach, Mrs. Hibbens quarreled with Mr. Crabtree about his fee for carpentry work. The final disagreement was not over wages, however, but over the unbrotherly manner in which Mrs. Hibbens pursued her disagreement. She did not deal with Mr. Crabtree face to face. Mrs. Hibbens was accused of not dealing with her workers in a Christian way; finally she was expelled from the church. Communal harmony was threatened and Mrs. Hibbens was silenced. There was conflict in early New England, but the people did not think it well to resolve conflict through law; in fact the society could not tolerate legal conflict. Auerbach puts it this way: "Litigation was perceived as a form of self-aggrandizement contrary to the best interests of the community. It was also un-Christian: law, in the words of one minister was 'a heart without affection, a mind without passion.'" Conflict was either suppressed or dealt with through mediation. The choice was between enforced harmony or open schism.

The same threads found in Auerbach's early New England are operative today among Southern Baptists of Hopewell, Georgia. In Carol Greenhouse's *Praying for Justice*, the people of Hopewell are characterized by law avoidance or law aversion. Greenhouse reconstructs the link between the Christian life and social harmony. She speaks of the shadow of conflict in a past that generates or motivates a studied harmony, and of present-day Hopewellian struggles for harmony as a sign of commitment to Jesus and fear of community disintegration. Studied harmony is the effort to reduce the rate of conflict. In Greenhouse's rendition of Hopewell beliefs, harmony is the twin of justice. And while harmony is valued as the measure of human worth, Greenhouse says, "harmony has a somewhat negative cast, in that its meaning has more to do with the silencing of disputes than with the absence of disagreement." This silencing of disputes that accompanies the harmony model has not received adequate attention except by those promoting rights by means of adversarial behavior.

This history of legal cultures in the United States is the history of conditions under which dispute settlement preferences are "shifting commitments." These shifting commitments usually involve a change from legal models based on har-mony to those characterized by adversarial models. Of course, no period is char-acterized by a single model. For example, it is fair to say that a prominent feature of legal culture in the 1960s was its adversarial mode. The adversarial legal model was used in the pursuit of justice, to deal with concerns of right and wrong. The 1960s have been remembered as confrontative, a time when many social groups felt encouraged to come forward with their agendas: civil rights, consumer rights, environmental rights, women's rights, American Indian rights. The decade has been described as a time of rights explosion.

The early 1970s was characterized by harmony rhetoric. The concerns were not with justice, but with harmony and efficiency. Harmony law models usually em-phasize programs that support nonjudicial means for dispute handling. The alter-native dispute resolution movement (known as ADR) came into being. Law schools shifted their training in the adversarial methods and began to include training in alternative dispute resolution mechanisms. The concern with harmony was accompanied by the silencing of disputes; Americans were told that they were too litigious. The production of harmony, the movement against the contentious, the movement to control the disenfranchised, and the loss of concern with rights created a model of law that was intolerant of conflict, its causes, and its expres-sion. An intolerance for strife seeks to rid the society of those who complain—"love it, or leave it"—and by various means attempts to create consensus, homo-geneity, and agreement. The harmony model of the 1970s and 1980s is a kind of cultural soma that tranquilizes potential plaintiffs who increasingly agree to con-sent to treatment by means of mediation or who are told, "Don't be negative." The rationalization for how well harmony works was often sought in the anthro-pological literature. The Kpelle of Liberia who have a moot court procedure, a therapeutic model to settle family problems (although in reality the Kpelle liti-gated many of their disputes), and the Zapotec of Mexico who followed a mini-max model as an ideal (give-a-little, get-a-little) rather than zero-sum game solu-tions (while they also litigated a good deal) were used as examples of how Ameri-can justice could become "more civilized."

The Roscoe Pound Conference, "Perspectives on Justice in the Future," held in St. Paul, Minnesota, in 1976, was a turning point indicating a cultural shift with ramifications far beyond the law. A way of thinking about the structural problems of inequality, about social relations more generally, and about solutions to these problems by cultural means was dramatized. The solution that emerged was a procedural reform whereby the harmony model would come to replace the adver-sarial model in law. The rhetoric at the conference extolled the virtues of alterna-tive disputing mechanisms governed by harmony and efficiency: the courts were overcrowded; American lawyers and the American people were too litigious; new tribunals were needed to divert cases generated by the regulated welfare state. Al-ternative dispute agencies were described as being agencies of settlement or recon-ciliation, and people who stood in the way of such procedural reforms were said to suffer from "status quoism."

In the years following the conference the public was immersed in alternative dispute resolution rhetoric. The language was formulaic; generalizations were repeated without grounding, authority and danger were invoked, and values were presented as facts. Because of his authoritative position as Supreme Court chief justice, Warren Burger carried considerable weight in setting the tone of the language that characterized the speeches and writings of the movement. Burger warned that adversarial modes of conflict resolution were tearing society apart and that alternative forums were more civilized. He claimed that Americans are inherently litigious. He argued that lawyers should serve as "healers of human conflicts," where plaintiffs are patients needing treatment, and claimed that training a lawyer as adversarial is anachronistic. Burger again warned that the loads on the courts were too great.

The framework of the harmony ideology is beginning to take hold, while the rhetoric and origins of the ideology go unquestioned. Most lawyers are not doing work that carries them anywhere near a courtroom context. There is no evidence for saying that Americans rely primarily on the adversary process for resolving all their disputes; Americans negotiate primarily and only rarely move to third party handlers. Further, Burger's argument that Americans are becoming increasingly litigious does not stand the test of numbers. In spite of evidence to the contrary, the chief justice proceeded relentlessly with his solution, privatization of law, which meant taking a large volume of private conflicts out of the courts and into the channels of arbitration, mediation, and conciliation.

The theory of harmony that undergirds the alternative dispute resolution movement conceptualizes harmony behavior as the keystone of community. Harmony, the same theory explains, causes the country to be more productive, more innovative, and more entrepreneurial. The harmony theorists believe that litigation causes loss of community, destroys trust and cooperation, and leads to problem solving based on emotion rather than on rationality and efficiency. Alternative dispute resolution is also seen as essential to democracy because the parties are afforded the opportunity to deal with the real issues rather than to be entrapped in lawyers' rhetoric. Embedded in this harmony theory is a belief that individual assertion of rights is evil. The harmony theorists are constructing a social order that exercises injunctions against conflict and even against voicing disputes.

Some critics have described the alternative movement as antilegal, antirights, and antijustice in the sense of an absolute justice orientation. It is preferable to talk about its consequences in terms of the view of conflict that is carried by mediation forums of the 1980s. The harmony theorists see conflict as dysfunctional and threatening to the social order, a phenomenon to be diffused. This notion of conflict presumes societal consensus about rights and values, which leads to the operation of mediation forums that have no explicit standards of justice. Furthermore the ideology of mediation is visualized as a process that brings people together; disputes are reshaped as communication problems rather than conflicts over values. Unequal power does not enter the paradigm, and disputes about facts and legal rights are transformed into disputes about feelings and relationships.

Rothschild observes that the harmony model is one where conflict is personalized, and where social problems become localized in the realm of emotion. Indeed, alternative dispute resolution such as mediation leaves no written record and no legacy, as do the courts whose recorded cases allow us to understand the etiology of injury and prevention.

Harmony theory predicts that consensus will build community, state, and business. The premise is that everyone shares (or ought to share) the same goals. In harmony discourse, the talk of rights and remedies is absent, while rhetoric about mythical litigation explosions becomes a way to explain American business failure, the high cost of insurance, and more. In the minds of some analysts alternative dispute arrangements represent a relatively new type of political domination. Harmony ideology serves to control confrontational politics; it also controls or suppresses criticism. The institutionalization of harmony models operates as an informal state embedded in the practices of everyday life, and intertwined with educational institutions, therapy communities, and management techniques more generally.

EDITOR'S NOTE

See also Kenneth B. Nunn, "Law as a Eurocentric Enterprise," 15 *Law and Inequality* 323–371 (1997), where Professor Nunn critiques "the law" from a theoretical position developed by African-centered scholars. He concludes that law, as it is understood in Western societies, is an instrument of cultural domination and control.

Chapter 8

Vantage Point

Pat K. Chew

There is the story, a version of which is told in many cultures, of the trickster and the neighbors.

Two longtime neighbors looked up from their fields—just as the trickster walked by on the dirt road between their farms. On the right side of the trickster's body, she was dressed in elegant red silk, but on the left side of her body she wore tattered rags.

The first neighbor observed to his neighbor, "What a rich and important person has come by!"

"Oh, no," said the other neighbor, "our visitor is a poor but pious soul."

"You blind fool," yelled the first neighbor, "can't you see?"

And so the neighbors argued and argued until it looked like they might actually come to blows.

Upon which the trickster turned around, revealing to the neighbors her two-sided attire—and abruptly halting the dispute. "Ah," said the trickster, "so it is—that you are both right, or . . ." paused the trickster, "you are both wrong."

Chapter 9

Toward a Theory of Conflict and Culture

Stella Ting-Toomey

Low- versus High-Context Cultures

It is the patterned ways of thinking, acting, feeling, and interpreting that constitute the fundamental webs of a culture. Conflict, as a form of intense, antagonistic communicative experience, is bounded by the cultural demands and constraints of the particular situation. This set of demands and constraints, in turn, implicitly dictates what are the appropriate and inappropriate ways of behaving and communicating in a given system.

In analyzing the relationship between conflict and culture, however, one cannot analyze conflict styles in all cultures simultaneously in the theorizing process. As a starting point, perhaps a more fruitful approach is to compare and contrast groups of cultures in relation to a particular set of conflict issues. Thus, on a conceptual level, Edward T. Hall's low- and high-context framework offers an attractive alternative for this theory-building phase in analyzing the interdependent nature of conflict and culture.

According to Hall, any transaction can basically be divided into three communication systems:

> Any transaction can be characterized as high-, low-, or middle-context. HC [high-context] transactions feature preprogrammed information that is in the receiver and in the setting, with only minimal information in the transmitted message. LC [low context] transactions are the reverse. Most of the information must be in the transmitted message in order to make up for what is missing in the context.

Although no one culture exists exclusively at one extreme, in general, low-context cultures (LCC) refer to groups of cultures that value individual orientation, overt communication codes (or "elaborated codes"), and maintain a heterogeneous normative structure with low cultural demand/low cultural constraint characteristics. Conversely, high-context cultures (HCC) refer to groups of cultures that value group-identity orientation, covert communication codes (or "restricted codes"), and maintain a homogenous normative structure with high cultural demand/high cultural constraint characteristics. For Hall, Germany, Scandinavia, Switzerland, and the United States are situated at the low-context end of the continuum; and the Chinese, Japanese, Korean, and Vietnamese cultures are loaded on the high-context end of the continuum. Whereas meanings and interpretations of a message are vested mainly in the explicit communication codes in the LCC system, meanings and interpretations of a message are vested primarily in the implicitly shared social and cultural knowledge of the context in the HCC system. As Okabe, in comparing the dominant modes of rhetoric in the United States culture and Japanese culture, cleanly summarizes:

> The digital is more characteristic of the American mode of communication. . . . The Japanese language is more inclined toward the analogical: its use of ideographic characters, its reliance on onomatopoeia, and its emphasis on the nonverbal aspect.
>
> The excessive dependence of the Japanese on the nonverbal aspect of communication means that Japanese culture tends to view the verbal as only *a* means of communication, and that the nonverbal and the extra-verbal at times assume greater importance than the verbal dimensions of communication. This is in sharp contrast to the view of Western rhetoric and communication that the verbal, especially speech, is *the* dominant means of expression.

In short, in the HCC system what is not said is sometimes more important than what is said. In contrast, in the LCC system words represent truth and power.

Hence, casting this conceptual framework in analyzing conflict and culture, conflict interaction takes on different meanings and interpretations depending on whether the conflict has occurred in the low-context system or the high-context system. In fact, we can begin to discuss conflict interaction from two foci: LCC conflicts and HCC conflicts. Specifically, what are the underlying characteristics of conflicts in LCC as compared with conflicts in HCC?

LCC versus HCC Conflicts

The four conceptual dimensions of why, when, what, and how of conflicts will be addressed in accordance with the LCC and the HCC definitions. According to Olsen, in any system conflicts occur primarily for either "instrumental" or "expressive" reasons. Instrumental conflict is marked by "opposing practices or goals," and expressive conflict stems mainly from "desires for tension release, from hostile feelings." In viewing the same conflict episode, for example, in an organizational setting concerning the rejection of a sales proposal by a North American supervisor in the LCC context, a North American subordinate will probably view the conflict episode very differently than a Japanese subordinate who has submitted the proposal. The North American subordinate will probably enter the conflict situation with heated discussion and issue-oriented arguments. He or she will probably produce facts, figures, and graphs to illustrate his or her case. In contrast, the Japanese subordinate will probably be dumbfounded by the direct, outright rejection and will then proceed to analyze the conflict episode as a personal attack or a sign of mistrust. In fact, he or she will probably resign as soon as possible.

In short, in the LCC system individuals are better able to separate the conflict issue from the person involved in the conflict. LCC individuals can fight and scream at one another over a task-oriented point and yet be able to remain friends afterwards; whereas in the HCC system the instrumental issue is closely tied with the person that originated the issue. To openly disagree with or confront someone in public is a severe blow and an extreme insult, causing both sides to "lose face." Especially in the case of superior-subordinate communication in the HCC system, individuals are supposed to engage in a normative process of "reciprocal sensitivity" toward one another, and ritualistically enact the roles of the *sempai-kohai* (senior-junior) relationship with a certain degree of respect and in accordance to the implicit, culturally written scripts.

Given the fact the LCC individuals (in accordance to Hall's LCC conceptual definition) are more likely to view the world in analytic, linear logic terms, and that issues and persons are commonly perceived as dichotomous concepts, persons in this LCC system would be more likely to punctuate the conflict event as primarily instrumental-oriented. Conversely, HCC individuals, who mainly perceive the world in synthetic, spiral logic terms, would be more likely to punctuate the same conflict event as expressive-oriented in focus. HCC individuals would have a much more difficult time in objectively separating the conflict event from the affective domain. For them, the conflict issue and the conflict person are the same, hardly separable from each other. To summarize the key points succinctly:

Proposition 1: Individuals in LCCs are more likely to perceive the causes of conflict as instrumental rather than expressive in nature.

Proposition 2: Individuals in HCCs are more likely to perceive the causes (or, more important, they tend to focus on the process) of conflict as expressive rather than instrumental in nature.

The second question of conflicts is concerned with the specific conditions in which conflicts are most likely to occur in the two cultural systems. Jackson's normative system model may be useful in answering this question. According to Jackson, a normative system is "any system of expectations by others for [the] actor's conduct." Social actions between two actors rhyme in synchrony when "the covert, symbolic responses of others to actor's conduct coincide, i.e. the expectations are 'shared.'" Hence, intercultural synchrony occurs when two strangers, coming from different cultures, actually synchronize their patterns of actions, interpretations, and expectations. Intercultural tensions and misunderstandings arise when normative behaviors and, hence, normative expectations are being implicitly or explicitly violated by either of the involved intercultural participants. The players in the unfolding drama are "out of sync" with each other—they have not abided by the fundamental rules of the game.

In fact, the rules of the game are quite different depending on whether we are discussing conflicts in an LCC system or conflicts in an HCC system. Given the fact that the LCC structure contains low cultural demand/low cultural constraint characteristics, a relatively high degree of uncertainty and risk prevails in each LCC interpersonal interaction. Conversely, given the fact that the HCC structure maintains high cultural demand/high cultural constraint characteristics, once the cultural scripts of the system are mastered, a relatively low degree of uncertainty and risk prevails in each HCC interpersonal encounter. Conflict potentials are relatively higher between strangers in the LCC situation than in the HCC context because the players in the LCC system usually play by idiosyncratic rules and only improvise coordination on the spot. Furthermore, the probability of making an interpersonal "interaction error" is also higher in the LCC system than in the HCC system because there are no specific collective (or cultural) normative rules to govern and guide the different interaction episodes. LCC misunderstandings and potential conflicts are most likely to occur when individual normative expectations of acceptable behaviors are being violated. HCC misunderstandings and potential conflict tensions are most likely to happen when the collective or cultural normative expectations of appropriate behaviors in a situation are being implicitly violated. As the HCC interaction rituals are more stringent and rule-bound than the LCC interaction rituals, it is clearly more noticeable when a stranger coming from a different culture unintentionally violates the HCC interaction routines than it is in an LCC situation. In short, interaction deviates from cultural normative expectations are more easily spotted in a normative homogeneous system (as in the case of HCC) than in a normative heterogeneous system (as in the case of LCC). To summarize, the two key points are as follows:

Proposition 3: Conflicts are more likely to occur in LCCs when individual normative expectations of the situation are being violated.

Proposition 4: Conflicts are more likely to occur in HCCs when collective or cultural normative expectations of the situation are being violated.

The third question concerning the normative relation between conflict and culture asks: What kinds of general attitude do the conflict players hold toward antagonisms and tensions in an LCC system and in an HCC system? If an individual's interpretive scheme is grounded in a particular culture and attitude is embedded in this interpretive process, culture also frames one's attitude. Individuals who are situated in different cultural systems would learn to hold different attitudes toward conflicts. In the LCC system, which is primarily characterized by an action- or doing-orientation, the conflict players are probably more likely to assume a direct, confrontational stance when differences of opinion occur. This doing-orientation approach will also serve as a normative force for both conflict parties to press for resolution and early closure. In the HCC system the predominant mode of conflict attitude can best be described as evasive and nonconfrontational. Players in the HCC believe in the use of implicit or restricted codes. A calculated degree of vagueness and circumlocution are typically employed when tensions and anxieties mount. Miyahara, in commenting on the communication style differences between North American managers and Japanese managers, used the following vivid example: If a North American supervisor must inform his or her subordinate that she or he is not satisfied with the sales proposal, she or he would probably use very explicit, direct response, such as: "I can't accept this proposal as submitted. You should come up with some better ideas";

whereas a Japanese supervisor would say: "While I have the highest regard for your abilities, I would not be completely honest if I did not express my disappointment at this proposal. I must ask that you reflect further on the proposal you have submitted to me." Hence, tactfulness and indirect speech are two modes of attitude and behavior treasured in an HCC system. In an LCC system open confrontation of ideas and direct, issue-oriented discussion are two valued modes of human expressiveness. Whereas revealment is vital to the low-context system, concealment is vital to the high-context system. Although HCC individuals may experience tremendous inner tensions intrapersonally (culturally or individually induced), these individuals will be unlikely to express their emotions openly and act on them publicly. Whereas LCC individuals will hold a more direct-active stance toward conflicts, such as confronting the conflict issue or changing some aspects of the conflict situation, HCC individuals will hold a relatively more indirect-inactive stance toward conflicts, such as avoiding or ignoring the conflict situation. Barnlund, in his classic piece on the communication style differences between Japan and the United States, noted the following:

> Regardless of social circumstances, Americans prefer to defend themselves actively, exploring and developing the rationale for positions they have taken. When pushed, they may resort to still more aggressive forms that utilize humor, sarcasm, or denunciation. Among Japanese, the reactions are more varied, but defenses tend to be more passive, permit withdrawal, and allow greater concealment . . . the Japanese may ritualize encounters to avoid the triggering of threat, Americans may find such situations an inevitable consequence of their greater expressiveness.

In sum, the general conflict attitudes of the conflict participants in an LCC system and an HCC system are as follows:

Proposition 5: Individuals in an LCC are more likely to assume a confrontational, direct attitude toward conflicts.
Proposition 6: Individuals in an HCC are more likely to assume a nonconfrontational, indirect attitude toward conflicts.

The final question on conflict and culture asks: How do the players actually "play" in LCC conflicts as compared with HCC conflicts? Communication attitude and style are interdependently linked. Style is the overt manifestation of one's cognitive orientation. Style here refers to the behavioral verbal and nonverbal means of expressing oneself. Style also embodies the attitudinal and affective components of one's reactions toward conflict management.

According to Glenn, Witmeyer, and Stevenson's study on cross-cultural persuasive styles, representatives from the United States typically engage in factual-inductive style of argument; the Soviet Union representatives typically use axiomatic-deductive style of logic; and representatives from the Arab countries primarily engage in the affective-intuitive style of emotional appeal. For Glenn et al., the factual-inductive style is based on the study of pertinent facts and moves inductively toward conclusions. The axiomatic-deductive style proceeds from general to the particular, from fundamental principles to their implications. Finally, the affective-intuitive style is based on affective, emotional messages to persuade

TABLE 9.1
A Summary of Basic Characteristics of LCC Conflict and HCC Conflict

Key Questions	Low-Context Conflict	High-Context Conflict
Why	analytic, linear logic	synthetic, spiral logic
	instrumental-oriented	expressive-oriented
	dichotomy between conflict and conflict parties	integration of conflict and conflict parties
When	individual-oriented	group-oriented
	low collective normative expectations	high collective normative expectations
	violations of individual expectations create conflict potentials	violations of collective expectations create conflict potentials
What	revealment	concealment
	direct, confrontational attitude	indirect, nonconfrontational attitude
	action and solution-oriented	"face" and relationship-oriented
How	explicit communication codes	implicit communication codes
	line-logic style: rational-factual rhetoric	point-logic style: intuitive-affective rhetoric
	open, direct strategies	ambiguous, indirect strategies

the audience. The affective-intuitive style of communication can probably be divided into two levels of analysis: the use of circumlocution or flowery speech to appeal to the emotional response of the audience and the use of ambiguity and understatement to diffuse the conflict topic.

Given the basic premises of the LCC system and the HCC system, LCC players will probably be more likely to engage in the hard bargaining rational strategies of factual-inductive style or axiomatic-deductive style in handling conflicts; HCC players will probably be more likely to use the soft bargaining strategies of affective-intuitive style in managing various conflict episodes. Where the LCC system values line logic, the HCC system treasures point logic; whereas LCC individuals tend to engage conflicts from the mind, HCC individuals tend to approach conflicts from the heart. The two systems represent two paradigms, two world views. In sum, the last two propositions are as follows:

Proposition 7: Individuals in an LCC are more likely to use factual-inductive or axiomatic-deductive style (or line logic style) of conflict management.

Proposition 8: Individuals in an HCC are more likely to use affective-intuitive style (or point logic style) of conflict management.

Due to different punctuation points (causal versus process, issue-oriented versus person-oriented) of the same event, different expectations of the same situation, and different attitudinal and communication orientations toward the same episode, initial intercultural interaction anxieties can create minor misunderstandings, and minor misunderstandings can develop into major intercultural conflicts. Without understanding the fundamental assumptions that LCC and HCC individuals hold toward the conflict episode, conflict begets conflict.

Table 9.1 presents a summary of characteristics of the why, when, what, and how questions of conflicts in the low-context cultural system versus conflicts in the high-context cultural system.

Chapter 10

Multimethod Probes of Individualism and Collectivism

Harry C. Triandis, Christopher McCusker, and C. Harry Hui

Individualism—collectivism constructs have been popular in most of the social sciences for about a century. For example, the terms *Gemeinschaft* (community) and *Gesellschaft* (society), in sociology, or relational versus individualistic value orientation in anthropology, have been used for some time.

Defining Attributes

Constructs such as collectivism can best be defined by means of several attributes. A person is most likely to be a member of a collectivist culture if the person has each of the attributes listed in Table 10.1. Theoretically, one can classify people by means of multidimensional schemes that are based on similarities in patterns of having or not having particular attributes. This means that, in addition to "pure collectivism," there are also many intermediate types, as well as types with *both* individualist and collectivist attributes. The following section presents the attributes of the pure collectivist-individualist types.

First, collectivists pay much attention to a certain ingroup and, compared with individualists, behave more differently toward members of that group than toward members of outgroups. The ingroup can best be defined by *common fate*. In prehistoric times the ingroup must have been the unit of survival, or the food community. If there was no food, all members of the ingroup starved together. As cultures evolved, the most important ingroup became the tribe, the work group, or the nation. In most cultures the family is the most important ingroup, but it is best to think of several concentric circles representing ingroups that influence an individual's actions to a greater or lesser degree.

Individualists also have ingroups and outgroups, but they do not see as sharp a contrast between them and do not behave as differently toward ingroup and out-

From 59 *Journal of Personality and Social Psychology* 1006–1009, 1020 (1990). Copyright © 1990 by the American Psychological Association. Reprinted (or adapted) with permission.

TABLE 10.1
*Attributes Defining Individualism and Collectivism and
Their Antecedents and Consequents*

Antecedents	Attributes	Consequents
Individualism		
Affluence	Emotional detachment from	Socialization for self-reliance
Cultural complexity	ingroup	and independence
Hunting/food gathering	Personal goals have primacy	Good skills when entering
Upper social class	over group goals	new groups
Migration	Behavior regulated by attitudes	Loneliness
Urbanism	and cost-benefit analyses	
Exposure to the mass media	Confrontation is OK	
Collectivism		
Unit of survival is food	Family integrity	Socialization for obedience
ingroup	Self-defined in ingroup term	and duty
Agriculture	Behavior regulated by ingroup	Sacrifice for ingroup
Large families	norms	Cognition: Focus on common
	Hierarchy and harmony within	elements with ingroup
	ingroup	members
	Ingroup is seen as homogeneous	Behavior: Intimate, saving face,
	Strong ingroup/outgroup	reflects hierarchy, social
	distinctions	support, interdependence

group members as do collectivists. When there is conflict between ingroup and individual goals in collectivist cultures, ingroup goals have primacy over individual goals; in individualist cultures, personal goals have primacy over ingroup goals.

In collectivist cultures behavior is regulated largely by ingroup norms; in individualist cultures it is regulated largely by individual likes and dislikes and cost-benefit analyses. Thus, norms are more important determinants of social behavior in collectivist cultures, and attitudes are more important in individualist cultures.

In collectivist cultures there is much emphasis on hierarchy. Usually, the father is the boss and men superordinate women. This is not nearly as much the case in individualist cultures. Furthermore, harmony and saving face are important attributes in collectivist cultures. The ingroup is supposed to be homogeneous in opinion, and no disagreements should be known to outgroups. In individualistic cultures confrontations within the ingroup are acceptable and are supposed to be desirable because they "clear the air." Thus, *hierarchy* and *harmony* are important defining attributes of collectivists.

Ingroup fate, ingroup achievement, and interdependence within the ingroup are emphasized in collectivist cultures. Personal fate, personal achievement, and independence from the ingroup are emphasized in individualistic cultures.

Self-reliance has a different meaning in these two kinds of cultures. In collectivist cultures it means "I am not a burden on the ingroup"; in individualist cultures it means "I can do my own thing."

Collectivists tend to think of *groups* as the basic unit of analysis of society. Individualists tend to think of *individuals* as the basic unit of analysis. Assuming that people in general have more cognitions that are ingroup than outgroup related, the tendency to think of individuals as the basic units of analysis will result in individualists thinking of ingroups as more heterogeneous than outgroups, as is usually found in the West. The tendency to think of groups as the units of analysis will result in ingroups being perceived as more homogeneous than outgroups in collectivist cultures. This tendency will become even stronger in collectivist cultures because the emphasis on ingroup harmony requires ingroup members to conform and to be homogeneous. Homogeneity in behavior is a virtue in such cultures, but people are free to think deviant thoughts, as long as they behave "correctly" (i.e., do what is expected by ingroup norms).

In collectivist cultures there is great concern about what happens in the ingroup and to ingroup members. This is also true in individualist cultures, but in such cultures, the ingroup is narrow, consisting only of first-degree relatives and a few "best friends," and there is much emotional detachment from most larger ingroups.

The self is defined as an appendage of the ingroup in collectivist cultures and as a separate and distinct entity in individualist cultures.

Collectivist cultures have few stable ingroups, and people are influenced very much by these ingroups. Behavior in individualistic cultures is rarely greatly influenced by ingroups, because there are so many ingroups and they often make contradictory demands. The individual decides which group to pay attention to and "picks and chooses" ingroups and forms new ingroups when convenient.

Vertical relationships (e.g., parent-child) that are in conflict with horizontal relationships (e.g., spouse-spouse) take priority in collectivist cultures, and vice versa in individualistic cultures.

Certain values such as achievement, pleasure, and competition are emphasized by individualists more than by collectivists, whereas family integrity, security, obedience, and conformity are valued more by collectivists.

Antecedents of Individualism

There appears to be a shift from collectivism to individualism in many parts of the world. The major determinant of this shift is affluence. Geert Hofstede found correlations of the order of .80 between the rank of a country, on his individualism score (based on responses to values), and gross national product per capita. As people become affluent, they become financially independent and independent from their ingroups. Affluence is also usually associated with industrialization and is related to cultural complexity (indexed by such variables as the number of distinct occupations, levels of political organization, and population density). Complex cultures tend to be more individualistic than simple cultures because there are many potential ingroups and individuals have an opportunity to choose whether to stay in or to leave these ingroups.

Affluence is related to having small families, including having only one child. Small families allow parents to raise their children individualistically, and children of such families tend to be idiocentric.

The method of making a living is also an important determinant of individualism or collectivism. In cultures where people make a living by gathering food, hunting, or fishing, self-reliance tends to be more functional than dependence on authorities. In such cultures child-rearing practices emphasize self-reliance and independence, and thus people conform less than in cultures that are based on agriculture. In agricultural cultures there is more collectivism and conformity because it is more functional to conform to authorities while public works (e.g., building of irrigation canals) are being performed. Similarly, in most cultures, but especially in complex industrial cultures, the upper classes emphasize self-reliance and independence and are individualistic, whereas the lower social classes emphasize obedience in their child rearing and tend to be conforming. Davidson, Jaccard, Triandis, Morales, and Diaz-Guerrero found that among lower-class women in Mexico, norms determined whether they intended to have additional children, whereas among upper-class Mexican and most American women, attitudes predicted whether they intended to have more children.

Exposure to the modern mass media also increases the shift from collectivism to individualism, because most television programs are produced in the individualistic cultures. Social mobility and geographical mobility also contribute to individualism. Those who have migrated to other countries are more individualistic. Movement from rural to urban centers also is correlated with individualism. Child-rearing practices that characterize individualist cultures emphasize the child's autonomy, creativity, self-reliance, and independence from family. In collectivist cultures, obedience, duty, and sacrifice for the ingroup are emphasized.

Consequences of Individualism

Socialization can be conceived of as both an antecedent and a consequence of individualism. Individualists raise their children to be self-reliant and independent, but self-reliance and independence also create individualism. Thus, circular causation is involved between the cultural syndrome and socialization. Among the consequences, the most important concern social behavior.

Collectivists behave toward their friends and coworkers with more intimacy (e.g., revealing personal information), and toward their outgroups with less intimacy, than do individualists. The hierarchical structure of collectivist cultures means that there is more subordination and less superordination toward ingroup members in collectivist than in individualist cultures; also, there should be less subordination and more superordination of outgroups by collectivists than by individualists. Because individualists must enter and leave many ingroups, they develop superb skills for superficial interactions, but do not have very good skills for intimate behaviors.

Further Comments

1. While there are still skeptics, the basic proposition that conflict is best understood in its cultural context is now widely applied. Sally Engle Merry, Austin Sarat, Susan S. Silbey, Richard Delgado, Richard Abel, and others pioneered work on various aspects of the relationship between culture and conflict. Recent examples of diverse applications include the innovative works by Mary Gentile, in managing conflict in an increasingly diverse workplace; by Mitchell Hammer and Gary Weaver, in cultural considerations in hostage negotiations, and by Peter Schuck, on how different academic disciplines have their own cultural approaches to environmental disputes. In analyzing marriage arrangements, Leti Volpp argues that we tend to blame a person's "culture" for what we deem as "bad behavior."[1] The work by Robert Ellickson and others on how norms rather than legal rules govern dispute resolution also illustrates the relevance of culture in understanding conflict. In these cases, it is, for instance, the cultures of rural landowners in Shasta County, the diamond industry, or sumo wrestlers that are relevant.[2]

2. As the readings in Part 1 suggest, however, there is ongoing dialogue on how to define fundamental terms and how to interpret their interrelationships. In their insightful 1998 review of the literature on conflict and culture, Michelle Le Baron and her colleagues describe how the more recent literature reveals a "dramatic shift of focus." They note the trend toward "progressive questioning, deconstructing, and stripping away of what were once-assumed foundations," as illustrated by the themes of culture-bound perceptions and cultural construction of identity and knowledge.[3]

> Although the terms perception and construction appear similar and often are used interchangeably, each term implies different assumptions about the nature of social reality. Perception suggests the presence of an objective social world which can be investigated and known. The hope is that an accurate knowledge of social reality may be accumulated that will help us to correct misperceptions and improve perception, enabling us all to "see" things in the same way. The term construction suggests that there is no objective social reality "out there." Rather, we collectively construct or define what we believe to be the objective social world. In other words, through various processes (culture being one such process) we socially construct reality.

As LeBaron explains, the earlier research and literature reflected a naive belief that culture is stable and assumptions of the transparency and accessibility by all of the "dominant" culture. In contrast, more recent research and literature acknowledge culture as a "dynamic that both shapes and reflects experience" and that both dominant and multiple minority cultures may be more "opaque" and complex than assumed. In addition, scholars now are revisiting the varied meanings of fundamental terms and concepts:

> What do we mean by culture? What do we mean by competence? What do we mean by knowledge? What do we mean by fair practice? Through which cultural lens will we evaluate the boundaries of ethical behavior? These questions flow not only from an acknowledgment of the complexity of multiculturalism, but also from the decline of modernity and the questions inspired by postmodernism, feminist theory and social constructionism. . . . Words and terms must be chosen carefully and explained thoroughly, and none stand autonomous or free from critique.

3. In addition to the constructs described in Ting-Toomey's and Triandis's chapters, there are numerous others. For example, Geert Hofstede has described three other dimensions, including (A) power distance (indicating how disparities in power and equality are perceived); (B) masculinity/femininity (indicating the extent to which individuals are expected to conform to designated social roles and characteristics for men and women); and (C) uncertainty avoidance (indicating how individuals react to the lack of structure and clarity and uncertain situations).[4] Cynthia Savage also describes value orientations originally developed by Florence Kluckhorn and her associates.[5] These values are organized around the six categories of self, family, society, nature, human nature, and the supernatural.

Though potentially useful tools, these constructs, of course, have their limitations. While there have many studies on individualism and collectivism,[6] for instance, scholars have questioned the limited number of nationalities studied and the fact that most of the research has been conducted by Western theorists.[7]

Teaching Ideas

1. Think of a heated dispute where different parties experienced and described the conflict differently. How did these differences come about? How did the individuals involved, the cultural norms, or the event itself contribute to these differences? How did the first person to describe the conflict shape the resolution process and outcome? If you were the mediator, how would these factors have influenced you, your way of handling the dispute, or the eventual outcome?

2. There are many ways in which we acquire our own, individual "culture," including the stories that we grew up with. Identify a favorite family story that deals with a conflict or dispute, either taken from a book or passed down orally. Reflect on how the story transmitted important values and approaches to resolving conflict.

3. Graphically depict your own "cultural map." You might begin by identifying key cultural groups to which you belong. For this exercise, you can define "cultural group" broadly to include groups that have influenced how you perceive the world and what is important to you. These might include your family, ethnic, religious, school, or occupational group. Be creative in how you depict your map. It might be a circle with free-flowing lines to depict the relative importance of and interrelationships between each group.

4. Using the constructs described in the readings, describe yourself according to the individualism-collectivism constructs and the high- and low-context constructs. Explore how these self-observations help explain your approach to conflict and conflict resolution. You might also ask someone else who knows you well to describe you. To what extent are your self-perception and her or his perception different?

NOTES

1. Mary C. Gentile, "Managing Conflict in a Diverse Workplace," Harvard Business School, Case No. 5-396-090 (1995); Mitchell R. Hammer and Gary R. Weaver, "Cultural Considerations in Hostage Negotiations," in Gary R. Weaver ed., *Culture, Communications and Conflict: Readings in Intercultural Relations* (Needham Heights, MA: Ginn Press 1994), 499–510; Peter H. Schuck, "Multiculturalism Redux: Science, Law, and Politics," 11 *Yale Law and Policy Review* 1 (1993); Leti Volpp, "Blaming Culture for Bad Behavior," 12 *Yale Journal of Law & the Humanities* 89 (2000).

2. Robert C. Ellickson, "Of Coase and Cattle: Dispute Resolution among Neighbors in Shasta Country," 38 *Stanford Law Review* 623 (1986); Lisa Bernstein, "Opting Out of the Legal System: Extralegal Contractual Relations in the Diamond Industry," 21 *Journal of*

Legal Studies 115 (1992); Mark D. West, "Legal Rules and Social Norms in Japan's Secret World of Sumo," 26 *Journal of Legal Studies* 165 (1997).

3. Michelle LeBaron, Erin McCandless, and Stephen Garon, *Conflict and Culture: A Literature Review and Bibliography (1992–1998 Update)* (Fairfax, Va: George Mason University Institute for Conflict Analysis and Resolution, 1998), 2. See also Michelle LeBaron Duryea, *Conflict and Culture: A Literature Review and Bibliography* (Victoria, British Columbia: University of Victoria Institute for Dispute Resolution, 1992).

4. Geert Hofstede, "The Cultural Relativity of the Quality of Life Concept," in Gary R. Weaver ed. *Culture, Communication and Conflict: Readings in Intercultural Relations* (Needham Heights, MA: Ginn, 1994), 131.

5. Cynthia A. Savage, "Culture and Mediation: A Red Herring," 5 *American Journal of Gender and the Law* 269 (1996).

6. E.g., Harry C. Triandis, *Individualism and Collectivism.* (Boulder: Westview, 1995).

7. Elizabeth Weldon and Karen A. Jehn, "Examining Cross-Cultural Differences in Conflict Management Behavior: A Strategy for Future Research," 6 (4) *International Journal of Conflict Management* 387–403 (1995).

Part II

Gender and Conflict

Introduction

While culture and conflict are interrelated, this part on "Gender and Conflict" and the next on "Ethnicity, Race, and Conflict" demonstrate the lack of agreement about the details of this interrelationship and about the significance of the connections. These parts illustrate that some fundamental issues are unresolved and offer varied perspectives on how they might be resolved.

Anita Taylor and Judi Beinstein Miller raise three basic propositions: (1) it is appropriate and, indeed, important to study conflict in consideration of gender; (2) gender should be studied as a social construct and not as a matter of biological sex categories; and (3) the nature of power in conflict and how gender modifies power should be carefully studied.

After this introductory chapter come two classic but controversial articles. Carol Gilligan argues that the process of conflict resolution, and in particular moral reasoning, cannot be described in general terms without consideration of gender. Critical of a model of moral reasoning that presumes that boys/men and girls/women have identical moral considerations, she proposes instead that males are more drawn to rights and logic-driven reasoning, whereas females are more drawn to relational and care-driven reasoning. Ironically, Gilligan's work is sometimes criticized as both overgeneralizing about women (given, for example, myriad ethnic and socioeconomic differences) and as static (given how moral reasoning may differ over time and across situations). But the fact remains that Gilligan's work was one of the first and the most visible to argue for gender differences in conflict resolution; and her work continues to be widely cited in many disciplines.

The second classic piece, by Trina Grillo, brings attention to the possibility that dispute resolution processes can pose inherent dangers to their participants. She posits that men and women may experience and be impacted differently by different processes. Her focus is on how mediation of custody disputes, particularly when mandated by the courts, may present disproportionate risks to women. She argues that women's inclination toward caring and their historical subservience in their domestic relations, for instance, are likely to result in a mediation in which women are dominated.

The next set of short readings continues to explore how gender and conflict are interrelated. As a group, they illustrate the range of inquiries: Do women and men approach conflicts differently, either cognitively (as Gilligan suggests) or behaviorally? Are the outcomes of conflict resolution different for women and men, and are the participants affected differently (as Grillo suggests)? Do men and women have different expectations and perceptions about each other in the conflict resolution process? What explains the commonalities and the differences between genders? In what ways are our perceptions and behaviors shaped by our life experiences? The readings indicate that we are in the early stages of our research on these topics—we are still deciding what questions to ask at the same time as we are formulating tentative answers. In the short excerpts that follow Grillo's chapter, James Grosch and his colleagues discuss a large-scale community mediation program in New York; Michele Hermann compares the judicial and mediation processes in New Mexico; Martha Chamallas summarizes her findings on tort law cases; and Loraleigh Keashly summarizes her literature review of the research. A number of these studies look at both gender and ethnic differences, thus allowing us to consider the interrelationship between these two characteristics. As you review these studies, in addition to their specific inquiries and findings, consider the implications of the studies and what follow-up questions they raise.

While much research considers the relationship of gender to conflict less directly, Phil Zuckerman explores a dispute where gender is the issue. His sociological study of a Jewish congregation arguing over how to "regulate" gender offers numerous firsthand accounts of differing perceptions of religion, gender, and loyalties. In contrast to the set of short readings above, this piece offers a detailed narrative of an evolving conflict and how the participants become increasingly vested in gender and religious symbols.

Finally, this part ends with a thought-provoking piece by Tracy E. Higgins that relates issues about gender and feminist ideology, culture, and disputes over international human rights. Feminists traditionally have argued that differences matter; but questions over international human rights for women force feminists to explore how far this principle of differences should extend. Higgins explores the tensions in two related philosophical and political debates: (1) those who advocate for a universal model of human rights (universalists) versus those who advocate that human rights and norms are specific to each culture and not cross-cultural (cultural relativists); and (2) those feminists who advocate that women throughout the world share some common concerns and experiences, such as oppression by the state or private customs, that should serve as the foundation for a global platform (feminist universalists or essentialists) versus those feminists who question these commonalities, suggesting instead that gender oppression needs a local, contextualized focus (feminist anti-essentialists). While noting that the cultural relativists and feminist anti-essentialists both share a skepticism of universal standards and focus instead on a cultural perspective, she distinguishes their varied views on the formation and role of cultural standards. Higgins's discussion reveals the complexities within feminist jurisprudence, while introducing the cultural relativist debate that is revisited at the end of Parts 3 and 4.

Chapter 11

The Necessity of Seeing Gender in Conflict

Anita Taylor and Judi Beinstein Miller

Our first proposition is that it is inappropriate to study social issues (including conflict) without considering the impact of gender. It is inappropriate because gender is one factor that pervades all aspects and levels of conflict. Gender carries expectations for conflict behavior and for rights and responsibilities in conflict negotiations. As such, it connects social context to specific conflicts while influencing conflict processes directly. But the pervasiveness of gender makes its influence, like the air one breathes, too often unseen. Gender becomes a kind of subtext or buried premise that then supports other axiomatic conclusions. That invisibility is nowhere more important than in the paradigms on which Western science and philosophy are based, paradigms shared by mainstream conflict theorists and practitioners alike.

Mainstream theorists and practitioners have seldom recognized the gender bias inherent in their worldview, or have not perceived many phenomena as effects of male dominance, even when they questioned the tenets of logical positivism. Feminist scientists, however, have identified gender bias throughout Western thought and science. They have identified bias in locations ranging from the selection of research questions and populations (e.g., focusing on studying heart disease in men, or concentrating research resources on "public" policy issues) to the premises that inform data interpretation (e.g., interpreting a tendency of women to dislike competitive situations as "fear of success"). Keller, Eisler, and others have shown how masculine perspectives have pervaded Western thought since Plato, elevating the need for linear thinking, rationality, and objectivity to axiomatic status. The premise that "man" is a competitive animal, for example, is widely accepted and underlies much of social science, lay and public philosophy, and interpersonal interaction. These kinds of observations lead us to the conclusion that gender must be included in studies of conflict. To exclude it is to ignore or misunderstand a central element in human behavior. Although gender will not be equally salient in all conflicts, it will be involved in some way if the social and political structure in which the conflict occurs is patriarchal.

From Anita Taylor and Judy Beinstein Miller, eds., *Conflict and Gender* (Cresskill, NJ: Hampton, 1994), 4–15.

In contrast to its background position in mainstream theory and research, gender occupies center stage in feminist theories, which argue that no phenomena can be properly understood without a consideration of gender. Gender organizes social life, social structure, and social beliefs and, according to gender schema theory, gender also organizes the way we process information about the world and hence influences communication in and about conflict. The term *schema* refers to a network of associations that organize or guide perception. Schemata include expectations or beliefs about things that go together, for example, attributes of friends versus enemies or, in the case of gender, what goes along with being female or male. Just as people infer attributes about a person from knowledge of a variety of characteristics (e.g., race, nationality, age), so does (presumed) knowledge of a person's sex evoke attributions about a person. Just as we use some attributes (e.g., spends time with me) to assign persons to a relationship category, we use other attributes (e.g., is nurturant or aggressive) to assess their femininity and masculinity.

The network of associations that constitute a schema not only enables interpretation, judgment, and prediction in situations in which information is unavailable or ambiguous, it also guides categorization and assignment of meaning to the objects of our senses. The associations are not random collections of expectations but rather are born out of regularities in experience, which are culture-bound. Dimensions of experience that matter in a culture are thereby reproduced in the schematic knowledge of its members. Gender schemata, although quite different from one culture to another, are fundamental schemata for humans. Girls and boys in most societies learn to make gender distinctions early in life and continue to elaborate their networks of gender associations because everyone around them makes these distinctions.

The research of Sandra Bem shows how we come to see the world more or less through gender-colored glasses, depending on how well socialized, or in her words how sex-typed, we are. The better we have internalized cultural expectations about gender, including their application to our self-concepts, the more we understand the world, including ourselves, in gendered terms. Our culture makes the distinction between male and female relevant to nearly all aspects of life, with nearly all aspects becoming gendered, including places, events, objects, and behavior. Consequently, the more gender-schematic is our information processing, the greater is our readiness to associate and remember places, events, objects, and behavior on the basis of gender.

Bem and others have provided convincing evidence for the organizing influence of gender schemata by comparing the information processing of sex-typed and non-sex-typed individuals. The subjects in her experiments first rate themselves on a series of traits (the Bem Sex Role Inventory) that are used to categorize them as sex-typed or non-sex-typed, and various aspects of information processing and memory are then compared among these groups of subjects. For example, in one experiment subjects were shown slides of words that had been previously judged to be masculine, feminine, or neuter and told that their memory for these words would later be tested. The recall of sex-typed subjects was expected to manifest an organization by gender to a greater extent than the recall of other subjects. Bem expected and found that sex-typed subjects recalled clusters of same-gender words to a greater extent than non-sex-typed subjects did, presumably because remembering one schema-related item enhanced retrieval of another with which it was associated. In another experiment, subjects listened to a recorded discussion between three males and three females, whose pictures were projected on a screen as they spoke. Afterward, the subjects were asked to match each statement in the discussion with one or another of the photographs. Bem expected that sex-typed subjects would confuse statements by same-sex discussants more often than would non-sex-typed subjects because of their tendency to sort people on the basis of gender. Here, as in other experiments, she found evidence that sex-typed individuals were particularly inclined to organize information on the basis of gender.

Another source of evidence for the pervasive influence of gender comes from language. Although the extent to which language influences perceptions remains controversial, it is clear that how people use language reflects how they perceive the world. Thus, it is significant that language reflects extensive gendering, both in the specific symbols used and in their organization. Phenomena that are irrelevant to sex (e.g., cars, ships, nations, tools) are extensively gendered. Cohn, in an analysis of language used by defense consultants to discuss deterrence, war, and nuclear weapons, provides one powerful example. Masculine-centered sexual imagery pervades this language—for example, "getting more bang for the buck," "losing your stuff by disarming," and in talk about erector launches, patting the missile, and deep penetration. Successful detonation of the first nuclear bomb was announced, in in-house communications, as the birth of a baby boy. The specific situation discussed by Cohn reflects a general characteristic of our language: It "embodies" a gendered view of reality.

Needless to say, when we use language to think, we think with its connotations. Because language, although highly variable from one culture to another, is deeply gendered, it necessitates careful consideration of a second proposition: Gender should not be studied by studying sex—which has been so widely done. We find it troubling to develop this point because it raises questions to which no one has even tentatively satisfactory answers. The difficulty of finding answers, however, must not deter attention to such an important question—as has been the case with most research about conflict.

Most scholars recognize that gender (as distinguished from biological sex) is a social construction, and much feminist research and theory has concentrated on examining the nature of gender. But most social scientific research about gender, including almost all research that relates gender to conflict, does not reflect its socially constructed nature. Instead, most researchers use the term *gender* when what they have actually measured is whether a person is considered (or whether they report themselves) to be male or female—which in most cases corresponds to the person's biological sex. Yet, unless one assumes that what is meant by *sex* and what is meant by *gender* are in fact equivalent, we cannot know whether or not what has been measured is gender. Even in common discourse, most people recognize some differences between what they think of as biological sex and the category of gender, regardless of what words they use. They make distinctions that have more to do with being masculine or feminine, or with how men and women are supposed to behave, think, and/or feel, than with whether those people are male or female.

In short, the terms *sex* and *gender* are not equivalent and should not be used that way by scholars. Not only does equivalent usage lead to confounding of concepts, it raises other important questions about the phenomena we think we are studying. We do not mean that these questions invalidate previous research, but we do suggest that conclusions based on this research be reexamined. Moreover, we believe the ways in which gender influences human relations should be kept foregrounded in any discussion of conflict resolution and in any discussion involving gender.

Sometimes research and theory explicitly reflect the recognition that gender is a social construction; often they do not. In either case, implicit assumptions about gender should not remain unstated or unexamined. These assumptions are that there are two, and only two, genders, operationalized as man and woman; and that these two genders are invariable. These assumptions are made because gender is seen as inextricably related to two, and only two, invariable biological categories, male and female. Many scholars recognize that gender is not clearly demarked, but they operate on unstated assumptions that biological categories are. Thus, although they recognize that gender may be a variable construction, they conceive a person's sex to be discrete. But, because no good way of operationalizing the idea of gender has been conceived, scholars generally do so by "measuring" sex identifications. In writing, however, they nonetheless use the term *gender* to refer to what has been measured.

The difficulty with such a convention should be obvious: Concepts recognized as different (sex and gender) are not defined differently (either conceptually or operationally) and in fact are confounded in both measurement and reporting. It is widely believed that sex and gender correlate highly, and such a belief may be warranted. But even without precise measurements we know sex and gender do not correlate perfectly, and without a clear operationalization of gender, we have no way to assess the degree of confidence we can have in any conclusions about gender differences or similarities when they are measured by sex identifications.

Scholarship based on humanistic methods is only slightly less "guilty" of confounding sex and gender than that based on scientific methods. We have great sympathy with the arguments of many feminist scholars that humanistic methods are especially useful for gender research due to their focus on the complexities of individual experience. But humanistic writing is rarely freer than social scientific writing from the overarching confounding of sex and gender. Moreover, few scholars, regardless of discipline or method, have any clear concept of gender as other than an identity based on invariable, bipolar biological "realities." Few can say what it is that creates a sense of being male and female. Although all may recognize that the two "kinds" of gender are defined in relationship to each other, almost no one operationalizes that relationship in defining the concept. Many feminist scholars argue that a component of hierarchy exists between the (two) genders, but as we argue here, identifying and operationalizing that hierarchy has rarely been done.

Such thinking transfers buried assumptions about sex to gender without ever questioning the transfer, much less the original assumption. Having assumed two discrete, mutually exclusive sexes, we further assume that once identified, sex is unchanging. Although scholars (and most others) recognize that neither of these assumptions applies without qualification to gender, most thinking and research continues to be built around two discrete, mutually exclusive, and unchanging genders. Research about psychological gender may be an exception to such a conclusion, but even then a person's gender is thought to change only in relatively superficial ways (e.g., men may become more feminine as they age).

Several writers have shown that even the biological dichotomy between male and female humans is not as clear as assumed. Unless one defines a male as any individual with a Y chromosome and a female as anyone without a Y chromosome, the male and female categories are not mutually exclusive, regardless of whether the criterion is hormones or any of the sex markers including secondary sex characteristics. For example, men and women share the same hormones, although in different quantities, and there is great variation among both men and women in how much of each hormone an individual has, which in turn changes for each person with time and environmental influences. In the absence of biotechnological developments that science fiction may foreshadow, men cannot birth babies, nor can women inseminate men; but neither can all women birth babies, nor all men inseminate women. More significantly, many people with the "wrong" chromosomes develop female gender identities and some people with no Y chromosomes develop male gender identities. Although modern surgical techniques and modern media have permitted wider awareness of such "anomalies," such inconsistencies are not new phenomena. Nor have they been created by "modern" civilization. Some cultures have legitimated gender identities that were inconsistent with external genitalia; others have attributed special status to persons who possessed biological manifestations of both sexes.

Why then does our research about gender so rarely exhibit the appropriate caution in its generalizations? One (not the only) reason is that we do not see our conceptualization of gender as problematic. We may recognize that masculinity and femininity vary by degree, but we rarely extend that conception to our understanding of gender. If we recognize femininity and masculinity as being different from female and male, we may operationalize them as continuous variables and add the qualification "psychological" gender. Even then, we rarely see gender as influenced by situation, and we do not construe it as defined in part by relationships. Rather, we treat it as an identity that is discrete (two, invariable, mutually exclusive categories) and seldom think of doing research that conceptualizes it any other way.

From our perspective, gender is behavior and schematic processing of behavior more than it is a "thing." Gender attributions are made by each person in everyday life, without testing their biological basis. In ways most of us never consider, each of us is always "doing" gender—and drawing conclusions about it. In that way, each person is a gender researcher. Almost never does any of us meet another without deciding what gender she or he is. And, without ever noticing, we use verbal and nonverbal communication to cue those around us to the gender identity we wish them to perceive, noticing those efforts only when they fail. Yet the processes by which we make these gender decisions remain virtually unknown. Although some intriguing possibilities have been posed, little research explores these possibilities. Such research is essential for scholarship to illuminate adequately the nature of gender and the implications of gender difference.

Research about what leads to gender attributions can improve understanding of more than gender. It can be, for example, fundamental to developing theories about conflict and its management or resolution—for, inevitably, conflicts involve people who carry into all situations their gender schemata, which guide their behavior in and communication about the situations. Attributions of gender involve far more than a simple decision of whether individuals are male or female. Those attributions inevitably entail implications about appropriate behavior and what behaviors mean.

In essence, what we argue about gender here is that conceptual clarification is required. We need a conceptualization flexible enough to allow for more than two genders, for malleable gender behavior, and for change in what counts culturally as genderlike.[1] Women of color and some feminist scholars have pushed current feminist thinking a long way toward that goal. Feminists have largely recognized that no unifying "essence" unites all women and that we must accommodate differences among women if our thinking and research are to be accurate and useful. Similar recognitions need to inform conflict research. We cannot usefully continue the practice of measuring gender by sex.

The third proposition we believe necessary for adequate understanding of conflict and conflict resolution concerns power in conflict. Specifically, attention must be paid to the nature of power in conflict, the relationships of power to conflict, and the place of power in conflict, in each case as power is modified by gender. This proposition is not quite so problematic for conflict theory as our second because most conflict theory examines power. What feminist thinking contributes is a recognition of the ways in which gender and power merge.

Foremost among these points is the need to reconceptualize what we mean by power itself. Power in Western culture has been conceived of as the ability to control—whether the control is exerted on other people, the environment, or oneself. It is, as such, integral to maintaining order in a hierarchal social structure. Rarely recognized, however, is the link between such an understanding and the construal of hierarchy as essential to social structure. Control in a hierarchy inevitably involves a person or entity in a position to dominate those less powerful, whether that ability is exercised or simply accepted by those who are dominated. To conceive power as control might not be necessary in egalitarian systems.

Here again is a manifestation of the deeply buried assumptions that tie gender to conflict in usually unseen ways. Conceivably, hierarchy does not require a gender component. But in practice, most hierarchical systems that we know are patriarchal.[2] And in a patriarchy, gender is linked to power because the dominant entity is always male or identified with male, a conclusion demonstrated clearly by many feminist writers.

Schaef has proposed an alternative conception of power, one that is essentially feminist. Instead of construing power as power over others, she describes "power to" or "power with," which is the ability to empower oneself and others. These two concepts differ in important ways. The traditional conception of power as the ability to control (usually others) is of a limited entity. Any increase in power by the person or group being controlled involves a reduction in amount of power held by the controller. In contrast, the empowerment conception of power does not conceive of power as limited. Instead, in an empowerment construction power is unlimited, and to empower generates increases in one's own power as well as that of others. This type of power not only does not require hierarchy or dominance but is in fact thwarted by hierarchy and destroyed by dominance. This alternative conception of the nature of power is central to feminist thinking because equality is at the heart of feminism. Feminism rejects constructions of relationships between people that elevate one above the other and permit the domination of one by the other.

Clearly, whether one employs a power over or power with conception affects how power is seen in relation to conflict. Feminist analysis makes two points about power. The first (not a new idea to conflict theory) is that power asymmetry itself leads to conflict and thwarts its resolution. Control and domination thwart achievement of autonomy, which according to some scholars is a basic human need. When any basic need remains unmet, individuals will search vigorously for ways to meet it. Being dominated is not a need-satisfying way of living, and if the "history" of human cultures demonstrates anything, it is that the dominated must be controlled through actual or threatened coercion. Such a dynamic in large part explains why the history of hierarchically structured cultures is a history of forceful control of the dominated portions of the populace by successive elites. It also explains why that same history includes few examples of conflicts, even those ostensibly ended by wars, that have actually been resolved. Coercion as a means of conflict control is antithetical to the actual resolution of conflicts.

A second point made by feminist analyses of power and conflict is newer to conflict theory: Hierarchy is strongly linked to patriarchy. Patriarchy, a hierarchical system of social structure that elevates males and that which is male identified, involves a concomitant devaluation of the feminine—females and female-identified values, behaviors, or objects. In a patriarchy, people must be controlled through dominance, backed by force if necessary, and control is exercised by male or male-identified dominators. Thus, values that perpetuate the hierarchy and the system of control are identified with males and become masculine values. Values that are less useful in perpetuating hierarchy and control are identified with females and become feminine values. Among these feminine values are those essential to maintaining the species itself, but in a patriarchal culture they are not valued equally with masculine values. Moreover, enculturation processes ensure that these devalued feminine characteristics are not distributed at random through the population but found more among women than men.

Particularly important to remember when applying feminist ideas to an analysis of conflict is that the gendering of conflict through conceptions of power is not limited to situations of conflict between women and men. Patriarchal arrangements place whatever is defined as feminine in devalued (hence disadvantaged) positions. Thus, in patriarchy women are disadvantaged because they are less valued and/or less powerful than men.

The role of hierarchy in patriarchy is particularly complicated because it is influenced by other elements as well. Race and class inequalities also characterize many relationships and may be as salient or more salient to patriarchal power than gender. Gender in such cases remains important, but it is modified by race, class, or both. The experience of gender is then qualitatively different from race to race or class to class. Males ordinarily retain higher rank within the race or class, but the hierarchy distinguishes among them by race and class. Equally significant, although less often obvious, is the disadvantage of female-identified males. In a patriarchy, males within a class or race group retain their higher rank only when they embody masculine characteristics. Those who noticeably embody the feminine violate cultural prescriptions and may become the most disadvantaged of all. In modern U.S. culture, for example, it is possible—even desirable—for men to show sensitivity and to be caring toward their families. But, should they demonstrate female-identified qualities without sufficient balance of the traditionally masculine ones, they become among the most vilified people within the culture.

Feminist analysis raises the question of whether the use of power in conflict can ever be functional for resolving the conflict as opposed to managing it. Some conflict resolution theorists have noted how approaches to eliminating conflict have usually employed power and have ultimately resolved few conflicts. Our question is this: What would be the impact of bringing a feminist conception of power into conflict resolution theory and practice?

Clearly, conflict theory needs to identify means of empowering the disadvantaged as well as the advantaged. Some efforts at doing so have been made. More important is the need to learn how to transform existing patriarchal systems, because significant empowerment of disadvantaged groups will not be possible as long as power is conceived as limited and divisible rather than unlimited and generative. The conception of "power over" (coercive power) collides with outcomes of autonomy and equality for all parties.

This analysis of power and its place in conflict exposes the deeply radical nature of a feminist critique. Conflicts among unequals—inevitable as long as humans strive for autonomy—cannot be resolved in a hierarchy. This feminist analysis is consistent with ideas about engaging conflict constructively that are common in communication and conflict studies. In emphasizing that individual and relationship growth can occur through the constructive handling of conflict, both feminist analysis and relational communication theory eschew the power-over construction normally implied in the discourse about conflict. Feminist analysis goes further in that it links constructions of power and equality with gender and, we add, of necessity includes an understanding of the complexity of gender. Finally, we invite our readers to consider the implications of having the parties involved in conflicts—be they "ordinary" humans in personal relationships, supervisors in work relationships, "leaders" in governments, teachers in classrooms, mediators in disputes, or scholars in research academies—not only recognize the feminist conception of power but also share its absolute dedication to equality.

NOTES

1. Especially useful in recognizing the variability of the phenomena of gender are the distinctions Kessler and McKenna make among gender assignment (what infants are labeled at birth), gender identity (what one calls oneself), gender role, and gender attribution (what gender other people decide a person is). Notably, each of these groupings uses dichotomous categorization but does not rely on and is not consistent with the supposedly clear biological dichotomy. We feel the need to add a point: Gender identity has at least two facets, which are not invariable as they are much influenced by situation. Two aspects of gender identity are how one identifies oneself to oneself and how one identifies oneself to others.

2. Matrilineal social structures rarely refute this conclusion. Although familial ties and descent may associate with female, power structures in most such cultures reflect strong gender components that privilege males. Most important to recognize is that dichotomous categorization of cultures into hierarchical or not is as inappropriate as is dichotomous categorization of gender.

Chapter 12

In a Different Voice
Psychological Theory and Women's Development

Carol Gilligan

In this particular dilemma, a man named Heinz considers whether or not to steal a drug which he cannot afford to buy in order to save the life of his wife. In the standard format of Lawrence Kohlberg's interviewing procedure, the description of the dilemma itself—Heinz's predicament, the wife's disease, the druggist's refusal to lower his price—is followed by the question "Should Heinz steal the drug?" The reasons for and against stealing are then explored through a series of questions that vary and extend the parameters of the dilemma in a way designed to reveal the underlying structure of moral thought.

Jake, at eleven, is clear from the outset that Heinz should steal the drug. Constructing the dilemma, as Kohlberg did, as a conflict between the values of property and life, he discerns the logical priority of life and uses that logic to justify his choice:

> For one thing, a human life is worth more than money, and if the druggist only makes $1,000, he is still going to live, but if Heinz doesn't steal the drug, his wife is going to die. (*Why is life worth more than money?*) Because the druggist can get a thousand dollars later from rich people with cancer, but Heinz can't get his wife again. (*Why not?*) Because people are all different and so you couldn't get Heinz's wife again.

Asked whether Heinz should steal the drug if he does not love his wife, Jake replies that he should, saying that not only is there "a difference between hating and killing," but also, if Heinz were caught, "the judge would probably think it was the right thing to do." Asked about the fact that, in stealing, Heinz would be breaking the law, he says that "the laws have mistakes, and you can't go writing up a law for everything that you can imagine."

Thus, while taking the law into account and recognizing its function in maintaining social order (the judge, Jake says, "should give Heinz the lightest possible sentence"), he also sees the law as man-made and therefore subject to error and change. Yet his judgment that Heinz should steal the drug, like his view of the law as having mistakes, rests on the assumption of agreement, a societal consensus around moral values that allows one to know and expect others to recognize what is "the right thing to do."

Fascinated by the power of logic, this eleven-year-old boy locates truth in math, which, he says, is "the only thing that is totally logical." Considering the moral dilemma to be "sort of like a math problem with humans," he sets it up as an equation and proceeds to work out the solution. Since his solution is rationally derived, he assumes that anyone following reason would arrive at the same conclusion and thus that a judge would also consider stealing to be the right thing for Heinz to do. Yet he is also aware of the limits of logic. Asked whether there is a right answer to moral problems, Jake replies that "there can only be right and wrong in judgment," since the parameters of action are variable and complex. Illustrating how actions undertaken with the best of intentions can eventuate in the most disastrous of consequences, he says, "Like if you give an old lady your seat on the trolley, if you are in a trolley crash and that seat goes through the window, it might be that reason that the old lady dies."

Theories of developmental psychology illuminate well the position of this child, standing at the juncture of childhood and adolescence, at what Jean Piaget describes as the pinnacle of childhood intelligence, and beginning through thought to discover a wider universe of possibility. The moment of preadolescence is caught by the conjunction of formal operational thought with a description of self still anchored in the factual parameters of his childhood world—his age, his town, his father's occupation, the substance of his likes, dislikes, and beliefs. Yet as his self-description radiates the self-confidence of a child who has arrived, in Erik Erikson's terms, at a favorable balance of industry over inferiority—competent, sure of himself, and knowing well the rules of the game—so his emergent capacity for formal thought, his ability to think about thinking and to reason things out in a logical way, frees him from dependence on authority and allows him to find solutions to problems by himself.

This emergent autonomy follows the trajectory that Kohlberg's six stages of moral development trace, a three-level progression from an egocentric understanding of fairness based on individual need (stages one and two), to a conception of fairness anchored in the shared conventions of societal agreement (stages three and four), and finally to a principled understanding of fairness that rests on the free-standing logic of equality and reciprocity (stages five and six). While this boy's judgments at eleven are scored as conventional on Kohlberg's scale, a mixture of stages three and four, his ability to bring deductive logic to bear on the solution of moral dilemmas, to differentiate morality from law, and to see how laws can be considered to have mistakes points toward the principled conception of justice that Kohlberg equates with moral maturity.

In contrast, Amy's response to the dilemma conveys a very different impression, an image of development stunted by a failure of logic, an inability to think for herself. Asked if Heinz should steal the drug, she replies in a way that seems evasive and unsure:

> Well, I don't think so. I think there might be other ways besides stealing it, like if he could borrow the money or make a loan or something, but he really shouldn't steal the drug—but his wife shouldn't die either.

Asked why he should not steal the drug, she considers neither property nor law but rather the effect that theft could have on the relationship between Heinz and his wife:

> If he stole the drug, he might save his wife then, but if he did, he might have to go to jail, and then his wife might get sicker again, and he couldn't get more of the drug, and it might not be good. So, they should really just talk it out and find some other way to make the money.

Seeing in the dilemma not a math problem with humans but a narrative of relationships that extends over time, Amy envisions the wife's continuing need for her husband and the husband's continuing concern for his wife and seeks to respond to the druggist's need in a way that would sustain rather than sever connection. Just as she ties the wife's survival to the preservation of relationships, so she considers the value of the wife's life in a context of relationships, saying that it would be wrong to let her die because, "if she died, it hurts a lot of people and it hurts her." Since Amy's moral judgment is grounded in the belief that, "if somebody has something that would keep somebody alive, then it's not right not to give it to them," she considers the problem in the dilemma to arise not from the druggist's assertion of rights but from his failure of response.

As the interviewer proceeds with the series of questions that follow from Kohlberg's construction of the dilemma, Amy's answers remain essentially unchanged, the various probes serving neither to elucidate nor to modify her initial response. Whether or not Heinz loves his wife, he still shouldn't steal or let her die; if it were a stranger dying instead, Amy says that "if the stranger didn't have anybody near or anyone she knew," then Heinz should try to save her life, but he should not steal the drug. But as the interviewer conveys through the repetition of questions that the answers she gave were not heard or not right, Amy's confidence begins to diminish, and her replies become more constrained and unsure. Asked again why Heinz should not steal the drug, she simply repeats, "Because it's not right." Asked again to explain why, she states again that theft would not be a good solution, adding lamely, "If he took it, he might not know how to give it to his wife, and so his wife might still die." Failing to see the dilemma as a self-contained problem in moral logic, she does not discern the internal structure of its resolution; as she constructs the problem differently herself, Kohlberg's conception completely evades her.

Instead, seeing a world comprised of relationships rather than of people standing alone, a world that coheres through human connection rather than through systems of rules, she finds the puzzle in the dilemma to lie in the failure of the druggist to respond to the wife. Saying that "it is not right for someone to die when their life could be saved," she assumes that if the druggist were to see the consequences of his refusal to lower his price, he would realize that "he should just give it to the wife and then have the husband pay back the money later." Thus she considers the solution to the dilemma to lie in making the wife's condition more salient to the druggist or, that failing, in appealing to others who are in a position to help.

Just as Jake is confident the judge would agree that stealing is the right thing for Heinz to do, so Amy is confident that, "if Heinz and the druggist had talked it out long enough, they could reach something besides stealing." As he considers the law to "have mistakes," so she sees this drama as a mistake, believing that "the world should just share things more and then people wouldn't have to steal." Both children thus recognize the need for agreement but see it as mediated in different ways—he impersonally through systems of logic and law, she personally through communication in relationship. Just as he relies on the conventions of logic to deduce the solution to this dilemma, assuming these conventions to be shared, so she relies on a process of communication, assuming connection and believing that her voice will be heard. Yet while his assumptions about agreement are confirmed by the convergence in logic between his answers and the questions posed, her assumptions are belied by the failure of communication, the interviewer's inability to understand her response.

Although the frustration of the interview with Amy is apparent in the repetition of questions and its ultimate circularity, the problem of interpretation is focused by the assessment of her response. When considered in the light of Kohlberg's definition of the stages and sequence of moral development, her moral judgments appear to be a full stage lower in maturity than those of the boy. Scored as a mixture of stages two and three, her responses seem to reveal a feeling of powerlessness in the world, an inability to think systematically about the concepts of morality or law, a reluctance to challenge authority or to examine the logic of received moral truths, a failure even to conceive of acting directly to save a life or to consider that such action, if taken, could possibly have an effect. As her reliance on relationships seems to reveal a continuing dependence and vulnerability, so her belief in communication as the mode through which to resolve moral dilemmas appears naive and cognitively immature.

Yet Amy's description of herself conveys a markedly different impression. Once again, the hallmarks of the preadolescent child depict a child secure in her sense of herself, confident in the substance of her beliefs, and sure of her ability to do something of value in the world. Describing herself at eleven as "growing and changing," she says that she "sees some things differently now, just because I know myself really well now, and I know a lot more about the world." Yet the world she knows is a different world from that refracted by Kohlberg's construction of Heinz's dilemma. Her world is a world of relationships and psychological truths where an awareness of the connection between people gives rise to a recognition of responsibility for one another, a perception of the need for response. Seen in this light, her understanding of morality as arising from the recognition of relationship, her belief in communication as the mode of conflict resolution, and her conviction that the solution to the dilemma will follow from its compelling representation seem far from naive or cognitively immature. Instead, Amy's judgments contain the insights central to an ethic of care, just as Jake's judgments reflect the logic of the justice approach. Her incipient awareness of the "method of truth," the central tenet of nonviolent conflict resolution, and her belief in the restorative activity of care, lead her to see the actors in the dilemma arrayed not as opponents in a contest of rights but as members of a network of relationships on whose continuation they all depend. Consequently her solution to the dilemma lies in activating the network by communication, securing the inclusion of the wife by strengthening rather than severing connections.

But the different logic of Amy's response calls attention to the interpretation of the interview itself. Conceived as an interrogation, it appears instead as a dialogue, which takes on moral dimensions of its own, pertaining to the interviewer's uses of power and to the manifestations of respect. With this shift in the conception of the interview, it immediately becomes clear that the interviewer's problem in understanding Amy's response stems from the fact that Amy is answering a different question from the one the interviewer thought had been posed. Amy is considering not *whether* Heinz should act in this situation ("*Should* Heinz steal the drug?") but rather *how* Heinz should act in response to his awareness of his wife's need ("Should Heinz *steal* the drug?"). The interviewer takes the mode of action for granted, presuming it to be a matter of fact; Amy assumes the necessity for action and considers what form it should take. In the interviewer's failure to imagine a response not dreamt of in Kohlberg's moral philosophy lies the failure to hear Amy's question and to see the logic in her response, to discern that what appears, from one perspective, to be an evasion of the dilemma signifies in other terms a recognition of the problem and a search for a more adequate solution.

Thus in Heinz's dilemma these two children see two very different moral problems—Jake a conflict between life and property that can be resolved by logical deduction, Amy a fracture of human relationship that must be mended with its own thread. Asking different questions that arise from different conceptions of the moral domain, the children arrive at answers that fundamentally diverge, and the arrangement of these answers as successive stages on a scale of increasing moral maturity calibrated by the logic of the boy's response misses the different truth revealed in the judgment of the girl. To the question "What does he see that she does not?" Kohlberg's theory provides a ready response, manifest in the scoring of Jake's judgments a full stage higher than Amy's in moral maturity; to the question "What does she see that he does not?" Kohlberg's theory has nothing to say. Since most of her responses fall through the sieve of Kohlberg's scoring system, her responses appear from his perspective to lie outside the moral domain.

Yet just as Jake reveals a sophisticated understanding of the logic of justification, so Amy is equally sophisticated in her understanding of the nature of choice. Recognizing that "if both the roads went in totally separate ways, if you pick one, you'll never know what would happen if you went the other way," she explains that "that's the chance you have to take, and like I said, it's just really a guess." To illustrate her point "in a simple way," she describes her choice to spend the summer at camp:

I will never know what would have happened if I had stayed here, and if something goes wrong at camp, I'll never know if I stayed here if it would have been better. There's really no way around it because there's no way you can do both at once, so you've got to decide, but you'll never know.

In this way, these two eleven-year-old children, both highly intelligent and perceptive about life, though in different ways, display different modes of moral understanding, different ways of thinking about conflict and choice. In resolving Heinz's dilemma, Jake relies on theft to avoid confrontation and turns to the law to mediate the dispute. Transposing a hierarchy of power into a hierarchy of values, he defuses a potentially explosive conflict between people by casting it as an impersonal conflict of claims. In this way, he abstracts the moral problem from the interpersonal situation, finding in the logic of fairness an objective way to decide who will win the dispute. But this hierarchical ordering, with its imagery of winning and losing and the potential for violence which it contains, gives way in Amy's construction of the dilemma to a network of connection, a web of relationships that is sustained by a process of communication. With this shift, the moral problem changes from one of unfair domination, the imposition of property over life, to one of unnecessary exclusion, the failure of the druggist to respond to the wife

The contrasting images of hierarchy and network in children's thinking about moral conflict and choice illuminate two views of morality which are complementary rather than sequential or opposed. But this construction of differences goes against the bias of developmental theory toward ordering differences in a hierarchical mode. The correspondence between the order of developmental theory and the structure of the boys' thought contrasts with the disparity between existing theory and the structure manifest in the thought of the girls. Yet in neither comparison does one child's judgment appear as a precursor of the other's position. Thus, questions arise concerning the relation between these perspectives: What is the significance of this difference, and how do these two modes of thinking connect?

Chapter 13

The Mediation Alternative
Process Dangers for Women

Trina Grillo

Mandatory Mediation and the Dangers of Forced Engagement

Emma has been in a marriage which in its early years seemed to be a good one for both Emma and her husband. She has been the primary caretaker of the children, and she is very committed to them. She has lived much of her life through her husband and her children, and has not worked outside her home. Increasingly, however, she has begun to feel that she and her husband have grown apart, and that he does not see her as a person but rather as a repository of various roles. After much agony, she has decided to end her marriage. Her departure from the marriage is a first step toward seeing her life as having separate dimensions from her husband's and children's, but her right to individuation does not seem clear to her; in fact, there are many times when it seems selfish and wrong. It is hard for her even to find the language to describe what is propelling her to turn her life, and her children's lives, upside down, but propelled she is. The marital separation was an early step toward defining her own physical and psychological boundaries. She now finds herself, however, feeling guilty, frightened, and unsure of how she will survive in the world alone.

Joan has been in a marriage in which she has been physically abused for ten years. She and her husband David have two children, whom David has never abused. She is afraid, however, that if she leaves David, he will begin to abuse the children whenever he is caring for them. Joan has been afraid to leave her marriage because David has threatened to harm her if she does so. When she separated briefly from him previously, he followed her and continually harassed her. Each time David beats Joan he shows great remorse afterwards and promises never to do it again. He is a man of considerable charm, and she has often believed him on these occasions. Nonetheless, Joan has finally decided to leave her husband. She is worried about what will happen, economically and physically, to her children and herself.

Reprinted by permission of the Yale Law Journal Company and Fred B. Rothman & Company from *The Yale Law Journal*, Vol. 100, pages 1545–1610.

It might be that mediation would help Emma's family disengage and discover new ways of relating to one another. Mediation could be useful, even transformative, during the divorce process. Significant possibilities of damage to Emma also exist, however. For example, she might find herself traumatized by a forced engagement with her husband. Or, in the intimate mediation setting, she might find it difficult to withstand criticism of how she is conducting herself in life or in the mediation.

For Joan, the direct confrontation with her husband, with the safety of her children and herself at stake, would surely be psychologically traumatizing and might also put her in physical danger. Because of these possibilities, the chance—even the substantial one—of a beneficial result cannot justify the sort of intrusion by the state that occurs when mediation is mandatory.

While some of mandatory mediation's dangers affect men and women equally, others fall disproportionately on women. A study that compared people who chose to mediate with those who rejected the opportunity found that 44 percent of the reasons given by women who rejected mediation services offered to them centered around their mistrust of, fear of, or desire to avoid their ex-spouse. In contrast, those men who rejected mediation appeared to do so because they were skeptical of the mediation process or convinced they could win in court. Thus, the requirement of mandatory mediation that the parties meet personally with one another, usually without a lawyer present, presents troubling issues for women. Feminist analyses, looked at alone and together, clarify why this is so.

The Ethic of Care in Mediation

Several feminist scholars have suggested that women have a more "relational" sense of self than do men. The most influential of these researchers, Carol Gilligan, describes two different, gendered modes of thought. The female mode is characterized by an "ethic of care" which emphasizes nurturance, connection with others, and contextual thinking. The male mode is characterized by an "ethic of justice" which emphasizes individualism, the use of rules to resolve moral dilemmas, and equality. Under Gilligan's view, the male mode leads one to strive for individualism and autonomy, while the female mode leads one to strive for connection with and caring for others. Some writers, seeing a positive virtue in the ethic of care, have applied Gilligan's work to the legal system. But her work has been criticized by others for its methodology, its conflation of biological sex with gender, and its failure to include race and class differences in its analysis. Indeed, it is not likely that the male/female differences Gilligan notes are consistent across racial and class lines. The "ethic of care" has also been viewed as the manifestation of a system of gender domination. Nevertheless, it is clear that those who operate in a "female mode"—whether biologically male or female—will respond more "selflessly" to the demands of mediation.

Whether the ethic of care is to be enshrined as a positive virtue, or criticized as a characteristic not belonging to all women and contributing to their oppression, one truth emerges: many women see themselves, and judge their own worth, primarily in terms of relationships. This perspective on themselves has consequences for how they function in mediation.

Carrie Menkel-Meadow has suggested that the ethic of care can and should be brought into the practice of law—that the world of lawyering would look very different from the perspective of that ethic. Some commentators have identified mediation as a way to incorporate the ethic of care into the legal system and thereby modify the harshness of the adversary process. And, indeed, at first glance, mediation in the context of divorce might be seen as a way of bringing the woman-identified values of intimacy, nurturance, and care into a legal system that is concerned with the most fundamental aspects of women's and men's lives.

If mediation does not successfully introduce an ethic of care, however, but instead merely sells itself on that promise while delivering something coercive in its place, the consequences will be disastrous for a woman who embraces a relational sense of self. If she is easily persuaded to be cooperative, but her partner is not, she can only lose. If it is indeed her disposition to be caring and focused on relationships, and she has been rewarded for that focus and characterized as "unfeminine" when she departs from it, the language of relationship, caring, and cooperation will be appealing to her and make her vulnerable. Moreover, the intimation that she is not being cooperative and caring or that she is thinking of herself instead of thinking selflessly of the children can shatter her self-esteem and make her lose faith in herself. In short, in mediation, such a woman may be encouraged to repeat exactly those behaviors that have proven hazardous to her in the past.

In the story above, Emma is asked to undergo a forced engagement with the very person from whom she is trying to differentiate herself at a difficult stage in her life. She may find it impossible to think of herself as a separate entity during mediation, while her husband may easily be able to act on behalf of his separate self. As West Describes: "When a separate self must be asserted, women have trouble asserting it. Women's separation from the other in adult life, and the tension between that separation and our fundamental state of connection, is felt most acutely when a woman must make choices, and when she must speak the truth."

Emma will be asked to talk about her needs and feelings, and respond to her husband's needs and feelings. Although in the past her valuing relationships above all else may have worked to the detriment of her separate self, Emma will now be urged to work on the future relationship between herself and her ex-husband. Above all, she will be asked to put the well-being of the children before her own, as if she and her children's well-being were entirely separate. Her problem in addressing her future alone, however, may be that she reflexively puts her children before herself, even when she truly needs to take care of herself in order to take care of her children. For Emma, mediation may play on what are already her vulnerable spots, and put her at a disadvantage. She may begin to think of herself as unfeminine, or simply bad, if she puts her own needs forward. Emma may feel the need to couch every proposal she makes in terms of the needs of her children. In sum, if she articulates her needs accurately, she may end up feeling guilty, selfish, confused, and embarrassed; if she does not, she will be moving backwards to the unbounded self that is at the source of her difficulties.

For Joan, the prescription of mediation might be disastrous. She has always been susceptible to her husband's charm, and has believed him when he has said that he would stop abusing her. She has also always been afraid of him. She is likely, in mediation, to be susceptible and afraid once again. She may continue to care for her husband, and to think that she was responsible for his behavior toward her. Joan, and not her husband, will be susceptible to any pressure to compromise, and to compromise in her situation might be very dangerous for both her and her children.

Sexual Domination and Judicial Violence

Women who have been through mandatory mediation often describe it as an experience of sexual domination, comparing mandatory mediation to rape. Catharine MacKinnon's work provides a basis for explaining why, for some women, this characterization is appropriate. MacKinnon has analyzed gender as a system of power relations, evidenced primarily with respect to the control of women's sexuality. While MacKinnon recognizes the sense in which women are fundamentally connected to others, she does not celebrate it. Rather, she sees the potential for connection as invasive and intrusive. It is precisely the potential for physical connection that permits invasion into the integrity of women's bodies. It is precisely the potential for emotional connection that permits intrusion into the integrity of women's lives.

Men do not experience this same fear of sexual domination, according to MacKinnon; they do not live in constant fear of having the very integrity of their lives intruded upon. Men may not comprehend their role in this system of sexual domination any more than women may be able to articulate the source of their feeling of disempowerment. Yet both of these dynamics are at work in the mediation setting. It may seem a large leap, from acts of physical violence and invasion to the apparently simple requirement that a woman sit in a room with her spouse working toward the resolution of an issue of mutual concern. But that which may be at stake in a court-ordered custody mediation—access to one's children—may be the main reason one has for living, as well as all one's hope for the future. And because mandatory mediation is a forced engagement, ordinarily without attorneys or even friends or supporters present, it may amount to a form of "psychic breaking and entering" or, put another way, psychic rape.

There is always the potential for violence in the legal system: According to Cover "A judge articulates her understanding of a text, and as a result, somebody loses his freedom, his property, his children, even his life. . . . When interpreters have finished their work, they frequently leave behind victims whose lives have been torn apart by these organized, social practices of violence."

The reality of this background of judicial violence cannot be discounted when measuring the potential trauma of the mandatory mediation setting. Although the mediation system is purportedly designed in part to help participants avoid contact with the violence that must come from judicial decisions, in significant ways the violence of the contact is more direct. Since the parties are obliged to speak for themselves in a setting to which the culture has not introduced them and in which the rules are not clear (and in fact vary from mediator to mediator), the potential violence of the legal result, combined with the invasiveness of the setting, may indeed end up feeling to the unwilling participant very much like a kind of rape. Moreover, in judging, it is understood that the critical view of the quarrel is that of the judge, the professional third party. Mediation is described as a form of intervention that reflects the disputants' view of the quarrel. But having the mediation take place on court premises with a mediator who might or might not inject her prejudices into the process may make it unlikely that the disputants' view will control. Thus, a further sense of violation may arise from having another person's view of the dispute characterized and treated as one's own.

That many reportedly find mediation helpful does not mean everyone does. Consensual sex may take place in a certain setting in one instance, but that does not make all sex in that setting consensual; sometimes it is rape. And sometimes it may only seem to be consensual because forced sex is considered par for the course—that is, it is all we know or can imagine.

When I have suggested to mediators that even being forced to sit across the table and negotiate, unassisted, with a spouse might be traumatic, their reaction has been almost uniformly dismissive. Some mediators have denied that this could possibly be the case. Even mediators who acknowledge the possibility of trauma have said, in effect, "So what?" A few hours of discomfort seem not so much to ask in return for a system that, to their mind, serves the courts and the children much better than the alternative. But a few hours of discomfort may not be all that is at stake; the trauma inflicted upon a vulnerable party during mediation can be as great as that which occurs in other psychologically violent confrontations. As such, it should not be minimized. People frequently take months or years to recover from physical or mental abuse, rape, and other traumatic events. Given the psychological vulnerability of people at the time of a divorce, it is likely that some people may be similarly debilitated by a mandatory mediation process.

Moreover, because the mandatory mediation system is more problematic for women than for men, forcing unwilling women to take part in a process which involves much personal exposure sends a powerful social message: it is permissible to discount the real experience of women in the service of someone else's idea of what will be good for them, good for their children, or good for the system.

Alternatives to Mandatory Mediation

Sally Engle Merry and Susan S. Silbey have said that "[d]isputes are cultural events, evolving within a framework of rules about what is worth fighting for, what is the normal or moral way to fight, what kinds of wrongs warrant action, and what kinds of remedies are acceptable." The process by which a society resolves conflict is closely related to its social structure. Implicit in this choice is a message about what is respectable to do or want or say, what the obligations are of being a member of the society or of a particular group within it, and what it takes to be thought of as a good person leading a virtuous life. In the adversary system, it is acceptable to want to win. It is not only acceptable, but expected, that one will rely on a lawyer and advocate for oneself without looking out for the adversary. The judge, a third party obligated to be neutral and bound by certain formalities, bears the ultimate responsibility for deciding the outcome. To the extent that women are more likely than men to believe in communication as a mode of conflict resolution and to appreciate the importance of an adversary's interests, this system does not always suit their needs.

On the other hand, under a scheme of mediation, the standards of acceptable behavior and desires change fundamentally. Parties are to meet with each other, generally without their lawyers. They are encouraged to look at each other's needs and to reach a cooperative resolution based on compromise. Although there are few restrictions on her role in the process, the mediator bears no ultimate, formal responsibility for the outcome of the mediation. In sum, when mediation is the prototype for dispute resolution, the societal message is that a good person—a person following the rules—cooperates, communicates, and compromises.

The glories of cooperation, however, are easily exaggerated. If one party appreciates cooperation more than the other, the parties might compromise unequally. Moreover, the self-disclosure that cooperation requires, when imposed and not sought by the parties, may feel and be invasive. Thus, rather than representing a change in the system to accommodate the "feminine voice," in actuality, mandatory mediation overrides real women's voices saying that cooperation might, at least for the time being, be detrimental to their lives and the lives of their children. Under a system of forced mediation, women are made to feel selfish for wanting to assert their own interests based on their need to survive.

There are, then, many good reasons why a party might choose not to mediate. While some argue that mediation should be required because potential participants lack the information about the process which would convince them to engage in it voluntarily, this is not a sufficient justification for requiring mediation. If the state were committed only to making sure that disputants become familiar with mediation, something less than mandatory mediation—such as viewing a videotaped mediation or attending an orientation program—could be required, and mediators would certainly not be permitted to make recommendations to the court. That more than the simple receipt of information is required under a statutory mediation scheme demonstrates a profound disrespect for the parties' ability to determine the course of their own lives. Perhaps intrusion on the parties' lives might be justified if, in fact, children were demonstrably better off as a result of the process. There is no credible evidence, however, that this is so. The legislative choice to make mediation mandatory has been a mistake.

The choice presented today in California and in some other states is between an adversary process with totally powerful legal actors, in which clients never speak for themselves (and often do not know what is going on), and a mediation process in which they are entirely on their own and unprotected. The adversary system admittedly works poorly for child custody cases in many respects. There are, however, some ways to avoid damaging custody battles under an adversary system, such as enacting presumptions that make outcomes reasonably clear in advance, court-sponsored lectures on settlement, and joint negotiation sessions with lawyers and clients present. When in court, lawyers could be held to higher standards with respect to communicating with their clients, and judges could refrain from speaking to lawyers when their clients are not present. (It is difficult to imagine how a client can know whether to trust his lawyer when significant parts of the proceedings take place out of earshot.)

The only reason to prefer mediation to other, more obvious alternatives is that the parties may, through the mediation process, ultimately benefit themselves and their children by learning how to communicate and work together. Whether this will happen in the context of a particular mediation is something only the parties can judge.

Any reform proposals, of the adversarial system or of a mediation alternative, should be rejected if they result in further disempowerment of the disempowered. Reform must operate on two simultaneous levels: first, by changing the institutions and rules that govern custody mediation, and second, by encouraging the respect of each mediator for the struggles and lives of the individuals involved in mediation. Any reforms should evince a concern for the personhood of the mediation clients, a concern that is lacking under current mediation practices.

With respect to institutional changes, an adequate mediation scheme should not only be voluntary rather than mandatory, but should also allow people's emotions to be part of the process, allow their values and principles to matter in the discussion, allow parties' attorneys to participate if requested by the parties, allow parties to choose a mediator and the location for the mediation, allow parties to choose the issues to mediate, and require that divorcing couples be educated about the availability and logistics of mediation so as to enable them to make an intelligent choice as to whether to engage in it.

The second aspect of reform represents more of a personal dynamic, one which is harder to institutionalize or to regulate. But the mediator must learn to respect each client's struggles, including her timing, anger, and resistance to having certain issues mediated, and also must learn to refrain, to the extent he is capable, from imposing his own substantive agenda on the mediation.

Conclusion

Although mediation can be useful and empowering, it presents some serious process dangers that need to be addressed, rather than ignored. When mediation is imposed rather than voluntarily engaged in, its virtues are lost. More than lost: mediation becomes a wolf in sheep's clothing. It relies on force and disregards the context of the dispute, while masquerading as a gentler, more empowering alternative to adversarial litigation. Sadly, when mediation is mandatory it becomes like the patriarchal paradigm of law it is supposed to supplant. Seen in this light, mandatory mediation is especially harmful: its messages disproportionately affect those who are already subordinated in our society, those to whom society has already given the message, in far too many ways, that they are not leading proper lives.

Of course, subordinated people can go to court and lose; in fact, they usually do. But if mediation is to be introduced into the court system, it should provide a better alternative. It is not enough to say that the adversary system is so flawed that even a misguided, intrusive, and disempowering system of mediation should be embraced. If mediation as currently instituted constitutes a fundamentally flawed process in the way I have described, it is more, not less, disempowering than the adversary system—for it is then a process in which people are told they are being empowered, but in fact are being forced to acquiesce in their own oppression.

Chapter 14

Role of Ethnic and Gender Difference in Mediated Conflicts

James W. Grosch, Karen G. Duffy, and Paul V. Olczak

Overview of Study

The New York government-sponsored dispute resolution program was founded in 1981 and currently has mediation centers in all sixty-two counties of the state. Mediators at these centers are volunteers from the local community who have undergone at least a twenty-five-hour training program and served an apprenticeship with an experienced mediator. From 1990 to 1992, a total of almost twenty-eight thousand mediation hearings took place statewide. Of these hearings, 69 percent were referred to mediation from the court system, 9 percent were walk-ins, and the remainder came from a wide variety of sources, including private attorneys, schools, legal aid, and other public agencies. The types of problems dealt with in mediation included charges of harassment, assault, housing disputes, personal/real property disputes, family disputes, and breach of contract.

Discussion

The results of this study provide support for the six hypotheses we examine. With respect to ethnicity, Whites were under-represented in community mediation relative to their presence in the general population, whereas Hispanics and Blacks (but not Asians or Native Americans) were over-represented (Hypothesis 1). Disputes reaching mediation tended to be largely intraracial (Hypothesis 2) and involved a greater likelihood of violence if the claimant was Black, Hispanic, or Asian (Hypothesis 3). Additional analyses suggest that White participants became involved in mediation under circumstances much different from those of other ethnic groups. White claimants were less likely to be in disputes involving criminal behavior, and were more likely to be self-referred (or walk-ins) and have a relationship high in intimacy with the respondent. Compared to Whites,

From 6 *International Journal of Conflict Management* 48, 52–53, 65–66 (1995).

the differences between Blacks, Hispanics, and Asians were relatively small, suggesting that these three groups were involved in similar types of conflicts that led to mediation.

With respect to gender, female claimants were similar to Black, Hispanic, and Asian claimants in that they were over-represented compared to the general population (Hypothesis 4) and were more likely to be involved in disputes having at least a potential for violent behavior. These findings are consistent with theories of social interaction that explain ethnic or gender differences in terms of social status. Groups that historically have experienced lower levels of social status, such as women and Blacks, are more likely to be involved, as either claimants or respondents, in criminal disputes that have at least some potential for violence. Unlike Blacks, Hispanics, and Asians, however, females were more likely to have a relationship high in intimacy with the respondent (Hypothesis 5), particularly in mixed-gender cases. Female claimants were also more likely to reach a consent agreement than male claimants (Hypothesis 6). Although the percentage difference was small, these findings are consistent with social psychological research indicating that women tend to be more cooperative and more concerned with developing and maintaining relationships.

It is important to note that gender difference can vary as a function of ethnicity (and vice versa). This type of relationship between gender and ethnicity has also been found in laboratory and criminal justice research, and indicates that each variable should not be viewed in isolation from the other. Females may be more likely to be claimants in mediation, but the magnitude of this difference depends on ethnicity. This finding suggests that ethnic groups may have different cultural views of mediation as well as the roles males and females should play in attempting to resolve interpersonal conflicts.

Although support was found for all six hypotheses, an important question remains as to why these ethnic and gender differences exist. We examined the role of three possible explanatory variables: source of referral, claimant education, and claimant income. Source of referral did not appear to change the main findings with regard to violence and intimacy, although some interesting results emerged across the different referral sources. For example, the likelihood of reaching a consent agreement was greatest in disputes referred by social/private agencies, followed by court-referred disputes and walk-ins. In fairness to critics of mandatory mediation, our analysis did not include variables, such as compliance rate or quality of the consent agreement, that have been predicted to suffer when mediation is court-referred. Clearly, additional research is needed to determine how referral source affects the mediation process and expectations of the disputants.

As for claimant education and income, [our] analysis indicated that these two variables were associated with the dispute and outcome measures, but were not by themselves responsible for the observed ethnic and gender differences; [and] that other variables, such as geographical setting of the dispute (e.g., rural vs. urban setting) and age, employment status, and family background of the disputants, may also contribute to the observed differences. As Betancourt and López and Nkomo caution in their critique of ethnicity research, group differences need to be interpreted carefully with a concern for possible cultural variables, such as values, norms and historical forces, that may contribute to the observed effects of demographic variables. The data presented in this study suggest that ethnic and gender differences do exist in mediation. However, the factors underlying these differences are complex and cannot be reduced to just education and income.

Chapter 15

New Mexico Research Examines Impact of Gender and Ethnicity in Mediation

Michele Hermann

Professors and students from the University of New Mexico Schools of Law and Sociology are collaborating on a research project under a grant from the Fund for Research on Dispute Resolution to study the effects of race and gender on mediation and adjudication of cases in Albuquerque's small claims court. This court, the Bernalillo County Metropolitan Court, is a non-record court with jurisdiction to hear civil cases in which the amount in controversy is $5,000 or less. During the time of data collection for the study, the court had three judges in the civil division who handled approximately nine thousand cases per year. All three judges are male; one is African American, one is Hispanic American, and one is European American. The court contracts with a local mediation center to operate the court's mediation program, under which all civil filings are screened for potential metabolite [dispute resolution developments and processes] and about one-third of the cases are referred to mediation.

The research project randomly assigned more than six hundred cases to either adjudication or mediation, and tracked both the case results and the participants' reactions.

A great deal of useful information has been gained from the data analysis to date. Perhaps the most startling finding is that in the objective outcomes of both adjudicated and mediated cases, disputants of color fared worse than did white disputants. These disparate results were more extreme in mediated than in adjudicated cases. An ethnic-minority plaintiff could be predicted to receive eighteen cents on the dollar less than a white plaintiff in mediation, while an ethnic-minority respondent could be predicted to pay twenty cents on the dollar more. When examining how the ethnicity of the co-mediators affected outcomes, the study found that when there were two mediators of color, the negative impact of the disputant's ethnicity disappeared. The ethnicity of the mediators did not change the objective outcomes of white disputants' cases.

The negative outcomes found for ethnic-minority participants were not replicated when the data were analyzed for gender. For the most part, neither the gender of the

From *Dispute Resolution Magazine* 10–11 (Fall 1994). ABA Publishing. Reprinted with permission.

claimant nor that of the respondent had a statistically significant effect on monetary outcomes in either adjudicated or mediated cases, except that female respondents did better in mediation than male respondents, paying less than their male counterparts.

The examination of procedural and substantive satisfaction produced interesting contrasts to the objective outcome analysis. Despite their disparately poorer outcomes, ethnic-minority disputants were more likely to express satisfaction with mediation than were white disputants. Female disputants, on the other hand, were more likely to express satisfaction with adjudication. Indeed, white female respondents, who had the most favorable objective outcomes in mediation, reported the lowest level of satisfaction. Furthermore, compared to other mediation respondents, white women were less likely to see the mediation process as fair and unbiased. Women of color, on the other hand, reported the highest level of satisfaction with mediation, despite their tendency to fare the worst in objective outcomes as either claimants or respondents.

The evidence that disputants of color fare significantly worse in mediation than do white participants raises important questions about whether the traditional mediation process is appropriate in disputes involving ethnic minorities, as well as members of other groups who are traditionally disempowered in American society.

Chapter 16

The Architecture of Bias
Deep Structures in Tort Law

Martha Chamallas

As in so many other areas of the law, formal equality on the face of the law of torts bears little connection to gender and race equity as measured by real-world standards. Most empirical studies indicate that women of all races and minority men continue to receive significantly lower damage awards than white men in personal injury and wrongful death suits. Some of these data have been generated by the movement to study gender and race bias in the courts, with the predominant focus being on disparities between men and women. These data confirm that in the realm of torts a higher value is placed upon the lives of white men and that injuries suffered by this group are worth more than injuries suffered by other, less privileged groups in society.

For example, my calculations from tort judgments and settlements reported in a 1996 guide for personal injury lawyers indicate that, in the aggregate, male plaintiffs received awards that were 27 percent higher than those of female plaintiffs. Similarly, a study of wrongful death cases between 1984 and 1988 conducted by the Washington State Task Force on Gender and Justice in the Courts found that the mean damage award for a male decedent was $332,166, compared to a mean award of $214,923 for a female decedent. A nationwide study of jury awards in personal injury cases, conducted by Jury Verdict Research, Inc., showed that in virtually all age groups, women received significantly lower mean and median compensatory damage awards than did men. Although there are fewer data analyzing tort awards along racial lines, a Washington study of asbestos cases in the 1980s found substantial disparities between settlement amounts of minority and nonminority plaintiffs.

My primary contention is that contemporary tort law devalues or undervalues the lives, activities, and potential of women and people of color. Applying critical theory, I argue that this devaluation is accomplished by subtle means, through the social construction of legal categories that purport to describe types of injuries and types of damages. I look for the hidden gender or racial dimension in basic legal categories, such as "physical harm" or "pecuniary loss." When these "neutral" categories of injuries and damages are ranked in importance, there is often a

From 146 *University Pennsylvania Law Review* 464–467 (1998).

negative impact on nondominant groups. Specifically, I assert that injuries of low value are more often associated with women, while injuries of high value are more often linked to men. The devaluation process can also work to contaminate the very neutrality of the categories themselves. My research suggests that the gender of the victim plays an important role. In deciding how to categorize a loss, the law looks not only in some abstract way at the nature of the injury or loss, but also at who is suffering the loss. In this way, the gender of the prototypical plaintiff affects how we conceptualize the nature of the harm.

EDITOR'S NOTE

See also Carlos Villarreal, "Culture in Lawmaking: A Chicano Perspective," 24 *University of California Davis Law Review* 1193 (1991), where Professor Villarreal argues that the biases in tort law have had a disparate negative impact on Chicanos.

Chapter 17

Gender and Conflict
What Does Psychological Research Tell Us?

Loraleigh Keashly

Studies provide evidence of influences and norms that may affect and influence conflict and behavior. In the realm of intimate, ongoing, personal relationships, Burggraf and Sillars suggest "the intimacy and temporal permanence of family relationships allow spouses to abandon culturally determined standards for behavior and replace them with personally negotiated norms." Similarly, within the organizational context, structural bases of power, experience, and job status are stronger influences on behavior than is gender per se. To discover these more specific norms requires research methods and measurement strategies that are sensitive to conflict at different levels of analysis (e.g., intrapersonal, interpersonal, group, and intergroup) and that capture its dynamic nature in specific situations. Little research to date has used such methods or measures.

Evidence suggests that the experience and meaning of conflict may differ for women and men. Several studies highlight gender-linked differences in experiences of conflict. In focused interviews with women and men clerical and maintenance workers, Patricia A. Gwartney-Gibbs and Denise H. Lach found that the origin, processes, and outcomes of workplace disputes differed somewhat for women and men. Although both spoke of conflicts about family and day care, benefits, and grievance, women more often reported interpersonally oriented conflicts that were not being managed by institutionalized dispute resolution methods. Some women chose to make lateral moves to get out of the situations that affected their movement hierarchically in the organization.

Weingarten and Douvan spoke with equally well-known and well-respected female and male mediators about how they viewed and carried out their roles as mediators. Women viewed their goal to be an understanding of parties and their differences, whereas men saw their goal to be the development of an agreement. Men believed they should be neutral, whereas women believed they should facilitate balance between conflicting parties. Miller's work on women's and men's interpersonal conflict scripts found little difference in the components of the script but differences in how the components went together. Men perceived the offended to be

From Anita Taylor and Judi Beinstein Miller, eds., *Gender and Conflict* (Cresskill, NJ: Hampton, 1994), 185–186.

the one who decides when the conflict is over, whereas women perceived that both the offended and the offender needed to agree. Each of these studies indicates the importance of looking not only at "outcomes," whether in behavioral or perceptual terms, but also at processes of "achieving" outcomes and the interpretation of these outcomes by those involved.

Finally, worth attention is the persistence of beliefs in gender-linked behavior even when these behaviors are not found in research. Similarly noteworthy are differences in how women and men are treated and perceive themselves to be treated when their behavior differs little. The existence of perceived differences in behavior in the absence of observed differences promotes consideration of the impact of others' expectations on interactions in conflict. Do we deal with women and men differently as a result of these expectations? Do we assume "differences" are natural and inevitable and use them as a basis for discrimination? How do we deal with men and women who behave in sex-role incongruent ways, that is, those who behave "out of character"? Such questions need to be addressed more than researchers have done to date.

It is within a dynamic interplay of expectations, perceptions, and behavior that the role of gender in conflict lies. To speak of "gender differences" is a misnomer. To speak of "gendering" and "conflicting" may be more accurate. By far the majority of our research in gender and conflict is static and contextless. Our measurements and our research methods need to reflect this more dynamic nature in order to transform our description and understanding of conflict and of gender.

Chapter 18

Gender Regulation as a Source of Religious Schism

Phil Zuckerman

This paper explores a case of religious schism in which a struggle over gender regulation was central in the splitting apart of a Jewish congregation in the Pacific Northwest. While there were several factors and various latent sources of conflict that precipitated this case of religious schism, the struggle over gender regulation was the most prominent and ultimately decisive. Members of this small Jewish community disagreed about how men and women should worship together publicly and what roles are appropriate for males and females in a Jewish religious context. Unable to compromise, they parted ways.

Based upon more than a year's worth of participant observation among Northweston's Jewish community, as well as in-depth interviews with twenty-nine involved informants, this paper will explore the struggle in Northweston's Jewish community over gender regulation, and how and why this struggle resulted in schism.

Gender Regulation and Religious Conflict

Gender regulation is the process by which a community (in this case, religious) attempts to define, institute, and justify "masculine" and "feminine" behavior and roles for its members. Gender regulation is distinct from "sexual regulation" in that the former is concerned with public roles and practices, while the latter is concerned with private encounters between individuals, usually involving sexual/physical intimacy.

Recent research has examined the way in which gender regulation is understood and negotiated within contemporary western religious life. Neitz and Goldman persuasively argue that religious identity "is inextricably tied to understandings of gender and sexuality." Furthermore, the regulation of gender is at the heart of religion, that is, gender is "central to the meaningful interpretation

From 58(4) *Sociology of Religion* 353 (1997). Copyright © Association for the Sociology of Religion, Inc., 1997.

of contemporary American religious organizations and markets." According to Caroline Walker Bynum:

> It is no longer possible to study religious practice or religious symbols without taking gender—that is, the cultural experience of being male or female—into account. And we are just beginning to understand how complex the relationship between religion and gender is.

It is in the spirit of furthering such understanding that this study illustrating issues of gender as a source of religious schism has been undertaken.

Susan Sered's recent study of feminist challenges to patriarchal authority within Israeli society offers an important paradigm for understanding gender regulation and religious conflict. According to Sered, there are two ontologically different sets of issues at play within patriarchal religious systems: "women," which designates "female people who have varying degrees of agency within specific social situations," and then "Woman," which designates "a symbolic construct comprised of allegory, metaphor, fantasy and (at least in male dominated religions) men's psychological projections." According to Sered, when someone or something challenges a religious system's assumptions of "Woman" the result is often religious conflict, because "'Woman' as a symbol is often associated with some of the deepest and most compelling theological and mythological structures in the religious tradition." The case of Northweston's Jewish community lends support to Sered's insight, for the battle over gender regulation was more than just a community disagreeing over random policies or principles, but was a situation in which members within a religious system disagreed over central structures and meanings within that system: structures and meanings of gender.

Background

For decades, there was only one synagogue in Northweston, Washington. Now there are two.

When a Jewish congregation splits up in a city full of many different Jewish congregations, the communal ramifications and sociological implications may not be so profound. However, in the case of Northweston, this was the only synagogue in town. The schismatic rift thus represented more than just the diversification of a growing religious community. It represented the break-up of a small Jewish enclave that, for decades, had sought strength and comfort in its unity and solidarity.

Rather than a mutually-respectful parting in which both sides gracefully recognized the rights and needs of the other group, the split in Northweston's Jewish community was quite painful, characterized by damaging gossip, severed friendships, divided couples, tense confrontations, and a myriad of personal attacks.

The Northwest Temple Evolves

The Northwest Temple was initially founded in the 1950s as a Conservative congregation.[1] It was during the 1980s, under the liberal influence of Rabbi Kohner
(originally ordained a Reform Rabbi who later became Reconstructionist), that
the Northwest Temple steadily transformed into a progressive, egalitarian congregation that sought to embrace relatively radical practices and doctrines that were
quite innovative and unique.

Some of the major changes that the Northwest Temple underwent throughout
the 1980s (which constituted a clear break from the Conservative movement's
form of Judaism to which the Northwest Temple had been originally committed),
included the changing of the wording of one of Judaism's most traditionally sacred prayers, the Aleynu, to be more universal and less ethnocentric; the allowance of musical instruments to be played in the sanctuary on Shabbes; the acceptance of patrilineal descent as sufficient for complete Jewish identity; an openness toward inter-married couples; and so forth. As mentioned above, all of these
policies were latent sources of division, which precipitated the eventual schism.

The most significant changes instituted by Rabbi Kohner throughout the 1980s
were specifically gender-related. First came the construction and institution of
egalitarian prayer. For most Jewish congregations, whether Orthodox, Conservative, or Reform, all major prayers recited throughout the weekly Sabbath services
and important holidays are characterized by the reference to God as a man; God is
exclusively referred to as "Lord" or "King," and the pronoun to refer to God is
invariably "He." Rabbi Kohner, with the support of several members of the
Northwest Temple congregation, decided that male-specific allusions to God were
inappropriate; he made it Temple policy to eliminate or change any overt references to God as male. Thus, rather than translate various names or references to
God from the ancient Hebrew into obviously masculine terms, the prayers would
be translated into gender-neutral wording; "Oh Lord" thus became "Oh Eternal
One," and so on. The most important Yom Kippur prayer Avinu Malkaynu was
initially translated into the literal English of "Our Father, Our King." Rabbi
Kohner changed it to the gender-neutral "Our Parent, Our Source." All male-
based prayers were reshaped, not just those referring to God. Thus, "God of our
fathers" became "God of our ancestors." One traditional prayer recited weekly is
the Amidah in which the Jewish patriarchs are named (Abraham, Isaac, and
Jacob). Rabbi Kohner, in his desire to make all prayers as gender-neutral as possible, re-wrote the prayer to include the Jewish matriarchs (Sarah, Rebecca, Rachel,
and Leah) as well.

The changing of masculine-based prayer to egalitarian prayer was a major
source of congregational division. There were those who greatly appreciated the
institution of egalitarian prayer (regardless of how non-traditional it may be), and
then there were those who felt that the changes in prayer were unacceptable. According to these individuals, ancient prayers should not be changed simply to fit
modern political trends, namely, feminism. Thus, the social sensibilities of the former group had initially been offended by the male-centered (albeit traditional)

language, while the religious sensibilities of the latter group were subsequently offended by the "tinkering" with traditional (albeit patriarchal) prayer. As one male member of the Northweston Minyan, age forty-five, who was disturbed by the new egalitarian liturgy, explained:

> One reason I wanted to embrace Judaism is because it is an ancient tradition which flourishes still . . . and I believe that if people do something . . . observe certain religious rites for a few thousand years, then there's probably something right about doing that. . . . And what I saw at the Northwest Temple was a casting aside of this very tradition that I saw valuable. I found it arrogant and repugnant to tinker around with prayers that were—depending on what prayer it was; it may have been a prayer that was a thousand years old or two thousand years old—to tinker with a prayer or custom because it didn't seem politically correct in 1990 or 1995, it just seemed the height of intellectual arrogance.

A woman in her late forties, also of the Minyan, agreed:

> They were very big on gender issues. So, you know, you could never say "He" for God . . . it seemed like the more Jewish I was getting, the less Jewish they were getting. Yeah, it was really bizarre. . . . To me it got to be embarrassing because they would start off services and they would say, "Okay we're gonna go by the prayer book except any time you see this word, substitute this word" . . . and . . . I said, "But you know, the Hebrew word is masculine" . . . you know . . . I just thought it was kind of stupid. . . . It seemed to be more concerned with current political correctness than it did with traditional Judaism.

A further innovation was the inclusion of women as equal participants in public prayer, followed by the allowance and encouragement of both men and women to wear the same holy garb. In many Jewish congregations (to a greater degree in more Orthodox congregations and to a lesser degree in Conservative or Reform congregations), there are differences in the prescribed roles of men and women during the weekly Shabbes service. These differences manifest themselves in a distinct division of labor, different appropriate clothing for each gender, and sometimes separate seating arrangements. For example, in many congregations, only men are called up to read from the Torah; only men give drushas (interpretive talks on readings from the Torah); only men wear kippot (skullcaps); only men wear tallisim (prayer shawls); only men count as part of a minyan (gathering of ten members necessary to take out the Torah for the Shabbes service); men and women sit separately, often divided by a mehitzah (partition); only men may chant/sing prayers out loud; only men recite the most holy prayers; women are encouraged to wear dresses or long skirts, wear long-sleeved blouses, wear scarves over their heads if married; and so forth.

Over the course of the last decade, as he was drawn closer to the Reconstructionist vision of contemporary Judaism, Rabbi Kohner instituted a strict policy of egalitarian practice within the congregation; there were to be no role distinctions between men and women. Both men and women could wear the same holy garb (kippot and tallisim); both men and women could be called up to read from the Torah; both men and women could give interpretive talks and lead prayers;

women didn't have to wear dresses or long skirts; and so forth. In short, the traditional division of labor based on gender was abolished, as well as gender-based seating arrangements and dress codes.

As with the changes in prayer, the change that transformed the Northwest Temple from a Conservative congregation marked by a modest level of traditionally enforced differential gender roles into a staunchly egalitarian congregation was a major source of division. Many people were supportive of the changes, others were offended. As would be expected, the people who felt uncomfortable with the changes in the prayers, were the same people who were disenchanted with the institution of egalitarian practice in public worship.

The Northwest Minyan Emerges

Unhappy with the above-described changes that the Northwest Temple underwent under the auspices of Rabbi Kohner, several active members of the congregation decided to form their own separate prayer group to meet in the back of the Temple. At this stage, breaking away to form a separate synagogue was not in mind. Rather, these congregants simply wanted to pray in a more traditionally structured manner within the walls of the Northwest Temple, which they still considered their synagogue.

The disgruntled group initially coalesced around one individual, Abe Shibel. Abe Shibel had nothing to do with the Northwest Temple—a fact that was well known in the community. He was an elderly university professor who also happened to be an ordained Orthodox Rabbi, though never employed as such. To him, the Northwest Temple was "treyf" (not kosher; unclean). He had been offering a Wednesday night Talmud class in his home for twenty-five years, with consistently sparse attendance. However, with the growing disenchantment over at the Northwest Temple, attendance at his classes suddenly began to swell. Abe Shibel did not actively recruit a following, by any means. Rather than a resourceful leader who garnered a following, the opposite was the case: a group of disgruntled members of the Northwest Temple found themselves under Abe Shibel's reluctant tutelage; his Talmud class was simply the only structured Jewish activity within Northweston outside of the Northwest Temple. (Indeed, once the Minyan group began having separate services, Abe Shibel refused to act as leader or Rabbi.) Anyway, it was in his home, during his weekly Talmud classes, that people began expressing their shared dissatisfactions with the Northwest Temple, and it was here that the assembled individuals first became aware of themselves as a separate group with common dissatisfactions regarding the Northwest Temple.

Eventually, these individuals decided that they wanted a more traditional Saturday morning prayer service. For them, the services at the Northwest Temple had gotten far too liberal, far too experimental, far too loose. They wanted to "get back to tradition." They wanted what they considered to be "real," "authentic" Judaism, not some watered-down, egalitarian, "politically correct" Judaism. And, in a reactive manner, these individuals did not just want to get back to a regular

Conservative style of worship (as the Northwest Temple once had offered), but they sought a decidedly Orthodox approach. If the Northwest Temple was going further and further into its own interpretations of what Judaism should be and how it should be practiced, then this traditionally-minded group would go in just the opposite direction: not progressive innovation, but back to strict tradition. If the Northwest Temple was going to change, up-date, and "modernize" Judaism, this group would get "back to the roots." If the Northwest Temple's gender regulation was getting more egalitarian, then this group would enforce a hierarchical form of gender regulation that was decidedly non-egalitarian.

So the group began having Saturday morning services in a back room of the Northwest Temple. Thus, simultaneous services were held on Saturday mornings: in the main sanctuary was the egalitarian service with re-written prayers, non-gender-specific liturgy, and men and women wearing the same holy garb, conducting the same practices throughout the service, and sitting together. In the back room was an Orthodox, halakhik (lawful) service, with only men leading traditional (i.e., non-revised) prayers, only men wearing certain holy garb, only men conducting various practices, and men and women sitting separately—divided by a mehitzah (partition). According to one male member of the Northwest Temple in his early fifties:

> There were a group of people . . . who had gotten together and wanted to be a little bit more traditional . . . what they wanted to do was they wanted to pray and use the temple—they were just pleased to use the back room . . . but a lot of the members of the temple no longer wanted to allow the Minyan to use the back of the facility as a sanctuary. We were in a political time where there was a lot more recognition of women in Jewish events here, and basically in terms of our community, women and men are equal. So . . . I think the straw that kind of broke the camel's back was the fact that the Minyan was using the mehitzah—women and men were separated.

The Mehitzah Dispute

According to a male in his forties:

> I think the issue that actually caused the split was the separation of men and women, the mehitzah. The Orthodox group wanted women separated and wanted a division, and a very significant [non-Orthodox] membership [within the Northwest Temple] said, "That is morally repugnant to me. I could not belong to a synagogue—we cannot allow a division of men and women in prayer in our synagogue." And I think that's the issue that sent one group packing.

A woman in her early fifties agreed:

> I think the mehitzah was the linch-pin from the point of view of our community ejecting that group—um, and they ejecting themselves. Such sentiments were shared by Rabbi Kohner's wife. . . . The issue of sitting apart, polarized the whole community. You know, the issue of mehitzah.

Norma Baumel Joseph contends that "this particular issue [the mehitzah] has become the hallmark of the divisions that exist among American Jewry." Judith Plaskow agrees, noting that the separation of the sexes by a mehitzah is a "highly contentious issue, which has split many a U.S. congregation."

Although various individuals within the Northwest Temple had been divided over many issues over the years, they had always considered themselves one congregation. Even when the small group, unhappy with the changes implemented by Rabbi Kohner, began holding separate, traditionally Orthodox Saturday morning prayer services in the back room, the congregation was still one. However, it was the mehitzah dispute around which the two groups actually became separate and a chasm widened that would never be repaired.

When it was realized by certain members of the Northwest Temple that the Orthodox group in the back room had erected a mehitzah, the controversy truly flared. Several outspoken members of the Northwest Temple made it known to the rest of the congregation that they could not tolerate the existence of a mehitzah, even in a back room. It was their position that the small, newly Orthodox group had to either get rid of the mehitzah, or get out of the Northwest Temple. It didn't matter that many of them were integral members of the Northwest Temple (ex-presidents and current board members included), it didn't matter that they were practicing a traditional form of Judaism, and it didn't matter that they were in a separate back room. They had erected a mehitzah, which to some egalitarian-minded members of the Northwest Temple represented destructive hierarchy, patriarchal oppression, and sexism—the very trends which the Northwest Temple had fought so hard to counter over the last decade.

It was stressed by these egalitarian-minded congregants that with the erection of the mehitzah came additional severely anti-egalitarian regulations. In addition to the physical barrier of the mehitzah, women would not count toward assembling a minyan (religious quorum); only men count in the quorum necessary for taking out the Torah; women could not be heard during services; women could not be called up to read from the Torah; and so forth.

Under the leadership of Rabbi Kohner, diversity, universalism, and egalitarianism were the core values of the Northwest Temple. And to these members of the Northwest Temple, the mehitzah stood for just the opposite: segregation, oppression, and sexist domination. The mehitzah and all the regulations on women's participation that went with it were unacceptable.

The demands of this egalitarian-minded group were clear: the mehitzah had to go, or they—the newly formed Orthodox group praying in the back room—would have to find another place to put it, outside of the confines of the Northwest Temple. One man, age forty-five, who was part of the Orthodox group praying in the back, explained it this way.

> There were about a dozen of us who found the politics and religious practices of the Northwest Temple repugnant . . . so a few of those people started meeting . . . to daven [pray] traditionally, that is, with men and women separated and to have the whole service in Hebrew. . . . Now simultaneously, our practices infuriated a group of

people at the Northwest Temple, uh, mainly—the mehitzah, which separates men and women in the service became a hated object by a small group of people at the Northwest Temple. Now, of course, there was never any talk of having that mehitzah at the Northwest Temple, in the main sanctuary . . . [and] there was certainly never any program or mission to try to get people to quit going to the Reform service. But this mehitzah became a symbolic fixation for the most leftist types at the Northwest Temple . . . it was a ludicrous situation. Everybody who went to the—except Rabbi Shibel—who went to the Minyan service was a member of the Northwest Temple, and for what it's worth, about half the people who went were women who are highly articulate, educated, serious people, professional women and mothers who are perfectly aware of what they are doing and what they want to do, and in my humble opinion, ought to be able to choose how they daven. But then there was another group of people, the Northwest Temple people, who thought that wasn't relevant that these people chose to daven in this way, that it shouldn't be allowed because it was inherently oppressive.

To be sure, some members of the Northwest Temple weren't bothered by the separate Orthodox services being held in the back room on Saturday mornings, and really didn't care about the mehitzah. After all, it was Jewish (it wasn't as if the small group were in the back room holding communion or praying to Buddha), and furthermore, it was voluntary—women weren't forced to participate; if they didn't like sitting on the women's side of a mehitzah they were free to come into the main sanctuary and enjoy the egalitarian service. As one woman, age thirty-seven, expressed:

> If they want to have a mehitzah, fine, let them have it. I mean, I just didn't see like what the big deal was, that much. . . . I kind of felt like, let 'em do it. I mean, it did not offend my feminist principles in the least. I don't want to do it, but I—this is what Orthodox Jews do, so if you don't like it, don't be an Orthodox Jew. . . . If you don't like it, don't go.

However, the small "anti-mehitzah group" was vocal and influential, and also enjoyed the support of Rabbi Kohner. As one woman in her forties, who was part of the Orthodox group, recalled:

> The ultra-feminists at the Northwest Temple became very alarmed, including Rabbi Kohner's wife, that there was a mehitzah anywhere on Northwest Temple property . . . that this was an offense to God and to all, you know, politically correct Jews, and it couldn't be allowed. And it was really quite a big hoo-ha. A petition against the Orthodox group was drawn up and circulated. It read, in part: "We support the principle of egalitarianism at the Northwest Temple, including the full participation of men and women in the minyan and other aspects of Jewish life; and we are opposed to any religious services at the Northwest Temple that exclude members on the basis of gender or sexual orientation . . . and we are opposed to mehitzah barriers that segregate women from men in our synagogue . . . and we oppose the use of our Torah scrolls in any services that deny access to some of the Jewish people [i.e., women] . . . and we oppose the use of the Northwest Temple, which is a public facility of the Jewish community, for any religious services that enforce sexual discrimination."

Rabbi Kohner signed the petition, along with twenty-five others. One man, in his late fifties, explained his feelings:

> Jane Frankel created a petition declaring we will not have—any organization that wants a mehitzah cannot be a part of the Northwest Temple, or affiliated with the Northwest Temple. I signed it. . . . I said, Fuck it. I don't work for this organization, I'm not on the board. I'm gonna say what I think: that is disgusting, those people are disgusting.

Another informant, a woman in her late thirties, wasn't so sure about her position:

> Somebody started passing around this petition . . . saying the Northwest Temple shall only allow egalitarian davening. So, by signing the petition you're saying the Minyan needs to get out of here. And I had a really hard time because these are all my friends, I mean, I had friends on both sides. And I felt really stuck in the middle. And they asked me to sign the petition. And I felt like if I didn't sign it, I was siding with the Minyan and I was like not an egalitarian Jew. And if I did sign it, then I was not allowing the Minyan to daven in our temple. So I did not sign it.

The actions of this small anti-mehitzah group which generated the petition inevitably served only to reinforce the identity of the small Orthodox group, and it was under the pressure of the former that the latter first began to imagine leaving the Northwest Temple to form their own separate congregation.

Symbols and Religious Conflict

Why the mehitzah? Why did this issue, when so many others had caused controversy over the years, finally sever the community? Most likely, it was the symbolic nature of the mehitzah. The mehitzah is a symbol, a tangible, mundane thing in and of itself, yet imbued with spiritual meaning and moral value. As Susan Sered notes, "Religious conflicts tend to be, by definition, conflicts over symbols (symbols are, after all, the currency of religion)."

For members of the split-off Orthodox faction, the mehitzah was a symbol of tradition. For those opposed to the mehitzah, it was a symbol of oppression. And at the heart of it, the mehitzah is a symbol—first and foremost—of gender regulation. Those wanting a traditional religious communal affiliation based on unequal gender division were ultimately unable (or not allowed) to remain under the same roof with those seeking gender equality, and the mehitzah served as the symbol around which both sides could rally. These two approaches to gender regulation could not be reconciled, and it was within this lightening rod symbol of the mehitzah that each faction's fears and aspirations were invested.

One woman, age forty-nine, a member of the Northwest Temple, explained her position and what the mehitzah symbolized for her.

> [The Northwest Temple was] progressively becoming more and more egalitarian . . . and so this was a real shocker that there was a mehitzah in this building, in this house

. . . and it was seen as offensive and some women would even use the word abominable. It was an abomination. . . . And it's really ugly to me, because I also hold the view that before the patriarchy we actually had a sane society. And then there was this wave of migration of people who had iron, and who practiced unbelievable atrocities called war, who destroyed a world-wide, maybe . . . ten thousand year old matriarchal, pacifistic, agrarian society, where women had been honored, where God had been honored but in a female form, where the earth had been seen as a mother that brought forth life, women were held in reverence . . . and so I have a whole deep and very well-thought out rage at the patriarchy in general, and what the mehitzah represents to me is that control of women, the silencing of women. . . . So the patriarchy is the source of all evil—that's a given—the mehitzah is the symbol of keeping women suppressed.

Another woman, who prefers davening at the Northwest Minyan, explained:

There really is an image of the mehitzah as just like treating blacks—to sit in the back of the bus . . . the Northwest Minyan would get a hundred new members tomorrow if there wasn't a mehitzah. It touches those nerves and those buttons in such a powerful way, in terms of women being silenced, women not having to take responsibility . . . those issues are very big because they are at odds with how women are evolving in our own society. It creates a real chasm. It's really hard to say, here's this woman who's the CEO of a company and she's behind the mehitzah and she cannot partake of the greatest honors . . . it's a slap—is how my friends see it. They are shocked that I don't feel that way. I don't feel that way at all. I think the mehitzah's fine. . . . I think it serves a valuable purpose; I think that men and woman are different. I just kind of like my own space . . . [I find] the mehitzah to be, on a personal level, fairly liberating. Um, though I also really understand why people have a problem with it.

Since Émile Durkheim's classic study of totemism, scholars have been exploring the ultimate importance of symbols in religious life, especially within religious conflict. Fred Kniss argues that "ideas and symbols play a central role in most religious conflicts"; Kniss characterizes religious symbols as "cultural resources" and suggests that "[s]ince concrete cultural resources are not likely to be divisible, they are more likely to result in intense, all-or-nothing battles ending in schism rather than compromise." In his study of Mennonite history, Kniss found that struggles which involved concrete cultural resources were nearly three times as likely to end in schism than those over abstract resources. The schism of Northweston's Jewish community offers further support to Kniss's insight.

The potential power of symbols within a religious cultural context is further strengthened when those symbols involve gender regulation. As Howard Eilberg-Schwartz argues, "[G]ender is not just another subject that intersects with religion, but is central to the work that religion accomplishes and the ways in which it goes about it." Since gender regulation is central to religious systems, symbols which encapsulate gender regulation are that much more controversial; they speak to the ultimate cultural/religious meanings of what it means to be "male," "female"—in short, human. In the case of Northweston's Jews, the mehitzah was just such a symbol.

Discussion: Two Oppositional Camps

Hunter describes a general cultural division between groups of people with an "impulse toward orthodoxy" versus those with an "impulse toward progressivism." What is at stake between these two groups is "competing systems of moral understanding." According to Hunter (drawing upon Durkheim), problems exist between these two camps because "not only does each side of the cultural divide operate with a different conception of the sacred, but the mere existence of the one represents a certain desecration of the other." Hunter's characterization of these two ideal-types (orthodox/progressive) fits Northweston's Jewish community: the traditionalists of the Minyan and the anti-mehitzah group of the Temple, respectively. The "orthodox" group could not tolerate a synagogue which instituted full gender equality; to them, this was a desecration of something they considered sacred: traditional Judaism. The "progressive" group could not tolerate a prayer service within their Temple which enforced gender inequality; to them, this was a desecration of something they considered sacred: egalitarian Judaism.

Most members of the Northwest Minyan say they were kicked out. Most members of the Northwest Temple say that the Orthodox group wanted to leave on their own volition. Either way, it is no accident that this sectarian group went on to call its newly established Orthodox congregation the Northwest Minyan—as noted above, a "minyan" is a traditionally understood as a quorum of ten men necessary to take out the Torah. Women do not count toward the making up of a minyan.

Conclusion

Hunter speaks of a newly-emerging cultural/religious rift within the United States. The rift is characterized not so much by inter-religious tension, but by a social division which cuts across religious denominations separating liberal/progressives from conservative/orthodox within given denominations. The case of Northweston's Jewish community offers sound qualitative data to support this paradigm. Additionally, this case study adds ethnographic data from a Jewish community to previous research concerned with the centrality of gender within religion, and confirms that struggles over gender regulation have great potential for contemporary religious conflict and change, especially when that struggle involves symbolic representations of a given religious system's form of gender regulation. By illustrating the cultural significance of gender within contemporary religious life, and the potential for religious schism it entails, this case offers support to those who argue that understandings of gender cannot be separated from religiosity; attempts to challenge or change the former, inevitably involve the latter.

NOTE

1. My typological use of the three main American Jewish denominations represents a

continuum, with Orthodox representing the most traditional, strict, and sect-like congregational style; Reform representing the most modern, liberal, and church-like congregational
style; and Conservative falling somewhere in the middle of the two poles. A fourth denomination, Reconstructionist, by far the smallest denomination, is difficult to place on the continuum. While known for being progressive, egalitarian, and innovative, the Reconstructionist denomination is unique. Reconstructionist Judaism is deeply committed to Jewish
tradition (unlike Reform, which was created to simply mimic German Protestantism of the
1800s), and yet it is highly creative in liberal ways that distinguish it from Orthodoxy and
Conservativism, resulting in a denominational style sui generis that does not fall neatly
within the Reform-Conservative-Orthodox continuum. However, Reconstructionism is
noted for its progressive social values, such as its acceptance of homosexuals.

Chapter 19

Anti-Essentialism, Relativism, and Human Rights

Tracy E. Higgins

Feminism is the fire that melts, but does not destroy.
—Dr. Nahid Toubia[1]

During the Fourth United Nations World Conference on Women, cultural differences among women presented a series of practical and theoretical problems. The practical problems arose out of the enormous task of negotiating among a large group of people a single, albeit complex, document that would set an agenda for addressing the problems of women globally. Differences in culture, language, religion, and education presented complications at every stage of the process. As a theoretical matter, such differences presented a less immediate but in some ways more difficult and persistent problem: In the face of profound cultural differences among women, how can feminists maintain a global political movement yet avoid charges of cultural imperialism?

This theoretical dilemma has become a serious political hurdle for global feminism as the challenge of cultural relativism permeates the politics of any discussion of women's rights on the international stage.

Feminist responses to this charge are complicated and sometimes conflicting. On the one hand, feminists note that culture and religion are often cited as justifications for denying women a range of basic rights, including the right to travel, rights in marriage and divorce, the right to own property, even the right to be protected by the criminal law on an equal basis with men. Women have much to lose, therefore, in any movement away from a universal standard of human rights in favor of deference to culture. On the other hand, feminists acknowledge that feminism itself is grounded in the importance of participation, of listening to and accounting for the particular experiences of women, especially those on the margins of power. Indeed, much feminist criticism of traditional human rights approaches has focused on the tendency of international policymakers to exclude women's

From 19 *Harvard Women's Law Journal* 89–105, 111–115 (1996).

experiences and women's voices. Thus, the claim that Western concepts of women's equality are exclusionary or imperialist strikes at the heart of one of feminism's central commitments—respect for difference.

In short, both the move to expand universal human rights to include those rights central to women's condition and the move toward a relativist view of human rights are consistent with and informed by feminist theory. Indeed, the tension between them reflects a tension within feminism itself, between describing women's experience collectively as a basis for political action and respecting differences among women.

Cultural Relativism versus Universalism

The debate over the universality of human rights is almost as old as the movement toward universal human rights standards in international law. Following World War II, as the Universal Declaration of Human Rights was being drafted, the Executive Board of the American Anthropological Association (AAA) warned that the Declaration would be "a statement of rights conceived only in terms of the values prevalent in the countries of Western Europe and America." The Board added that "standards and values are relative to the culture from which they derive" and thus "what is held to be a human right in one society may be regarded as anti-social by another people." A global audience found this position of moral relativism particularly troubling in the wake of the Nazi Holocaust and feared that it would wholly undermine the nascent human rights agenda. Thus, notwithstanding the efforts of the AAA and the emergence of conflicts of values among participating nations, the Declaration embraced the assumption of the universality of human rights.[2]

Despite the general consensus reflected in the Declaration, differences have persisted over the scope and priorities of the international human rights agenda, differences that are translated with surprising frequency into the rhetoric of universality versus cultural relativism, imperialism versus self-determination. Notwithstanding the language of universality, the question remains: To what extent may a state depart from international norms in the name of culture? Both the Covenant on Economic, Social and Cultural Rights and the Covenant on Civil and Political Rights contribute to this tension in their recognition of the importance of the collective right to self-determination. These documents do not clearly resolve the degree to which citizens, exercising their right of self-determination, may subordinate other protected rights in the interest of security, development, or culture.

Apart from any ambiguities in human rights instruments themselves, non-Western states have argued that the very hierarchy of human rights established in those instruments privileges civil and political rights over economic, social, and cultural rights in a way that is biased toward both Western political traditions and the wealth of Western states relative to the rest of the world.[3] Strategic enforcement of existing standards, coupled with the persistence of discrimination and economic inequality in Western nations, have further called into question the adequacy of

Western concepts of civil and political rights to ensure human well-being. Finally, postmodernism and identity politics within the academy have contributed to the critique of universalism by questioning its very philosophical foundations.[4]

Located within this political and intellectual milieu, contemporary defenses of universalism range from natural rights arguments to positivism to utilitarianism to social contract theories. Regardless of which form the arguments ultimately take, assertions of the universal nature of such claims tend to rest upon an epistemological assumption about the universality of human reason rather than a metaphysical claim about their correspondence with a reality independent of human understanding.[5] Under such immanent universalist theories, truth is a product of the right functioning of human reasoning. This claim about human knowing, in turn, has the consequence of privileging the thinker, the philosopher, the scientist, or the lawyer in the debate over the meaning of human experience. The truth claims that emerge are normative and are understood as substantially independent of history, individual choices, and human experience. Disagreements over human rights are errors in reason, logical mistakes which can be resolved through better thinking.

Opposing the various theories offered as justifications for the existence of universal human rights, cultural relativism reflects skepticism about the availability of universal norms. Like universalism, cultural relativism takes a number of different forms. Generally speaking, however, cultural relativists are committed to one or both of the following premises: that knowledge and truth are culturally contingent, creating a barrier to cross-cultural understanding; and that all cultures are equally valid. Combined with the empirical observation of cultural diversity worldwide, these two premises lead to the conclusion that human rights norms do not transcend cultural location and cannot be readily translated across cultures. The two premises of cultural relativism deprive human rights advocates of both a transcendent justification for human rights standards (i.e., notwithstanding disagreement, human rights exist as a product of the human condition) and a hope for consensus (by bridging the barriers of cultural difference). Cultural relativism raises the possibility that the category "human" is no longer sufficient to enable cross-cultural assessment of human practices or the actions of states.

The Challenge of Feminist Anti-Essentialism

Feminist concerns with difference and exclusion have created some of the same dilemmas within feminism that cultural relativism has generated in the realm of international human rights. Indeed, debates within feminism concerning the degree to which women's condition transcends boundaries of culture, race, and class parallel the struggle between universal and culturally specific visions of human rights. Not surprisingly, therefore, feminist theorizing on the global level is often divided between relativist and universalist approaches. This section explores the assumptions that feminist theory shares with both universalism and cultural relativism. It first describes the emergence of feminist anti-essentialism as a challenge to the universal scope of feminist politics and the persistence of essentialist theories of women's oppression in the face of this challenge. It then discusses the implications of anti-essentialism for feminist human rights activism.

Global Feminist Politics and the Appeal of Essentialism

Feminism has long been concerned with questions of difference. Initially, this concern focused almost exclusively on gender difference: how women may differ from men; how to account for those differences; whether and how those differences do (or should) matter in private life and public policy. Although feminist theory continues to develop around these issues of gender difference, the question of difference has multiplied.

Much incisive and insightful criticism, particularly by feminists of color, has revealed that treating gender difference as the primary concern of feminism has had the effect of reinforcing gendered categories and collapsing differences among women. These critics have argued convincingly that early feminist descriptions of women's experience focused on white, middle-class, educated, heterosexual women. Consequently, the political priorities of the women's movement in the West (e.g., equal access to education and employment, abortion rights) have reflected the most urgent concerns of a relatively more powerful group of women. Moreover, even shared concerns, such as domestic violence and rape, have often been described and addressed based on the experiences of a relatively narrow group of women. Accused of essentialism, feminists who theorized a commonality among women were criticized for committing the dual sin of reinforcing patriarchal assumptions about women as a group and marginalizing some women along the lines of race, class, and sexual orientation.

Despite its theoretical and political vulnerabilities, the practical appeal of essentialism, like the appeal of universalism, persists. Essentialist assumptions offer the promise of uniting women in a way that transcends or precedes politics. Ellen Rooney has suggested that essentialism reflects a "desire that what unites us (as feminists) pre-exist[s] our desire to be joined; something that stands outside our own alliances may authorize them and empower us to speak not just as feminists but as women." This desire may be felt even more urgently on the international level where differences among women threaten to outweigh commonalities.

Much feminist activism on the international level has been premised on two assumptions, both of which may be characterized as essentialist: first, that women share types of experiences and are oppressed in particular ways as women; and second, that these experiences are often different than those of men. These assumptions have led feminists to challenge the traditionally narrow definition of human rights and attempt to expand it to cover experiences shared by women as a group. Like universalist descriptions of human rights or human well-being, feminist essentialism has lent political coherence to the feminist movement and has provided a foundation for Western feminists' expansion of their political vision. Indeed, feminist progress in reshaping the scope of the international human rights agenda stands as an important example of the power of organizing around assumptions of commonality.

Perhaps feminism's most significant contribution in this context has been to expand the scope of human rights to include not just what nations do to one another or what nations do to their citizens, but what citizens do to one another. Although some violations of women's rights fit easily into a civil liberties analysis, much of the abuse of women is part of a larger cultural and economic framework that renders women systematically vulnerable to private power. Abuses of women's rights that are not attributable to state action narrowly defined fall outside a definition of human rights violations as solely a matter of state infringement of civil and political liberties. In contrast, the insistence at the United Nations Conference on Human Rights in Vienna and again at the Women's Conference in Beijing on the inclusion of violence against women as a human rights issue has roots in the insight that countries create and sustain the conditions under which women are victimized and therefore should be accountable for the level of gender-based violence.

Feminists have therefore criticized the traditional focus on political rights, or negative rights against the state, in international human rights instruments as reflecting the view that the greatest threat to the life and liberty of a citizen is the state. According to many feminists, that view does not reflect the realities of women's lives. Rather, the private exercise of male power, often reinforced by the state, more often threatens women's lives and liberty.[6] Thus, by focusing on women's common experience of private oppression, feminist work in international human rights has revealed a potential inconsistency between a vision of human rights as limiting state power and the need for state intervention to limit abuses of private power. In this sense, feminism has offered an external challenge to the adequacy of traditional human rights analysis.

Anti-Essentialism, Cultural Relativism, and Feminist Human Rights Activism

Although feminists have criticized the adequacy of traditional human rights, they have less frequently attacked the universality of those rights. Rather, recognizing the threat that cultural defenses pose to women's rights, as defined from a Western feminist perspective, feminists have most often argued for an expansion of both the scope and the applicability of human rights standards. Indeed, feminist efforts to expand the scope of human rights violations to include harms women suffer as a result of cultural norms or religious practices pose an even greater threat to cultural integrity than do traditional human rights standards. This increased scrutiny of the culture and its most central institutions, the church and the family, has made advocates of a global feminism a target of cultural relativists.

In addition to criticism from cultural relativists, this cross-cultural approach to women's oppression has not been immune from criticism within the feminist community. Such cross-cultural analysis depends upon very broad assumptions about women's lives and experiences and therefore raises important empirical questions regarding the extent to which women's oppression is similarly constituted across cultures. It also raises issues about the formulation of those empirical questions themselves. An essentialist approach generally begins with the experiences of white, middle-class, educated, heterosexual women. Such an approach tends to attribute commonly shared forms of oppression to gender and specific forms of oppression to other sources such as race, class, or sexual orientation. Consequently, an essentialist approach risks becoming a least common denominator approach, allowing relatively privileged women's experiences to define the feminist agenda. This tendency, in turn, creates division among women. In short, when feminists aspire to account for women's oppression through claims of cross-cultural commonality, they construct the feminist subject through exclusions, narrowing her down to her essence. And, as Judith Butler has observed, "those excluded domains return to haunt the 'integrity' and 'unity' of the feminist 'we.'"

Responding to this division, anti-essentialist feminists have attempted to rethink both the various descriptions of gender oppression that have been offered and the assumption that gender oppression can be described meaningfully along a single axis. Instead, they have focused on local, contextualized problems of gender oppression. In this sense, anti-essentialism's criticism of general accounts of women's oppression parallels cultural relativism's critique of universal theories of human rights. Like cultural relativism, feminist anti-essentialism seems to lead to the conclusion that gender inequality cannot be explained cross-culturally.

Thus, despite the general inclination of feminist human rights activists to side with universalists, feminist theory, specifically anti-essentialism, does resonate with relativists' concern over cultural imperialism. Indeed, global feminists' tendency to take for granted the adequacy of their own standards—reflected in their simultaneous insistence on both the inadequacy of traditional human rights norms and the universal application of amended, feminist standards—is precisely the tendency that generated the anti-essentialist critique within feminism itself.

Notwithstanding this resonance, some feminists have cautioned that radical anti-essentialism, like cultural relativism, threatens to undermine the central goal of feminist human rights advocacy: to identify and criticize systems of inequality and injustice that transcend cultural, political, and geographic boundaries. The assumption that gender is culturally contingent not only calls into question universalist notions of gender justice but also renders problematic a feminist critique of legal institutions and legal reform outside of narrow, localized experience. To the extent that feminist anti-essentialism questions the use of cross-cultural categories, it threatens to undermine the identification of broad structures of inequality premised on gender.

It is perhaps this concern that has left feminist advocates on the international level much more reluctant than feminists within the United States to accept the implications of anti-essentialism. At least within a single state, cultural commonalities and legal institutions provide a common framework within which difference can be contained. On the international level, the parameters of such a framework are much more difficult to identify. Moreover, adherence to a universalist approach has been relatively successful for feminist human rights advocates. Although the effort to develop Western notions of justice has proceeded largely without women's participation—and indeed at times with the assumption that they are incapable of reason—women have made identifiable legal gains on the international level by resorting to claims of justice and equality. Feminists therefore fear that without an objectively defensible basis for evaluating the status of women, women will be left with power alone to dictate the outcome of competing claims of truth. That prospect most frightens those who are most oppressed.

A feminist approach to international human rights therefore leads in two apparently conflicting directions at once: (1) increased awareness universally of the importance of cultural and economic rights for women, including such issues as the structure of the family; and (2) increased respect for cultural difference based on an awareness of the partiality of perspective, a skepticism of universal claims of authenticity. Is the tension irreconcilable? Does a feminist commitment to resist imperialism, a commitment born of women's own experience of powerlessness under patriarchy, leave us without a standard by which to condemn abuses of women throughout the world?

Increasingly aware of the diversity of women's experience, sympathizing with the claim that universalism may be barely disguised ethnocentrism, and embracing in large part a position of epistemological skepticism, feminists are faced with a dilemma. Should they move to expand human rights to encompass women's experience as though it were monolithic or, recognizing women's differences, reject the universality of human rights divorced from cultural context? The latter conclusion risks undermining feminist critiques of cultural practices that are deeply harmful to women. Women are economically disempowered in the name of culture. They are denied the right to be educated, to travel, to seek paid employment, to divorce. They are denied legal protection against domestic violence, including spousal murder. They are subject to painful, often dangerous surgery to ensure female chastity. Together these practices and countless others create and sustain cultures of male privilege across the globe. Feminists must therefore respond to relativist or anti-essentialist arguments and take seriously issues of cultural difference without surrendering a critical stance toward the many forms of women's oppression.

Two Views on Culture and Coercion

Although sharing a concern with cultural difference and a lack of faith in the availability of universal standards, feminist anti-essentialism and cultural relativism nevertheless reach different conclusions regarding the possibility of cross-cultural evaluation. As the preceding section suggests, cultural relativists and feminist anti-essentialists are each concerned with the implications of cultural difference and the problem of coercion, yet they view both culture and coercion differently. This section examines the concepts of coercion and culture as they are used in both feminist anti-essentialist and cultural relativist arguments and suggests that, despite its commitment to tolerance, the relativist view of culture tends to obscure issues of coercion at the heart of gender politics.

Cultural Relativism: Essentializing Culture, Obscuring Coercion

Feminists have questioned arguments based on a simple assertion of cultural integrity for several reasons. First, cultural relativists may inadequately attend to the degree to which power relationships within the culture itself constrain the ability of individuals to renegotiate cultural norms. Yet this inattention is inconsistent with a concern about coercion. The relativist cannot criticize Western imperialism and at the same time ignore non-Western states' selective use of the defense of culture in the service of state power. The risk of such intra-cultural coercion seems especially great when that selective invocation of culture has differential effects on groups within the state such as minority ethnic or racial groups or women.

Second, cultural relativist arguments may oversimplify the complexity and fluidity of culture by treating culture as monolithic and moral norms within a particular culture as readily ascertainable. Yet a single, inward glance at Western culture reveals the absurdity of this assumption. The multiplicity of beliefs in the United States (or even within a single community or family) about the legitimacy of abortion or the role of women in the family illustrates the complexity of translating imperfectly shared assumptions into evaluative standards. Such oversimplification seems inconsistent with the very premises of cultural relativism. Indeed, cultural relativists' tendency to describe differences in terms of simple opposition—Western versus non-Western—without exploring how specific cultural practices are constituted and justified "essentializes" culture itself. Treating culture as monolithic fails to respect relevant intra-cultural differences just as the assumption of the universality of human rights standards fails to respect cross-cultural differences. Cultural differences that may be relevant to assessing human rights claims are neither uniform nor static. Rather, they are constantly created, challenged, and renegotiated by individuals living within inevitably overlapping cultural communities.

This oversimplification of culture may lead relativists to accept too readily a cultural defense articulated by state actors or other elites on the international level, actors that tend not to be women. Yet it seems unlikely that a cultural defense offered by the state will adequately reflect the dynamic, evolving, and possibly conflicting cultural concerns of its citizens. Given the complexity and multiplicity of culture, the ability or inclination of heads of state to identify and translate cultural practices into specific defenses against the imposition of Western human rights norms is questionable. Feminists in particular have cited example after example in which culture has been selectively and perhaps cynically invoked to justify oppressive practices.

The apparent inconsistency between cultural relativists' fear of inter-cultural coercion and virtual neglect of intra-cultural coercion must be understood in light of relativists' assumptions about the relationship between culture and the individual. If culture is understood simply as a reflection of human will, then the existence of any particular social organization tends to become its own legitimation. Focused on defending cultural integrity from external encroachment, cultural relativists tend to be much less concerned with the way culture determines or limits the individual's possibilities for self-definition.

Feminist Anti-Essentialism: Complicating Coercion

Although cultural relativists and universalist defenders of the existing human rights regime are fundamentally opposed in their approaches, they find common ground to the extent that the existing regime embraces values of self-determination, both cultural and political. Yet it is precisely this privileging of autonomy that triggers feminism's departure from both liberal pluralism and cultural relativism. The version of cultural relativism that is informed by liberalism's concern for autonomy and self-determination treats cross-cultural critique as an encroachment on cultural integrity. To the extent that cultural relativists are concerned with coercion or cultural imperialism, they tend to associate an absence of cross-cultural critique with human freedom; thus, they confine moral judgments about intra-cultural coercion to the only standards that they deem coherent: local standards.[7] This argument privileging social autonomy creates an unlikely alliance between cultural relativists and liberal universalists, particularly with respect to issues emerging from the private as opposed to the public sphere.

In contrast to cultural relativists and liberal pluralists,[8] feminist anti-essentialists are centrally concerned with the interplay between culture and self, exploring ways in which culture constructs gendered individuals. Unlike the cultural relativist model, which privileges the action of the individual or group in the creation of culture, much of feminist theory assumes a more complicated connection between culture and limits on human subjectivity.[9] Unlike the liberal pluralist view, which focuses on state power and privileges private ordering, feminism emphasizes the role of private power. The most important premise of this feminist view is that the sex/gender system is substantially a product of culture rather than divine will, human biology, or natural selection.[10] Implicit in this assumption is the claim that cultural norms—language, law, myth, custom—are not merely products of human will and action but also define and limit the possibilities for human identity.

Connected with this view of cultural limitations on human subjectivity is the notion that cultural norms function as a source of power and control within modern society. Consistent with this recognition, many feminists have rejected a theory of power that posits monolithic control held by a coherent or unified sovereign. Yet it is precisely this model of power that traditional human rights standards are designed to regulate and to which cultural relativists often defer when exercised within cultural boundaries. In contrast, feminists, influenced by Michel Foucault, have emphasized the degree to which power is exercised both from above, by sovereigns, and within concrete social interactions and relationships—in short, through culture. For feminists, culture itself becomes a source of control and a site of resistance, a form of power that feminist human rights activists must engage directly along with more traditional public and private forms.

Feminist anti-essentialists' emphasis on culture's role in creating and regulating human beings helps to explain their departure from both liberal pluralism and cultural relativism. Although feminism, liberal pluralism, and some forms of cultural relativism share a concern over coercion, for feminists, simply preserving self-determination on either the individual or the cultural level is an inadequate response.

A focus on external coercion privileges a traditional model of power exercised by elites and treats local manifestations of that power, such as family relationships, as by-products of individual ordering. Yet, if the self is constituted by culture, as many feminists assume, equating emancipation from external coercion with individual freedom is problematic. Instead, feminists must consider a more complex process of emancipation that involves transformation of the self.

NOTES

1. Nahid Toubia, foreword to *Women of the Arab World: The Coming Challenge*, ed. Nahid Toubia, trans. Nahed El Gamal. (1988), xii.

2. The Declaration states:

The General Assembly [p]roclaims this Universal Declaration of Human Rights as a common standard of achievement for all peoples and all nations, to the end that every individual and every organ of society . . . shall strive by teaching and education to promote respect for these rights and freedoms and by progressive measures, national and international, to secure their universal and effective recognition and observance, both among the peoples of Member States themselves and among the peoples of territories under their jurisdiction.

GA Res. 217(A)(III), U.N. Doc. A/180 (1948).

3. The circumstances under which [the Declaration] was drafted support the perception that early human rights documents, reflect a Western bias. The membership of the drafting committee, the Commission on Human Rights, was overwhelmingly Western. In addition, the U.S. Department of State orchestrated the early drafting of a proposed constitution. Finally, most of the critical meetings took place in the United States, and American NGOs were extremely influential in the process. See John P. Humprey, "The Universal Declaration of Human Rights: Its History, Impact and Juridical Character," in *Human Rights: Thirty Years after the Universal Declaration*, ed. B. G. Ramcharan (1979), 21.

Despite the dominance of the United States in the drafting process, the degree to which the document reflects Western rather than universal norms is contested. According to some, the notion that the standards embodied in the document are uniquely Western is itself profoundly racist. See Richard Schifter, "U.S. Dep't of State, Human Rights: A Western Cultural Bias?" in *Current Policy No. 1105*, 2–3 (1988).

4. See Steven Seidman and David G. Wagner, introduction to *Postmodernism and Social Theory*, ed. Steven Seidman and David G. Wagner (1992). Seidman and Wagner explain:

Central to postmodernism is its critique of the claim that scientific knowledge is universal and can be justified in a noncontextual way. Postmodernists contend that standards of truth are context-dependent. . . . Postmodernists tend to favor forms of social inquiry which incorporate an explicitly practical and moral intent, that are contextual and restricted in their focus (local stories are preferred over general ones), and that are narratively structured rather than articulating a general theory.

5. Richard Rorty in "Human Rights, Rationality, and Sentimentality" in *On Human Rights: The Oxford Amnesty Lectures* 41 (Stephen Shute & Susan Hurley eds. 1993) describes this movement away from metaphysical realism as reflecting the waning relevance of moral philosophy to the human condition:

Why has knowledge become much less important to our self-image than it was two hundred years ago? Why does the attempt to found culture on nature, and moral obligation on knowledge of transcultural universals, seem so much less important to us than it seemed in the Enlightenment? Why is there so little resonance, and so little point, in asking whether human beings in fact have the rights listed in the Helsinki Declaration? Why, in short, has moral philosophy become such an inconspicuous part of our culture?

6. This is not to suggest that women are not also the victims of traditional human rights violations—they are. Women are imprisoned, tortured, raped, killed, and silenced by state authorities in the same way men are. Yet women are more commonly imprisoned, tortured, raped, killed, and silenced by their own spouses, lovers, and families.

7. It is important, of course, to keep in mind the possibility of intra-cultural critique and rebellion. Anthropologists and other defenders of cultural relativism who have tended to idealize non-Western cultures have had to confront the abuses by post-colonial regimes in Cambodia, Uganda, and Ethiopia, and the emigration of many citizens of those states to formerly colonial states in the West.

8. I use the term "liberalism" or "liberal pluralism" to refer to a commitment to the basic political framework that underlies existing human rights standards. "Universalism" refers to a commitment to universally applicable human rights norms, though not necessarily to those currently embodied in international law.

9. Although generalizing, I would argue that most feminists, whether or not they define themselves as anti-essentialists, posit an important role for culture in constraining women's subjectivity. It is this constraint in its many forms, and the belief that it is malleable, that animates much of feminist politics.

10. Feminist theorists sometimes express this relationship between subjectivity and culture as the distinction between sex and gender, a distinction perhaps first emphasized by Simone de Beauvoir in her claim "One is not born, but rather becomes, a woman" (Simone de Beauvoir, *The Second Sex,* ed. and trans. H. M. Parshley, 1949; reprint, New York: Alfred A. Knopf, Inc., 1953), 267.

Further Comments

1. Others have described how dispute resolution processes can be "gendered" and the consequences of such gendering. Deborah Kolb and Linda Putnam, for instance, have explained that a process such as negotiation can be gendered if "attributes more commonly associated with one gender are more valued for effectiveness in conducting the process; thus rendering attributes associated with the other gender as devalued." Thus, current analysis of the negotiation process tends to value traits stereotypically associated with males—such as competition, individuality, analytic rationality, and strategic thinking. In contrast, traits stereotypically associated with females—such as cooperation, intuition, emotionality, and reasoning based on the particular situation—are devalued or ignored. Kolb and Putnam argue that by considering alternatives and questioning the dominant "masculine" perspectives on negotiation, we can uncover fundamentally different and potentially more constructive and effective ways of negotiating and resolving problems.[1]

While recognizing that there is no single feminist theory but many feminist theories, Elizabeth Schneider posits that there are some common crucial aspects to all feminist theories that affect how process is viewed. For instance, a feminist perspective emphasizes that process is dynamic and constantly unfolding, that process has transformative potential to make a significant change (both positive and negative) in individual lives, and that process and results are linked. "Methods of institutional practice and decision-making affect who is silenced and who can speak; the context in which rules are applied affects their meaning. So when we think, for example, about what process is due, or consider the various values of process, we must consider who can speak, the way in which procedural rules allow or deny access to courts and the way in which process is experienced by the individual."[2]

2. The materials in Part 2 raise many issues about both the usefulness and the dangers of generalizing on the basis of gender. Gilligan's constructs of care and justice, for instance, have been applied to a range of settings. Carol Rose has extrapolated these constructs, describing the impact of people's perception that women have a "taste for cooperation." She hypothesizes that employers and others are inclined to offer women less or be more demanding of women because they perceive women will, in the interest of being cooperative, accept those terms.[3]

Others question whether one can generalize Gilligan's findings to different ethnic groups. Carol Stack, for instance, studied whether Gilligan's categories would be applicable to African Americans. She found that African American boys and girls were equally likely to consider "justice" and "care" factors; the result was the same for African American men and women. In other words, there were no gender differences.[4]

Dangers of generalizing also apply to men. Recall that Gilligan describes a male "voice" as well as a female one. On the one hand, one can question whether she is overessentializing boys and men. On the other hand, she raises the possibility that the male voice is distinct. In the same way that we cannot generalize a universal voice to women, we cannot generalize a universal voice to men. In what ways have the male gender's approach to conflict been socially constructed?

3. A common perception is that alternative dispute resolution (ADR) processes such as mediation have many positive attributes. Compared to litigation, ADR is viewed as faster and cheaper, while allowing the parties to resolve their disputes creatively. Richard Delgado was one of the first to suggest that despite its positive potential, ADR also has some inherent dangers.[5] He suggests, for instance, that unlike more formal and regulated processes such as litigation, informal processes such as mediation do not have the procedural and legal safeguards to protect participants from racial and other social prejudices. Grillo's article similarly questions the appropriateness of mandatory mediation in family and custody disputes.

4. As suggested by the readings, research results on gender are equivocal. Meanwhile, the existing research is being utilized. Patricia Gwartney-Gibbs and Denise Lach have described a conceptual and theoretical model for understanding how dispute resolution in the workplace contributes to gender differences in employment. Drawing on multidisciplinary research, they propose that gender differences do exist in the origins, processes, and outcomes of disputes. Furthermore, they link the differences to gender roles and institutional structures such as industries and occupations.[6]

Recognizing that the workforce is increasingly diverse, Mary Gentile focuses on how businesses, managers, and employees can most constructively and productively work together. In her case analyses illustrating aspects of diversity-related intra- and interpersonal conflict, she considers such issues as the differences between intent and perception, power and access, equality and fairness; the role of bystanders and third parties; and the implications of involvement.[7]

5. Research also is emerging on the intersection between conflict and sexual orientation. For example, Isabelle Gunning describes how the mediation process and mediation programs can be a preferable alternative to the court system for gay and lesbian communities. Given the bias and ignorance of the court system, gay and lesbian disputants may find that disputes around organizational conflict, property, and family and custody issues may be better resolved in mediation. "Lesbian and gay mediators, with their intimate and textured understanding of lesbian and gay lives and cultures, are an important part of encouraging the use of mediation in the lesbian and gay communities. . . . [S]traight or unconnected mediators who are interested in providing quality, unbiased mediation services . . . also have important roles to play—if they can connect with those communities in both professional and personal ways."[8]

6. Philosopher Uma Narayan also has discussed issues of cultural essentialism and relativism. She explains, for instance, that one of the problems with cultural

relativism is definitional: what constitutes "culture" is both arbitrary and constantly shifting. There also may be sharp differences among those supposedly in the same culture (and commonalities among those in different cultures). While culture is the result of social evolution, it also is a reflection of the times and those in power. Those in power may selectively label some customs as essential, so that attacks on these customs are viewed as betrayals.[9]

Higgins's article describes the feminist debate between cultural essentialism and cultural relativism. Terrell Northrup writes about another area of tension within feminist ideology: the divergences between conflict resolution theory and feminist theory. Northrup notes that conflict resolution theorists emphasize that alternative dispute resolution processes should be efficient (speedy and less expensive) and that increased efficiencies lead to just results because the parties can resolve their disputes quickly. Northrup suggests, however, that feminist theory sees a kind of "schizophrenia" between efficiency and justice. Feminists define justice in broad terms, arguing that structural, institutional, and historical causes and correlates of inequities must be addressed. Structural justice requires long-term solutions and may well be a longer, messier, and less manageable than the ADR processes that conflict resolution theorists envision.[10]

Conflict resolution theorists also view the neutrality of third-party processors, such as mediators, as essential and achievable. With a neutral mediator, the presumption is that power imbalances between the parties diminish in importance. But feminist theorists are wary of the notion of impartiality. Citing the work of Iris Young, Northrup raises several concerns, some of which are also identified in other readings in this book:

> First, the problem of culture as an obstacle to neutrality is often couched as a problem not of power but of difference. That is, culture must be taken into account because a mediator cannot understand a party fully if her cultural understandings are different from his. Remedies suggested by the conflict resolution literature include warnings for the mediator to become aware of her biases, to learn about cultural differences, and to create as neutral a setting as possible for the mediation sessions. In spite of cultural differences, the mediator should remain as objective as possible and help the disputants find common ground, conflict resolution proponents argue. In effect, differences are reduced to a unity. To the extent, however, that the cultural grounding of the mediator guides her behavior—her interventions, comments, suggestions—the process of the mediated negotiation may be propelled in a particular direction by the mediator, a direction that is untrue to the meanings, norms, or practices of the party whose culture is different. That is not simply a problem of difference, but also one of power. For example, Anne Donnellon and Deborah M. Kolb argue that in U.S. organizations conflicts involving gender, race, and ethnicity are handled in ways that reflect a predominant ideology of meritocracy that is based on individual success, a Western and masculinist model that masks the role of difference in creating conflict situations. They state that the idea of "constructive conflict" is used in the field as if it were an absolute, while in reality some methods and solutions [are] only "constructive" for some.

> Second, mediators are not only products of their own culture, but are also products of a "culture" of Western conflict resolution proponents. That culture is learned

when a mediator is subjected to training sessions, reads mediation related materials, and interacts with other mediation professions and/or paraprofessionals. In some ways this could be seen as an indoctrination into one view of approaching conflict, presumably a Western middle class approach at that. Again, the mediator-as-process-guide in many ways will be affected by the norms and values of this second "culture." Susan Goldstein, in a discussion of the particular claims of the Western conflict resolution literature, contrasts some of the undisclosed aspects of this practice with the norms of conflict management in Asian cultures. Face-to-face confrontation, for example, which is assumed and unquestioned in Western conflict management practice, is in some cultures highly undesirable if not rude. The acceptability of a third party varies by cultures as well, so that in some Asian cultures only family members perform a mediating role. Further, the Western model of human nature gives priority to individualism that, according to Lisa Adler and Lily Ling, is not typical of many cultures. "The majority of civilizations in the world," they contend, "value a collective subjectivity (family, clan, tribe, nation, state) over a individual one." The message of these writers is that not all aspects of the Western model are easily or even ethically transportable across cultures. Further, the idea of mediation is itself a cultural product, not necessarily common to all cultures. This position stands in sharp contrast to the contention of some of the major conflict resolution theorists that "generic" and universal principles of conflict management can be found and applied across the board to any conflict.

Third, there is a danger that defining the mediator role in terms of neutrality exalts the status of the role, making the mediator one who is outside the conflict and therefore "objective" and better able to see the "true" nature of the dispute. In effect, the mediator becomes an expert who has an elevated viewpoint from which to perform his analysis. Linda Alcoff and Laura Gray have dealt at length with the problems inherent in such contexts as that of the psychotherapy office or the confessional where a person with a problem exposes its details to an "expert." The expert then interprets the person and her story, rewriting the conflict using codes of what is seen as "normal" according to the dominant discourse, and then "gives it back" in its altered form. This, then, is not a problem of guiding the process in more productive directions, but one of placing specific value on some things and devaluing others from the privileged role of expert.

Teaching Ideas

1. Explore how conflict and conflict resolution might be "gendered." Consider a particular dispute. What difference would the sex and gender of the following individuals make?

> the parties to the dispute (What if they were both women, both men, or one of each sex?)
> the third-party decision maker or facilitator (e.g., the judge, mediator, or village elder)
> the representatives of the parties (e.g., the lawyers)
> those most affected by the process or the outcome, either directly or indirectly

How do our stereotypes about men and women, masculinity and femininity, affect our answers? In what ways can the procedural and substantive rules, institutions, or issues be gendered?

2. Using Gilligan's dichotomy, identify a problem, perhaps a legal case, and analyze the dispute under her "justice" and "caring" approaches. How would the outcomes differ? How does each approach compare to a legal analysis?

3. Katharine Bartlett, Sandra Janoff, and others[11] have considered how men and women experience and are impacted differently by law school. Janoff considered how law school socializes students to approach problems in a certain way. For instance, in her study, while women were more likely to approach problems with a care orientation, the law school experience tended to reshape their approach to a more rights-oriented, emotionally neutral approach. Bartlett has suggested that law school emphasizes competitiveness and being adversarial, which tends to disadvantage women students and reinforce male dominance. Do you agree with Janoff and Bartlett?

Reflect on your educational experience. In what ways have the particular academic discipline, school philosophy, or peer values affected the way in which you approach problems? What are the consequences of not conforming? Are certain groups of students more affected by the socialization process than others?

NOTES

1. Deborah M. Kolb and Linda L. Putnam, "Through the Looking Glass: Negotiation Theory Refracted through the Lens of Gender" (paper presented at "Gender Issues in Negotiation and Conflict Resolution," Harvard Law School, October 12–13, 1995), 8–12.

2. Elizabeth M. Schneider, "Gendering and Engendering Process," 61 *University Cincinnati Law Review* 1223, 1226–1228 (1993). See also American Bar Association Committee on Women in the Profession, *Elusive Equality: The Experiences of Women in Legal Education* (Chicago, 1996).

3. Carol M. Rose, "Bargaining and Gender," 18 *Harvard Journal of Law and Public Policy* 547 (1995).

4. Carol B. Stack, "Different Voices, Different Visions: Gender, Culture, and Moral Reasoning," in Faye Ginsburg and Anna Lowenhaupt Tsing, eds. *Uncertain Terms: Negotiating Gender in American Culture* (Boston: Beacon Press, 1990), 19–27.

5. Richard Delgado, Chris Dunn, Pamela Brown, Helena Lee, and David Hubbert, "Fairness and Formality: Minimizing the Risk of Prejudice in Alternative Dispute Resolution," *Wisconsin Law Review* 1359, 1387–1391, 1400–1404 (1985).

6. Patricia A. Gwatney-Gibbs and Denise H. Lach, "Gender and Workplace Dispute Resolution: A Conceptual and Theoretical Model," 11, 28(2) *Law and Society Review* 265–296 (1994).

7. Mary C. Gentile, "Managing Conflict in a Diverse Workplace," Harvard Business School, Case No. 5-395-090 (1995) and Teaching Note No. 5-396-008 (1995).

8. Isabelle R. Gunning, "Mediation as an Alternative to Court for Lesbian and Gay Families: Some Thoughts on Douglas McIntyre's Article," 13(1) *Mediation Quarterly* 47–52 (1995). See also Annette Townley, "The Invisible-*ism*: Heterosexism and the Implications for Mediation," 9(4) *Mediation Quarterly* 397–401 (1992).

9. Uma Narayan, "Rethinking Culture: A Feminist Critique of Cultural Essentialism and Relativism" (presentation at the University of Pittsburgh, February 25, 1999). See also Uma Narayan, *Dislocating Cultures: Identities, Traditions and Third World Feminism* (New York: Routledge, 1997).

10. Terrell A. Northrup, "The Uneasy Partnership between Conflict Theory and Feminist Theory" (unpublished paper, Aug. Syracuse Univ. 1995), 7–8.

11. Katharine T. Bartlett, "Feminist Perspectives on the Ideological Impact of Legal Education upon the Profession," 72 *North Carolina Law Review* 1259–1270 (1994); Sandra Janoff, "The Influence of Legal Education on Moral Reasoning," 76 *Minnesota Law Review* 193–238 (1991).

Part III

Ethnicity, Race, and Conflict

Introduction

It is both particularly challenging and promising to study the intersections of ethnicity, race, and conflict. As in the gender and conflict area, scholars and dispute resolution practitioners are still in the early stages of determining the research agenda and the most constructive inquiries. As illustrated in Part 2, some researchers study gender and race concurrently in an attempt to understand their interrelationships. Meanwhile, the fluid nature of inquiries about ethnicity and conflict is apparent. The composition and characteristics of ethnic groups change, dependent on such factors as immigration patterns. In addition, the types of disputes and issues evolve, as illustrated by the readings on the various forms of racial conflict.

While our multiethnic and multiracial communities offer interesting and valuable ways of resolving conflicts, as illustrated by Manu Aluli Meyer's reading near the end of this part, they also create societal conflicts throughout the country with which we continue to struggle. The first set of readings explores some of the realities, tensions, and complexities in this area. Howard Gadlin and Janie Victoria Ward both talk about interracial conflict, mostly Black-White disputes, but offer very different perspectives. Gadlin, reflecting on his experiences on college campuses, describes how White Americans and people of color have fundamentally different understandings of what racism is and how it is manifested. These different perceptions both prompt conflict and inhibit resolving the conflict. Ward, through the narratives of African Americans, discusses themes of justice and caring in interracial conflict.

The next two readings, by anthropologist Kyeyoung Park and legal scholar Taunya Lovell Banks, consider conflict between ethnic minority groups, focusing on disputes between Korean Americans and African Americans. Park's work looks at the hostility and violence in South Central Los Angeles, also played out in a number of other American cities, between Korean American store owners and African American residents and customers. She describes how culture is intertwined in these disputes, affecting how the two groups perceive the problems and each other. Discussing a film depiction of a dispute (spurred by an interracial romance) between Asian Indian Americans and Black Americans in Mississippi, Banks observes obstacles to coalition building between ethnic groups. While the disputes in Los Angeles and Mississippi might appear to involve only two ethnic groups, both Park and Banks suggest that White society plays a role in prompting and resolving the conflicts. Completing this set of readings is Mary Patrice Erdmans's description of intragroup conflict within the Polish American community.

She contrasts the values and priorities of immigrant groups with the more established ethnic community. Her work vividly documents how culture is dynamic and how the societal perception that the members of an ethnic group are homogeneous should be questioned.

The next piece, by Manu Aluli Meyer, offers a change of pace, in presentation and in content. Her description of the native Hawaiians' process of peacemaking, *ho'oponopono*—meaning "to make right"—illustrates the rich range of approaches to dispute resolution in our multicultural American society. At the same time, her article captures both the spirituality and practicality of this ancient yet still utilized practice.

This part ends with Doriane Lambelet Coleman's article on the "cultural defense"—offering evidence of cultural beliefs or practices to explain what might otherwise be unacceptable or criminal conduct. Here we explore further issues of cultural relativism versus universal norms, as introduced in Higgins's essay at the end of Part 2, but in a different context and from a different perspective. Coleman poses the following dilemma: If we are sensitive to the defendant's culture, which is often shaped by her or his immigrant background, how do we reconcile the rights (and injuries) of the victims? Stated more broadly: In our increasingly multicultural society, when should divergent cultural values be accommodated or rejected?

El respeto al derecho ajeno es la paz.
Respect for the rights of another, that is peace.
—A Mexican American proverb

Chapter 20

Conflict Resolution, Cultural Differences, and the Culture of Racism

Howard Gadlin

Rituals of Racism

In a recent book, Marc Howard Ross refers to culture as "the practices and values common to a population living in a given setting." Culture organizes and is constituted by beliefs, norms, behaviors, and institutional practices. Agreement and disagreement, conflict and cooperation are all dependent upon and given meaning by the culture within which they occur. In contemporary America, we have become so accustomed to thinking about differences and conflict between different racial and ethnic groups, not to mention men and women, gays and straights, and so forth, that we almost forget the common cultural base that structures and gives meaning to these conflicts. Let me explain why I have begun to think in terms of a culture of racism.

After some years of work as an ombudsperson, I began to notice a certain predictable quality to the stories related to me by disputants where race or gender was the issue or at least an element. Furthermore, I could often foresee what would occur when the disputants were brought together. It was almost like watching a carefully choreographed dance and marveling at the harmony of movements: each dancer's steps smoothly coordinated with the other dancer's steps in a way only multiple rehearsals could achieve. To an observer, these are disputes in which people know their parts very well and, although they have not actually rehearsed their particular lines, they are drawing from a well-understood repertoire of attitudes, emotions, cognitions, beliefs, and statements about the other. (When I say that they know their parts, I do not mean to imply a self-conscious choosing of which lines to use in which circumstances. Rather I am referring to something analogous to the way we, even well into adulthood, find ourselves being children when we interact with our parents.)

This ritualistic playing of a role is most apparent in large group disputes. Each side in such disputes becomes an exaggerated, almost caricatured version of itself. If accused of not doing enough in relation to affirmative action and racial equality,

From 33 *Negotiation Journal* 35–42 (January 1994). Plenum Publishing.

the faculty and administration both retort with a well-rehearsed script crafted to exonerate them even before the charges have been spelled out. Frustrated with what they perceive as resistance, denial, equivocation, and backsliding, critics of the university substitute demands for plans, interpret every action or proposal in the worst possible light, and develop arguments crafted only to persuade those they have already convinced. It is as if everyone is committed to the conflicts as they are currently constituted. No one is prepared to go beyond defending their initial position in the dispute. One reason for the rigidity of these conflicts is a profound suspiciousness regarding the abilities, character, and intentions of the parties on the other side of the dispute.

In today's campus climate, this means that many women and people of color assume that the white men who numerically dominate the administration and faculty: (1) got there because of their skin color and gender privilege; (2) are at the very least insensitive to, and more typically, hostile to, the concerns, difficulties, and aspirations of those women and minorities attempting to move up; and (3) have selected as their colleagues in the upper echelons only women and people of color who have sold out to the white male establishment, compromising their personal identity and group affiliation. These assumptions are almost the mirror image of the assumptions made by most white males about people of color and, to some extent, women in positions of power or status: (1) that they are there only for reasons of affirmative action; (2) that they will be especially adept at understanding and dealing with the concerns, difficulties, and aspirations of those traditionally excluded from the upper levels of the academic hierarchy; and (3) that they will probably be indifferent, if not downright hostile, to the needs of white male colleagues and students.

But there is more. In these conflicts, each disputant's identity is intimately tied up with the conflict itself, and requires the maintenance of the conflict as a means to conserve his or her identity. Now those of us who work with conflict know that among the most intractable conflicts are those that have engaged some aspect of the identities of the disputants. But I believe that race is such a core feature of identity that conflicts where race is a factor become, among other things, conflicts that challenge each person's sense of who she or he is. It appears as if the disputants' identities are so bound up in the conflict that if the conflict were to be resolved, diminished, or even controlled, then their identities would be threatened. Especially for the subordinate groups, the maintenance of the conflict seems to sustain the identity which has been forged by racism. To me as a white man, it is almost as if the members of the dominated groups say to themselves, "If I am not in conflict I am not facing the reality of the discrimination that has helped shape who I am."

For the dominant groups a somewhat different dynamic pertains, but here too, identity plays a key role. Most people who are successful experience their accomplishments as a result of their abilities and effort, even if they have a fairly sophisticated understanding of social forces and the differences in opportunity between majority and minority groups. They interpret their success as a confirmation of the standards by which their accomplishments have been measured. (Within universities I have encountered few, if any, white people who have not at some level bought into standards by which their privilege or dominance is maintained.) For these people then, a fundamental internal conflict emerges in the face of recognizing the reality of racism; a conflict between acknowledging their own privilege and denigrating their own accomplishments. One cannot accomplish the former without also achieving the latter. Often this is made even more complicated by the conflict between the need to defend what one wants to believe is the "nonracist nature" of one's own actions or positions and the need to address the issue at hand. Even those of us who begin discussions of race by acknowledging that none of us can avoid being touched by racism are trying to borrow a bit of transcendence through that acknowledgment.

Let's look at some of the features of racial and ethnic conflicts and their resolution. At first glance there is the effect of what is often referred to as the cultural background of each of the disputants and the mediator. (The campus where I work is wonderfully multicultural—more than 50 percent of the undergraduate student body is other than Caucasian. The same can be said for a considerable proportion of the staff. The faculty and upper administration are the least integrated segments of the campus.) Cultural background is usually referred to as one of the contributing factors that goes into the make-up of the personality or character of the disputant, added on to or integrated with the particulars of family size and history, early childhood experiences, relationships with parents, socioeconomic class, and so on.

Obviously, disputants of different racial or ethnic backgrounds will vary in their ways of entering into, participating in, and resolving conflicts. One group will be more aggressive than another; this group makes more eye contact than that; saving face will be manifested differently in different groups; and expectations of the mediator will also differ for different groups. For that matter, noticeable differences emerge from one culture to the next in the preference given to group versus individual identity. Similarly, gender differences can be treated as cultural differences: those coming from women's culture handle conflict differently than those coming from men's culture. (An enormous literature, some of it specific to conflict resolution, some of it quite general, identifies the differences in those cultures. There are even translation guides for those who try to communicate across the cultural divide that separates men and women.)

Much of the literature on cultural differences in conflict is valuable for alerting us to the ethnocentricities inherent in many of the styles, concepts, values, and practices of contemporary western dispute resolution. However, this work also serves to particularize the alleged differences between races in ways that may, in the long term, serve more to uphold divisive stereotypes than undermine them. For example, while any honest discussion of the race issue in the United States must address the question of differences, there is no way of discussing difference that is not also problematic. However well intended, attempts to associate particular styles or traits with racial or ethnic groups that are, in fact, quite large and diverse can result in a stereotyping that is just as distorting and misleading as conventional derogatory stereotyping. Thomas Kochman's *Black and White Styles of*

Conflict is an example of such work. Attempting to make sense of some of the misunderstandings and miscommunications that characterize certain black-white conflicts, he winds up attributing many of the central features of these conflicts to differences in black and white cultures. The deficiencies in this kind of approach can be appreciated only if we first briefly examine the complexity of the issue of difference in American race relations.

Over the past four decades, efforts to ameliorate inequality have bounced between the denial and appreciation of difference. Historically inequality has been "justified" by reference to differences and deficiencies that dominant groups attribute to subordinate groups. Rejecting these attributions, advocates of equality have often downplayed intergroup differences and been suspicious of those who assert or acknowledge their existence. Referring to differences while justifying the advantages of the dominant group or opposing proposals intended to reduce inequality is taken either as a sign of malevolence or as the mere reflex of the powerful protecting their privilege. Indeed, the issue of the interpretation of difference is at the heart of many of the conflicts I see as an ombudsperson; a student who believes he has been graded unfairly by comparison with others in the class or a staff member who believes her performance evaluation is more harsh than those of her fellow employees will often attribute the poor grade or evaluation to race. At the same time, the faculty member or supervisor will deny that race had anything to do with the evaluation.

The Surplus Meanings of Racial Differences

Any discussion of racial differences, at the level of individual cases or at the level of sociological generalizations, is charged with surplus meaning. Every dispute about difference where race is a factor, even when it is not the issue, evokes the entire history of differentiation and discrimination. This was once illustrated for me at a conference for ombudspeople that included in the program a session on campus codes against hate speech and a separate session on the problems of international students. The discussion of speech codes was cautious and inhibited—each person speaking demonstrated a wariness of taking a position that might be taken as a sign of not being committed to racial equality, not being prepared to take every step necessary to promote greater equality. No one was willing to offer up any examples of a situation where she or he had used language in an offensive way. By comparison, the discussion of international students was relaxed and free flowing, with people practically competing to tell the most outrageous story of cross-cultural insensitivity. In this context, attributions and acknowledgment of difference were seen as providing the opportunity for greater understanding and offenses of insensitivity based on ignorance of difference were easily tolerated and assumed to be easily remedied. Differences were assumed not to be about race, but about culture, even though the people involved were often of different races. But the discussion of racial differences at home can never achieve the ease of discussion of cross-cultural differences because racial differences in the United States are as much a reflection of our common culture as they are of the cultural differences among the various racial and ethnic groupings. The differences discovered in discussions with people from different cultures are indicators of the separateness of our cultures, or at least we can take them as such. The differences discovered in discussions among people of different racial or ethnic groups within the country are differences shaped in part by the history of interrelationship among the different racial groups, and those interrelationships include slavery, segregation, internment, discrimination, exclusion, hostility, charity, condescension, and so on.

Every discussion of difference is problematic in some way and necessarily enters into racial conflicts even while offering a way to understand them. The boundary between an appreciative description and a reified stereotyping of a group is both thin and elusive. When Kochman speaks about black styles of conflict, he attributes the style he is describing to the culture of black people as if that culture existed in isolation from white culture. Any effort to describe and take into account cultural differences in dispute resolution, or any other endeavor for that matter, necessarily risks compartmentalizing the phenomenon of racial and gender conflict and separating the psychological dynamics from their social context, which actually heightens discrimination. My quarrel with Kochman is not with his effort to describe the difference between black and white styles of conflict but with his failure to understand these differences in the context of black-white relations. Observed differences between groups are understood in terms of attributes derived from some essential features of the groups to which people belong. Once we have ascribed certain qualities to whole groups, we tend to explain those qualities by emphasizing what is in the minds of individual disputants, as if that were the only way culture could affect an individual, and to de-emphasize the contribution of interactive and social factors.

We need to understand conflict as a social relation composed by the disputants. Similarly, the qualities of the disputants themselves are constituted by their conflictual relationship. Furthermore, efforts to understand the effects of culture, or more specifically cultural differences, on conflict and conflict resolution when the conflict is about or related to race fail to take into account the crucial contribution of the shared culture that provides the framework within which cultural differences assume the significance that they do. Conflict over race does not derive merely from the differences among groups but equally and importantly from what they share. This constellation of commonality, conflict, and difference is what I refer to as the culture of racism. By referring to a culture of racism I wish to differentiate that from what is often described as racist culture.

Racism and the Culture of Racism

Usually the term "racist culture" is used to describe a culture in which there is a clear hierarchical structure in which one racial group dominates all other racial groups on the basis of differences—real or imaginary—that the dominant group defines, reifies, assesses, and valorizes. "Racist" here is an adjective, a descriptor.

By the culture of racism I am referring to the entire constellation of social relationships, beliefs, attitudes, and meanings that develop among those living within a racist culture. A certain circularity exists in these definitions because the culture of racism is built around the validation of differences. Of course, multiculturalism is also built around a validation of differences, albeit with very different emphases and interpretations of those differences.

Racism is embedded in relations of domination and oppression or domination and subordination. These relations create and impose a dynamic of their own on all who live within them and who then, themselves, reproduce those relations. When intercultural conflict (conflict between members of different races within a racist society) occurs, it cannot be understood by looking only at the cultural differences between the conflicting groups because these differences themselves, in part, constitute the very racism of which the conflict is one of many expressions. Notice that when I refer to a culture of racism as something we all share, I am not suggesting that the experiences of different groups in the culture of racism are identical; quite the contrary. Racial conflict often reflects differences about difference.

At the same time, we cannot blithely assume that these conflicts serve only to divide the groups who share in the culture of racism. On the contrary, these conflicts are part of what unites them in a common culture. The culture of racism, like any culture, is built around a set of shared assumptions. By "shared" I am referring not to a conscious consensus but rather to commonly held, but not necessarily consciously recognized, beliefs and attitudes. For example, in American society, race is a fundamental structuring force of almost every major dimension of experience. We define people racially and we are defined racially, even if not always explicitly, even without our assent. New immigrants to the country very quickly learn the racial schemes and hostilities that compose our social landscape. Similarly the disagreements we have about race would not make sense without a common history, even though that common history was experienced differently by different groups depending on their location in the racial hierarchy of the country. It is this common history that makes both consensus and lack of agreement possible.

Charles R. Lawrence III, in an article on unconscious racism, made a similar observation about racism when he wrote:

> Americans share a common historical and cultural heritage in which racism has played and still plays a dominant role. Because of this shared experience, we also inevitably share many ideas, attitudes, and beliefs that attach significance to an individual's race and induce negative feelings and opinions about nonwhites. To the extent that this cultural belief system has influenced all of us, we are all racists. At the same time most of us are unaware of our racism. We do not recognize the ways in which our cultural experience has influenced our beliefs about race or the occasions on which those beliefs affect our actions. In other words, a large part of the behavior that produces racial discrimination is influenced by unconscious racial motivation.

In American culture, lack of agreement is structured into the very ways people of different races experience themselves as well as their interaction with those of different races. At the core of this culture is a structurally-based antagonism between the races—everyone is socialized into it, even if their individual upbringing emphasizes values that challenge the underlying hierarchical arrangement of racial groups. The culture of racism then ensures differing experiences not only of race, but of racial conflict itself, and hence, the perpetuation of ongoing racial antagonism.

Drawing from impressions gleaned while working with disputes where race is a factor, and at the risk of falling into the same trap in which I earlier located Kochman, I will attempt to characterize some of the features of these different experiences. White people and people of color begin with fundamentally different understandings of what racism is and how it is manifested. Whites almost always understand racism in terms of individual prejudice and attitudes. Racism, in the white scheme of things, refers to actions and beliefs which are directed, often intentionally, toward harming, insulting, or discriminating against people of color. These days, most whites believe, racism is the exception. Despite the continuation of quite blatant *de facto* segregation—in housing, education, and transportation, for example—whites believe people of color have come a long way from the 1950s, when segregation was still legal and where outright discrimination was openly and widely practiced. While there is some acknowledgment of institutional racism, most whites seem to believe at the same time that there is a preference for people of color; it is *they* who have the advantage when it comes to admission to schools or applications for employment.

For the most part, most whites see racist acts or events as the exception to an egalitarian norm, an aberration or a sign of pathology. When a charge of racism is made, white people respond with the same conceptual framework they would if charged with any other individually-based criminal or immoral act. They examine the particular instance, uncover the related reasoning and attitudes, and look to see if bias was shown against the person of color or the proposal or whatever was under consideration. Intent, not impact, governs their assessment of the degree to which racism was a factor. They fail to take into account the culture of racism.

But, as Claude Steele has observed:

> [t]erms like prejudice and racism often miss the full scope of racial devaluation in our society, implying as they do that racial devaluation comes primarily from the strongly prejudiced, not from "good people" like us. But the prevalence of racists—deplorable though racism is—misses the full extent of the burden of people of color, perhaps even the most profound part.

For people of color, racism is embedded in the structure of everyday life, grounded in institutions and culture, inseparable from even the most laudatory features of American society. Successful or not, most people of color experience themselves as living in a culture organized around white privilege—a set of assumptions whites have about the culture being theirs, about belonging and taking for granted, that is rarely if ever available to people of color. Peggy McIntosh describes these assumptions as white privilege. Describing her growing awareness of white privilege she observes:

> I was taught to recognize racism only in individual acts of meanness by members of my group, never in invisible systems conferring unsought racial dominance on my group from birth.

For the dominant group, this recognition means confronting constant reminders that point to their complicity in the subordinate status of the other, even while the dominant group strives to remain guilt-free. For the subordinate group, this recognition provides powerful impetus for assuming the stance and psychology of the victim. Even when not taking the victim's stance, people of color who vociferously critique the perpetuation of racial hierarchy are often dismissed as exploiting the role of the victim. Confrontations between dominant and subordinate groups are permeated by the interplay of attributions of blame and denials of guilt.

So, for example, when a predominantly white administration rejects a proposal for a program intended to reduce inequalities between people of color and whites, it often finds itself accused of being racist. Since the individual reasons the administration held for its decision were rarely prejudiced ones, it finds the accusation unfair and almost incomprehensible. For the people of color, the rejection represents yet another thwarting of efforts to challenge structural inequality and is therefore, whatever the motivations of individual decision makers, thought to be racist. White identity, especially white liberal identity, is built around the denial of responsibility, almost guaranteeing that a failure to appreciate the depth and breadth of structural racism will occur. At the same time, racial identity for nonwhites almost guarantees an inference of personal prejudice as the motivation for racist acts, which also almost guarantees that the extent of structural racism will be under-appreciated even when it is being responded to.

From these differences in the experience of racism emerges another assumption—that of an insurmountable incommensurability of each other's experience. Each group assumes not just that its experience cannot be understood or appreciated by the other, but also that even the best efforts at communicating would not allow for a significant understanding of the other's position in the social world. When conflict emerges, it is taken as just another of the many indicators of an unbridgeable chasm rather than as a sign that it is time to work on the process of communication. Conflict provides the stimulus to withdraw from communication rather than to engage in it. Eventually some features of a particular dispute might be resolved, but the fundamental, underlying conflict is untouchable.

Chapter 21

"Eyes in the Back of Your Head"

Moral Themes in African American Narratives of Racial Conflict

Janie Victoria Ward

I was trained as an adolescent psychologist, and much of my education included immersion in the life-span developmental literature, particularly in the areas of identity and moral development. However, as an African woman, I soon came to realize that the issues traditionally addressed in the literature seldom reflected the shared concerns of those of us for whom the visibility of skin color makes us easy marks for denigrating and discriminatory practices. I have always found it curious that there are so few empirical studies specifically examining race-related morals and values, particularly as the terms "moral behavior" and "African Americans" have been inextricably linked since our arrival on these shores—from the ultimate immorality of human bondage to contemporary arguments concerning the use of compensatory affirmative action to redress past wrongs. African Americans are frequently at the center of these concerns. In addition, often in the minds of (some) Euro-Americans, when one thinks of black folks, issues of moral behavior frequently spring to mind, for example, the escalating crime statistics (the immorality of delinquency and violent behavior) or teen pregnancy, single motherhood, and welfare recipiency (the immorality of sexual promiscuity and traditional family breakdown).

Yet African Americans know that while some of our behaviors to others may seem self-contemptuous, when we turn our moral gaze inward, we have a different story to tell. Christian ethicist Katie Cannon argues that throughout our history, blacks have developed different ethical values in response to perilous social conditions. Given our subordinate social positionality and the existing conditions of oppression under which we must live, for African Americans many of the values reflected in the construction of our moral beliefs must be explicitly associated with issues of power and victimization. However, despite the fact of unequal power relations between white and black Americans, there has been very little systematic investigation of the development of core values specific to our culture and socially

From 20(3) *Journal of Moral Education* 267–280 (1991). Reprinted by permission of Taylor & Francis Ltd., P.O. Box 25, Abingdon, Oxfordshire, OX14 3UE.

marginalized position in society, and our differences in moral perspective are rarely taken seriously by researchers and thus are seldom sought.

This paper analyzes African Americans' narratives of inter-racial conflict. I believe that our personal beliefs and the moral convictions we hold about the world evolve from our past experiences, particularly the choices we make and our reflections upon them. By focusing particular attention on the relational nature of racial conflicts, I am more able to consider the complex socio-political context in which racial knowledge develops and moral judgments regarding racial differences are formed. The political socialization inherent in racial socialization requires the development of a unique relational knowledge base, and necessitates the ability to identify and analyze issues of power and authority embedded in interpersonal relationships between black and white individuals. Moreover, it requires the ability to develop effective and healthy resistance (both psychological and social) to the negating effects of racial and often economic oppression.

The narratives I have selected to illustrate the two relational voices of justice and care address issues representative of the everyday social situations in which, from a black perspective, racial conflicts are seen to occur and moral judgment and choices must be made. In addition, I will explore in these narratives issues specific to the psychological development (moral and identity) of African Americans and to the transmission of race-related morals and values in black cultures. The first narratives presented constitute a group; all of the stories are organized around the themes of justice and fairness.

Themes of Justice

Mrs. Brown, a school teacher, described a work-place dilemma in which she and another black female co-worker arrived a few minutes late to school. They were surprised to discover that a colleague, a white female teacher, entered the building at the same time as the two black women but, unlike them, she was not marked late. Mrs. Brown, upon challenging the differential application of school policy, was informed that the white teacher was a personal friend of the principal, and she was warned never again to question school practice. Over time the rankling between the outspoken and defiant Mrs. Brown and her principal reached a crisis point and the principal forwarded to the School Department an official letter of reprimand. Although she was officially exonerated from any wrongdoing, following this tense period of what she considered undue and severe harassment, Mrs. Brown transferred eventually to another school.

The psychology of justice is concerned with people's beliefs about fairness and justice and is seen as a form of equilibrium between conflicting interpersonal claims. As I listened, I heard Mrs. Brown employ justice concerns to frame this racial conflict—"If you have a policy about being late, then everyone should be marked late." Opotow's work on moral community suggests that individuals exclude others from the moral domain when they are perceived as outside the boundary in which moral values, rules, and consideration of fairness apply. Mrs. Brown, as defined, is positioned outside of her headmaster's moral community and, as she is undeserving of justice, he is thus justified to create a double standard—different sets of moral rules and obligations for different categories of people. Externally positioned, not only are her claims to justice delegitimized, but she is outcast—labeled a troublemaker and targeted for persecution and elimination.

When the narrative is read for representations of self and I attend to the "I" in this story of relational conflict, Mrs. Brown emerges as a resister, one who stands up for her rights even when standing up is perceived as threatening to others and potentially threatening to herself. There is no question that she is aware of her position as subordinate (principal to teacher, white male to black female) and as being external to his moral sensibility of entitlement—a potentially disempowering positionality to be sure. Yet how is it that Mrs. Brown could resist being disempowered and act in her own behalf? Embedded in the narrative is an important clue as she paused and said, "You know how it is when you're a slave . . . whether it was right or wrong, you don't have a right to question why, you just accept it." It is in this temporally disjunctive moment that Mrs. Brown flashes back in time—not her time (as in a specific moment in her life) but "our time," the collective history of African American people. She connects to a communal consciousness of our slave past—the degradation, dehumanization, and humiliation of being completely controlled, in body, mind, and spirit. In that moment of temporal suspension, in which she simultaneously was attuned to her present situational conflict and was spiritually connected to those of us whom slavery had silenced and disempowered before, Mrs. Brown summoned the transformative clarity and courage to make a moral judgment and take a moral stand. The evocation of communal memory as evidenced in this narrative identifies a key element in Mrs. Brown's development of self as both political resister and moral agent.

Although she was subsequently labeled arrogant by her principal—"That's a label they're gonna put on a black female . . . when you speak out," she explained—at a later point in the interview, Mrs. Brown claims that arrogance as a sign of her acknowledgment of her own individual self worth and intrinsic moral value and as a member of a larger moral community than certainly her employer could envision. When I asked her how she knew she had done the right thing, her response was a fitting example of moral connectedness—she viewed her challenge to the school policy which eventually brought about system change not only as a personal victory but a victory for all: "Because it made changes for everybody, not just me. We made it better for everyone, not just myself."

Mr. Davis described a workplace racial conflict in which a white man with no prior experience in a particular blue collar profession was hired at a higher salary and placed in a higher level than Mr. Davis, who in his ten years with the company was the oldest and most experienced employee and had during this time risen to the rank of "head man." "So," explained Mr. Davis, "I had a choice to make. Be head man again or leave. Because it wasn't fair." True to his word, Mr. Davis left the work-site and shortly thereafter received a phone call from his boss at home asking him to reconsider.

When I asked Mr. Davis why he thought his boss hired the unqualified white man, I was told, "I think the prejudice. Just to keep, you know, just to have a white face out front. It couldn't have been no other reason. He didn't know nothing, not about the bread business."

Later it became apparent that nepotism played a major role in this work-place conflict; the new man hired was the boyfriend of the sister of somebody in a position of authority. The telephone conversation went back and forth between Mr. Davis and his boss, who finally asked Mr. Davis what he (the boss) should do.

> You've got other white boys that's been here, you know. Move these guys up. You get a person out of the street, bring him in, put him on top and then ask me to train him? I won't take it, no way. Not me. So all the drivers back there, they said, "What are we going to do?" Put him in the back of the line, let him come up like the rest of us come up, man.

There's no question that Mr. Davis felt a kinship with his white fellow co-workers, and despite their racial differences, his operant principle seemed to imply that hiring and promoting an inexperienced and unqualified outsider as supervisor was not only a personal affront but was an injustice to them all. Following the racial conflict, I asked my next question, "If you were to create a racial survival kit, what would you put in it?" Mr. Davis answered,

> A set of eyes in the back of your head. [And what would the eyes be looking at?] Watching the whitey behind you. Because they're sneaky people. You see they're talking and laughing with you, and deep inside, they're feeling—just going about their business. . . . They're good people when you're watching them, but if you turn—you have to keep your eyes on them.

Here Mr. Davis provides evidence that he recognizes and responds to what he sees as white people's inclination to act in their own self-interest, no matter whom they step on in the process. But Mr. Davis's sense of when and whether it's proper to act on the basis of a cultural group's self-interest is far more complicated, as I was to discover in the interchange that followed.

"Do you think you did the right thing?" I asked. "Sure," he explained. "Why should I let him come in and take over? If he had been a brother, I might have went, you know, but I would have still been upset. It wouldn't have bothered me as bad." I asked him what would have been the difference had it been a black man who had been chosen to be on top.

> I would have felt that—give him a chance, you know. But you know, like I say, we've got to help our brothers and sisters, we've got to help them as best we can. So, I would have—I would have gave him (in) a little.

Several questions regarding moral community are generated from Mr. Davis's exchange: is it okay to bend the rules for another black, and if so, why and when? As mentioned before, Mr. Davis made it clear that he saw himself connected to his fellow white workers with whom, no doubt, he had built and secured genuine and mutually respectful relationships. However, he also indicates that he sees himself connected to other blacks, presumably blacks with whom he has had no prior relationship. In addition, not only does he claim cultural connection, but he also tells us he is willing (begrudgingly, but willing none the less) to allow these unknown blacks to advance at his expense. So, we have the appearance of a moral inconsistency: it is okay for a black to be advanced over Mr. Davis but not all right for a white man to do the same.

One way to interpret the unevenness in his moral perspective might be to consider that from Mr. Davis's perspective, in the act of stepping aside to allow another black man to get ahead, he doesn't see himself diminished, and, I might argue, based on this articulated sense of connection to other blacks, that he may actually see himself enhanced. But I still have two articulated relational connections present (to his fellow white co-workers and to the imagined black "brother" whom he'd be willing to step aside for) which we can assume, given the current state of race relations in the USA, will at times present conflicting claims (e.g., rules must be fair and we must all play by the same rules as opposed to the idea that because blacks are so frequently shut out of the game, sometimes they have to break the rules just to get in to play). This raises interesting questions related to moral psychology and how Mr. Davis maps his moral domain. What are his criteria for moral community and what is its relationship to the relational world in which the socio-political implications of racial sameness and difference hold critical meanings in our lives? When do connections to one moral community take precedence over one's connection to the other? From the perspective of African Americans, when, if ever, is it appropriate to restrict our moral community to blacks or the experiences of black people and when should the moral community include the experiences of all people (black and white)? Mr. Davis's unwillingness to allow a white to be advanced over him, and yet proclaiming his willingness to make a personal sacrifice for the advancement of a "brother" and for the implied group advancement of the race, concurs with Cortese's position that members of ethnic groups "develop and support different and sometimes contradictory systems of ethical thought, each of which are valid within its particular sociohistorical and cultural setting." Finally, how, through parents, do the moral imperatives associated with the African American's bicultural (black and white) existence get communicated across the generations? Mr. Davis's mixed moral message (fairness requires that you play by the rules but sometimes, to do the right thing, black folks should be willing to break the rules), which at least on the surface appears to betray a moral inconsistency, draws attention to the complexity of race-related morals and values in the racial socialization of black children.

A situation in which "ignoring" the problem was the strategy of choice is offered by Ayesha [a young woman, aged sixteen], the last respondent in this group of moral conflicts which center around justice concerns. Ayesha offers two short but powerful conflicts. In the first, she tells a story of her treatment in a department store. Rather than helpful assistance, her presence is frequently met with suspicion and distrust.

> Because a lot of times people in the stores, they stare you down, they stay on your tail, they'll watch you the whole time that you're in the store. You don't see them walking around following white people walking around in stores. But you will see them follow the black person when they walk around the stores.

What is the conflict for Ayesha in these instances?

> Whether I should go ahead and buy it and give them the money or whether I shouldn't. And sometimes I (say) I'm not going to find it anywhere else, so I've got to get it here and I get it. A lot of times I ignore the fact, the fact that you're not helping me, (I) just go on about my business.

Ayesha's narrative account of racial suspicion raises concerns for me as a researcher and as a member of the black community. Unlike the previous narratives, I was drawn into this young woman's dilemma in a particularly intimate way. Ayesha, in discussing her treatment in white-owned department stores, was bringing to light one of those everyday indignities African Americans face regularly and my familiarity with these degrading events was unsettling at a deeply visceral level. Yet, though familiar with the situation and the feelings provoked by such suspicion and/or indifference, Ayesha's account of the event and the choices she felt were available to her were particularly troubling to me for the following reasons.

Ayesha seemed able to acknowledge her moral exclusion and could even envision a sense of agency in response to this undue character assault. She recognized that she had something that the store owner wanted (money) but which she could choose to withhold, thus she possessed some power. Ultimately, however, rather than utilize her power, she proceeds to disempower herself, "I just ignore the fact." But before I could ask her if she could imagine another way to deal with this situation, Ayesha offered another, even more chilling example of how insidiously cunning the notions of white superiority/black inferiority which permeate this country serve to control attitudes and behaviors in our nation today.

> Sometimes we'd (she and her black friends) go to the pizza house after games and you had to pay before you could get in. You couldn't even come in the building. You had to order outside the pizza house what you wanted. And then you had to give them a dollar before you even sat down to eat. And you couldn't get in unless you were ordering something. And I can understand that standpoint because a lot of times, after games, a whole bunch of black people go in there and start a lot of commotion, they're in there fighting with the managers and stuff like that. So I can understand sometimes. But this really upset me because I was standing there that Friday and a white person came up and she said, "We're going to get something," and they let them come on in . . . and yet and still when we came to the door, they made us stand out and figure out what we were going to order. [What do you think they should have done?] The whites should have stood outside just like we stood outside. I think we're all in the same position, we're all going to order. I might not have been with that crowd. They don't know whether or not I was in with that crowd or not.

Ayesha has the perspective-taking skills to imagine why such a rule was initially implemented. However, Ayesha's ability to understand and accept the white restaurant owner's perspective doesn't get her out of the dilemma of being unfairly victimized. In fact, one can argue, Ayesha's solution—to make the white kids stand outside the pizza parlor with the blacks—rather than solve Ayesha's problem of victimization, would simply add a new class of victims. Yet Ayesha is unable to imagine another alternative, one in which neither she nor the white kids are systematically oppressed. Michelle Fine discusses how social ideologies of justice, in facilitating and obscuring exclusion, rationalize exclusionary practices and justify existing boundaries. The operant implied rationale here is the determination that black teens, all black teens, pose a public safety threat to the restaurant and, based on that fact, it is in the public's best interest to enforce policies which control blacks' behavior and limit their use of public facilities. Ayesha has taken in this exclusionary practice and she identifies this situation as a problem to which the solution lies in the suggestion that both whites and blacks should be treated the same (i.e., unfairly). Unfortunately Ayesha fails to see the injustice in the creation of a policy which classifies all black teens as a group, characterizes them as troublemakers, and singles this group out for unjust, exclusionary practices. Ayesha's psychological vulnerability lies in her inability to see the potentially disabling effects such exclusional practice has on the development of her healthy self-esteem and self-respect.

The developmental question thus becomes, What does Ayesha need yet to know? For example, in the first situation in which she knew in the department store that she was being followed with suspicion and distrust (and she believed white customers are not treated in this way), and she was aware of her own "veto" power—she could act on her disapproval of the treatment she had received and withhold her cash—how can Ayesha be helped to claim her moral perspective and assume responsibility to act on its behalf. How can Ayesha and other African American teens be helped to see through the social ideologies of justice which, instead of fostering fairness and equity for all, instead serve to promote moral exclusion through thinly veiled socially acceptable policies which work to enforce white superiority and black inferiority?

Themes of Care

The next group of narratives suggest that rather than seeing conflict on a continuum of bi-polar opposites with conflict at one end and harmony at the other, it is possible for some racial conflict to be constructive rather than destructive.

The ethic of care as defined by Gilligan, Noddings, and others is "rooted in receptivity, relatedness and responsiveness." It is based on an assumption of interpersonal interconnectedness, and moral concerns tend to focus on problems of detachment, disconnection, abandonment, and indifference. Mrs. Crosby told a short story about a difficult moment in her life as a parent. She collapsed an untold number of similarly disturbing conflicts—"it's always those sorts of things"—into this one event. Her children were planning a joint birthday party and they wanted to invite some white children from an extra-curricular program that they all attended. Because her home is in a black neighborhood, Mrs. Crosby was afraid the white children wouldn't show up. "I had no problem with the inviting," she explained. "But I didn't want them to be disappointed because the white kids wouldn't come. If I invited the white children," she explained, "and these white kids didn't show up, it could be a message that somehow they (her black children) were not worthy of them coming. That's the way they would interpret it." In addition she worried about how she would handle the situation, since then she'd have to talk about it (meaning racism and racial exclusion). "I was always being protective, you know, it was a protective measure so they wouldn't be hurt." She resolved the conflict by agreeing to invite the white children, who surprised her in that they all showed up and had a good time. But what begins as a story of fear and an expression of one woman's moral injunction against hurt shifts suddenly into a testimonial of her personal growth and empowerment. "I'll tell you something," she said to me in quite literally the next breath:

> Over the last 10 to 15 years, there were little things I may have equivocated about. I don't do it anymore. Now it's definite. When I walk into my job and say, "OK folks—we're hiring a black (employee)"—that's it. I'm the strong, black bitch in that office, so don't mess with me. That's who I am and I deliver on it.

In an instant, gone were the insecurity and self-doubt that had framed her story of indecisiveness and dread and replaced in its space was an image of self that was strong and unequivocating, racially decisive and proud. Riessman argues that narrators do not arbitrarily choose their narrative types, and as such there exists a relationship between form (the how) and function (the understanding that one wants to convey); between the meaning of the event and the problem the narrator selects to address. Mrs. Crosby, in choosing to tell me a story of her life in which she, as a black woman and mother, begins in one place (unsure and equivocating) and ends in another (strong and defiant) is as important as the actual transformation itself. Mrs. Crosby used her racial identity both as a central organizing theme for her life choices and as an organizing theme for her professional work. How she or any African American individual moves from a position of personal insecurity to a positive sense of one's racial identity and personal power has yet to be answered, as does the question of how believing in, espousing, and acting upon an ethic of care (especially the belief that one must always protect and prevent harm despite the limitations such protective behaviors may unwittingly place on others, particularly one's children) might work to enable or disable women from effectively achieving personal empowerment and self-development.

The last story which centers around an ethic of care illuminates another set of issues. Ms. Wayne told a story of a work-place conflict in which a tense personality clash between the only other African American secretary in the department and a white secretary blew up into a serious confrontation.

> I don't know what sparked it, but there was a particular day that the black secretary came over from her building to, what did she say, "beat that white bitch's ass." I went, "Oh Susan, no! No!" Because I knew . . . there wasn't no doubt that she could wipe the floor with the girl, you know. But I knew that if she did that, that she would lose her job. She was a single parent raising two children. She had recently relocated

there, and had just gotten that job, so she was the new kid on the block. And she couldn't afford it, for whatever satisfaction it would give her to beat this girl up, the consequences was too great. I just couldn't let her do it.

Ms. Wayne went on to explain that the white secretaries who had come to tell her of Susan's fury had frozen with confusion and fear, so Ms. Wayne knew she had to take action.

> So I got up and met Susan down the hall . . . and she was steaming. I grabbed her by the arms, and it took all my might to push her backwards as she was going forward . . . and then talking to her and struggling with her, "Susan, you can't do this. Let's go outside and talk."

Outside Ms. Wayne negotiated with her friend, convincing her that a violent response to this white secretary's acts of disrespect would only lead to unemployment and with her responsibilities as a single mother—"it just ain't worth it." The situation was resolved in that the black secretary agreed to an effort toward conciliation and the white secretary agreed, essentially out of fear, to behave politely toward her from then on, given that they had to work together. In the course of her narrative, Ms. Wayne explained,

> The fact that she was white, I mean they'd fire her (the black secretary) just like that, she'd be gone (so) I couldn't let her do it. I couldn't let my girl go down like that . . . she needed the job . . . if I could help her to keep that job, then . . . don't even think about it, just get up and whatever it is, you've gotta do it—just do it.

This narrative is a poignant illustration of how operating within an ethic of care, Ms. Wayne connected to the new black secretary as a single mother (like herself) responsible for the economic survival of her children, and as a woman who can be made so angry that she would consider a violent response, yet when in such a state can be calmed down and behave reasonably if someone takes the time to listen and respond. In addition, she connected with the new secretary as another black woman, a potential friend with whom she could survive what she had described as "the sea of whiteness." Necessity of care as a moral imperative felt by Ms. Wayne and her urgency to intervene if she could to prevent an impending disaster and prevent pain, are features of the ethic of care previously identified in a study of the moral concerns of urban youth.

Perspective and Representation

How will what I have learned from this exercise inform my interpretative process and aid my understanding of race-related socialization in African American families today? First, in appreciation of the range of knowledge that African Americans possess about the relational world and, in particular, our relationship to and with Euro-American populations, I am now adding a new reading to the process of interpretation of racial conflict narratives—that is, a reading for representations of whites and blacks from the black perspective of the narrator. For example, when I read for whites, I ask the questions, How are whites represented and in whose terms? Based upon representations of whites in the narrative, when are blacks articulating and making choices from existing knowledge claims (white folks are sneaky and you need eyes in the back of your head), and when does it seem that new knowledge (negative or positive) about whites has been gained and has become incorporated into one's existing relational knowledge base? And what are the implications of this knowledge that constrain or enable our personal agency? Combining the racial conflicts offered from the perspectives of blacks which focus specifically on whites with whom they are in conflict, moral contradictions and ethical inconsistencies in the attitudes and actions of white people are frequently brought to light. For example, when the conflicts are organized around a moral opposition to unfairness, what emerges is a profile of whites as people who design and apply rules to suit themselves; who sometimes use rules to harass, exclude, and punish; who establish and enforce policies that favor other whites and promote self-interest, and who use policies to maintain power, to show it can be exerted, and to show blacks that they can be controlled. Therefore we can conclude that blacks learn through their racial conflicts in which they are the victims of unfairness and injustice that rules are man-made (by whites) and as such are subject to and often reflect whites' racist motivations and interventions. Warren has suggested that African Americans learn early in life that the political and legal systems treat them differently from whites and that depending upon one's skin color, there is little safety in policies, laws, and rules. Thus the philosopher's question "Why be just in an unjust world?" holds unique political significance to members of the African American community and holds important implications for the moral and political socialization of our children.

In understanding the world from the relational knowledge base of African Americans, what do we learn about whites when we focus on how they are represented in the (two) relational conflicts organized around a moral opposition to hurt, detachment, and abandonment? Whites are presumed to be fearful of blacks and black neighborhoods, and when whites engage in behaviors related to their fears and distrust, their attitudes and actions are believed able to inflict psychological harm. In the story with Ms. Wayne I see not only a white secretary exhibiting disrespectful behavior toward black women, but more interestingly, the other white secretaries are represented as confused by the differences found among blacks and are subsequently paralyzed into inaction. They were friendly to the interviewee because she was seen as calm, well-spoken, and familiar. The new black secretary, on the other hand, was seen as outspoken and aggressive and the white women didn't know how to handle her. She was the classic model of "other as stranger." Thus when there was a crisis in relationship, and the other was an unknown (and perhaps was assumed outside the moral community), the whites had nothing to fall back on, apparently not even their existing knowledge of relationships (i.e., that many conflicts can be mediated through dialogue), to resolve the dispute.

In conclusion, in this analysis of African Americans' narratives of racial conflicts I have combined selected events to create an episodic narrative, stitched together by the moral themes of justice and care, in order to make a larger point regarding the myriad dimensions of the relational world of interpersonal racial conflicts. Employing narratives as a conceptual tool, I have used these stories to make evident indigenous race-related assumptions held by African Americans which grow out of and in turn inform cross-racial social relations. Appreciation of these perspectives will lead to a fuller understanding of the African American's constructions of morality, racial identity, and personal instrumentality.

Chapter 22

Use and Abuse of Race and Culture
Black-Korean Tension in America

Kyeyoung Park

> They hope I don't pull out a gat and try to rob
> their funky little store, but bitch, I gotta job.
> So don't follow me up and down your market
> or your little chop-suey ass will be a target of the
> nationwide boycott.
> Choose with the people
> that's what the boy got.
> So pay respect to the Black fist
> or we'll burn down your store, right down to a crisp,
> and then we'll see you,
> 'cause you can't turn the ghetto into Black Korea
> —Ice Cube, "Black Korea"

Ice Cube's 1991 album *Death Certificate* was boycotted by Korean American community leaders, who said it contained lyrics that peddle bigotry and violence. In south central Los Angeles, on March 18, 1991, a black teenager, Latasha Harlins, was shot and killed by a Korean grocer, Soon Ja Du, in a dispute over a $1.79 bottle of orange juice. Superior Court Judge Joyce Karlin fined Du $500, put her on probation, and ordered her to perform four hundred hours of community service. While few killers are granted such an easy sentence, there was no reason to send Du to jail, said the judge. She was not a menace to society. The African American community of Compton rose up in anger. "You shoot a dog," they said, "and you go to jail. You shoot a black kid and you get probation." Committees were formed and rallies held.

The media described this Los Angeles controversy as a racial confrontation between blacks and Koreans. Headlines in the *Los Angeles Times* announced: "Boycott: Business Has Plummeted in a Store Where Korean American Owner Killed a Black Man"; "Korean Stores Firebombed; 2 of 3 Hit Have Seen Black Boycott";

From 98(3) *American Anthropologist* 492–497 (1996). Reprinted by permission of the American Anthropological Association from *American Anthropologist* 98, 1996. Not for further reproduction.

"Blacks Won't End Korean Store Boycott." An editorial in the same paper stated that protesters may feel they have a legitimate gripe, "but in the long run, boycotts rarely address the real, core problem and only add to community tension."

In this portrayal of the controversy, one needs to ask what and who are missing here. Where, for example, are white people in this interpretation of the conflict? Are Koreans simply another "white" group? What kind of racial discourse or structure is the media creating, and what role does race play in this conflict?

In contrast to the media's focus on race, black and Korean community leaders explain tensions in terms of culture. They claim that cultural differences account for the majority of the disputes involving merchants and customers. In addressing a boycott in New York, a Korean Human Relations staff member testified:

> Korean merchants' seeming attitudes toward their customers are the source of many tensions. . . . It is their frustration . . . they appear arrogant and rude. . . . Western culture is very open. It is kind, always smiling, that is the tradition. But we are very different. If a Korean woman smiles at an unknown man we would think she is a prostitute. Even if they don't smile it is not their intention to be rude or arrogant . . . they are not trained to smile.

While there are some real cultural differences between Korean merchants and African American residents, it is questionable whether these differences are the root of the problem.

Whereas community leaders emphasize culture and the media focus on race, scholars have stressed the importance of structural forces in race relations—for instance, the commercial role of minority middlemen. Korean merchants, when they operate outlets that serve as the intermediary between a local population and individuals in economic and political power, play a role similar to that of other ethnic minorities in third-world colonies. Middleman theory orients us to the conflict-ridden relationships between customers and merchants of different ethnic backgrounds. Although the middleman minority concept is a useful starting point for understanding the role of Korean merchants, the situation is far more complex.

The emergence of conflict among nonwhite minority groups has been explained as the direct consequence of increasing immigration and major changes in the social, economic, and demographic structure of American society that place minority groups in competition for scarce and valuable resources. Although economics may be at the base of potential conflicts, the problems between Korean merchants and black buyers are also social, because these roles are strongly defined along racial-ethnic lines. This conflict is further heightened by racially based and racially distinct perceptions and misperceptions, and by sharp cultural and linguistic differences, which produce a gulf of misunderstanding.

Black-Korean conflict is not only about economics but also about meanings. The clash of values and meanings happens in the context of a power relationship. Sylvia Yanagisako and Carol Delaney describe: "Inequality and hierarchy come already embedded in symbolic systems as well as elaborated through contextualized material practice." Douglas Massey and Nancy Denton's *American Apartheid* shows how whites develop a tangible stake in their whiteness through residential segregation. More recently, David Palumbo-Liu examined the white media construction of race relations in the aftermath of the Los Angeles uprising, showing how Koreans are deployed as surrogate whites in black-white conflicts. Here, I want to explore how white racism is reconstructed in the context of black-Korean tension.[1]

African Americans and Korean Americans in South Central Los Angeles

Tensions between Koreans and African American residents have developed in inner-city neighborhoods during the past two decades. Tensions between white, especially Jewish, merchants and African American residents in New York City have existed since the 1920s and were evident in the riots of the 1960s. However, the circumstances of conflict now are different from the 1920s and even from the 1960s. The increasing numbers of Asian Americans and Latin American immigrants living or working in inner cities as a result of the Immigration Act of 1965 complicate the political situation in ghetto areas.

Race has shaped and been shaped by U.S. politics. But the changes in south central Los Angeles have occurred in the context of post–civil-rights racial politics. Although race continues to be important in America, racial oppression has declined over the last half-century. However, this waning of oppression is not a linear, irreversible process. In fact, with the restructuring of the global order and the recurring economic crises in the United States, racially motivated state policies and hate crimes are once again on the rise. In the 1980s the Reagan administration attempted to reverse the political gains of the 1960s racial minority movements. The current attack on affirmative action has had effects in south central Los Angeles.

Disinvestment has occurred not only in the private sector but also in the public sector. Under successive Republican administrations, the federal and state governments withdrew funds for community-based organizations, thus undermining key institutions in the community. As in many other inner-city communities throughout the nation, the state abandoned the War on Poverty in South Central long before poverty was eliminated. The combination of New Federalism and declining dollars for community action led to increasingly scarce funds for social programs in depressed neighborhoods. The deindustrialization of America, accompanied by the flight of American capital, plant closings, and further transnationalization of capital flow and labor migration, has intensified the suffering of the urban poor.

Analyses of the political economy of south central Los Angeles show a community that has been increasingly isolated, politically and economically, from mainstream society. As the traditional industrial core of the city, South Central bore the brunt of the decline in manufacturing employment, losing seventy thousand high-wage, stable jobs between 1978 and 1982. Major companies such as General Motors, Goodyear, Firestone, and Bethlehem Steel closed plants in or around the area. According to a study by the United Way, a total of 321 plants or industries left the area over a fifteen-year period. The 1990 census shows that approximately one in three South Central residents lived in households with incomes below the official poverty line, a rate over twice that for the county as a whole. In 1990, only 59 percent of adults (ages twenty–sixty-four) in South Central worked, 16 percentage points lower than the rate for the county.

During this period of growing poverty and oppression for inner-city blacks, Korean immigrant merchants entered urban neighborhoods where the cost of starting or purchasing a business was relatively low. Korean Americans opened small businesses by relying on various sources of sociocultural capital, the Korean traditional financial system based on the *kye* (rotating credit association), and, to some extent, capital brought from Korea, as well as family labor and educational resources. As new immigrants they experienced downward mobility, from employment as white-collar professionals in Korea to small business owners in America. This was due to a combination of language and cultural barriers, nontransferable professional credentials, and discrimination in workplaces.

In Los Angeles, one in three Korean immigrants operates a small family business with few or no employees. According to a study by the Korean-American Grocers Association (KAGRO), there were 3,320 Korean American–owned liquor stores and markets in Southern California, with annual sales totaling $1.8 billion. In south central Los Angeles, a predominantly African American and Latino community, the NAACP [National Association for the Advancement of Colored People] estimates that up to 70 percent of the area's gas stations are now owned by Koreans. Korean business leaders report that as many as one-third of the community's small markets and liquor stores are Korean-owned. However, in the county of Los Angeles, the proportion of Korean business ownership in black neighborhoods accounts for only 10 percent of all Korean businesses.[2] This means that most Korean Americans run businesses in other low- or lower–middle-class neighborhoods in Los Angeles, including Koreatown. Despite their volume of business ownership in South Central, most Korean American merchants reside outside the area. In addition, despite the popular portrayal of Korean Americans as a model minority, they have little political power or wealth.

Construction of Race and Ethnicity among Korean Immigrants

Koreans believe themselves to be more civilized than any other people except the Chinese. Jeongduk Yi reports that Koreans dismissed whites as *yangi*, Western barbarians, until the late nineteenth century, when Korea was confronted by the military power of the supposedly inferior yangi and *waenom* (a derogatory term for the Japanese). After the turn of the century, whites occupied a higher position in the Korean conception of the world racial hierarchy because of their superior economic, military, and political power. Since 1945, the predominance of U.S.–educated Koreans in government and business and the presence of the U.S. Army in South Korea have contributed to this conception. The pervasive American cultural presence in South Korea, especially since the Korean War, has influenced Korean immigrants' racial attitudes. The experience of running small business enterprises also helps to structure Koreans' emergent ideologies of race and ethnicity. While some develop elaborate conceptualizations of the United States as a multiethnic society, others develop simpler notions—for example, the lighter one's skin, the better one is treated.

For Koreans operating small businesses, interethnic encounters arise in their day-to-day operations. Business proprietors become aware of their subordinate position to white Americans in the U.S. system of ethnic stratification. They recognize their role in replacing white American small business proprietors via "ethnic succession" and understand that whites are aware of this as well. In the United States, many Koreans experience discrimination as an ethnic minority for the first time, and some unfortunately reapply the treatment they receive to other minorities.[3]

In the current urban turmoil, African Americans have picketed and boycotted Korean merchants in South Central and complained about being overcharged and not treated with respect. In 1991 the Brotherhood Crusade, a vocal black organization headed by the charismatic Danny Bakewell, organized a boycott against Chung's Liquor Mart. Earlier, Tae Sam Park, the owner, had killed Lee Arthur Mitchell during an attempted robbery. What prompted the protest was a belief that the killing was unwarranted because Mitchell had been unarmed. There were further deaths on both sides, culminating in the looting and burning of Korean businesses during the Los Angeles crisis of 1992.[4]

The Instigating Role of Whiteness in Black-Korean Conflict

The African American–Korean American discourse is a triadic relation, not a dyad. It begins with their respective relationships to whites, and it puts Asians, in particular Koreans, in a paradoxical position in U.S. race relations. The triad is exemplified by the court's sentencing of Korean immigrant shopkeeper Du for shooting black teenager Harlins. Despite the fact that a gun was used, Judge Karlin, a white woman, argued that the rules against probation should not apply in the *Harlins-Du* case. The judge stated three reasons that this was an unusual case, thus justifying Du's lenient sentence:

> First, although the basis for the presumption against probation is technically present, that is, a gun was used, I find that it does not apply. The statute [Pen Code, 1203, subdivision (e)(2)] is aimed at criminals who arm themselves and go out and commit crimes. *It is not aimed at shopkeepers who lawfully possess firearms for their own protection.* Secondly, the defendant has no recent record, in fact, no record at all of committing similar crimes or crimes of violence. Third, I find that the defendant participated in the crime under circumstances of great provocation, coercion, and duress.

Racial inequality is routinely played out in judicial sentencing, usually in favor of whites against blacks. Blacks know well that whites who kill blacks get less rigorous sentences than blacks who kill blacks, and they know that blacks who kill whites get the most stringent sentences. Given this racialized formula, black community members could see that storekeeper Du got judicial treatment as a white because she killed a black. They could also see that she would have been sentenced as a black had she dared to kill a white. An African American male, a twenty-six-year-old United Parcel Service carrier, explained:

> Soon Ja Du should not have shot Latasha. If Latasha was another race, such as white, I do not think Soon Ja Du would have received a light sentence. I believe that Soon Ja Du thought that she could get away with it. Tension exists between the two groups because the Koreans have their stores in the black neighborhoods and do not employ blacks. Blacks have to shop at the Korean stores because they are in their neighborhoods. Members of Korean descent are different. Koreans have stereotypes of blacks from television.

An African American female graduate student states clearly:

> The role of race is high. The tensions have always been there and the last straw has broken the camel's back. The judge was unfair. A black postal carrier received six months in jail for beating a dog, but this woman receives probation for killing a human. The police and government officials have a code among themselves: Cover each other's ass. They avoid accountability and do not like to take responsibility for their actions. I do not trust cops.

These comments contrast with Korean merchants' evaluation of the role of race. Several of them indicated that race was not a real factor in a situation between a shopkeeper and a customer, and they felt that the media had injected race into a situation where it was not relevant. A fifty-two-year-old grocery market owner and former pharmacist in Korea, Mr. Kim, maintains:

> This Du Soon Ja incident has nothing to do with race. This is not so much a racial confrontation but rather a problem between merchants and customers. I see cultural differences as contributing to similar conflicts. I find fault with the American media. They kept spreading a message along racial lines and exaggerated the incident in order to satisfy themselves, which is often their job. It is like doctors who keep warning you that you are ill.

Similarly, many Korean merchants believe that for many years the mainstream media has inflamed the rage and passion black people feel toward Koreans through superficial, insensitive, and unbalanced coverage of incidents involving customers and shopkeepers. Kapson Lee, editor of *Korea Times, English Edition*, wrote:

> First, the media unduly emphasized the Korean ancestry of Du, thus, indirectly and perhaps inadvertently, contributing toward a negative image of Korean Americans in the eyes of Black people. Second, it played into the hands of those whose vested interest it was, and is, to exploit such fallacious images.

Unraveling "Culture"

Korean merchants attribute the main causes of these incidents to social and cultural differences—difficulties with merchant-customer communication, poverty in the African American community, situational or psychological factors, or the media. African American residents, despite their awareness of cultural differences, do not. In conflicts, the role of culture emerges in four different ways: (1) Korean Americans' approach toward business, (2) black and Korean Americans' perceptions of each other's cultures, (3) the impact of the dominant society's discourse on black and Korean relations, and (4) the social construction of race by both Koreans and blacks, mediated by the dominant cultural discourse. Here I present Korean shopkeepers' views first, then move on to African American ones.

Mr. Kim actually had known the Du family before the incident. His assessment of the shooting implicates the cultural traditions informing Korean Americans' approach to business. Their reliance on family labor means that individuals work long hours, a stressful situation that leads to fatigue and irrational responses.

> That shooting occurred is they were overworked and under lots of stress. They might be too tired to control themselves even over very trivial things. Like other Korean immigrant families, Mr. Du relied upon family labor, especially his wife, Du Soon Ja. I find it problematic to rely on family labor heavily. You might save some money on wages, but you do not realize that family members force themselves to work beyond their capability. I know it from my own experience with running a drugstore in Korea. That's why I do not allow my wife to work here. Mr. Du used to be in full feather, and always went to the bank and took part in other activities in the Korean community. Therefore, it was always Mrs. Du who ran the store. They own another store. In this context, I really want fellow Koreans to reflect on the way they operate their stores. Even a small store should hire at least part-time local help, if possible African Americans, instead of just exploiting family labor.

Another grocer, Mrs. Song, feels overwhelmed by difficulties in running a small business in a poor urban neighborhood. Nonetheless, she tells us that the dominant society, through mass media, can amplify interracial tension in a shopkeeper's store by focusing on shootings and boycotts involving Korean merchants and black customers:

> Even this morning a customer threatened us, mentioning a possible boycott. I am very scared. I do not want to cause trouble. If they do damage to goods, it is hard for me to be pleasant toward them. We try to treat and serve our customers, but sometimes they just expect us to serve them better. However, too much has been reported, and the media aggravated the whole matter.

In exploring the issue of culture, I asked my interviewees to describe themselves and their culture, and to show how their culture is similar to and different from other cultures. The shared and yet problematic opinion was that Koreans have more culture than blacks. References to "more culture" or "less culture" or "no culture" revealed popular notions of culture different from anthropological ones. Reflecting these notions, Mrs. Song compares Korean American culture with African American culture in the following way:

> We are enlightened not to steal, unlike African Americans in this neighborhood. Their parents do not pay attention to their children's education. Especially, since doing businesses in this south central L.A., I found that they do not have jobs. Lack of employment—they usually do not work.

Mr. Pai differs from others in that he has some structural understanding of African American history:

> I try to understand them better. Thanks to their civil rights movement, we Koreans, as *yakso minjok* [a lesser nation], are able to live now in America. As blacks have been oppressed for a long time, they have accumulated their hostility toward others, including us. Both Koreans and blacks are the same. However, our social background and way of thought are drastically different from theirs. For example, as far as children's education is concerned, it is common for Korean parents to sacrifice themselves to educate their children, which you cannot find either among whites or blacks. White parents do their duty to a certain extent but not fully like Korean parents, and black parents seem to ignore their children's education. For example, I raised my children to go to graduate school. In addition, strong family ties and respect for their parents are virtues, which one cannot find in America due to its welfare system.

While sharing some sentiments expressed by Korean shopkeepers, Jennifer, an African American woman, explains cultural differences as follows:

> They [Koreans] have more of a culture than Americans. They are not yet Westernized. They have rituals. They believe in Buddha. They have Buddhas in their stores and offer food to the Buddhas. I went into a nail salon. It freaked me out when I saw the Koreans worshiping Buddhas in the store. Koreans have a culture. We do not. I cannot speak African or Jamaican.

Here, culture becomes something foreign to America.

Racial and Cultural Discourses

Through their assumptions and ongoing constructions of race and culture, blacks, Koreans, and white institutions interpret black-Korean conflict in different ways. Blacks attribute problems to racist exploitation and discrimination; Koreans focus on business practices and communication; and the white establishment reflects the biases of capitalism (property owners over customers) and a white-Asian-black racial hierarchy.

Meanwhile, the media-led discourse portrays black-Korean conflict as a racial confrontation yet describes the details largely in terms of cultural differences, seldom mentioning the lack of public policy that deals with urban problems such as racism and poverty. Whether the media blame it on race or culture, their coverage is ahistorical. They further racialize black-Korean tension by conveying black intolerance of Koreans, which fuels Korean merchants' perspectives. At the same time they contribute to Koreans' negative portrayal of African Americans through stereotypical images of blacks. They reify and misrepresent the nature of interethnic tension by ignoring the historically situated social process that lies behind it.

The mass-media portrayal is interpreted differently by Koreans and blacks. In the view of many Korean Americans, the media's frequent showing of the videotape of the Harlins killing and the constant refrain of "the Korean-born grocer killing a black teenager" sowed the seeds of social conflict. They wondered whether there was a conspiracy among the white-dominated media to pit one ethnic group against another and then sit back and watch them destroy one another. For many African American viewers, the same videotape reminded them that the criminal justice system is grossly unjust to the black community. Indeed, in the *Harlins-Du* case, the judiciary system applied a racialized formula. As a consequence, black-Korean tension was more drastically intensified by state intervention than by the actions of blacks or Koreans.

In addition to the white media and judiciary, educational institutions construct an exclusionary public sphere. Here, Korean merchants lack an understanding of the alienation of African Americans from public education. Although Korean merchants have become skeptical of the way the media handle black-Korean conflict, they have not expanded this insight into an understanding of the judiciary or educational system. Nor do they seem to understand the structural linkage between white media, the court system, and educational institutions.

State agents, such as Judge Karlin in the *Harlins-Du* case, are major players in the development of racial tension. As David Goldberg argues, the state plays the role of articulating, legitimating, elaborating, and transforming racialized expression and racist exclusion, and rendering them acceptable. One result is that racial discourse has been confused with and replaced by cultural discourses. Here it is important to note the emergence of a new definition of race, replacing old concepts based on biology:

> Race is coded as culture, what has been called "the new racism," making no reference to claims of biology or superiority . . . [this is] a style of cultural self-construction that is not just nostalgic but future oriented, not simply static but transformative, concerned not only with similarity and continuity but also with difference and rupture.

Since neither blacks nor Koreans want to be criticized for racial bigotry, they attribute their conflicts to cultural differences. Korean community leaders can ignore their own responsibility by emphasizing the right to private property. African American community leaders can ignore broader issues by emphasizing maltreatment by Korean merchants.

Anthropological conceptualizations of culture give insufficient attention to problems of power and social conflict. My interviewees' cultural conception is along the line of Antonio Gramsci's proposition that "cultural processes unfold within a sharply divided society, a hierarchy of class domination backed by political power. Culture becomes part of the process of domination."

Rudeness, lack of smiles, and other bad manners of Korean merchants have been explained as cultural baggage from Korea. Do Koreans have such elements in their culture? Let us take the example of the smile. All of my Korean merchant interviewees worked seven days a week and often 16 hours a day—112 hours per week. Some said, "We are too tired to smile and be nice to our customers." Nonetheless, smiling must be studied in relation to the gender, class, and historical backgrounds of Koreans. For instance, if a woman is from the countryside, she tends not to smile in encounters with strangers. Given the fact that most new immigrants are from the cities and have professional backgrounds, this argument cannot be applied. I contend that if they ran businesses in middle- or upper-income neighborhoods in America, they might smile lest they be treated badly by affluent white customers. But most likely they do not smile in ghettos.

Koreans value themselves and explain their successes in terms of having "more culture" (family unity, ethnic solidarity, education) than blacks. Blacks also present Koreans as having more culture than themselves. Nevertheless, as Eric Wolf reminds us, culture is changing and manifold, not a fixed and unitary entity. As in the case of black-Korean conflict, cultural differentiation produces a politics of meaning. Though there is some grudging respect, there is also the implication that people with strange rituals and unknown Asian beliefs are in some sense not like "us" Americans. It would seem that the more American you are, the less culture you ought to have. Is the assumption that being deculturated is what being American is all about, and that therefore Koreans with their cultural richness have fewer claims to belong?

At the same time, the continuing black-Korean conflict is contributing to the creation of a new racial discourse: race as culture. This conflict focuses on relations between African Americans and Korean immigrant merchants, but it evokes larger issues: the reproduction of capitalist relations in contemporary America and the redefinition of race and culture in today's multiethnic society.

NOTES

1. For my ethnographic research, I focus on the geographical area of Figueroa Street to the east, Western Avenue to the west, the University of Southern California to the north, and Ninetieth Street to the south. A total of thirty African American and nineteen Korean American small business people were interviewed. Most of the interviews focused on the 1991 Soon Ja Du–Latasha Harlins incident. Most African American interviews were obtained at African American–run businesses such as hair salons and barber shops, and most Korean American interviews were collected at their stores, mainly liquor stores and grocery markets.

Korean merchants were receptive, with certain exceptions, toward the Korean American researcher. As expected, African American residents showed various responses. Some were glad to talk to us, a group of multiracial researchers. While one researcher interviewed an African American woman, the other people in the hair salon became very curious about the research. They began to ask questions, and soon others wanted to be interviewed as well. Another man was interviewed while he styled a patron's hair. The place was filled with excitement and laughter. Everyone had something to say, and it became difficult to interview just one person. Others whom I met on the street were quick to show their anger. A lady shouted to me, "Yeah, that's the treatment for a colored woman's death. Bullshit! I already sent a letter to request the judge's recall. That's all I can say." However, it was remarkable to see many others respond very calmly with a historical view of this tragic incident.

2. According to Professor Eui-Young Yu, the customer base of Korean-owned businesses throughout Los Angeles is 48 percent white, 22 percent Korean, 17 percent Latino, and only 10 percent African American (quoted in *L.A. Weekly* 1992).

3. Koreans in Japan have experienced severe discrimination; however, the Korean experience in Japan is not often mentioned in relation to the Korean American experience. Perhaps Korean Americans tend to view the Korean experience in Japan in terms of Japanese colonialism, a different context from the Korean American experience.

4. For instance, since January 1, 1990, at least twenty-five Korean American merchants have been killed by non-Korean gunmen (*Los Angeles Times* 1992). However, I argue that these statistics rhetorically serve activists and leaders in both communities and have little to do with race per se. Because many merchants in South Central are Koreans doing business in an African American community, any urban violence, including murder, automatically involves both groups.

Chapter 23

Both Edges of the Margin

Blacks and Asians in Mississippi Masala, *Barriers to Coalition-Building*

Taunya Lovell Banks

> When races come together, as in the present age, it
> should not be merely the gathering of a crowd; there
> must be a bond of relation, or they will collide.
> —Rabindranath Tagore[1]

> When spiders unite, they can tie up a lion.
> —Ethiopian proverb

Contemporary Barriers to Coalition-Building

[The film] *Mississippi Masala* provides the viewer with clues about coalition-building between communities of color in the United States. How [the film's key characters Demetrius,] Jay, Mina, and Kinnu view their condition in Mississippi illustrates the dilemma which American notions of race, racial hierarchy, and racial classifications pose for non-Black immigrants of color in this country. "[W]hites are powerfully absent in the film." [The film's director] Nair chooses not to explore the overt barriers to coalitions between communities of color imposed by the dominant culture, for that is old ground.

Director Nair, by focusing almost exclusively on the Asian Indian and Black communities in Mississippi, suggests that the really hard work is removing the barriers between communities of color. For example, although the Indian immigrants in the film are keenly aware that they are people of color in a White dominated community, there is only a false appeal to racial coalition with Blacks, when it serves the economic advantage of the Indian community. To the extent that non-White immigrant communities privilege their economic well being over securing economic, social, and political justice for all racially subordinated groups, coalitions between Blacks and other non-White groups are more difficult to maintain.

From 5(1) *Asian Law Journal* 7, 31–35 (1998).

The film suggests two other major barriers to racial coalition between these two groups. Both the Black and Asian Indian communities shape their external behavior and modify their culture to appease powerful Whites and gain some measure of equality, whether economic or social. Second, as I mentioned previously, group insularity within each community makes outreach to other racially subordinated groups difficult.

Appeasement of Powerful Whites

Nair uses the conflict over the romance between Mina and Demetrius to illustrate how both the Black and Asian Indian communities worry about appeasing powerful Whites even in their absence. The negative reactions of the Asian Indian and Black communities to the romance between Mina and Demetrius provide a lesson about coalition-building between these communities. In the end, Mina and Demetrius must leave Mississippi to maintain their relationship. Although each has different reasons for leaving, both reject their community's concern about appeasing powerful Whites.

Demetrius feels he must leave the state to survive economically. His father, stressing that Blacks need to appease powerful Whites, scolds him for violating "the rules [and] not knowing his place and staying in it." His fledgling carpet cleaning business has been destroyed because he dared to date interracially. Both powerful Whites and Asian Indians retaliate economically, contributing to the demise of Demetrius' business. Unsurprisingly, the White-owned bank threatens to call in Demetrius' loan. In addition, mirroring past practices by Whites, the Asian Indian motel-owners stop doing business with him.

Mina leaves for family reasons. Her relationship with Demetrius also violated "the rules." By dating outside her ethnic group, Mina broke caste and culture rules. In the film, Jay told Mina that she let down her family, her community and her "entire race." Mina's actions shamed not only her family, but also her community and race because they attracted the attention of the dominant White community. Jay seemed concerned not only about the family's standing in its community, but also with the community's standing in the eyes of the dominant society. There was a similar reaction in the Black community.

Group Insularity

Group insularity within the Black and Asian Indian communities also accounts for some of the negative reactions to the romance between Mina and Demetrius. In a confrontation between Jay and Demetrius, Jay states that people should stick to their own kind, adding, "You're forced to accept that as you grow older." Thus, Jay accepts rather than challenges the status quo or current racial hierarchy. No doubt he remembers how his challenge of General Amin caused his departure from Uganda almost two decades earlier. Jay still is not critical of how the group insularity within his own community contributes to the problem. In Uganda he blamed Blacks; in the United States he implicitly blames the dominant (White) culture.

The full range of reasons for resistance within the Asian Indian community to the romance between Demetrius and Mina is unclear. Perhaps Nair did this intentionally, or perhaps the film's lack of clarity simply illustrates the potential for cultural miscommunication that results from racial insularity. For example, Mina's relatives and Jay's friends, on finding the couple together, assault Demetrius saying that he, a Black man, should leave "their women" alone. Black viewers may interpret this statement as disapproval of interracial dating based on Asian Indian notions of racial superiority over Blacks. On the other hand, Asian Indian viewers may interpret the statement as disapproval of *any* outgroup dating, even with Whites.

Demetrius' friends and contemporaries within the Black community raise analogous culturally insular concerns. Jerome, his business partner, tells Demetrius to "leave those *foreigners* alone, they ain't nothing but trouble." Jerome asserts the prerogative of nativism to stress the status difference between native-born Blacks as U.S. citizens, and immigrants as foreigners. This status distinction allows native-born Blacks to overlook the common link of racial subordination as they attempt to privilege their status as citizens, *even* second class, over non-citizens.

Historically, native-born Blacks and Whites responded similarly to nativist fears. Sometimes, Blacks condemned discriminatory treatment directed at non-White immigrants. A few Black leaders saw the parallels between Black slavery and the subservient labor conditions connected to contract labor.[2] Even Blacks who opposed foreign contract labor opposed immigration restrictions that limited Chinese, but not Europeans, from entering the United States as "free" immigrants, seeing a racial motive. "[W]hile [W]hite workers slowly rallied in support of restriction[s on Chinese laborers], Blacks formed a near solid front in demanding that Chinese be accorded rights granted other newcomers." By drawing on their experiences with racial discrimination, Blacks have the capacity, but not always the vision, to see and attack racial injustice against other non-Whites.

Nativism is a continuing problem among segments of the Black community. A contemporary study by Scott Cummings and Thomas Lambert suggests that Black "attitudes toward Asian and Hispanic Americans are very similar to those held by the Anglo American majority." This finding may explain why exit polls indicated that among Black voters, 47 percent voted in favor of California's Proposition 187, a referendum restricting state assistance to undocumented immigrants. Frank H. Wu suggests that the Proposition 187 campaign asserted that "Asian and Latino immigrants were taking jobs from [B]lacks or using government services intended for underprivileged citizens," and falsely implied that Blacks would benefit if Asian and Latino immigrants were excluded. The willingness of nativist Blacks to act upon these claims and disadvantage non-White immigrants is a form of simultaneous racism. On the other hand, non-White immigrants also continue to capitalize on their treatment as non-Black. This too is simultaneous racism.

NOTES

1. Rabindranath Tagore, "On Education," in *A Tagore Reader*, ed. Amiya Chakravarty (1961), 216.

2. David J. Hellwig, "Black Reaction to Chinese Immigration and the Anti-Chinese Movement: 1850–1910," 6:2 *Amerasia* 25, 27 (1979). Frederick Douglass recognized that the importation of Chinese laborers was the way for the White aristocracy to maintain a slave-like labor force. John M. Langston, a law professor and later the Dean of Howard Law School agreed. Not all Blacks were sympathetic to Chinese immigrants. For example, during the anti-Chinese movement in the mid-nineteenth century, some native-born Blacks opposed Chinese immigrant laborers for fear they would compete with them economically, especially in the South. *Id.* at 26–27. The Black California press, although initially supportive of free immigration for Chinese, by the 1880s did not join the bulk of the Black press in condemning the Chinese exclusion laws because of economic pressures on Blacks created by the presence of Chinese laborers on the West Coast. *Id.* at 31–33.

Chapter 24

Not Our Problem

Margaret Read MacDonald

The [Queen] sat with her Adviser eating honey on puffed rice. As they ate they leaned from the palace window and watched the street below. They talked of this and that. The Queen, not paying attention to what she was doing, let a drop of honey fall onto the windowsill. "Oh sire, let me wipe that up," offered the Adviser. "Never mind," said the Queen. "It is not *our* problem. The servants will clean it later."

As the two continued to dine on their honey and puffed rice, the drop of honey slowly began to drip down the windowsill. At last it fell with a plop onto the street below. Soon a fly had landed on the drop of honey and begun its own meal. Immediately a gecko sprang from under the palace and with a flip of its long tongue swallowed the fly. But a cat had seen the gecko and pounced. Then a dog sprang forward and attacked the cat!

"Sire, there seems to be a cat and dog fight in the street. Should we call someone to stop it?" "Never mind," said the Queen. "It's not our problem." So the two continued to munch their honey and puffed rice.

Meanwhile the cat's owner had arrived and was beating the dog. The dog's owner ran up and began to beat the cat. Soon the two were beating each other.

"Sire, there are two persons fighting in the street now. Shouldn't we send someone to break this up?" The Queen lazily looked from the window. "Never mind. It's not *our* problem."

The friends of the cat's owner gathered and began to cheer him on. The friends of the dog's owner began to cheer her on as well. Soon both groups entered the fight and attacked each other.

"Sire, a number of people are fighting in the street now. Perhaps we should call someone to break this up." The Queen was too lazy even to look. You can guess what she said. "Never mind. It's not *our* problem."

Now soldiers arrived on the scene. At first they tried to break up the fighting. But when they heard the cause of the fight some sided with the cat's owner. Others sided with the dog's owner. Soon the soldiers too had joined the fight.

"Not Our Problem" is from *Peace Tales: World Folktales to Talk About* (North Haven, CT: Linnet Books), 18–20, © 1992 by Margaret Read MacDonald. Reprinted by permission.

With the soldiers involved, the fight erupted into civil war. Houses were burned down. People were harmed. And the palace itself was set afire and burned to the ground. The Queen and her Adviser stood surveying the ruins. "Perhaps," said the Queen, "I was wrong? Perhaps the drop of honey WAS our problem."

—A Tale from Burma and Thailand

Chapter 25

Immigrants and Ethnics
Conflict and Identity in Chicago Polonia

Mary Patrice Erdmans

After the annual Polish American parade in Chicago in 1988, a group of new Polish immigrants marched to the Polish consulate to demonstrate. Along the way, one immigrant told me about the problems she was having with "old Poles," that is, the established Polish American community. Among other things, she felt that Polish Americans were unwilling to help the new immigrants and provided as an example her attempt to enroll her children in a private grade school:

> [When I arrived at the Catholic school] I see that the principal's name is Polish. I think, I am lucky, she will understand. I ask her if she is speaking Polish and she says she is. This is very good for me. I think there is no problem. So then I explain how my husband is looking for a job and when he finds a job then we will pay tuition. Then I ask: "It is possible to enroll my children?" She got very angry and started yelling at me: "You can get a job anywhere, don't you want to work? You are here 6 months and you don't have a job!! When my mother and father came here they worked immediately. My father swept the streets and my mother cleaned tables." I said to her, "Your parents were peasants. We are not." She got very angry at me and I left and never saw her again. I enrolled my children in a magnet school.

The new immigrant identifies with the principal because they share a language and a label ("she is Polish"), but they are unable to form an allegiance based on these shared traits. In their interaction, the ethnic principal and the immigrant parent try to explain why the cultural identity does not work. The ethnic blames it on the work ethic of the immigrant who arrived from a communist country; the immigrant blames it on the rural roots of the ethnic's ancestors.

In the United States, ethnic identities are created and recreated in two ways: through time, as second and subsequent generations reinterpret their collective identity in specific historical contexts, and across space, as immigrants carry culture from one place to another. New immigrants may settle near established ethnics from their homeland, but their incorporation into this community is by no means certain because their identities are constructed in different cultural contexts and through different processes. First, if several decades separate the early and

From 36(1) *Sociological Quarterly* 175–76, 179–82, 190 (1995). Midwest Sociological Society, by permission.

later arrivals, homeland and destination conditions are not likely to be similar. The immigrants and ethnics then only superficially share an ancestral homeland. Second, the re-creation of ethnicity over generations produces a different identity than the construction of an immigrant identity through movement across borders.

Immigrant and Ethnic Cultures in Chicago's Polonia

Differences between immigrants [foreign-born Poles] and ethnics [native-born Americans of Polish heritage] are expressed in each group's languages, religious rituals, and political beliefs. The dramatic changes in Poland over the last one hundred years—Poland was a partitioned nation until 1918, an independent nation between the world wars, and a communist satellite country between 1945 and 1989—have led to different types of immigrants. Peasant transoceanic migrant laborers, war refugees, and anticommunist exiles constituted the three main immigrant cohorts in the early twentieth century, post–World War II, and post–1965 respectively.

The early cohort emigrated from a Poland that did not exist on the map; it was partitioned into regions controlled by Russia, Prussia, and Austria. Therefore, national consciousness was very low among the early immigrants. The decision to emigrate was usually economic and connected to the diminishing availability of land and an increasing surplus of labor. As a result, this cohort was composed mostly of uneducated peasants. The post–World War II cohort, by contrast, left an independent Poland (1919–1939) and had a strongly developed national consciousness. Many of these emigres had fought in World War II, and their decision to emigrate (or not to return to Poland after the war) was a political decision. These Poles arrived as refugees in America, not as economic immigrants. Conflict in Polonia in the 1950s was a result of the differences in national identity and socioeconomic class between the early cohort and the post–World War II cohort.[1]

The most recent cohort emigrated from a communist Poland for both economic and political reasons. Some, discouraged by the failing economy of communist Poland, came to America seeking financial gain. Others, especially the refugees who had been involved in the *Solidarność* movement, were escaping political repression. These refugees, who came mostly in the 1980s, had a strong commitment to their national identity, and in America they remained actively involved in the political and social changes in Poland in the 1980s. Also included in this newest cohort were the *wakacjusze*, Poles in America on temporary tourist visas working illegally.

In general, the political, economic, and geographic faces of Poland changed throughout the twentieth century, and therefore the composition of the cohorts differed. Table 25.1 summarizes these differences. Today's descendants of the early immigrants are generally working-class ethnics who have an emotional attachment to the folk culture of Poland as presented to them by their parents and grandparents.

TABLE 25.1
Differences among Polish Immigrant Cohorts

	Early Cohort (1870–1913)	War Cohort (1939–1959)	New Cohort (1965–1989)
Poland's political state	Partitioned	Interdependent	Communist
Main motives for emigrating	Economic	Political	Economic/Political
Cohort educational level*	Low	High	High
Cohort size	Large (1,500,000)	Small (190,000)	Small (350,000)

*Low levels of education refer to less than high school education—many of the early immigrants were illiterate, and few had attended school beyond the eighth grade. High levels of education refer to high school diploma and beyond—between a third and a half of the two latest cohorts had post-secondary degrees.

The post–World War II cohort and the most recent immigrant cohort are better educated and more urbanized than the earlier cohort and, hence, identify with the intellectual components of an evolving Polish nation and culture. The different meanings of Polishness are, at times, a consequence of class differences. Some express it as a preference for Chopin versus the polka. New immigrants describe it as "not having anything in common" with the "early peasants" who were "mostly uneducated laborers" who "signed their name with an X."

Historical events, such as World War II, industrialization, and the imposition of a communist system, have changed not only Poland's political and economic systems, but its culture as well. Thus Polish Americans and Polish immigrants have different historical memories and different cultural expressions. Immigrants have stated: "There are differences in language, in the way of thinking, in remembering about Poland, our experiences in Poland, experiences with Germans, with Russians. We have only a few common topics because we have had such different experiences." Moreover, they add: "We have different values. We came from a different country. Before, it was farmland, now it's industry. We cannot even talk to them. Everyone here is having polka parties. In Poland no one polkas."

Immigrants think Polish ethnics are marooned in the past. One immigrant complained about a Polish American organization that was sponsoring a new edition of a nineteenth-century novel: "It's really stupid. It would be compared to something like a novel about the wild west. It was great when I was fourteen, but they consider this a great novel. OK, at some point in Polish history it was an important book, but not right now. We have world-recognized writers, why don't they sponsor those writers? Why? Because they don't know about them." Another said: "For me it's a pity that Polish Americans don't know Polish culture. Do you know W——? Well, he brings groups from Poland over here. It's stupid because some people think that those actors or performers represent Polish culture. Baloney. They [Polish Americans] don't even know that Polish theater was considered the best in the world in the 1970s."

For both immigrants and ethnics, political heroes and cultural icons are embedded in the time period of emigration. Current Polish American ethnic culture is the creation of the turn-of-the-century wave shaped within a U.S. context. Thus Polish ethnics write pamphlets about, name streets after, and celebrate the holidays of

Casimir Pulaski and Thaddeus Kosciuszko—generals in the American Revolution (the spellings of both names have been anglicized). New immigrants value Polish culture as it has evolved in Poland. Political heroes for new immigrants include the *Solidarność* leaders Father Jerzy Popieluszko and Lech Walesa. Cultural heroes include the science fiction writer Stanislaus Lem, political satirist Jan Pietrzak, and poet Stanislaus Baranczak.

Language, too, divides immigrants and ethnics. Immigrants point to the "archaic Polish" spoken by the ethnics. One said, "The language wasn't too common, they were from that old old Polonia." Another noted, "He spoke that old Polish you can only read about in literature classes in Poland." The Polish spoken by ethnics differs from that spoken by immigrants for two reasons. First, the ethnics often speak a rural dialect that is no longer spoken in contemporary Poland. Anti-immigration sentiment and the 100 percent American movement in the early twentieth century did not encourage the children of immigrants to retain their native language. Language classes sponsored by Polish fraternal organizations at that time were English language classes. If children learned Polish they learned the dialect of their parents. Language differences also exist because ethnics speak a hybrid Polish-English. For example, Polish Americans use English syntax and Polish vocabulary (i.e., the sentences are likely to follow the English noun-verb-object pattern). Or they conjugate American verbs along Polish patterns (e.g., *parkowac* means "to park"). The language of ethnics is not "dead," but its regenerative source is America, not Poland. In the shadow of the "crusade for Americanization" the ethnics created a unique culture.

The Roman Catholic Church, while serving as a nexus for social interaction between immigrants and ethnics in Chicago, is also a site of conflict. Roman Catholicism is the dominant religion of Poland. Historically, the Church has been a source of unity for the Poles; many believe that Polishness, as a national identity, survived in the Church during the years of partition (1795–1918) and communist rule. For early twentieth-century Polish immigrants in Chicago, the Church was both a unifying institution in local neighborhoods and the source of internecine struggle among the various political factions. In the 1980s, the Church was an arena of conflict because ethnics and immigrants disagreed on roles and behavior within the Church. For example, the *Solidarność* refugees felt that the Church should be more politicized. Many priests in Poland supported *Solidarność* in words and deeds. In the United States, however, refugees had disagreements with Church officials in Chicago who refused to allow political banners to be hung in churches. In addition, immigrants said they thought of priests as educated, but were surprised to find Polish American priests speaking a colloquial "low" level of Polish. Immigrants were critical of Polish American priests' weekly sermons, which they saw as fundraising efforts, rather than as an interpretation of scripture. Polish American priests criticized new immigrants for not formally registering with the parish and for not contributing sufficiently to the weekly collection. Finally, the immigrants and ethnics had different religious rituals. For example, in Poland, Catholics can go to confession before or during mass in order to give them an opportunity to cleanse their soul before receiving communion. In the

United States, confessions are often heard only once a week, usually on Saturdays, and most American Roman Catholics take communion even if they have not been to confession. The Roman Catholic Church provides a context that brings immigrants and ethnics together; however, differences in expectations and behavior lead to minor annoyances and squabbling.

Some ethnics describe the conflict between themselves and the new immigrants in political terms. Polish Americans assert that immigrants "have a communist mentality, they don't understand how things work over here," they are "brainwashed," and that "communist rule changed the psychology of those people." These kinds of statements are used to criticize the work ethic of the new immigrants. Ethnics believe that the welfare state in Poland destroyed Poles' willingness to work and their ability to find jobs on their own initiative. They believe that the immigrants "came here expecting a handout because that's what they got from the communist government. . . . Their mental attitude is one that accepts the welfare system." Polish Americans describe the effects of communism in several ways:

> These people came from a communist country where everyone was guaranteed a job and a house. And when they come here they have to struggle, and this is where the problems start. They have been indoctrinated in Poland for over thirty years—the state gives you a job, the state gives you medical insurance, the state gives you an education.
>
> They came from a communist system, it is different. I'll give you an example. A young fellow came to me and said, "What kind of country is this, there is no office that gives you an apartment?" You know I started laughing and then I picked up the weekend edition of the paper and I said, "Look here, one, two, three, four pages of apartments for rent. What kind of apartment do you want?"

New immigrants do not agree with the ethnics' assessment. In fact, use of public assistance by Polish refugees is low. Still, many ethnics attribute the differences between them and immigrants to the effects of communism.

In summary, the divisions within Chicago's Polonia are in part a result of these different interpretations of Polishness and are expressed in language, musical and literary preferences, sacred rituals and heroes, and social values and attitudes. For immigrants, Polishness is shaped by contemporary communist Poland, while for ethnics it emerges from the context of being a white ethnic group with roots in nineteenth-century rural Poland living in pluralist America. As a result of these differences, Polish Americans and Polish immigrants frame their relations in an "us/them" debate rather than a "we" dialogue.

Conclusion

The process by which an immigrant becomes an ethnic occurs over time. In the initial stages, however, the two populations are different in that their identities produce different demands. Cultural identities, social needs, and political interests emerge from and are shaped by a population's country of birth. These differences in culture, needs, and interests play a more determinative role in group relations than shared ancestry. While shared ancestry leads the groups to believe they "ought" to work together, it does not always function well as a basis for solidarity between immigrants and ethnics.

This research supports recent work on cultural identities, reinforcing the notion that culture is not a static representation of artifacts. Polishness in the United States is neither a Chopin sonata nor Stan's Polka Band. Ethnicity is not a museum that preserves cultural traditions. Instead, Polishness is forged by a multitude of contexts that cross temporal, national, and ideological borders: rural nineteenth-century and industrial twentieth-century Poland; anticommunism and democratization; the 1960s ethnic revival in the United States and anti-Semitism in Poland. The dynamic nature of Polish ethnicity emerges within American society and through the integration of the multiple waves of new Polish immigrants, who bring with them "updated" versions of the homeland culture. Each version of the culture is shaped by the political and economic evolutions of the homeland.

The findings move us away from what Paul Gilroy identifies as a "dogmatic focus on national cultures." The era of ethnic nations and national ethnicity has passed. Nations are not always built on ethnic unity, and ethnic unity does not always emerge among groups who emigrated from the same geographic region. Movements across borders have always resulted in constructed cultures that have roots in numerous hemispheres and nations. A transnational approach to culture recognizes the diasporic nature of these identities.

As cultural studies and multicultural curriculums take hold in American universities, we need to recognize the heterogeneous, complex, multidimensional, and dynamic nature of cultural identities. The borders of "Asian," "Latino," "Black," and "White" identities are contested and evolving. We cannot simply box up identities. As Gilroy suggests, "absolutist conceptions of culture" are erroneously simplistic and lend themselves to ethnocentric and racist ideologies. Such absolutist and essentialist notions become susceptible to proprietorship. "Polishness," like "Blackness" or "Chineseness," is not a property to which one group can lay claim. The claim to cultural ownership, and the discounting of the "other" for not being Polish enough, or Black enough, or Chinese enough, simply creates the opportunity to reproduce or newly produce exclusionary power structures. Rey Chow warns that groups escaping subordinate status positions should be careful not to simply reconfigure the power relations with themselves on top. When identities are used as weapons to wield power over other groups, "the new solidarities are often informed by a strategic attitude which repeats what they seek to overthrow."

As we move toward an increasingly inclusionary political and academic agenda, it becomes even more important that we understand the forces behind the construction of ethnicity rather than quibble over which version of the ethnicity is represented. Our focus should center on understanding the political and economic forces propelling identity construction, including colonialism, industrial transformation, political transitions, and state immigration policies, as well as ethnicity-based social movements and national revolts. Focusing on process will move us away from the simple catalog-style analysis of naming the content of ethnic cultures.

NOTE

1. The effects of political changes in the homeland on the identities of the immigrant cohorts were also evident in the Serbian community in Milwaukee. Serbs arriving in the early 1990s left from provinces ruled by the Austro-Hungarian empire and had not developed a strong national consciousness. The post–World War II Serbs were political refugees, many of whom had been affiliated with the Serbian nationalist Chetnik movement, who were fleeing from the recent communist take-over. This group was highly nationalistic. Deborah Padgett suggests that when post–World War II Serbian emigres arrived in Milwaukee, they were thrust into an "Americanized" second-generation Serbian ethnic community that was "alienated by the newcomers' call for renewed support of Serbian nationalism." The conflict stemmed from the different weight given to the issue of nationalism within the Serbian community.

Chapter 26

To Set Right
Ho'oponopono, a Native Hawaiian Way of Peacemaking

Manu Aluli Meyer

Ho'oponopono, which literally means "setting to right" or "to make right," is an ancient Hawaiian communication practice based on the physical and spiritual need for members of a family to work together and aid in one another's well-being. Historically, ho'oponopono was practiced only between immediate family members. Because each member played an important role in the survival of the family, maintaining harmony was vital to keeping the family alive and well. Ho'oponopono was the means with which that harmony was maintained.

In 1994, the Native Hawaiian Bar Association established Na'au Pono, a ho'oponopono demonstration project that received its first referrals from family court about a year ago. Although members of most families no longer depend on one another for physical survival, the need for a process that peacefully resolves conflicts among family members is as pressing as ever.

Key Conditions

The first step in the ho'oponopono process is the choice of a *haku* (facilitator). In ancient Hawaii, the haku was usually a male member of the healing, professional class, known as the kahuna. Today, haku are most often respected elders—male or female—who are not involved in the issues that have given rise to the ho'oponopono. The haku plays a vital role in setting a tone of *aloha* (love, affection), the spirit that ties the family together.

Once the haku has been chosen, the participants must understand and agree to the following before the ho'oponopono can begin:

1. Each individual in the *'ohana* (family) is committed to being part of the problem-solving process.
2. All words and deeds that are part of the ho'oponopono will be shared in an atmosphere of *'oia i'o* (the essence of truth).

From *Compleat Lawyer* 30–35 (Fall 1995). ABA Publishing. By Permission.

3. A spirit of aloha is shared by the participants, or they are committed to reinstating that spirit.
4. Everything said in the ho'oponopono will be kept in confidence; nothing will be repeated outside the ho'oponopono.
5. The chosen haku is a fair and impartial channel through which the ho'oponopono can be done. (All participants must agree.)

The purpose of the five conditions is to ensure an ethos of commitment, honesty, privacy, and fairness, and to provide a foundation and structure for the discussions that will follow. It is these five conditions that set the stage for a successful, relationship-centered resolution process.

A part of the haku's role is to "ritualize" a tone of sincerity and commitment for the ho'oponopono by asking each participant whether he or she understands and agrees to the five conditions. The haku has the right to pause and assess a particular participant's sincerity, and to end, postpone, or continue the process based on what he or she feels is appropriate. A ho'oponopono will not begin if the haku determines that the participants are unwilling to agree to the five conditions.

The extent to which a haku will need to establish the necessary tone of sincerity will vary greatly from family to family. Families that have long experience with ho'oponopono will come to the process fully aware of the five conditions and fully prepared to accept them. (They know already that the ho'oponopono will not proceed without such acceptance.) For modern Hawaiian families, however, for whom the specifics of ho'oponopono are vague, a clear presentation of the five conditions will be necessary.

The ho'oponopono will begin with a *pule wehe* (opening prayer), said by the haku and addressed to family *'aumakua* (god or gods) to ask for guidance, strength, clarity, and healing. After or during the pule wehe, the haku will "say" the *kukulu kumuhana*, the meaning of which can be understood in two ways.

Kukulu kumuhana means both a clear, objective statement of why the ho'oponopono was called—a useful starting point for discussion—*and* a form of spiritual solidarity in which people focus on one person or one problem and, in doing so, unify their spiritual strength for positive ends. Kukulu kumuhana can be understood as the pooling of the emotional, physical, and spiritual strength of family members for a shared purpose. Whether conscious or unconscious, it *always* is present in a successful ho'oponopono.

The haku may facilitate the spirit of kukulu kumuhana during a ho'oponopono if one of the participants becomes "stuck in hostility." In doing so, the haku will ask all of the family members to spiritually and mindfully help break the barriers that are keeping the one member stuck.

It is interesting to think about why kukulu kumuhana refers both to the pooling of strength and the stating of the problem, and whether that dual meaning has something to do with the success of ho'oponopono. Stating the problem in the hopeful context of spiritual solidarity is much like planting a seed in fertile soil—the very nature of kukulu kumuhana provides the context for resolution.

Mahiki

Mahiki is the process of examining one layer at a time, of inching toward the source of trouble to untangle emotions, actions, and motivations, which will, in turn, uncover yet another, deeper layer of the same. In the process of mahiki, the haku deals with only one problem at a time, tracing it from start to finish until it can be fully understood. Imagine mahiki as peeling back the layers of an onion. It is the heart of a ho'oponopono, the process that enables the family to come closer to *mihi* (forgiveness) through the identification of *hala* (fault or transgression) and *hihia* (entangled emotions).

During mahiki, the participants may speak only when given permission and only to the haku. This gives the haku an opportunity to deflect the anger and clarify the emotions or thoughts of participants who may be too *hihia* (entangled) to speak clearly. Generally, hakus agree that anger and emotions are important and valuable in ho'oponopono, but should not run unchecked or misdirected.

Time Out

Another phase of a ho'oponopono is *ho'omalu*, a time for the participants to gather strength and think. It is a silent time and usually is called by the haku to quell mounting tension or provide a rest and time for silence and reflection. Ho'o-malu is a valuable and useful tool in ho'oponopono as it serves to ritualize the time when family members eat, gain individual strength, or pool their energies for the benefit of the group. It can last a few minutes, a few hours, or days.

Although every ho'oponopono must end in resolution, the path to that ending is not always amicable. There is an option in ho'oponopono called *mo ka piko*, which means "to sever the umbilical cord." An example of when mo ka piko might be used is a situation in which one member of the family refuses to participate in the problem-solving process or to embrace the family with any sense of aloha. As a result, he or she may be cut off from the ho'oponopono and, if restitution is not made, asked to leave the family for good. Mo ka piko is used only when all other options have failed.

One of the last phases of ho'oponopono is *mihi*, a phase of forgiveness, apology, and confession. It usually is charged with sincerity and strong emotions. During mihi, the haku no longer acts as the mediator of words and emotions but allows members to talk directly to one another. The character of that talk is *'oia i'o*, one of the five conditions of the ho'oponopono to which the participants agreed.

'Oia i'o is absolute truth, sincerity, and the spirit and essence of truth. Among its many aspects is "total truth"—truth without innuendo, intentional omission, or slanting of facts and presentation. It also is truth that can be sensed emotionally; a person will know by what he or she is feeling whether his or her statement

FIGURE 26.1
Glossary to Ho'oponopono

'Ohana: Family blood ties or, more recently, a very close grouping
Haku: An unbiased mediator, one that is respected by all
'Aumakua: Family god, often represented by a living creature or plant
Pule Wehe: Opening prayer, usually said to the family 'aumakua
Kukulu Kumuhana: A pooling of *mana* (energy or strength) directed toward a positive goal; a unified
  force. This also is the clear, objective statement of the problem
Hihia: A tangling of emotions that hinders forgiveness
Mahiki: The discussion of the problem, a time to unravel, to peel away the layers of acts and feelings
  that have created the hihia
Hala: Fault or transgression
Ho'omauhala: Period of unrest, the continued holding of a grudge, feelings of hostility
Ho'omalu: A silent period, a "time out"
'Oia I'o: The flesh of truth, absolute truth, the essence of truth
Mihi: Forgiveness, repentance, apology, confession
Kala: To release, untie, free, unbind
Mo Ka Piko: To sever the umbilical cord; symbolically, to cut off an 'ohana member
Pule Ho'opau: Closing prayer

---

is 'oia i'o. This kind of truth, no matter how painful it may be to others, is what is expected in ho'oponopono because the essential element of ho'oponopono is the total revealing of what really happened. Until everyone involved knows clearly who did what to whom and why, it will not be possible to remedy the situation.

The phase of *kala*—to release, untie, free each other completely—follows the phase of forgiveness. Kala represents an ideal that is not easy to attain. In ho'oponopono, it is expressed in the phrase: *Ke kala aku nei 'au ia 'oe a pela noho'i 'au e kala ia mai ai* (I unbind you from the fault, and thus may I also be unbound by it).

The kala process of forgiving and releasing is not the same as the more familiar "forgive and forget," in which an incident that is forgotten has actually been repressed. Kala seeks instead to strip the incident of its pain-causing attributes. It may be remembered, but if mihi and hala have been sincere, it will be remembered as "no big thing anymore."

Although the specific experience of kala will vary with each ho'oponopono, some of its aspects will be common to all: a sense of releasing, a deep and profound emptying, a feeling that something has been lifted from the group, a lightness, and an upwelling of aloha. All of this is healing.

Another Prayer

A successful ho'oponopono ends with a drained yet united and uplifted family. The process closes with a *pule ho'opau*, a prayer that gives thanks for guidance and asks for continued support. Prayers are essential to the Hawaiian peacemaking process. Denying the need for guidance from a spiritual source is denying the truth of what makes ho'oponopono work.

TABLE 26.1
Ho'oponopono and Mediation: Examining the Differences
Victoria Shook and Leonard Ke'ala Kwan

Ho'oponopono	Mediation
The setting	
• Family home or other intimate setting that is familiar to family and haku	• Office or other site that is unfamiliar to disputants
• The process is private; limited to family members and the haku.	• The process is public; it includes many outsiders in central roles, e.g., mediators, and in peripheral roles, e.g., accountants, lawyers, counselors, etc.
• Time is extended, marathon-like; the process can last hours or even days; multiple sessions are possible; sessions are scheduled close to time of the problem.	• Sessions may last between two and four hours; multiple sessions are possible; a time lapse is likely between the grievance process and settlement.
How conflict is understood	
• Conflict is disruptive to harmonious relationships.	• Conflict is normal, potentially positive, and can lead to personal growth.
• Boundaries of conflict extend beyond the family to the spiritual and natural world, as do repercussions.	• Boundaries of conflict are narrow, defined by those directly involved.
• View of self as relational; in conflict, the focus is the affects of individual behavior on the group; "security" and self-worth are achieved through relationships.	• Self is seen as autonomous, individuated; can speak of "self-interests" in conflict; "security" of self comes with individual achievements, e.g., economic success.
• Conflicts bind people tightly through hihia.	• Conflict is divisive and separates people.
How conflicts are resolved	
• Problems are dealt with holistically; there are no limits on the scope of resolution that is possible.	• Problems/conflicts can be compartmentalized in such a way that some issues are "mediatable" and some are better taken care of by other specialists.
• Traditionally, island societies allowed "no exit"; entangled, conflicted relationships needed to be straightened out.	• Urban societies are mobile; "exits" are easier if conflicts are unresolved; it is possible to settle the issues in conflict without creating or destroying good relationships.
• Purpose of ho'oponopono is to "clear the way," restore harmonious relationships; "straighten" things out	• Purpose of mediation is to make agreements
• Family process is to restore harmony, maintain integrity	• "Family mediation" is almost synonymous with "divorce mediation"; it helps the family restructure in as rational a way as is possible.
The role of the participants	
• Participants share cultural assumptions; traditionally everyone is familiar with the process and the ritual.	• Participants don't necessarily share an ethnocultural background.
• All parties have a connection to one another; the family system is the focus.	• Parties are segmented; individuals are the focus, e.g., "Disputant Party #1" and "Disputant Party #2."
• Family members deal with all aspects of the problem; there is no need for outside assistance.	• Disputants make their own decisions, but may need expert advice regarding the details of the agreement (and approval by lawyers and the court in family cases).
• Hierarchal structure—the haku has special status in relation to the family (although within the family, the relationships between the parents and children are more egalitarian than usual).	• The structure is egalitarian (nonstatus oriented); mediator has no ascribed status.
• Haku is known to family, is a respected elder, who has intimate knowledge of the parties.	• Mediator has no prior knowledge of or acquaintance with parties.

TABLE 26.1 *(continued)*

Ho'oponopono	Mediation
• Haku's authority is based on substantive knowledge (wisdom), skill, and status as an elder.	• The authority of the mediator has been gained through the obtaining of credentials and skills (via training); he or she has procedural knowledge.
• Haku's power is direct; he or she can influence, counsel, and advise; spiritual power also is available.	• Mediator's power is indirect and procedural; he or she can plan communication strategies and invoke leverage of "state" to boost influence, e.g., "What happens if you don't agree?"

Rules

Ho'oponopono	Mediation
• Based on an oral tradition (The parties are receptive to the power of the word; general intentions can cover broad range of matters; there is no need to spell out details.)	• The process is based on a written tradition (written files and notes; agreements must be written down with full details).
• A discussion about emotions and the quality of relationships is essential to understanding problems and resolving them.	• Talk about emotions is necessary at first, but is peripheral to the main focus: negotiating concrete agreements. (Further exploration of emotional issues is referred to counseling.)
• Direct emotional expression, particularly anger, is discouraged.	• Emotional expression is allowed; in "forum" stage, participants are expected to "ventilate" their feelings.
• Communication among family members is indirect and controlled by the leader.	• Direct communication is encouraged; indirect communication, i.e., mediator-controlled communication, is used only if necessary.
• No secrets; discussions occur with all members present.	• Secrets allowed in caucus.
• Self-scrutiny is key. (How have I transgressed? Will you forgive me?)	• Naming, blaming, and claiming of grievances by individuals ("This is what you did, this is what I want you to do for me.")

Stages

Ho'oponopono	Mediation
• Opening prayer and statement of problem by haku	• Opening statement by mediator, then the parties' first joint statements
• Discussions (mahiki)—the examination of all layers of the problem takes place with the whole family present.	• Discussions "get at the issues" by encouraging the parties to move from positions to interests; discussion occurs in joint *and* private sessions.
• Discussion is focused on the past to uncover the thoughts, feelings, and actions that have led to the conflict.	• Forum gives some focus to past actions, but only in the service of negotiating future actions.
• Through discussion there is understanding of hihia (tangled emotions), which makes possible the moving toward resolution.	• Discussion furthers negotiation by "reducing bargaining range" and "expanding the agreement zone" between parties.
• Resolution comes from mutual apology and forgiveness; admission of guilt, or contribution to hihia and hala are important.	• Resolution comes through negotiations that lead to a written agreement; agreements avoid admitting guilt or attributing blame.
• Session ends with prayer and socializing (a meal).	• The process ends with the parties receiving a copy of the agreement; then they disperse.

Chapter 27

Individualizing Justice through Multiculturalism
The Liberals' Dilemma

Doriane Lambelet Coleman

In California, a Japanese-American mother drowns her two young children in the ocean at Santa Monica and then attempts to kill herself; rescuers save her before she drowns. The children's recovered bodies bear deep bruises where they struggled as their mother held them under the water. The mother later explains that in Japan, where she is from, her actions would be understood as the time-honored, customary practice of parent-child suicide. She spends only one year in jail—the year she is on trial.

In New York, a Chinese-American woman is bludgeoned to death by her husband. Charged with murder, her husband explains that his conduct comports with a Chinese custom that allows husbands to dispel their shame in this way when their wives have been unfaithful. He is acquitted of murder charges.

Back in California, a young Laotian-American woman is abducted from her place of work at Fresno State University and forced to have sexual intercourse against her will. Her Hmong immigrant assailant explains that, among his tribe, such behavior is not only accepted, but expected—it is the customary way to choose a bride. He is sentenced to 120 days in jail, and his victim receives $900 in reparations.

A Somali immigrant living in Georgia allegedly cuts off her two-year-old niece's clitoris, partially botching the job. The child was cut in accordance with the time-honored tradition of female circumcision; this custom attempts to ensure that girls and women remain chaste for their husbands. The State charges the woman with child abuse, but is unable to convict her.

In these cases, the defense presented, and the prosecutor or court accepted, cultural evidence as an excuse for the otherwise criminal conduct of immigrant defendants. These official decisions appear to reflect the notion that the moral culpability of an immigrant defendant should be judged according to his or her own cultural standards, rather than those of the relevant jurisdiction. Although no

This chapter originally appeared at 96 *Columbia Law Review* 1093, 1099, 1156–1165 (1996). Reprinted by permission.

state has formally recognized the use of exonerating cultural evidence, some commentators and judges have labeled this strategy the "cultural defense."

The cultural defense (and the issues it raises about the rights of immigrants to retain aspects of their cultures when they come to the United States) is an important part of the larger debate about multiculturalism which currently is prominent in academic, social, and political circles. In particular, this larger debate concerns whether there is and should be a unifying American culture that guides our institutions, including the justice system, or whether the United States is and should be a culturally pluralistic nation in all respects, including in the law.

The introductory illustrations exemplify this debate in the legal arena with an unusual clarity, because they pit foreign customs and cultural practices directly against essential elements of contemporary American legal culture, including the antidiscrimination principle that is central to equal protection doctrine and related principles of universal rights that are at the foundation of feminist legal doctrine.

Allowing sensitivity to a defendant's culture to inform the application of laws to that individual is good multiculturalism. It also is good progressive criminal defense philosophy, which has as a central tenet the idea that the defendant should get as much individualized (subjective) justice as possible. The illustrations that introduce this article may be interpreted as reflecting this sort of sensitivity on the part of some prosecutors and judges.

For legal scholars and practitioners who believe in a progressive civil and human rights agenda, these illustrations also raise an important question: What happens to the victims—almost always minority women and children—when multiculturalism and individualized justice are advanced by dispositive cultural evidence? The answer, both in theory and in practice, is stark: They are denied the protection of the criminal laws because their assailants generally go free, either immediately or within a relatively brief period of time. More importantly, victims and potential victims in such circumstances have no hope of relief in the future, either individually or as a group, because when cultural evidence is permitted to excuse otherwise criminal conduct, the system effectively is choosing to adopt a different, discriminatory standard of criminality for immigrant defendants, and hence, a different and discriminatory level of protection for victims who are members of the culture in question. This different standard may defeat the deterrent effect of the law, and it may become precedent, both for future cases with similar facts, and for the broader position that race- or national origin–based applications of the criminal law are appropriate. Thus, the use of cultural defenses is anathema to another fundamental goal of the progressive agenda, namely the expansion of legal protections for some of the least powerful members of American society: women and children.

Margaret Fung, Executive Director of the Asian-American Defense and Education Fund, provided what is perhaps the best evidence of the tension that is created for progressives by these cases. When Ms. Fung first publicly addressed the decision in *People v. Chen*, the New York spousal killing case described above, she is reported to have expressed her concern that the result was bad for Asian women and for the image of Asian-Americans: "You don't want to import [immigrant] cultural values into our judicial system. . . . We don't want women victimized by backward customs. . . . We don't want so-called cultural experts perpetuating certain stereotypes that may not be accurate, . . . and putting that out to the American public." Later, however, Ms. Fung was reported to have reformulated her position on the use of cultural evidence by criminal defendants: To bar the cultural defense "would promote the idea that when people come to America, they have to give up their way of doing things. That is an idea we cannot support."

In addition to highlighting the dilemma posed by these cases, Margaret Fung's reactions highlight the two-fold discriminatory effect of the cultural defense. First, to the extent that cultural evidence is used to determine the outcome of criminal cases and to excuse some perpetrators of crimes, it results in disparate treatment of immigrants and other members of American society. Second, the particular cultural norms at issue in these cases are also inherently discriminatory in that they incorporate values about the lesser status of women and children; these values are contrary to those the contemporary international progressive agenda embraces. When the American legal system chooses to recognize such traditions in the context of pursuing individualized justice for the defendant, it condones the chauvinism that is at the core of these traditions.

The question of how to resolve the competing interests that Margaret Fung's turnaround so clearly sets out—a question that I call the "Liberals' Dilemma"—is the focus of this article. Unlike existing scholarship in the area, most of which does not appear to recognize this dilemma, it is my premise that the answer for legal (rather than moral) purposes should not be made in an ad hoc fashion, based on political and professional affiliations. Rather, I believe the law must reflect a broader, more considered resolution of this question, and that this resolution can be accomplished only by engaging in a balancing of the two substantial and conflicting interests. Thus, the defendant's interest in using cultural evidence that incorporates discriminatory norms and behaviors must be weighed against the victims' and potential victims' interests in obtaining protection and relief through a non-discriminatory application of the criminal law. Contemporary jurisprudence favors just this sort of balancing, which considers the interests of the two parties in a given case, as well as those of society generally, in determining the outcome. Using this approach, I conclude that victims' interests in this area are more compelling than those of defendants. In the process, I acknowledge that my position is contrary to that pure vein of multiculturalism that decries ethnocentrism in any form; and I agree that it also is contrary to those aspects of the liberal agenda that traditionally have sought to embrace (at least in theory) simultaneously both cultural pluralism and individual rights, including the rights of defendants and of the women and children who are often their victims. In this context, I believe that there are several reasons for choosing rights over culture.

First, the criminal justice system already affords defendants substantial opportunities to raise established, non-discriminatory arguments in support of their innocence or of a reduced sentence.

Second, permitting the use of culture-conscious, discriminatory evidence as part of the defendant's case-in-chief distorts the substantive criminal law and affords little or no protection to victims, whose assailants are left, as a result of this distortion, relatively free from broader societal strictures. There presently is no acceptable alternative to cure this deficiency.

Third, the use of cultural evidence risks a dangerous balkanization of the criminal law, where non-immigrant Americans are subject to one set of laws and immigrant Americans to another. This is a prospect that is inconsistent not only with one of the law's most fundamental objectives, the protection of society and all of its members from harm, but also with the important human and civil rights doctrines embodied in the Equal Protection Clause. Thus, society as a whole is best served by a balance that avoids the use of discriminatory cultural evidence.

Fourth, despite the benevolent interpretation I earlier afforded the modern acceptance of immigrant cultural evidence by some prosecutors and judges, there also is the substantial concern that culture consciousness—at least of the sort that leads to discriminatory results—may not be a good thing for a judicial system that is already plagued by a racist and sexist history. As Justice William Brennan commented in his dissenting opinion in *McCleskey v. Kemp*, "Formal dual criminal laws may no longer be in effect, and intentional discrimination may no longer be prominent. Nonetheless . . . 'subtle, less consciously held racial attitudes' continue to be of concern." It is at best ironic that progressive forces would purposefully give back to the system a new and lawful opportunity to treat immigrant women, children, and other minority victims of crimes as less valuable. At worst, this trend may foreshadow a return to overtly racist decisionmaking by some prosecutors and judges.

The acceptance of discriminatory cultural evidence at the very same time that laws are being developed to protect women and children from gender-related violence does more than set up a theoretical conflict. For example, in 1994, Congress enacted the Violence Against Women Act that, *inter alia*, provides grants for state court judges and other court personnel to be trained to identify and reject arguments about, among other things, cultural stereotypes. This statute, and recently issued asylum guidelines that define the political circumstances warranting asylum as including crimes of sexual violence, are based upon broad international declarations concerning the universality of a woman's right to be free from gender-motivated violence. These federal initiatives incorporate the very broad equal protection and rule-of-law principles that are at the core of the argument against the use of cultural evidence. They are at least inconsistent, if not in direct confrontation, with the development of state common law that incorporates gender-discriminatory cultural evidence.

Balancing

The law ought to be based upon a rational process that weighs the relative merits of both positions, taking into account the general interests of society. While the balancing doctrine is not flawless, it provides us with an analytical tool that addresses these concerns. Balancing is popular with the courts; moreover, it is inherently more objective, and thus more legitimate, than the political instincts that appear to have guided most prior discussions about the cultural defense.

While different versions of the balancing approach have been formulated by different courts in the context of different doctrines, the broader outline of the doctrine is constant; balancing requires analysis and weighing of the various interests being asserted, including an examination of alternatives and of the interests of society in the process and the outcome of the analysis.

We have seen that victims of immigrant crime have an important interest in ensuring that the criminal justice system works both to protect them from immigrant-on-immigrant crime in the same way that others in society are protected from the same kinds of crimes, and to vindicate them where those protections are ineffectual. On the other hand, we have seen that defendants in the cultural defense cases have a substantial interest in having their initial culpability as well as any ultimate sentence determined subjectively, with express consideration of the cultural factors that might be relevant to these separate analyses.

For conservatives and, ironically, some feminists, these competing interests and burdens are easily reconciled. "When in Rome, do as the Romans do!" is the conservative cry whenever multiculturalism appears to threaten established institutions in American society. The response to the cultural defense has not been different. Feminists generally do not align themselves with conservatives; however, because our "Rome" is a better place for women from the Western perspective, they do stand aligned—at least for the moment that it takes to articulate the anti-multicultural position—in regard to the cultural defense cases. Because this position inherently incorporates the judgment that the (female) victim's rights are paramount, it neither addresses nor solves the liberal dilemma.

However, for many liberals who do face the dilemma, including feminists of color, a full discussion of the competing positions in the cultural defense cases does not easily dispose of the problem. For this group, the evidence of interest and burden might be said to be more-or-less in equipoise. Further analysis focusing on two components of the balancing doctrine—namely possibly less burdensome alternatives and the best interests of society—is thus necessary to reach a consensus on the cultural defense cases. It is my view that this further discussion and analysis tips the scales in favor of the victims of immigrant crime.

As to the question whether less burdensome alternatives exist or could be developed, the answer is that at least one substantial, less burdensome alternative already exists for defendants, while there does not readily appear to be any solution for victims short of eliminating the option of the cultural defense. The Supreme Court has recognized, in some contexts, the defendant's right to present mitigating evidence during the sentencing phase of the proceedings. Information about how the defendant's culture would view his conduct could be considered in this context, and could lead to a reduced sentence. For example, it is not difficult to imagine that a court or a sentencing jury, after hearing evidence about the custom of marriage-by-capture, might set a relatively low term of incarceration for Mr. Moua, the Laotian Hmong refugee who abducted his victim from the Fresno State

University campus. The rationale for this reduction would be the sentencing authority's determination that, taking subjective factors into consideration, Mr. Moua is less morally blameworthy than a European-American defendant who has committed the very same crime, and whose explanation is, for example, that he was fulfilling a fraternity hazing rite. This alternative would not, of course, remove the stigma of a conviction, but the conviction's practical effect would be reduced significantly. It also has the advantage of being consistent with existing approaches to mitigation.

The criminal law also provides established defenses that in many cases allow the defendant to make culture-neutral arguments that are based on the same facts that would be used to establish the cultural defense. For example, a defendant who killed his wife upon discovering that she had strayed from the marital bed could interpose the traditional defense of provocation that is used—and that has been used since time immemorial—in the Anglo-American legal system in these circumstances. Of course, the defendant would not get the benefit of arguing that in his particular culture, the shame and devastation is elevated; nevertheless, the basic argument could be made. The defense of diminished capacity when properly used, that is, when not controverted by an effort to transform it into the cultural defense, also provides a viable option for immigrant defendants who commit crimes when they are despondent. Thus, for example, the defense of diminished capacity could, depending upon the circumstances, be used in mother-child suicide cases.

On the other hand, there is no analogous option for victims when the cultural defense is used to exonerate immigrant defendants. These defendants are returned to their communities with the imprimatur of what is in essence a multicultural law, a law that incorporates the custom or cultural practice at issue. The victims simply are left dead, beaten, raped, and mutilated, and potential victims may be convinced that the United States is not a place where they can hope to be protected from discriminatory culture-based crimes.

Indeed, other than the federal civil rights cause of action created by the Violence Against Women Act, there is no legal recourse for victims in these cases. The argument that these remedies constitute a viable alternative to eradicating the cultural defense from the strategic arsenal of defendants is not viable for one critical reason: The federal remedy clearly is meant to supplement existing state criminal laws. Because of this, the federal statute does not contain a criminal component, and thus is not sufficient to provide female victims and potential victims with either strong protection or vindication. In addition, by its very nature this remedy does nothing to protect children or other victims of immigrant crime who are not women.

Finally, the education option that has been suggested by one commentator, Nilda Rimonte, is also necessarily supplementary. While it may be true that educating immigrant communities about inconsistencies between their culture and United States law is ultimately necessary, I do not agree that alone it is sufficient to resolve the issues presented in the cultural defense cases for the simple reason that the defense is premised on the notion that our law ought not be ethnocentric in its application. Thus, while education may be helpful for those immigrants who wish to assimilate into the larger American culture, it is not likely to help with those individuals who have no desire to do so. As Jane Hansen and Deborah Scroggins suggest, a perfect example of this flaw in the education option is the response some Somalis give to the suggestion that immigrants who genitally mutilate their girls should be counseled against the customary practice: "The Somali woman doesn't need an alien woman telling her how to treat her private parts. . . . The decision must come from the Somalis." Another flaw in this option is that the failure to criminalize immigrant conduct that contravenes the criminal laws itself teaches immigrants the wrong lesson about the United States legal system. The Chinese-American community's reaction to the decision in the Chen case—women expressed fear that the decision would be read as an official sanction of gender-motivated violence—highlights this function of the law. A formal educational program seeking to teach immigrants the converse message would be hard-pressed to counter the powerful signal sent by the law's silence.

An evaluation of the social utility of the competing interests also supports the victims' position. The defendants' argument is based on the pure multiculturalist position that it is in society's interests to move toward true cultural pluralism in all institutions. The victims' argument is that a cultural pluralism that involves incorporating discriminatory cultural practices into the criminal laws will lead to a balkanized legal system that is inconsistent with equal protection principles we otherwise espouse. Leaving aside the relative constitutional merits of these conflicting positions, I do not believe that it is in the interests of society to reform our laws in a manner that is so eerily reminiscent of our history of gender and racial apartheid.

For those who do not believe that adopting the cultural defense would have this effect, and thus who believe that my analogy is overly dramatic, I would simply suggest that they look carefully at the cases where a version of the cultural defense has been effective, and ask themselves both about the results of those decisions, and how they would be compounded if the defense were formally to become law in jurisdictions across the United States. Such a transformation in the law would create, on a large scale, the very sort of legal distinctions we have only recently rejected.

Finally, an end note: Pure or strong multiculturalists may not be persuaded by this analysis. They may argue that, contrary to the view of conservatives and some feminists, a "Rome" where only Western values are prized is not a better place; and that contrary to the view of some liberals and feminists of color, there is no equipoise between immigrant defendants and victims of immigrant crime, because the goal of a multicultural society is always paramount. It is to these adherents of multiculturalism that I address this note and its caveat: Although my reasons may be slightly different, I, like Stanley Fish, believe that this strong adherence to multiculturalism eventually breaks down. In the cultural defense context, the strong multiculturalist position breaks down in at least three ways.

First, the notion that a culture or a cultural norm or practice can be identified objectively is simply anthropological and legal fiction. Second, the notion that culture is permanent is also fiction. Using these fictions to decide cases where lives—

both physical and emotional, of individuals and communities—are at stake is no more true to the objective of ultimate justice than is a system that does not permit the use of cultural evidence. Third, we—and here I include strong multiculturalists—are not seriously willing to extend the cultural defense to non-immigrant Americans. However, there is simply no viable rationale for carving out this distinction, at least not one that will support the heavy burden the cultural defense would place upon our legal institutions and the people they are intended to protect and govern.

The first point, that we cannot objectively and precisely define culture, raises two sets of problems. First, there is the problem of the existence of the custom or practice—that is, does it exist at all, and if it does, is it culturally acceptable in the minds of all or merely some segments of the foreign society at issue? Second, there are difficulties in interpreting the custom or practice—that is, is the custom or practice as the defendant has described it, or are there nuances that he has not described that are relevant to a full understanding of its value for purposes of legal analysis? If, for example, it could be demonstrated that a substantial portion of a foreign society did not accept a custom or practice—mother-child suicide in Japan is one such example, wife beating and killing in various parts of the world are another—how should an American court rule when asked to accept the practice as part of a cultural defense? And if customary views about a practice such as forced sexual relations or rape vary within a culture—for example among men and women within Hmong culture—how should a prosecutor and/or a court view a particular defendant's argument that his personal rendition of the practice should govern? This last example is made poignantly in *Minnesota v. Her*, where the parties and the witnesses disagreed on the question of whether rape was even a concept in Hmong culture.

The second point, that culture is incapable of being defined permanently, is equally troublesome. It is an anthropological fact that almost every culture is being modified, constantly. As Stuart Hall has noted, "Cultural identities come from somewhere, have histories. But, like everything which is historical, they undergo constant transformation. Far from being eternally fixed in some essentialised past, they are subject to the continuous 'play' of history, culture and power." Nilda Rimonte has described culture as "a force that . . . shapes and is shaped by its members." Culture is thus neither stagnant nor immutable; rather, it evolves over time to adapt to changing historical, political, and social circumstances. And while certain ingrained aspects of a culture may be said to withstand such evolution, even at its core a culture will be different in one historical period than in another. As Anh T. Lam puts it another way, culture "consists of the learned ways of behaving and adapting, as contrasted to inherited behavior patterns or instincts. A change in culture can be conscious and directed. People have the capacity to react to their culture."

Given these anthropological explications of the nature of culture, it should not be viewed as antithetical to strong multiculturalism for Americans to engage in a debate about the substance of a culture when we are asked through the criminal laws to make aspects of that culture part of our own. The contrary argument, that it is only legitimate for the substance of a culture to be debated among members of the culture itself, necessarily falls apart when elements of that culture are imposed upon a broader society. The justification for this inquiry is not founded in cultural elitism, but rather upon the truism that all culture is always changing, and that customs come and go depending upon various societal forces.

We have engaged in this cultural debate and selection process on many occasions in our own history, a clear example being the evolution of the role of women in society. While American culture during the nineteenth century provided a limited role for women, our culture has since evolved to provide a more expansive one. Our culture has evolved in this respect, for the most part leaving behind conventions, traditions, and customs—all derived from the various cultures that make up the American anthropological landscape—that subjugated and dehumanized women. It is significant that changes in our legal culture in the area of women's rights played a substantial part in the transformation of our broader culture, much in the same way that the Supreme Court's decision in *Brown v. Board of Education* to integrate the public schools is said to have paved the way for the integration of other public facilities. In both instances, the law was instrumental in instigating a cultural evolution (some would say revolution) that allowed us to parse out and reject many oppressive aspects of the culture.

This leads me to my third point: Based upon our evolution in the area of gender equity in particular, I surmise that even the purest and strongest of multiculturalists would recoil at a cultural defense case where the defendant was not an immigrant, but a European-American who argued that in his mind and in the community where he is from—"in his culture"—it continues to be appropriate for men to beat and rape their wives. This in fact may be true, as true as the same argument when made by the immigrant defendant. However, I do not believe that it would occur either to liberals generally, or to multiculturalists in particular, to believe in the inherent value of this argument. The reasons for this distinction are unclear; indeed, I am unable to conceive a basis for it that could survive scrutiny. It may be that most Americans expect conformity to contemporary legal principles from those we consider to be "our own," in a way that some of us may not from "others." And yet from the multicultural perspective, this distinction is not a viable one. If you respect cultural diversity, there simply is no coherent rationale for making the ad hoc decision to exclude certain cultures from pluralism's embrace. In the end, the decision may turn more on the value we place on the victim or on our higher expectations for the defendant.

Further Comments

1. Carrie Menkel-Meadow questions whether the American culture of adversarialism (based on our legal system) is adequate in a multicultural world.[1]

> My critiques are briefly as follows. . . . Binary, oppositional presentation of facts in dispute is not the best way for us to learn the truth. Polarized debate distorts truth, leaves out important information, simplifies complexity and obfuscates where it should clarify. More significantly, some matters (mostly civil, but occasionally even a criminal case) are susceptible to a binary (right/wrong, win/lose) conclusion or solution. This may be so because we cannot with any degree of accuracy determine the facts, because conflicting, but legitimate, legal rights give some entitlements to both (or all) parties, or because human or emotional equities cannot be sharply divided (parental rights in child custody, for example).

2. Isabelle Gunning suggests that studying other ethnic approaches helps us to confront possible value conflicts and to identify shared values on which to build solutions.[2] Manu Aluli Meyer's article only begins to describe the variety and richness of multiethnic and multiracial perspectives on dispute resolution. As Gadlin reminds us, however, there are risks in overgeneralizing or oversimplifying how ethnic groups approach conflict and dispute resolution. Also recall that the samples of research described in Part 2 on "Gender and Conflict" often considered the role of ethnicity in different disputes and conflict-related issues.

Thomas Kochman writes about differences between Black and White linguistic and cultural patterns, perspectives, and values that are likely to manifest themselves in conflict.[3] He advocates that these differences should be reciprocally acknowledged, respected, and considered valid. In working through disagreements and disputes, for instance, Kochman describes Blacks as more likely to use "sincere" argument and to interact in a confronting, personal, advocating, and issue-oriented cultural style. In contrast, Whites are more likely to use discussion and be nonconfronting, impersonal, representing, and peace or process oriented. Struggle or contentiousness is unifying for Blacks while polarizing for Whites. Cynthia Mabry also describes how African American culture may resolve family and custody disputes differently than advocated in current practice, particularly through the use of the extended family.[4]

Diane LeResche has researched in detail the informal dispute resolution processes used by Korean Americans. As she explains: "The supreme goal for Korean-Americans is to have harmonious relations among all persons within one's network of family, friends, and colleagues." They perceive conflict "as negative situations that represent a shameful inability to maintain harmonious relationships." Thus, Korean Americans seek a solution that does not "engender bitterness for the long term, helps all to save face, and preserves customary proper conduct between people in defined role relationships."[5] In what ways are LeResche's descriptions consistent or conflicting with Park's observations of Korean Americans in South Central Los Angeles?

3. Gadlin describes a "culture of racism." Derrick Bell dramatically illustrates his belief that racism is both a permanent and important component of our culture in a number of chronicles in his book *And We Are Not Saved*. He argues in each of these stories that White superiority has become the norm.[6]

Society's image of a particular ethnic group certainly shapes how we interpret disputes in which that group is involved. I have written, for instance, about the flawed societal image of Asian Americans as a successfully assimilated minority group who are represented throughout American society and do not experience discrimination. While this may describe some Asian Americans, it does not accurately describe the group as a whole. This image, however, colors our interpretation of disputes; so, for instance, it is more difficult for society to find Asian Americans' claims of employment discrimination credible.[7]

4. While some write about interracial conflict, the intensity and pervasiveness of interracial conflict in society apparently also affect the contents and characters used in books. Bernice Pescosolido and her coauthors studied racial images in children's picture books between 1937 and 1993 and examined the relationship between culture, gatekeeping, and conflict in society. Among a number of interesting conclusions, they found that the amount of interracial strife in society and African American challenges to the dominant societal norms (as measured by the number of conflicts, protests, and legal actions) are linked to the portrayal of Blacks in children's books. "When Black-White relations are stable—before and after the dramatic increase in Black insurgency—Black characters are more visible, whereas during the time of contested Black-White relations, Blacks and Black-White interactions were virtually deleted from children's books." What explains this result? The authors suggest that perhaps publishers want to avoid books about troublesome issues and groups or that publishers and writers are uncertain how to depict Blacks given concerns about negative stereotyping.[8] One wonders, however, about the lost opportunity for books to explore and educate about interracial strife while children are experiencing and observing it in their own lives.

5. While scholars and students of race relations once focused almost exclusively on Black-White relations and conflict, there is increasing attention to the relationships between non-white groups. The conflicts between Asian Americans and African Americans described by Park and Banks are merely illustrative of interethnic disputes. Both Eric Yamamoto, discussing the evolving dynamics in a post–civil rights America and a future "nation of minorities," and Bill Piatt, discussing Black-Brown relations in their historical and social context, offer insights to interethnic conflict.[9]

As I have discussed in the context of conflict between critical race scholars of different races and ethnicities, conflict and competition between the groups can be resolved in various ways. One option is for all minority groups to be considered "Black." Until about ten years ago, for instance, critical race scholars often equated "minority" with "Black," either not accounting for other minority interests or assuming they were synonymous with African American interests. This kind of generalization, however, ignores the diversity among minority groups (and, indeed, within a minority group). Another alternative is for the groups to compete directly with one another, to fight over resources and status. This approach, however, may degenerate into "racing to the bottom," where the different groups argue that they are the most disadvantaged, most discriminated against, and hence most worthy of attention. Finally, the parties could try to work constructively and collectively toward goals that in the aggregate and in the longer term would benefit each group and society in general.[10]

6. But how do you get groups with such different political agendas and historical memories to work together constructively and collectively? Francisco Valdes suggests that the process begins with a commitment to a philosophy of "interculturalism."[11] Interculturalism rejects polarized social and legal visions and instead recognizes that

> As Americans, we are bound together by heritage and circumstance; as Americans, we live under the same Constitution and occupy the same land; as Americans, we must find ways to live together. An Intercultural approach therefore would place a premium on acceptance and accommodation (not merely toleration) as overarching values of the law's commitment to liberty/equality ideals. Interculturalism thus would combine the commitment to liberty/equality for all in fact with a self-conscious use of the law and its processes to mediate the nation's historic and continuing non-liberty/inequality conflicts.

Eric Yamamoto proposes a four-dimensional approach:[12]

> [W]hat follows are the dimensions of an approach for inquiring into and acting on intergroup tensions marked both by conflict and distrust and by a desire for peaceable and productive relations. These dimensions of interracial justice inquiry are characterized by the four "Rs." The first dimension is *recognition*. It asks racial group members to recognize, and empathize with, the anger and hope of those wounded; to acknowledge the disabling constraints imposed by one group on another and the resulting group wounds; to identify related justice grievances often underlying current group conflict; and to critically examine stock stories of racial group attributes and interracial relations ostensibly legitimating those disabling constraints and justice grievances. The second is *responsibility*: It suggests that amid struggles over identity and power, racial groups can be simultaneously subordinated in some relationships and subordinating in others. In some situations, a group's power is both enlivened and limited by social and economic conditions and political alignments. Responsibility therefore asks racial groups to assess carefully the dynamics of racial group agency in imposing disabling constraints on others and, when appropriate, accepting group responsibility for healing resulting wounds.
>
> The third dimension is *reconstruction*. It entails active steps (performance) toward healing the social and psychological wounds resulting from disabling group constraints. Those performative acts might include apologies by aggressors and, when

appropriate, forgiveness by those injured and a joint reframing of stories of group identities and intergroup relations. The fourth dimension, closely related to the third, is *reparation*. It seeks to repair the damage to the material conditions of racial group life in order to attenuate one group's power over another. This means material changes in the structure of the relationship (social, economic, political) to guard against "cheap reconciliation," in which healing efforts are "just talk."

7. Erdman's article on Polish Americans can be studied in a number of ways. While American society tends to view an ethnic group as homogeneous, static in their values and traditions, and generally amicable as a community, her study illustrates how inaccurate these generalizations may be. In addition, Erdman's study can be used to initiate a discussion on immigrants—the conflicts they encounter and the dispute resolution systems they create to resolve them.

Jerold Auerbach has written extensively about the experiences of immigrants from Europe and Asia during the early years of the twentieth century. Prompted by unfamiliarity, discomfort, and often distrust of the American legal system, immigrant communities developed their own dispute resolution systems. Italian, Greek, Turkish, and Bulgarian immigrants, for instance, often relied on a *padrone* system to ease their transition to America. The *padrone*, a powerful authority figure, often acted as employment broker, provider of social services, and arbitrator of disputes. Scandinavian American communities in North Dakota and Minnesota often resorted to a conciliation process based on their cultural heritage. In Norway, for instance, "good men" had served as conciliators in private proceedings from which lawyers were excluded. Chinatown in the United States developed internal mediation processes that were often organized around the clans and villages from which the Chinese immigrants had come. And Jewish immigrants from Eastern Europe created arbitration and conciliation courts that at times served as centers for community and religious cohesion.[13]

While many consider Asians a single ethnic group, there are myriad ethnicities within this larger category. Eiichiro Azuma tells of the interethnic conflict between Japanese immigrants and their other Asian immigrant neighbors in Walnut Grove, California, between 1908 and 1941. Azuma documents the successive influxes and interethnic conflicts between Chinese, Japanese, East Indian, and Filipino immigrants into a small farming community where a white elite monopolized the town property and farm areas. As a means of survival, the Japanese immigrants found it "necessary to ingratiate themselves with the ruling class by demonstrating their profitability and desirability in the local economy." The interethnic conflicts also caused them to construct "negative ethnic/racial biases" against the other Asian groups.[14]

8. Recent years particularly have witnessed increased writings on Native Americans and their approach to dispute resolution. With more than five hundred tribal nations in the United States, there are many variations in traditions. Navajo concepts of justice, as described by Chief Justice of the Navajo Nation Robert Yazzie, illustrate one.[15] He distinguishes between "vertical" justice in the Anglo-European judicial system and "horizontal" justice used in traditional Navajo peacemaking.

A "vertical" system of justice is one which relies upon hierarchies and power. That is, judges sit above the parties, lawyers, jurors and other participants in court proceedings. The Anglo-European justice system uses rank, and the coercive power which goes with rank, to address conflicts. Power is the active element in the process. Judges have the power to directly affect the lives of the disputants for better or worse. Parties to a dispute have limited power and control over the process. A decision is dictated from on high by the judge, and that decision is an order or judgment which parties must obey or else face a penalty. The goal of the vertical system or adversarial law is to punish wrongdoers and teach them a lesson. For example, defendants in criminal cases are punished by jail and fines. In civil cases, one party wins and the other party is punished with a loss. Adversarial law offers only a win-lose solution; it is a zero-sum game. The Navajo justice system, on the other hand, prefers a win-win solution.

The "horizontal" model of justice is in clear contrast to the "vertical" system of justice. The horizontal justice model uses a horizontal line to portray equality: no person is above another. A better description of the horizontal model, and one often used by Indians to portray their thought, is a circle. In a circle, there is no right or left, nor is there a beginning or an end; every point (or person) on the line of a circle looks to the same center as the focus. The circle is the symbol of Navajo justice because it is perfect, unbroken, and a simile of unity and oneness. It conveys the image of people gathering together for discussion.

Horizontal justice thus emphasizes group solidarity and restoring the welfare of the community.

There also have emerged some intriguing descriptions of traditional Native Canadian tools for conflict resolution, such as Michelle LeBaron Duryea and Jim Potts's article on the uses of stories and legends, Marg Huber's explanation of the medicine wheel, and Teresa James's materials on "circle sentencing."[16] Some pieces address the conflict between Native American priorities and the priorities of competing groups, such as Douglas Ackerman's piece on the scientific community's and Native Americans' differing perspectives on ancient human remains and Jennifer Nutt Carleton's piece contrasting the U.S. government and Native Americans' interpretation of the "best interest" of Indian children.[17]

While these authors describe distinctly different approaches to dispute resolution, a parallel trend is for indigenous communities to rely increasingly on formal court systems modeled after the Anglo-American legal system. Robert Porter explains what he thinks is at stake:[18]

Because of the disparity in the fundamental cultural values underlying native and American societies, it is reasonable to conclude that Indian nations that have adopted litigation as their sole or primary means of formally resolving interpersonal conflict increase the likelihood that their members will focus exclusively on the vindication of their individual rights, and thus, marginalize their relationship to each other and their communities.

As this process continues and individual tribal members continue to adopt this defining aspect of American cultural behavior, it is likely that tribal communities . . . will become increasingly indistinct from American society at large. Ultimately, tribal nationhood and sovereignty will deteriorate to the point where the dominant society, and maybe even the native people themselves, will no longer desire disparate treatment of indigenous people as members of separate sovereign nations. When that time comes, assimilation will have reached the point where the indigenous population has become extinct.

9. The cultural defense has been used in domestic abuse cases, as described in Coleman's article. Domestic violence, prototypically abuse of women by their male partners, is of concern to American society generally but also to particular ethnic groups. Researchers have explored, for instance, how Latina/o, Native American, and Asian American cultures offer distinct explanations for why abuse occurs and suggest remedies that incorporate cultural norms.[19]

10. Coleman's article on the cultural defense and Higgins's article on international women's rights in Part 2 offer some interesting comparisons. While both authors recognize arguments for localizing or contextualizing conflicts involving women, they are ultimately critical of cultural relativism. Both articles, however, discuss cultural relativism in situations where women are typically the victims or socially restricted by cultural norms, so one wonders to what extent their critiques of cultural relativism can be generalized to other situations. Part 4 offers yet another perspective on issues of cultural relativism in the context of ethical dilemmas in international business.

Teaching Ideas

1. Explore how conflict and conflict resolution might be "racialized." Consider a particular dispute or consider in general: What difference would the race or ethnicity of the following individuals make?

    the parties to the dispute (What if they were both White, both Black, or one of each race? What if one or both are Latino/a, Asian American, or Native American?)

    the third-party decision maker or facilitator (e.g., the judge, mediator, or village elder)

    the representatives of the parties (e.g., the lawyers)

    those most affected by the process or the outcome, either directly or indirectly

In what ways can the procedural and substantive rules, institutions, or issues be racialized?

2. What stereotypes do you have about each of the major ethnic groups? How do our stereotypes about these groups affect how we perceive disputes in which they are participants? What if you could show that some of these stereotypes are accurate for the ethnic group as a whole? What are the problems with using these generalizations to predict a given individual's behavior, attitudes, or values?

3. Identify your own ethnicity. Perhaps you would describe it as Latino/a, African American, Native American, or European American—or perhaps in more specific terms, such as Haitian American, Mexican American, Cambodian American, Seneca Indian, Jewish American, or Irish American.

In what ways has your ethnicity affected your approach to dispute resolution? What ethnic values and traditions have you incorporated into your own dispute resolution philosophy?

4. Consider the following prediction: based on current immigration and growth trends, Americans of African, Hispanic, and Asian ethnicity will constitute approximately half of the U.S. workforce of major U.S. cities within the next twenty years. How will this demographic profile affect the kinds of disputes in the United States and the ways in which these disputes will be resolved?

5. Identify a controversial dispute at your law school or in your community. Discuss how the conflict would be analyzed and resolved under the principles described in Manu Aluli Meyer's article about ho'oponopono. Better still, role-play resolving the dispute by going through the stages described in the article and having students in the roles of the haku and other participants in the peacemaking process.

6. Mary Gentile describes nine reasoning patterns and cognitive strategies that make it difficult for us to understand alternative ways of viewing the world. These patterns—based on the work of Mary Ann Glendon, Deborah Tannen, Shelby Steele, Cornel West, Chris Argyris, and others—often restrict our problem-solving in issues triggered by the impacts of race, ethnicity, and gender.[20]

7. Finally, Ellen Summerfield, in *Crossing Cultures through Film*,[21] describes how to use films to explore cultural differences and suggests specific films for various purposes.

NOTES

1. Carrie Menkel-Meadow, "The Trouble with the Adversary System in a Post-Modern, Multi-Cultural World," 1 *Journal of the Institute for the Study of Legal Ethics* 49 (1996).

2. Isabelle R. Gunning, "Diversity Issues in Mediation: Controlling Negative Cultural Myths," *Journal of Dispute Resolution* 55 (1995).

3. Thomas Kochman, "Black and White Cultural Styles in Pluralistic Perspective," in Gary R. Weaver, ed., *Culture, Communication and Conflict: Readings in Intercultural Relations* (Needham Heights, MA: Ginn Press, 1994), 285–304.

4. Cynthia R. Mabry, "African Americans 'Are Not Carbon Copies' of White Americans—The Role of African American Culture in Mediation of Family Disputes," 13 *Ohio State Journal on Dispute Resolution* 405 (1998).

5. Diane LeResche, "Comparison of the American Mediation Process with a Korean-American Harmony Restoration Process," 9 *Mediation Quarterly* 323 (Summer 1992).

6. Derrick Bell, *And We Are Not Saved: The Elusive Quest for Racial Justice* (New York: Basic Books 1987), chaps. 4, 5, 9.

7. Pat K. Chew, "Asian Americans: The 'Reticent' Minority and Their Paradoxes," 36 *William and Mary Law Review* 1 (1994).

8. Bernice A. Pescosolido, Elizabeth Grauerholz, and Melissa A. Milkie, "Culure and Conflict: The Portrayal of Blacks in U.S. Children's Picture Books through the Mid- and Late-Twentieth Century," 62 *American Sociological Review* 443, 460–462 (1997).

9. Eric K. Yamamoto, *Interracial Justice: Conflict and Reconciliation in Post–Civil Rights America* (New York: New York University Press, 1999); Bill Piatt, *Black and Brown in America: The Case for Cooperation* (New York: New York University Press, 1997). See also Lisa C. Ikemoto, "Traces of the Master Narrative in the Story of African American/ Korean American Conflict: How We Constructed 'Los Angeles,'" 66 *Southern California Law Review* 1581 (1993); and R. L. Robinson, "The Other Against Itself: Deconstructing the Violent Discourse between Korean and African Americans," 67 *Southern California Law Review* 15, 17–35, 64–85 (1993).

10. Pat K. Chew, "Toward a Community of Critical Race Scholars: Racing to the Bottom . . . or What?" (paper presented at the Yale Law School, November 1997). See also J. M. Balkin, "The Constitution of Status," 106 *Yale Law Journal* 2313 (1997), describing status conflict and status competition among various social groups, including groups defined by race, religion, gender, and sexual orientation; and Alexandra Natapoff, Note: "Trouble in Paradise: Equal Protection and the Dilemma of Interminority Group Conflict," 47 *Stanford Law Review* 1059 (1995), describing different approaches to constructing a multiminority jurisprudence including color-blindness, bipolarity, and ranking.

11. Francisco Valdes, "Diversity and Discrimination in Our Midst: Musings on Consti-

tutional Schizophrenia, Cultural Conflict, and 'Interculturalism' at the Threshold of a New Century," 5 *Saint Thomas Law Review* 293, 352 (1993).

12. Yamamoto, *Interracial Justice*, 174–175.

13. Jerold S. Auerbach, *Justice without Law?* (New York: Oxford University Press, 1983), 69–93.

14. Eiichiro Azuma, "Interethnic Conflict under Racial Subordination: Japanese Immigrants and Their Asian Neighbors in Walnut Grove, California, 1908–1941," 20(2) *Ambrosia Journal* 27–56 (1994).

15. Robert Yazie, "Life Comes from It: Navaho Justice Concepts," 24 New Mexico Law Review 175, 177, 180 (Spring 1994). See also Philmer Bluehouse and James W. Zion, "Hozhooji Naat'aanii: The Navajo Justice and Harmony Ceremony," 10 *Mediation Quarterly* 327 (Summer 1991); Carole E. Goldberg, "Overextended Borrowing: Tribal Peacemaking Applied in Non-Indian Disputes," 72 *Washington Law Review* 1003 (1997); Chief Justice Tom Tso, "The Process of Decision Making in Tribal Courts," 31 *Arizona Law Review* 225 (1989).

16. Michelle LeBaron Duryea and Jim Potts, "Story and Legend: Powerful Tools for Conflict Resolution," 10 *Mediation Quarterly* 387 (Summer 1993); Marg Huber, "Mediation around the Medicine Wheel," 10 *Mediation Quarterly* 355 (Summer 1993); Teresa M. James, *Circle Sentencing* (report to the Supreme Court of the Northwest Territories, April 23, 1993) (on file with the editor).

17. Douglas W. Ackerman, "Kennewick Man: The Meaning of 'Cultural Affiliation' and 'Major Scientific Benefit' in the Native American Graves Protection and Reparation Act," 33 *Tulsa Law Journal* 359 (1997); Jennifer Nutt Carleton, "The Indian Child Welfare Act: A Study in the Codification of the Ethnic Best Interests of the Child," 81 *Marquette Law Review* 21 (1997).

18. Robert B. Porter, "Strengthening Tribal Sovereignty through Peacemaking: How the Anglo-American Legal Tradition Destroys Indigenous Societies," 29 *Columbia Human Rights Law Review* 235, 273–274 (1997).

19. E.g., Jenny Rivera, "Domestic Violence against Latinas by Latino Males: An Analysis of Race, National Origin, and Gender Differentials," 14 *Boston College Third World Law Journal* 231 (1994); Gloria Valencia-Weber and Christine P. Zuni, "Domestic Violence and Tribal Protection of Indigenous Women in the United States," 69 *St. John's Law Review* 69 (1995); James W. Zion and Elsie B. Zion, "Hozho'Sokee'—Stay Together Nicely: Domestic Violence under Navajo Common Law," 25 *Arizona State Law Journal* 407 (1993); Donna Coker, 'Enhancing Autonomy for Battered Women: Lessons from Navajo Peacemaking," 47 *UCLA Law Review* 1 (1999); Karin Wang, Note: "Battered Asian American Women: Community Responses from the Battered Women's Movement and the Asian American Community," 3 *Asian Law Journal* 151 (1996).

20. Mary C. Gentile, "Ways of Thinking about and across Difference," Note No. 9-395-117, Harvard Business School (1995).

21. Ellen Summerfield, *Crossing Cultures through Film* (Yarmouth, Maine: Intercultural Press, 1993).

Part IV

Global Perspectives

Introduction

Part 4 explores different global perspectives on culture and conflict, drawing from a range of geographical contexts. I have grouped readings on conceptually linked topics that raise issues with transnational implications. All the works also share a common purpose: they prompt us to reflect, to question, and at times to reframe our own cultural model of conflict. As John Paul Lederach urged in Part 1, there are professional and personal benefits not only to trying to understand and respect another cultural perspective but to trying to perceive the dispute within the other culture's frame of reference—to move from sympathy to empathy with another culture.

Some of the readings directly compare and critique the "Western" model of conflict with other cultural models. Other readings explore constructs, such as "face" or apology, that play integral roles in conflict resolution in some cultures but are ambivalently viewed in other societies. Some articles describe cultural values and dispute resolution mechanisms, such as those in the Gypsy culture, that are alien to most cultures but are internally coherent to Gypsy culture. Some make comparisons between cultures in more philosophical terms, while others, such as the reading on cultural relativism in international business decision making, consider issues in concrete and practical fact patterns.

We begin with the inquiry: Why is it that the norm in some societies is peace and in others it is conflict? Bruce D. Bonta's insightful analysis of dozens of peaceful societies reveals that these societies hold particular fundamental worldviews. Many make different assumptions about what is effective in deterring conflict, questioning, for instance, Western views on the role of punishment or the need for outside authorities such as armies or formal governments.

The next set of readings offers further opportunities to compare our Western view of conflict with others. At the same time, these readings introduce various disputes between groups in a particular region, namely, the Middle East—illustrating both the complexities and the difficulties of resolving some long-standing historical disputes. Paul E. Salem's article juxtaposes premises of Western conflict resolution with those from an Arab perspective. He believes, for instance, that the West, as a present successful "empire," is likely to adhere to an ideology of peace because such would reinforce a status quo that is favorable to its dominant position. In contrast, the Arab and Islamic world is in a time of comparative decline, and thus the prospects of conflict, instability, and transitions in power are attractive. At the same time, some major currents of modern political Arab thinking view conflict and struggle as progressive and purifying. Mohammed Abu-Nimer follows with a case analysis of conflict in a Middle Eastern context and shifts our attention to a community dispute in a Palestinian village in northern Israel. The dispute is between the Druze community, which tends to support Israeli government policies, and the minority Christian community, which tends to identify with the broader Palestinian identity and the Arab world. It is interesting to note, however, how the process of resolution focuses more on restoring order to local community relationships than on broader political agendas.

In intransigent conflicts in the Middle East and elsewhere, it sometimes seems that increased communication between the parties worsens rather than facilitates the resolution process. Z. D. Gurevitch offers a basic but intuitively compelling explanation. Suppose that two individuals hold fundamentally different assumptions about a conflict; they do not share a "common world of understanding." In order to make progress, Gurevitch proposes, the individuals must have the "ability to *not* understand," that is, to recognize that the other is perceived as "strange." To illustrate, he describes an attempted dialogue between Jewish-Israeli and Arab-Palestinian teachers who are meeting to discuss the two cultural and political worlds that exist within their educational system, yet oppose each other with respect to the Arab-Israeli conflict. Marc Howard Ross also offers an explanation of intransigent conflicts, particularly long-standing ethnic conflict. While relevant to the Middle Eastern context, his comments also can be extrapolated to many other parts of the world. Describing what he calls a culture of ethnic conflict, Ross explains that psychocultural dynamics often prompt ethnic groups to tighten the boundaries between their group and all outsiders and to interpret past and current events in ways that fuel fear and anger toward one another.

This part then shifts gears and explores two topics that, at least ostensibly, are considered very "foreign" to American society. The first set of readings considers "face" and apology, particularly in the Chinese context. The second set of readings considers the Gypsy culture and dispute resolution especially as it deals with the concepts of impurity (*marime*).

Legal scholar Mari Matsuda recalls an experience in Micronesia that suggests alternative ways of thinking about such things as apology and fault determination as part of the dispute resolution process. The next piece by anthropologist Hsien Chin Hu is the often-cited seminal piece on "face." Although there have been more current research and writings on the topic, this classic piece continues to capture particularly well the sometimes obscure concept and its nuances. She describes the concept of face as Chinese, yet one wonders how universal (albeit under different labels) the underlying construct is. Glenn R. Butterton's piece briefly explains the concepts of *li* and *fa*. Butterton's and Hu's pieces together offer us a framework from which to understand some key principles in traditional Chinese dispute resolution processes.

The readings on the Roma, more commonly known as the Gypsies, ask us to shift gears again. Because of the Gypsies' steadfast desire for cultural insularity, it has only been relatively recently that detailed information about Gypsy culture and their approaches to dispute resolution has become available to non-Gypsies. Unlike cultures that have defined territorial jurisdictions, Gypsies are transnational in that their "communities" are in numerous countries and may even be migratory. But Gypsy culture is distinguished in other ways as well. Walter Otto Weyrauch and Maureen Anne Bell's article explains the core Gypsy concept of *marime*, a highly undesirable state of impurity linked to sexual taboos and hygiene. It then describes a dispute resolution system for various problems, including *marime*-related violations. Finnish sociologist Martti Gronfors's account of the Finnish Roma illustrates variations among Gypsy groups. He describes "blood feuding" as the primary mechanism for serious harms, the institution of nonmarriage, and the indispensable and functional relationship between the two.

In Thomas Donaldson's piece, we revisit cultural relativism in the context of international business. He offers guidelines for U.S. managers doing business abroad who face ethical dilemmas created by the cultural norms of the foreign country in which they are operating. Rather than a general rule for all situations, Donaldson suggests a case-by-case approach that acknowledges both American values and the values of the foreign country.

Finally, from a book by Marjorie Shostak, an articulate African woman named Nisa recounts her marriage and other interpersonal relationships. As she describes various disputes she has with her husband Besa, we are struck by how the type of intramarital conflict she describes could occur in virtually all cultures. Yet while the type of conflict is universal, Nisa's description of how she, her husband, their families, and !Kung society deal with the disputes is unique to her tribe and specific culture. Nisa's narrative allows us to reflect on how one's culture shapes the underlying assumptions, values, and approaches one brings to conflict.

Chapter 28

Conflict Resolution among Peaceful Societies
The Culture of Peacefulness

Bruce D. Bonta

And forgive us our trespasses
As we forgive those who trespass against us.
—From "The Lord's Prayer," Matthew 6:12

Nyam, the articulate son of a former headman, had been accused of planting durian trees on lands that traditionally belonged to others. In recent years the Semai, peaceful aboriginal people who live in the rugged mountains of the Malay Peninsula, have been harvesting durian fruit and packing it out to the road which comes up from the lowlands, so they can sell it and buy the consumer goods that have become essential to them—tobacco, machetes, radios, and so forth. Planting trees on other properties threatened and angered Nyam's neighbors, some of whom belonged to different families. Tensions were mounting.

Tidn, the headman of the village affected by Nyam's actions, recognized the potential for conflict so he convened a *becharaa'*, a proceeding which the villagers use to try to resolve disputes. Nyam and his relatives were invited to attend to discuss and settle the matter. Since his land also had been invaded by Nyam, Tidn was a party to the dispute; he invited Entoy, headman from a nearby valley, to preside over the *becharaa'*. Nyam arrived near dusk at the Semai village.

Conversation was casual, as everyone was well acquainted and was generally familiar with the nature of the conflict. Nyam, a picture of studied indifference, talked animatedly with various people. After a while, the villagers gathered in a circle and the formal discussions began with preliminary speeches about the importance of settling the dispute before it got out of hand. Each of the parties to the conflict gave his version of events, justifying his actions in an unemotional manner. Nyam denied some of his trespasses and sought to rationalize others. Speakers advanced their points of view, but no one acted as witnesses except for the principals in the case; there was no direct confrontation or cross-examination. The

Reprinted by permission of Sage Publications Ltd. from B. D. Bonta, *Conflict Resolution among Peaceful Societies: The Culture of Peacefulness*, vol. 33(4) *Journal of Peace Research*, 403–406, 406–416 (Sage Publications Ltd., 1996).

speeches went on and on, with people frequently talking past one another and not answering the comments of others.

When no one had anything more to say—points had been emphasized and re-emphasized until all were exhausted from the proceedings—the *becharaa'* was ready to be concluded. It was obvious to everyone that Nyam's actions were wrong, but the consensus was that he could keep and use the trees that he had already planted, though he must plant no more. Entoy could have levied a small fine on Nyam but everyone felt it was more important for the group to keep its harmony than to treat the guilty party too roughly. Entoy lectured the assembled people on the importance of their tradition of unity, peacefulness, sharing food, and not fighting. He made it clear to all that the matter had been completely settled and that no one was allowed to bring it up again.

The Semai are among more than forty societies that have evolved highly peaceful lifestyles, that rarely if ever resort to violence. U.S. citizens are among the thousands of societies that do use violence, if need be, to settle their differences. The processes of settling disputes in the USA, such as the jury trial, are based on assumptions about conflict that differ from those of the peaceful societies. The goal of this article is to explore those differences. The basic issue is to gain an understanding of why dozens of peaceful peoples are able to resolve conflicts nonviolently virtually all the time, while the rest of the world is not so successful. As the examination of conflict resolution in these small-scale societies proceeds, one fundamental fact emerges: the peacefulness of their conflict resolution is based, primarily, on their world-views of peacefulness—a complete rejection of violence. That argument may appear to be circular, but a careful look at conflict resolution in those societies seems to support it.

In contrast, the Western world-view boils down to all acceptance of the inevitability of conflict and violence. Peace and conflict studies, for Western scholars, is frequently a process of understanding the reasons for conflict, and the study of conflict resolution often focuses on strategies for preventing and resolving disputes. Some of the major facets of Western beliefs that will form a framework for this essay include the following concepts: [(1) conflict is a normal aspect of all societies; (2) punishment deters conflict and violence; (3) armies are necessary to deter external conflict; and (4) conflict is best managed through political structures].

The purpose of this investigation is therefore to examine conflict and conflict resolution among the peaceful societies and to compare them with the corresponding Western beliefs. Since much of the literature of conflict resolution is based on the experiences of the thousands of relatively violent societies, a balance is needed from the perspective of peaceful peoples. In this paper I attempt to show that conflict resolution in peaceful societies is founded on overarching world-views that conflicts are the exception, not the norm, and that they are neither reasonable nor desirable. Conflicts, to these peoples, must be avoided as much as possible, resolved as quickly as possible, and harmony restored as soon as possible in order for people to live peacefully with one another and with outsiders. In order to achieve nonviolent conflict resolution in practice, individuals and groups of people should rely on themselves to settle disputes within their groups as well as conflicts with other peoples; furthermore, they should use resolution strategies that dissipate tensions as well as settle the issues. This resolution should be achieved as much as possible without the threat of punishment (other than ostracism).

Strategies of Conflict Resolution

Peaceful societies use a variety of strategies to try to prevent, control, manage, and resolve the conflicts that do come up, such as the Semai *becharaa*.' An examination of these various strategies provides an overview of the common processes used by these peoples to resolve conflicts, and helps set the stage for the discussion that follows.

Self-Restraint

The literature explicitly describes the ways that the Ifaluk, Tahitians, Paliyan, and Toraja use variations of self-restraint as a means of moving away from conflict situations once they arise. (Their approach is doubtless followed by other peaceful societies, such as the Amish, Mennonites, and Hutterites, though the literature about those peoples is not as explicit on the subject.) These peoples feel that heightened emotional states lead quickly to further trouble, so they actively try to dissipate their emotions whenever a conflict seems possible. A first-stage approach for a Toraja individual experiencing heated emotion is to remind himself or herself that any open expression of the feeling might be dangerous: the expression of such feelings would be ridiculed, might lead to hostile supernatural actions, and would open oneself to serious illness.

Negotiation

Negotiation is often considered in a positive light by Western writers, particularly when it is broadly defined as the interaction between parties to a dispute who work toward an agreement without the intervention of third parties who might make compulsory decisions. But the literature on the peaceful societies has little to say about direct negotiations by disputants. People in many of these societies do not want to confront one another directly, and they prefer indirection rather than assertion, inference rather than confrontation. The parties to a conflict are encouraged to settle their problems on an internal level, through self-restraint, but not necessarily through the confrontational tactics of direct negotiation. Other techniques are more effective.

Separation

At least ten of the peaceful societies separate in order to avoid conflicts (which is equivalent to resolving them). Clearly, walking away from a dispute is one of the most favored ways of resolving conflicts among these peoples. Among the

Malapandaram, Paliyan, Birhor, Buid, and !Kung, individuals, including spouses, separate when a quarrel cannot be easily resolved, and whole communities will split apart to avoid conflicts. The literature about these peoples is filled with examples of individuals or whole communities moving away from an area, in some cases quite abruptly, because they faced conflicts. Among the Toraga and Balinese, separations to avoid conflicts appear from the literature to be somewhat less permanent than among the other five peoples mentioned above. The historical literature about some of the Western peaceful peoples—the Amish, Hutterites, and Mennonites—makes it clear that they moved away from domination and conflict by stronger societies numerous times. While they would doubtless not abandon their communities and flee on a moment's notice because of a minor conflict, there is no question that they might well move again if faced with an unresolvable conflict with the larger society.

Intervention

Western writers on conflict resolution concentrate heavily on the importance of third-party intervention in disputes. Among peaceful peoples, intervention by others is an effective technique for resolving conflicts. In several of these societies, the ethic of avoiding conflicts is so strong that it is incumbent on bystanders to become involved in virtually any circumstances where controversies threaten to become serious or where a conflict situation seems to be developing. Among some peoples, certain individuals are noted as being particularly skilled at helping defuse conflicts, but in others the literature indicates that any bystander will step in to mediate. The common thread of these mediators is their desire to get a dialogue going—and keep the potential contestants talking until the tensions are defused.

Meetings

Humor and meetings, such as the Semai *becharaa'* mentioned earlier, are specific techniques used by third parties, but they deserve to be mentioned separately because they are frequently used by several peaceful societies. As with the other strategies, the purpose of the meeting is to lessen tensions more than it is to confront or decide, though those elements may also be present. These meetings provide forums for the airing of hostilities: frequently the simple discussion of grievances is enough to defuse problems. The meetings also serve to contain conflicts before they can disrupt society, either by minimizing issues as private rather than public concerns, or by restricting involvement in order to allow informal mechanisms of social control to operate.

Humor

Humor is undoubtedly a useful strategy for reducing tensions and resolving conflicts in many societies, but it has been mentioned only a few times in the literature of peaceful peoples. The !Kung try hard to maintain a joking atmosphere in their camps, frequently pointing out one another's faults in a facetious manner to resolve their tensions. When a leader in a Paliyan community becomes involved in helping to resolve a conflict, he will often use joking or soothing to defuse the situation. If a Tristan Islander ever lost his temper in a quarrel he would have that scar on his reputation for life; people who defuse tense situations with jokes gain general respect. The Inuit joke to avoid and defuse conflicts; joking also allows them to confront problems with enough ambiguity that grievances can be aired without fear of provoking others. In the past, the Inuit had song duels to resolve conflicts in a humorous fashion before they became serious enough to provoke violence, and to laugh off animosities and return to friendship, or at least restraint.

These strategies seem to dissipate tensions and resolve issues effectively when conflicts do arise in the peaceful societies. In some societies authority figures make judgments while in others the people decide by consensus, but the overall effect is the same—healing, continuation of the community, or separation. Furthermore, the traditional forms that those strategies take among these peoples appear to be important factors in their success. That is, peoples are conscious of their own traditional ways of handling problems and seem able to keep the peace in part through the force of their traditions. For these peoples, the ways they resolve disputes are logical and effective—and they seem to work. When the traditional ways are not used, conflicts can result. For instance, the failure of a group of Buid to follow their traditional meeting-style of conflict resolution (called a *tul-tulan*) on one occasion resulted in tragedy.

Conflict Is a Normal Aspect of All Societies

Some scholars have maintained that conflict and violence is the normal condition of small-scale societies, which typically rely on a superior state authority to prevent warfare. Others argue that all societies have to contend with violence. The literature on the peaceful peoples flatly contradicts these assertions. While violence exists in very modest amounts in some of these societies, in others it appears to be rare or completely absent.

There are a few basic differences in strategies for resolving conflicts among these twenty-four societies. Some of the ones that experience occasional violence use moderately aggressive techniques for resolving disputes, such as stylized rhetorical speaking referred to as "talking" by some anthropologists. When the !Kung are discussing a contentious issue and their emotions begin to rise, they may pour out their thoughts at a very rapid rate—a sudden, spontaneous discussion by the various people involved with the issue. When the G/wi have a conflict that is threatening to escalate, one party to the problem will talk out the difficulty to a third person within the hearing of the whole band, and the other party may answer to a fourth, again so everyone will hear. When the Temair become too angry for mediation to work, instead of a face-to-face confrontation the angry people may conduct night time harangues so everyone in the longhouse can hear without specifically naming individuals. These practices allow everyone to be a party to the dispute, to get feelings about an issue into the open without provoking direct confrontations, and to settle the contentious issues. They also save face for all participants, a universal need according to some.

On the other hand, many of the societies that almost never experience any violence tend to be meek and to have world-views that advocate meekness. For instance, the highly peaceful Chewong, Ifaluk, Paliyan, and Semai generally describe themselves as fearful people; the Batek, Chewong, Paliyan, and Semai flee from violence; and the Amish, Hutterites, Chewong, Semai, Tristan Islanders, and Yanadi are notable for their belief in nonresistance (not resisting aggression by the state or other individuals). But, while the most highly peaceful peoples are strongly characterized by a general fearfulness, passiveness, meekness, flight from conflict, and a belief in nonresistance, the societies which appear to take a more active role in promoting peacefulness do have patterns of occasional violence. There are elements of aggressiveness in these peoples—perhaps it could be described as an aggressive pursuit of nonviolence in resolving conflicts.

Punishment Deters Conflict and Violence

Western peoples believe that punishment is necessary to deter crime and violent conflict. They feel it creates fear in potential offenders that they will suffer as a result of their actions, and it is a just retribution for violations of the normal moral order. It seemed reasonable to look for evidence of punishment in the literature about these twenty-four societies to see if it is part of their conflict resolution practices. As it turns out, except for the punishment that parents in a few of these societies use for disciplining their children, these peoples use very little adult punishment. In fact, the absence of punishment appears to be one of the defining characteristics of a peaceful society. These peoples seem to rely on the strength of their other mechanisms to prevent and resolve conflicts peacefully and effectively. The threat of punishment is not needed, except for the practice of ostracism, a form of punishment. Ostracism is practiced by a range of societies worldwide to enforce social standards, according to Margaret Gruter and Roger D. Masters, who define it in general terms as "the general process of social rejection or exclusion." From the perspective of the peaceful peoples, ostracism may be defined as complete banishment from the society or, perhaps less severely, as rejection by a people of an individual's participation in some or all of the group's activities. The societies that use it at all use it quite infrequently, but the possibility is always there.

Probably the most dramatic practice of ostracism in this body of literature is the Amish strategy of shunning. If an Amish person has a problem accepting one of the rules of their church, and he or she refuses to give in to the will of the group, the individual will be ostracized by all members of the community, including the spouse, children, parents, siblings, and friends. No one may speak to the shunned person or hand food or other goods to him or her—food or other articles will be placed on a table for the shunned person to pick up. The person may continue to live at home and try to carry on a normal life—though that is, of course, nearly impossible. The Hutterites have a similar style of excommunicating members without expelling them from their colonies.

A comparable example can be found in Ladakh, where again ostracism does not necessarily mean the person is sent away from the community. If someone refuses to stop provocative or offensive behavior, the lamas may cease serving the religious needs of the individual, which would be highly demoralizing to a Ladakhi. No one would visit the ostracized person; no one would help the offender or his family in any endeavor; no one would offer food to, or accept food from, the individual; and there would be no possibilities of marriage alliances with other families. A harsh punishment such as that could be relieved only when the offender sought the pardon from the village civil and religious leaders.

Ostracism in other societies usually means totally excluding offenders from the group—for example, the Nubians—though in some cases it is done very gently. When a member of a G/wi band does not heed the consensus judgment of the group about a conflict, and when he ignores the barbed comments of others and does not mend his ways, the people may have to ease the offender out. This is done not by overt antagonism, but rather by subtly frustrating the offender, by misunderstanding his wishes on purpose, by not hearing him: by, in effect, rejecting him without causing him to feel rejected or offended. The process prompts the offender to feel disgusted with his life in the band, so that he'll leave of his own accord without feeling a need for revenge. Sometimes the offender will find another band to be more compatible and will settle into acceptable behavior patterns. Some G/wi, of course, never adapt and move about from band to band, accepted by all as individuals who have to be tolerated for a time.

Armies Are Necessary to Deter External Conflict

Many Western writers maintain that the existence of armies and the threat of military force is the only thing that keeps the peace between nations. States would invade one another constantly in their egocentric drives to acquire more territory, goods, trade markets, resources, and security, according to this argument, if it weren't for the certainty that the invaded state would fight back. This kind of argument is also extended to peaceful societies, which, it is argued, exist only in relation to, and through the sufferance of, more aggressive neighboring societies. These peaceful peoples must have relatively peaceful neighbors, live where they are relatively isolated from attack, live where flight from attack is a reasonable option, or be much stronger than potential attackers so that others wouldn't dare try an attack.

Some of the twenty-four peaceful societies under consideration here follow this generalization, at least superficially. The problem with the idea is that it views the relationship of the nonviolent society and the aggressive society only from the perspective of the latter: the peaceful society MUST be isolated from the strong society or it can't exist; it MUST be able to flee quickly from an attack by the neighboring violent people or it would quickly be destroyed. The literature on these twenty-four peoples and their relationships with dominating societies provides insights into this issue of peaceful peoples getting along with aggressive peoples—and it allows the simple generalizations to be challenged. Some of the peaceful societies fit those stereotypes but others do not.

Clearly, a few of the twenty-four peoples live in very isolated locations, such as the Ifaluk and the Tristan Islanders, who inhabit, respectively, islands in the Pacific and Atlantic Oceans. Other societies solve problems with outsiders, particularly with more powerful outsiders, by fleeing from danger. At the first sign of conflict, these peoples will abandon their villages and melt back into the forest, where they may stay for weeks or even years. But it is a mistake to assume that their relationships with their more powerful neighbors or the nations that they live in can be characterized only by isolation or flight from danger. They take their nonviolence seriously—as a positive approach to human relationships and as the basis of their lives—and avoiding conflict is only part of their logic. Conflict resolution, such as the Semai *becharaa'*, is more complex and ingenious than the simple term "separation" would imply. The Semai are highly committed to their peaceful ways, and they try hard to resolve conflicts with their more powerful neighbors, the Malay people, nonviolently. They have been invaded, dominated, and enslaved by the Malays for a long time, but they still agonize over the dilemma of how to continue to maintain their own ethic of peacefulness in the face of this domination; they do not easily accept the ethic of the aggressor.

A number of the peaceful peoples do have frequent contacts with outsiders and have been able to maintain their peacefulness despite it. The literature on these peoples suggests that they are able to get along with larger and more aggressive societies. Not all conflicts with people and government officials from outside their societies can be avoided, of course, yet they handle conflicts with outsiders in a similar fashion to their handling of internal conflicts—that is, peacefully.

The peaceful Anabaptist peoples that live in North America—the Mennonites, Hutterites, and Amish—have been persecuted for centuries but they have tried to settle conflicts with the larger societies in the same spirit of nonviolence that characterizes their internal relationships. For instance, during World War I draftees from these groups were punished, beaten, and tortured in U.S. military prisons, and civilians who refused to contribute money to the war effort through the purchase of war bonds were named in local newspapers, harassed, and physically abused by the local citizens. As a result of these experiences, the controversial Civilian Public Service program (CPS) of World War II, and a range of other factors, the basic beliefs of most Mennonites in nonresistance have been slowly changing. From the 1960s through the 1980s Mennonite commitment to "nonresistance" (taken from Matthew 5:39, "Do not resist one who is evil") has changed into a belief in "peacemaking," the feeling that they have a responsibility to engage the broader American and Canadian societies and work actively for peace, rather than avoid outsiders a nonresistance had previously implied.

The two other Anabaptist peoples, the Hutterites and the Amish, have not developed a spirit of engaging the larger societies of the USA and Canada as the Mennonites have done; but they still have conflicts or the threats of conflicts with outsiders to deal with. The Hutterite colonies try to prevent conflicts from arising by fostering frequent contacts with their farming neighbors and by generous exchanges of farm produce. The Amish have problems resolving individual conflict situations with outsiders since they cannot file lawsuits against others—that would violate their belief in nonresistance. Business competitors, buyers, and suppliers, knowing of that prohibition, take advantage of them by cheating and exploiting them.

Much as they say they do not deal with the outside society, in fact the Amish have developed a pattern of adjustments to external conflicts. Non-Amish leaders and supporters of the Amish help them informally to resolve their conflicts with outsiders in positions of power and influence, sometimes through helpful advocacy, sometimes through finding creative solutions to their problems. If an Amish person were taken into court, he would never contest charges and hire an attorney because of his belief in nonresistance, but an attorney friend might go along, just to sit there and make sure the courts acted fairly. The lawyer would not be paid, but the Amish would give him some garden vegetables or freshly baked bread. When the Pennsylvania government passed a new state requirement that all teachers had to be certified and had to meet minimum educational requirements, which the Amish teachers in their one-room schoolhouses couldn't do, the Amish got around the regulation by declaring that all their teachers were substitutes, and thus exempt from the regulation. The rural Amish people have little concern or interest in these pressures, counterpressures, and maneuverings—they believe in nonresistance and, if necessary, migration to avoid problems. Even their leaders do not frame their advocacy in the terms of the outsiders: rather, they see their activity as "working things out," being helpful in resolving issues, and liberating officials from their constant need to obey rules.

Conflicts with outsiders are thus resolved by peaceful peoples in a variety of ways, but the conclusion from these examples is that armies, killing, or other forms of violence are never part of their thinking, as they are to the rest of the world. The non-Western peaceful peoples likewise, such as the Yanadi, try to resolve their conflicts with outsiders in fashions that are consistent with their overall commitments to peacefulness. The cumulative story is thus of peaceful peoples resolving conflicts with larger, more aggressive societies through meekness, active involvement, and attempts to resolve difficulties peacefully—in complete accord with their world-views.

Conflict Is Best Managed through Political Structures

Kenneth F. Boulding sees conflict management as extending from the family to the tribe, to the nation, to the superpower, to the evolving world government. "Conflict control is government," he writes, "and though government has broader functions than this, conflict control is perhaps its most important single task." The literature about the peaceful peoples suggests that avoiding governments may also provide a viable model for peacefully resolving conflicts.

In many traditional societies, people avoid calling in outside authorities and try to settle their internal conflicts themselves. Outside police are to be avoided if at all possible. The peaceful societies likewise try to keep their conflicts to themselves. The idea that an outside government or political structure is an essential part of solving their conflicts, or would even be helpful in such situations, would be alien to these peoples. They see government agencies as highly threatening and they avoid such outsiders as much as possible during conflicts, though there are some exceptions.

For instance, a peaceful Zapotec town avoids having government officials involved in the affairs of their community since people feel that they would be treated much as any other Mexican town—and they are convinced that their town is different from the rest in its opposition to violence. Likewise, Nubian communities don't reveal serious problems to outsiders, particularly to authorities such as the Egyptian police; they feel that the best chance for their villages to survive is to be ignored by authorities. The Amish also settle their conflicts within; an instance where an Amish man sued his own church officials in court because he was ostracized was exceedingly unusual. In fact, none of the peaceful peoples included in the group of twenty-four, to judge by the available literature, appear to rely on intervention by outside agencies of any kind, with the possible exception of the Mennonites, many of whom today no longer feel the strict need to remain absolutely separate from all government functions, particularly in Canada.

In the peaceful societies, conflicts are handled by the individual parties to the conflict and by the group—rarely by outsiders. Individuals are expected to deal with conflict situations by walking away from them, by laughing them off, by displacing their feelings of anger in various ways, by smiling and being pleasant to everyone, by actively socializing with people with whom they may have unpleasant inner feelings, and so on. Individuals should try to solve their problems internally if they can.

When that doesn't work, the parties to a conflict should resolve the issues between themselves, or, more frequently, bring them to larger groups of people or authority figures within the society for discussion and resolution. But even group resolutions of conflicts, such as the Semai *becharaa'*, rely on the group to foster the dissipation of tensions so that individual, personal controls may keep the peace. None of these societies rely on the power of people as a political body to enforce the peace, with the sole exception of the threat of ostracism. But if the ultimate approach to resolving difficult conflicts for Western peoples is outward, to the next larger political or government body, as Boulding asserts, the ultimate focus for the peaceful peoples (and many other traditional societies) is inward, toward individuals and the group.

World-View of Conflict Resolution

"Conflict is . . . inevitable in human life. . . . Eliminating conflict is clearly impossible, and likely undesirable, because of the close link between conflict and creative, constructive change" described David W. Augsbergur. Two decades earlier, Morton Deutsch expressed similar ideas, and popular writers often reflect this thinking: "Conflict is a necessary part of *every* marriage. . . . If there is no conflict . . . it is a sign that something is wrong with the marriage." Other scholars, though not necessarily so enthusiastic about conflict as those writers, consider it simply a cultural behavior, and as such not to be judged desirable or undesirable. These ideas reflect the predominant world-views of Western societies that proclaim the ideology of love, peace, cooperation, and generosity, but accept conflict, aggression, competition, and violence as inevitable aspects of human nature and human societies.[1] Conflict resolution, in this view, is just a process—a strategy or series of strategies for settling disputes.

Such attitudes toward conflict would not be shared by peaceful peoples. While many of them would recognize that conflict is a problem at times in their societies, none would see it as beneficial. The purpose of this section is to look at the (mostly) positive ways these peaceful societies view their lack of conflict—their world-views of peacefulness—and to compare those views with the thinking of Western writers.

To start with some Western thinking, scholars using cross-cultural data have sought to explain the phenomenon of conflict and conflict resolution based either on the structural factors in societies or on psychological/cultural elements. The social structural analysis concentrates on economic, political, and social organization as the source of conflict; the psychocultural approach focuses on deep-seated "we-they" conceptions of human opposition. The former argues that stronger ties, such as kinship, will reduce conflicts, while the latter sees ambiguity in social actions, and thus tries to explain why some disputes are far more intense than others. Based on his own extensive cross-cultural analysis, Marc Howard Ross feels that both have validity: psychocultural factors may determine the intensity of a conflict, while structural factors may point out the targets of hostile actions and the ways conflicts are organized. He argues that low-conflict societies are characterized by both a psychocultural atmosphere of warmth and affection and cross-cutting social structures.

These arguments, and the impressive amount of cross-cultural data assembled, make a lot of sense but are not completely supported by the literature on peaceful societies. Ross's description of the strong sense of interpersonal trust that exists in low-conflict societies, with a corresponding lack of fear of isolation and abandonment, is contradicted by Jean I. Briggs's writings on peaceful Inuit groups, Catherine A. Lutz's descriptions of the Ifaluk, Unni Wikan's work on the Balinese, and other writings about nonviolent people. These societies try to eliminate expressions of anger and aggression by developing fears, anxieties, and uncertainties in children about other people. If others are not to be depended on to love them, if affection and support can never be taken for granted, the children internalize a constant need to live up to the society's peaceful values.

Conflict resolution among the twenty-four peaceful societies, their culture of peacefulness, is based on more than psychocultural and social structures: just as significant are their world-views of peacefulness. Thomas Gregor touches on this when he points out that the ideologies and symbolic values that societies hold to are also critical elements in providing the basis of a peaceful (or a violent) society. Deutsch makes the same point in his so-called "crude law of social relations," namely that "the characteristic processes and effects elicited by a given type of social relationship (e.g., cooperative or competitive) also tend to elicit that type of social relationship." In other words, cooperation breeds cooperation, competition breeds competition. Likewise, Signe Howell and Roy Willis, introducing the peaceful societies included in their anthology, conclude that these peoples all place an emphasis "on peaceful interaction among the members of the society, and this emphasis is cosmologically constructed and morally embedded in a cosmological universe of meaning." The literature on the twenty-four societies considered for this essay shows that their peaceful conflict resolution practices are fostered by their beliefs in peacefulness, which are in turn bolstered by the successful practices. To Western analyst Herbert C. Kelman, "the goal of conflict resolution is to shape new political and social arrangements. . . . To the members of these peaceful societies, the goal of conflict resolution is to maintain social harmony through traditional means of prompting individuals to remember and act on their shared beliefs."

The basic reason for peacefulness in these societies is that the people are strongly opposed to actual physical violence and firmly in favor of nonviolence, in contrast to neighboring, and sometimes very similar, communities that may only pay lip service to the ideals of peace and are, in actual practice, far more violent. The peaceful peoples not only believe fervently in their world-views of nonviolence: in general, they have internalized those beliefs and adhere to them very strictly, using primarily internal controls to prevent and resolve conflicts, as has been discussed earlier. In other societies that claim they have nonviolent values, but have not really internalized them; people rely primarily on external controls for preventing and resolving conflicts.

In addition, the point can't be emphasized too strongly that the peacefulness of these societies is not based on utopian thinking. People such as the Semai do not conceive of nonviolence as an ideal they should strive for; rather, they think of themselves as nonviolent. According to Robert Knox Dentan the Semai would not describe anger as bad in the abstract, instead they would say, "We do not get angry." The practice of nonviolence of these peoples combines their world-views of peace with a very realistic, pragmatic understanding of the results of violence. For instance, the Anabaptist societies and the Tristan Islanders see a constant, practical benefit to themselves in maintaining their meek, nonconfrontational, peaceful relationships with each other and with outsiders. The literature on the peoples who live on the fringes of Indian society—the Ladakhis, Paliyan, Malapandaram, Birhor, and Yanadi—emphasizes the practical ways their economic and social structures are integrated with their peacefulness.

To sum up this section, the peaceful peoples are intolerant of internal strife; they do not rationalize conflict and would not accept the possibility that violence is excusable in some circumstances. Few individuals in these societies would admit that, while they know they *should* be peaceful, sometimes they just have to use violence—that's the way humanity is. To them, other peoples are obviously violent, aggressive, and filled with conflicts and warfare; but they themselves are peaceful and highly conscious of it. Peacefulness is an absolute commitment for them. Most of their social, religious, mythical, cultural, psychological, and educational beliefs are derived from this world-view of their own peacefulness.

Conclusion

How do the conflict resolution strategies and beliefs of the peaceful peoples relate to the complex societies of today's world? On a practical level, professionals in the dispute resolution field might find some of the techniques used by these societies to be applicable at times, such as relying more on humor to defuse tensions, or placing more emphasis on building up individual restraints on hostility in conflict situations.

But the peaceful societies exemplify a more basic lesson about resolving conflicts without violence. They demonstrate that peaceful conflict resolution, in order to be an integral part of modern social life, must be based on a fervent commitment to nonviolence. If the examples of the peaceful peoples have any validity, nonviolence has to be accepted as one of the highest ideals, one of the most strongly accepted beliefs, of today's societies. We can gain glimpses of a world which resolves conflicts nonviolently through the vision provided by the peaceful peoples: a vision of individuals who always prefer peaceful behavior over aggression, and who always avoid confrontation and conflict; a vision of societies which look to their widely varying ethical, religious, and social traditions to support world-views of peace; and a vision of humanity successfully building and reinforcing peaceful beliefs into nonviolent social lives.

The example of the peaceful societies cannot be extended too far—they do not provide clear answers to many of the complex issues of conflict in today's world. The peaceful peoples do, however, provide a basis for understanding successful conflict resolution and they do inspire a vision of a potentially peaceful world. Arguments about the complexity of modern societies (compared to the small-scale peaceful peoples) may try to justify conflict as inevitable, but these are rationalizations which fade under the vision of peacefulness provided by these peoples: that human societies CAN be peaceful, that people CAN build virtually fail-safe structures for avoiding and resolving conflict, that punishments and armed conflicts are NOT essential for keeping the peace. The answer is for us to build, in our societies, world-views of peacefulness that are as strong as those of the peaceful peoples. This is the first step.

NOTE

1. I would define "world-view" as a system of thoughts and emotions about individual, social, and spiritual life which includes the human actions guided by those thoughts and emotions, while "ideology" is a system of beliefs which may or may not influence individual acts.

Chapter 29

A Critique of Western Conflict Resolution from a Non-Western Perspective

Paul E. Salem

The following are reflections on the premises and assumptions of Western conflict resolution as viewed from another cultural perspective, in this case, Arab. They derive from exposure to conflict resolution writings and simulations in a Western milieu and the experience of teaching conflict resolution in a non-Western context, namely in Beirut. The article aims to present a tentative critique of some hidden assumptions in the Western approach to conflict resolution, and to provide some insights into the macro-cultural framework to which Western conflict resolution approaches must adapt if they are to be used in the Arab world—or perhaps also in other areas of the non-Western world.

One must make clear from the beginning that any attempt to make broad generalizations about two diverse and loosely defined cultural and social groupings as "the West" and "the Arab world" is fraught with dangers of reductionism, essentialism, and simplification, to say nothing of Edward Said's Orientalism. The effort of finding general cultural patterns and tendencies, however, is, I think, well worth the risk and the effort; and the generalizations presented are only intended as food for thought signposts for further research rather than as definitive conclusions. Also, it should not be understood from the text that Arab society does not have effective conflict resolution methods of its own. Indeed, such methods are widespread and considerably effective. This article, however, is more strictly concerned with the comparative perspective rather than with exploring indigenous Arab methods of conflict resolution.

Peace and Empire

The Western community of conflict resolution theorists and practitioners operate within a macro-political context that they may overlook, but which colors their attitudes and values. This seems remarkably striking from an outsider's point of view and is largely related to the West's dominant position in the world. All suc-

From *Negotiation Journal* 361–368 (October 1993). Plenum Publishing.

cessful "empires" develop an inherent interest in peace. The ideology of peace reinforces a status quo that is favorable to the dominant power. The Romans, for example, preached a *Pax Romana,* the British favored a *Pax Britannica,* and the Americans today pursue—consciously or not—a *Pax Americana.* Conflict and bellicosity is useful—indeed essential—in *building* empires, but an ideology of peace and conflict resolution is clearly more appropriate for its maintenance.

Indeed, for many outsiders, it is quite common to view Western international conflict resolution policies, whether in the Arab-Israeli peace process, the UN Security Council, or elsewhere, as merely stratagems for defusing opposition to and rejection of the status quo. To the dominated members of a "pseudo-imperial" world system, peace may be something that they might indeed seek to *avoid,* and conflict may be an objective that they might seek to invigorate in order to destabilize the world system and precipitate its crisis or collapse. They may prefer to burn the temple down, rather than succumb to the worship of a foreign god.

The Debatable Virtues of Peace and the Underestimated Virtues of Battle

Other than the interest a triumphant West naturally has in peace, the concept of peace itself has a particular and positive cultural valuation in the West. The centrality of the idea that peace is necessarily "good" and war is "bad" is, to some degree, peculiar to the Christian worldview. This is not to say that other religions do not value peace or that the Church in history did not succeed in devising intricate theological arguments for a theory of the Just or Good War; in its central precepts, however, the Christian religion does specifically exalt the category of peace over, for example, other quite important categories, such as socio-political justice or obedience to a strict moral code. This exaltation—or over-valuation—of peace and blanket denigration of war and the traditional military virtues is, to a considerable degree, characteristic of the Christian worldview; but it is not a central part of the ancient Greek, Babylonian, Roman, Jewish, or Islamic worldviews.

In addition, early Christianity adopted outward doctrines of peace partially to insinuate itself throughout the Roman Empire; Islam, however, openly declared a sacred political program, and set out unapologetically from the beginning to back up its proselytization with military force. The Prophet himself and all the Rightly Guided Caliphs were proud warriors. In this context, war in itself is not shameful, nor is peace necessarily and always good. With regard to conflict resolution, the Western assumption that working for peace is always a good thing might be questionable in other cultural contexts.

Conflict without Struggle and the End of History

The Western world of the post–World War II era has largely abandoned the ideal of struggle which characterized its earlier history. Pre–World War II Western history, on the other hand, is largely marked by intense and often violent struggles to establish national unity, national independence, socio-economic equality, and/or popular government. The more successful among Western nations also prospered by conquering other nations and struggling for world supply and consumer markets.

The ideal of struggle was especially exalted in the nineteenth-century philosophies of Hegel, Marx, and Nietzsche; it was lent a pseudo-scientific basis by Darwin and bastardized by the national supremacism of German and Italian fascism. Moreover, among the decisive events that shaped modern Western political history—the revolutions of 1776, 1789, 1848, and 1917; the wars of Napoleon; and the First and Second World Wars—it was the ideal of struggle that was held in highest regard.

As Francis Fukuyama describes, however, many in the West today enjoy an indeterminate satisfaction that they have somehow reached "the end of history." This may not be completely illusory: in politics the "West" has achieved stability, orderly transitions of power, widespread freedoms, protection of basic rights, and participation in government; in economics it has achieved high levels of wealth and reasonable patterns of wealth distribution; class conflict has been more or less resolved in favor of a large middle class; in other social matters, education and literacy are widespread, health care is adequate, and popular culture through various media offers amusement and enjoyment of leisure time to a majority of the population. The West, in other words, may see nothing major that it still needs to struggle intensely in order to secure. It has reached a situation of relative self-satisfaction. From the West's perspective, what is, in a broad sense, is good, and should be preserved.

Outside the context of struggle, however, conflict is an overwhelmingly negative phenomenon, notable only for its harmful side-effects of violence, suffering, and general discomfiture. If the macro picture is indeed positive, as described earlier with regard to the West, then conflicts are, in a sense, troublesome brush fires that need to be put out rather than incipient struggles that need to be fanned. Obviously, from the outside—for example, Arab—perspective, wherein major and, perhaps, revolutionary change seems, to many, necessary at the level of political, economic, and social affairs, the side effects of conflict are not nearly as significant as the value of the struggle itself if it succeeds.

Indeed, in the major ideological currents that have defined political thinking in the modern Arab world—nationalism, Marxism, and Islamic fundamentalism—struggle has been held in high regard. In the thought of Arab nationalism (and indeed various regional nationalisms such as Syrian nationalism and Egyptian nationalism) the struggle—often violent—against external colonial powers and internal collaborationist forces was at the center of the nationalist worldview. In the Marxist and leftist currents that swept the Arab world, especially during the 1950s and 1960s, an irreducible struggle between the working class on the one hand and the local and international capitalist classes on the other was central. In Islamic fundamentalism of the radical type such as that challenging power in Algeria, Egypt, Jordan, Syria, Lebanon, and other Arab countries, a central struggle is posited between the minority of true believers and the majority of the population that is Muslim in name only.[1] In each of these cases struggle, and the conflict that comes with it, is central to the group's political view and is regarded, in some cases, as a progressive, invigorating, and purifying process.

Utilitarianism and the Comfort Culture of the Twentieth Century

Western conflict resolution relies heavily on the assumption that pain is bad and pleasure, or comfort, is good. It is accepted as obvious that the suffering, physical or otherwise, associated with conflict is one of the main inconveniences that conflict resolution practitioners try to eliminate. First, this assumption in itself—that suffering is bad and comfort is good—required a significant philosophical revolution in the West to become accepted. It was the task of nineteenth-century utilitarian philosophers like Jeremy Bentham and John Stuart Mill to make this principle a fairly widely accepted premise of modern Western culture. It flew—and still flies today among other cultures—against the more original principle that *"good* is good and *bad* is bad," where the first usages of good and bad in this phrase are defined in general moral or religious terms having nothing to do with pleasure or pain. The focus of Western conflict resolution theorists on the suffering generated by conflict rather than on the justice or morality of the cause may not strike resonant philosophical chords in other cultures. To the contrary, suffering itself in many cultures, including pre-modern Western culture, enjoys a fairly high valuation as a means for moral or spiritual purification or a necessary divinely-ordained component of life.

Second, the belief that discomfort is an isolatable evil and one that can be eradicated seems a characteristic of twentieth-century postwar Western culture. With advances in health care, economic standards of living, and home appliances, plus a vigorous media culture of consumerism and immediate-needs satisfaction, the modern Western urbanite or suburbanite lives in a world where comfort is achievable and discomfort is limited and eliminatable. In this context, suffering associated with conflict stands out. In other societies, however, where levels of socio-economic development in virtually all spheres are still considerably behind those of the West, comfort itself is the aberration, and discomfort and suffering are more familiar companions of life. In that context, the suffering or discomfort associated with conflict does not stand out; it blends in with a fabric of discomfort and suffering that embraces most aspects of life. The Western conflict resolution emphasis on the necessity of resolving conflict because of the salient discomfort that it brings with it may not be relevant in a social setting in which discomfort is widespread. People there may give less importance to the discomfort generated by the conflict and more importance to the justice or outcome of the dispute.

Third, there seems to be a hidden assumption among the Western conflict resolution community that physical suffering—to be precise, physical violence—is in a category of unacceptable suffering all its own. This assumes a valid and clear-cut distinction between physical and nonphysical suffering along the continuum of suffering. The confusion here stems partly, I think, from the pleasure-pain utilitarian philosophy and the acculturation to physical comfort, both described earlier. Is physical pain indeed more painful than nonphysical pain? Is a serious flesh wound worse than a serious injustice? If we gave a person a choice between getting punched in the face or having their home taken away from them, which would they choose? If we gave them a choice between losing their life or losing their country? Injustice, economic need, political need (struggles for liberty or freedom from oppression) are all in many cases experienced as acute nonphysical suffering. The definition of suffering itself, therefore, needs considerable clarification and specification. It may not mean the same thing from one culture to the next. In the Arab world as well, suffering is not something necessarily to be shunned, nor is physical pain or sacrifice particularly worse than nonphysical losses like loss of honor, loss of patrimony, loss of face, and so on.

Prometheus and Sisyphus

The West is riding at the crest of a wave of success at many levels. It is enjoying the later stages of a period of astoundingly rapid advances that began with the Italian Renaissance and expanded with the Industrial Revolution. With a record of Promethean achievement in technological, economic, political, social, and intellectual spheres, and with a modern history of continuous development, the West enjoys a basic optimism that things can be changed, and that that change can be for the better. World War I, World War II, the German holocaust, and the development of nuclear weapons have dampened but not extinguished this optimism.

The Arab and Islamic world, by contrast, is in the trough of a wave of decline and defeat. The heydey of Arab-Islamic culture, politics, economics, and technology began to fade in the twelfth and thirteenth centuries; the history of the past seven centuries has largely been one of stagnation and decline from that apogee. The legacy of this period is partially a pessimism that things cannot easily be changed, that change may often be for the worse, and that the forces that determine change are beyond one's control. For conflict resolution, the optimism of Westerners who approach conflicts with the confidence that they can be managed and resolved contrasts sharply with the pessimism of others that may regard conflicts as inherently unresolvable or unmanageable, and for whom the whole project of conflict resolution may smack of naive, over-optimistic enthusiasm.

Conflict Resolution and the "Scientific" Worldview

Western culture has internalized the natural mechanistic universalism of Thales and the atomism of Democritus, both of which provided a large part of the philosophical foundations on which the West's scientific and technological advances were built. Both allow a view of conflict resolution in which conflict is seen as the result of a clash of natural forces among discrete and independent units. The forces can be understood and resolved, and the atoms can be independently identified and dealt with. This is a particular worldview, and is profoundly different from others, such as a truly religious worldview in which conflict is the result of a struggle between divine and devilish or profane forces; a moralistic worldview, in which conflict is the result of a natural struggle between good and evil; or a superstitious worldview, in which conflict is the result of magic, unknowable forces. A neutral, "objective" approach to conflict assumes a certain neutral and "objective" view of the world. The collapse of the religious and moralistic worldview was a painful process that the West took centuries to pass through; it cannot be assumed that other cultures are at the same stage of advanced areligiosity and amorality.

The Descent into Psychology

In the nineteenth century, Nietzsche made it no longer possible to easily float religious, moralistic, or even historicist explanations of events. His grand nihilism reduced the world to the individual and his individual will. Furthermore, his attack on the idea that reason and morality are the fundamental guiding lights of the individual led to a revived interest in psychology. Freud's "discovery of the unconscious," followed by Skinner's behaviorism and other explanations of human motivation and action, provided the intellectual tools for an entirely *human* explanation of human attitudes and behavior, downgrading religious, ideological, moralistic, and other explanations.

With regard to conflict resolution, this intellectual legacy of the modern West encourages it to perceive conflict as the result of the thoughts and impulses of the individual, the causes of which are largely within that individual. In other cultures that have not yet gone through this process of nihilism and psychologization, it may be far more difficult to interpret conflict by reducing it to a set of perceptions, attitudes, and behavior patterns exhibited by autonomous individuals.

The Convenience of Postmodernism

The postmodern perspective that took hold of Western intellectual life after World War II abandons virtually all systematic philosophies in favor of an attitude of vague relativism. Being right—indeed rights themselves—is a matter of perspective and may differ from culture to culture or from individual to individual. Within their own contexts, more than one person or culture could be "right," even if their positions are contradictory to one another—never mind Aristotle's logical premise on which most Western thought was subsequently built, that a thing must be either "A" or "Not A"; from the postmodern standpoint, it could be "A" here, and "Not A" somewhere else.

This is a great boon to modern approaches to conflict resolution in which it is essential for parties to a conflict to be open to the possibility that while they may be right, so may the other parties. Postmodernism's mood of relativism allows an easy acceptance that the interplay of right and wrong is not necessarily a zero-sum game. In other, more traditional cultures (that could best be described as pre-modern or modernizing, rather than postmodern) there are more strict codes of right and wrong and more rigid accounts of truth. From their perspective, the interplay of right and wrong is more likely to be a zero-sum game: "I am either right or wrong; and to the degree that I am right, my opponent must be wrong, and vice versa." This mode of thinking makes several aspects of modern conflict resolution techniques (such as, for example, formulating a problem in a way that satisfies all parties) difficult to carry through.

"Flower Power" and the New Negotiation

The credo of individual openness that was part of the cultural revolution of the 1960s and 1970s in the West has found its way into Western conflict resolution techniques. Most Western conflict resolution manuals start with several exercises in which opponents are supposed to "open up," talk about their "personal experiences," "feelings," or "deep interests," and develop "relationships" with their opponents "as individuals." This segue into the negotiation proper may seem natural and comfortable to Westerners, but it may go against the grain of members of many other cultures. "Opening up," rather than maintaining and reinforcing formal roles, may be a highly distressing and counter-productive process that may alienate the participant from the negotiation process and from his negotiation partners and opponents. In many non-Western negotiation situations, it might be wiser to increase the level of formality and social role-playing in order to get the negotiations going, rather than to increase the level of personalization and individual self-revelation or to engage in game-playing to supposedly bring out the Jungian "inner child."

The Role of the Good Citizen

The West has already undergone the processes of centralization, bureaucratization, atomization, rule-formation, and rule-acceptance that were described by Weber as characteristic of modernization. One of the results of this process is the production of the "good" citizen/subject who generally accepts authority and rules (even if fairly anonymous), pays taxes, stops at red lights (even at midnight on a deserted crossroads), and so on. In the Western conflict resolution context, this usually means a relatively easy acceptance of the role of the anonymous moderator, facilitator, mediator, or other such central figures in the negotiation process; also, it may facilitate an easy acceptance of freshly-devised rules to guide the negotiation process.

In other contexts, the attempt of an anonymous (i.e., nontraditional) moderator/facilitator to establish leadership and authority over a negotiation process may cause resentment and may become part of the problem in the form of a struggle for power between the moderator/facilitator and various participants. The same may be true of new, nonlegitimized negotiation rules and guidelines; the imposition of rules may in itself be resented and resisted as an imposition of inappropriate authority. It is in this context that the importance of a traditional authority figure as moderator/facilitator and traditionally accepted rules of conflict resolution becomes apparent.

Militarization, Industrialization, and the Team Player

The grand factories brought on by industrialization and the mass citizen armies inaugurated by Napoleon eventually brought the majority of the population in the West into large group enterprises. This continued in the twentieth century with the growth of bureaucracies and large corporations that employ the bulk of the new middle class. Through these formative experiences, many Westerners have internalized the benefits of team work and the costs of uncooperativeness or prisoner's dilemma profiteering. In more fragmented societies organized around the family, the clan, or the small enterprise, the world appears far more competitive and large-scale team work has very few exemplars. Large-scale group work there may often be perceived as a formula for getting duped, and prisoner's dilemma profiteering is often regarded as rewarding and rarely punished. As a result, the seemingly natural appeal of "working together" toward reaching an agreement does not resonate as positively elsewhere as it does in the West. Working together, as opposed to working separately, in other contexts may cause apprehension as control is ceded to a group in whom the individual has little inherent trust.

Hobbes and the Problem of Enforcing Agreements

In the seventeenth century, Hobbes identified the difficulty of negotiating a social contract, or building trust, without a coercive power to enforce it; he argued that for parties to participate in negotiating an agreement without the guarantee that there will be a power to protect and enforce it would be irrational.[2] He also pointed out how dangerous it would be for parties to participate in such an agreement if the guarantee was not provided; it might even be worse than the state of nature in which you at least had a measure of freedom and equality as protection. In the West, most people have had the guarantee of strong government and the rule of law for a number of centuries now.

In the Western conflict resolution literature, the final phases of negotiation, those of "working toward agreement," have a breezy, relieved air to them, as if the most difficult and threatening part were over, and the parties would soon have an "agreement" on which they both could rely. In a political environment in which governmental authority is unstable and in which the rule of law is not necessarily paramount, moving toward "agreement," which is, after all, a situation of interdependence not only involving your adversary but also some external guarantor of the

agreement, may be in itself disquieting. It implies a giving up of control and autonomy and a limiting of one's freedom of action on the shaky grounds that the adversary can be trusted to fulfill his part of the bargain and that the "system" will help
protect his contract. But in the absence of an enforcer, it may be more preferable to
maintain a conflictual but known and predictable situation, than to try to construct
a less conflictual but much less predictable and transparent one.

Locke and Negotiating with Have-Nots

Another point to consider is that, in developing societies, people are mostly concerned with getting things they do not presently have rather than protecting what
they do have. John Locke's social contract, on which much of Western liberalism
is founded, was based on protecting what one has: life, liberty; and private property. It is a negotiation among haves for the protection and preservation of what
they have. Western conflict resolution is not too far from this perspective, based as
it is on some assumption that all parties to the conflict have something to lose,
something to preserve, and something to gain.

Negotiating with real have-nots, who have nothing to lose, nothing to preserve,
and everything to gain, might be quite different. Negotiating and bargaining assumes that each party has some number of "chips" that they can trade and shuffle
around with others to create a satisfactory resolution to some conflict; but what of
the party who has no chips at all, and whose only option in an uneven negotiation
situation is to seize the other party's (or parties') chips? Indeed, with some veiling
sophistication, this is what Marxist revolutionism proposes. Thus, Western conflict resolution through negotiation in a society of haves and have-nots may prove
problematic and, at times, impossible.

In Closing

I hope that in the paragraphs above I have raised some worthwhile questions
about the philosophical, moral, psychological, and cultural framework from
within which Western conflict resolution departs. It should be kept in mind that I
am not suggesting any judgments on Western or Arab cultures, but merely trying
to underline the serious diversity that exists at the deepest levels of different cultural and social formations. Value judgments only make sense from within one
cultural framework or another.

Moreover, I have attempted to present a tentative critique of some hidden
premises of Western conflict resolution and to point out a number of areas within
Arab political culture in which modern Western assumptions related to the theory
and practice of conflict resolution do not fully apply. I have tried to indicate that
some of the bases on which Western conflict resolution rest are not to be found, in
exact mirror image, in the Arab world, or perhaps also in other cultures. The conclusion to be drawn from this is not that the Arab world, for example, is more

conflict-prone or less conflict resolution-oriented than the West but that in transporting Western conflict resolution theories and techniques to the Arab world or elsewhere, they must undergo considerable cultural adaptation.

NOTES

1. A Quranic verse which is cited frequently by the main ideologue of modern Islamic fundamentalism, Sayyid Qutb, is "Fight them until persecution is no more, and religion is all for God." [Quran 2:93, quoted in Qutb, *ma'alim fil-tariq* (Signposts along the way) (Cairo: n.p., 1964), 152.]

2. "For the laws of nature, as justice, equity, modesty, mercy, and, in sum, doing to others, as we would be done to, of themselves, without the terror of some power to cause them to be observed, are contrary to our natural passions that carry us to partiality, pride, revenge, and the like. And covenants, without the sword, are but words, and of no strength to secure a man at all. Therefore notwithstanding the laws of nature . . . if there be no power erected, or not great enough for our security, every man will, and may, lawfully rely on his own strength and art for caution against all other men. And in all places where men have lived by small families, to rob and spoil one another has been a trade, and so far from being reputed against the law of nature, that the greater spoils they gained, the greater was their honor; and men observed no other laws therein, but the laws of honor, that is, to abstain from cruelty, leaving to men their lives and instruments of husbandry." From Thomas Hobbes' *Leviathan*, quoted in Ebenstein (1969: 377).

Chapter 30

Conflict Resolution Approaches
Western and Middle Eastern Lessons and Possibilities

Mohammed Abu-Nimer

Conflict Resolution in a Middle Eastern Context

A community dispute resolution process in a Palestinian village in Northern Israel reveals a set of conflict resolution assumptions.[1]

There are about fourteen thousand people in the village, 60 percent Druze, 23 percent Christians, and 17 percent Moslems. Although the Druze are the predominant group in the village, in this largely Moslem region, they are minority. The balance of power changed in this village in 1952, when, due to a new Israeli policy, young Druze males started joining the Israeli army. Still, today, only the Druze are obliged to serve in the Israeli army. Christians and Moslems in Israel are exempt from mandatory military services because of security considerations stated by the Israeli defense minister in 1952. Members of the Druze community who have fought in the Israeli army against Palestinians and Arab armies found it difficult to associate their political identity with such groups. This factor divided the village into two political camps, those who supported Israeli government policies, and those who opposed them.

As a result of intensive confiscation of lands, this village, like other Arab villages in Israel, is no longer agricultural. The community is economically at a transitional level in which people do not depend on agriculture as their main source of income and there is a relatively high level of education among the younger generations. Army service is the essential source of income for the Druze. Christians rely on small businesses and on administrative and educational positions in the village for their income, while Moslems work outside the village in the Israeli construction companies. In comparison with other communities in the area, this village is certainly considered more traditional than the surrounding communities.

The social structure of the three communities in the village is based on clan units. However, the Druze emphasize community interests and religious identity more than the other two communities. Moslems and Christians are less unified on the basis of their religious affiliations, but they identify themselves with the broader national Palestinian identity and the Arab world.

From 55(1) *American Journal of Economics and Sociology* 35, 41–46 (1996).

Since the establishment of Israel in 1948, the relationship between the three religious groups has been perceived as being peaceful and respectful. This was reflected
in mutual visits among the leaders of the communities particularly during weddings
and funerals, and other social events. Younger generations attended ethnically integrated schools and their members were separated only for religion classes.

The dispute arose when a group of Druze youths threw stones at a wedding of a
Christian leader's son. Two days later, some of the Christian clans' heads visited
the houses of the suspected Druze youths. They complained about the disturbance
at the wedding. The youth were warned by their fathers not to repeat this shameful behavior, which, as Christian leaders argued, could destroy the good relationship between the two communities.

One month later, a violent confrontation at midnight with a group of Christian
youths (not from the family whose wedding celebration was disturbed) resulted in
the hospitalization of two Druze young men. The incident began when some
Christian youths tried to convince a group of Druze youths to leave and return to
their homes, because they were screaming and disturbing the neighborhood's residents. The following day some of the Christian clans' leaders visited families of
the injured youths. They suggested beginning a process of reconciliation and apol-
ogized in an attempt to prevent further violence. The Druze families rebuffed their
apologies and announced that they would talk only when their sons were released
from the hospital.

The following day, as a result of a rumor that the two injured Druze had died,
approximately two thousand Druze attacked the Christian neighborhood. They
destroyed furniture in some houses, injured several Christians, and caused damage
to stores owned by Christians. As a result, many Christian families took shelter in
surrounding villages.

A few hours after this attack began, delegates from surrounding Moslem villages
in the area entered the village and stopped the Druze youths who were still threatening the Christian neighborhoods. During the disturbance, the Israeli police patrols
had left the village, and did not return until the morning of the next day.

Throughout the following week, Christian stores were closed, and Christian
students did not attend schools. Their neighborhood was paralyzed. This situation, of course, disrupted all aspects of village life. Meanwhile, the Druze leaders
of the attack were discussing in open meetings at the "Khilwi" (the Druze religious center) political, economic, and social sanctions against the Christians.
Many of the Druze elders and religious leaders did not attend these meetings, and
some of them (including the current and former mayors, and other clans' leaders)
even expressed their rejection of sanctions.

A few days later, many outside delegations (comprised of elders of major clans
from many of the surrounding villages) visited Druze leaders in an attempt to settle the dispute. Some of these delegations tried to intervene because Christian leaders asked them to, and others did so on their own.

The third party: A group of twenty-five regional leaders which was led by a
steering committee of seven members took the responsibility for settling this dispute. The committee visited several Druze houses, especially the leaders' houses

(mayors, heads of clans, and religious leaders). They also visited the Christian leaders' houses and inspected the damages caused by the crowd's attack.

The composition and strategies of the group gave it the credibility and legitimacy it needed to mediate successfully: (a) All of the group members were outsiders. They had no direct clan relationship with any of the disputants, and did not include clan leaders from the village, except some Moslem religious and community leaders from the specific village. (b) The average age of the group was over fifty years old. Age is a very important source of respect in traditional Arab society, and provides legitimacy and credibility for intervention in social conflict, regardless of the nature of the dispute. (c) All religions were represented in the third party to illustrate balance and justice in the process. (d) Members of the group were very familiar with the history of this village, the history of mediation and third party intervention in the region, and the customs and norms of the three religious communities. (e) Several members of the third party were mayors of large villages in the region, and a few were members of the Israeli parliament, elected by the Arab minority inside Israel. Also among the group were several Druze who held high military positions.

Members of this third party group had no direct power to levy economic or political sanctions upon the parties (the specific families). However, their political and social standing in the community enabled them to influence the Druze community's willingness to dialogue with their Moslem neighbors. (f) The fact that some members of the third party had either a direct or indirect political or social stake in the dispute—solving such a dispute would add to the high social status of every member of the third party—encouraged them to take an active approach.

This seemingly minor incident came to involve increasing numbers of people because of the context in which it took place. Since there are other Christian and Druze villages in the region, the dispute was characterized by the third party, and by the parties directly involved, to have regional implications. It threatened the security and social order of the whole region. Also, the conflict escalated very rapidly to include the entire Christian and Druze communities. Therefore, neither the village's local Christian or Druze traditional mediators nor the leaders of the Moslem minority in the village were able to settle the conflict or even attempt to intervene without outside support.

The issues at dispute had no obvious economic implications nor related to explicit tangible resources, therefore, parties did not consider a legal battle in the Israeli court system. The issues as perceived by the parties and the third party were to involve the honor, shame, respect, and the dignity of both communities.

There was an asymmetric power relation between the parties. The Druze youths were backed by a wider community that possessed a substantial number of weapons and close connections to Jewish political parties, and the police and military forces. The Christian community influence was more localized through economic and administrative resources, and some members had strong ties to the Israeli security services.

The main intervention processes or stages employed by the third party were: (1) selection of committee; (2) fact finding (home visits) back and forth; (3) separate consultation and caucus with the parties; (4) several sessions of negotiation and bargaining conducted separately with each party; and (5) reaching the settlement.

Throughout the process, the interveners utilized a set of social and religious values and norms: (1) The importance of preserving and protecting the honor of the parties; the dispute threatened to bring shame and dishonor on many members of the village. (2) The unity of the families, village, and region should be maintained in order not to dilute power and solidarity in facing outside challenges. (3) The harmony of future generations is central to the socialization processes (religious and social). An individual and a community defined the meaning of their existence as working to create a positive environment for their children and the next generation. A conflict of this magnitude could disturb the expected future harmony. (4) Since disputants and third party members derived their social values from their religions, therefore, they emphasized that Christianity, Islam, and Druze are three religions that stress values of tolerance and respect of elders. (5) A tradition of peaceful and respectful relationships in the village in the past; the village had no violent confrontations between any of its three communities since the establishment of Israel in 1948. In addition, elders described in various stories the social and political harmony that existed among the villagers prior to 1948. (6) The Arab tradition of forgiveness and dignity, an important value which elders have traditionally utilized to encourage certain behaviors of tolerance and respect; while values of honor, shame, and dignity are adopted in this Arab village in Israel, nevertheless they are core values of contemporary social systems in the Arab world, whether in an urban, village, or bedouin community.

Throughout the mediation process, elders, particularly third party members from the three religions, shared historical stories to illustrate the application of these values. Also these stories stressed the contribution of reconciliation and mediation processes in restoring harmony and peaceful coexistence between disputing communities.

The intensive efforts of the third party committee produced a settlement which indicated that: (a) the Druze would allow the Christians to return to their houses; (b) Druze families would not receive money for their injured youths, but the Christian families ought to apologize directly to the youths; (c) Druze leaders would guarantee to prevent any further attacks on Christian neighbors; (d) economic sanctions should be suspended immediately; and (e) Druze students would stop disturbing Christian students in the schools.

After the Christian families fulfilled the conditions of the agreement, the Druze families permitted the return of all Christian families to their homes. However, partial economic and social sanctions continued, led by some leaders of the mob which had attacked the Christian community, and who opened several new stores near Christian stores. These actions incited debate within the Druze community on the validity and effectiveness of the sanctions, and over the next ten months the commitment to the sanctions faded away. The economic dependency of the village on the Christian businesses also was an important factor in the erosion of support for sanctions.

Just one year later, a Druze elder described the dispute as a part of the village's history. Students and children were advised to avoid mentioning it (since it was a shameful and a dangerous event).

Thus, the dispute management in this context was achieved through existing traditional social institutions, operated by the local social and political leaders. It was not based on a legal framework, although this was an option since Israeli law is used at every other level.

This case illustrates the use of dispute resolution processes to restore social order and the power relation between the parties. There was no substantial action, or even recognition of the need, to change the power disparity between the parties, in spite of the fact that both parties recognized the power disparity as one of the major causes of the conflict escalation. Avoidance of the issue reflects a major tendency among traditional dispute resolution interveners whose core values/motivations include values of harmony, avoidance of conflict, and maintenance of order.

Basic Assumptions of Middle Eastern Conflict Resolution Process

From the process of resolution in this particular Middle Eastern dispute, one can abstract several basic assumptions about settling disputes in the area. First, conflict resolution aims to restore social order and the disrupted balance of power, rather than to change power relationships or the status quo.

Second, even though a dispute might begin between two individuals or two families, it soon escalates to involve the entire communities or clans. The group, not individuals, is a central locus of action.

Third, the initiation and implementation of intervention are based on the social norms and customs of the society. These social codes are utilized to evaluate an individual's status, therefore they operate as a pressuring tool to reach and implement an agreement between two families. Bargaining moves to reach a settlement are conducted on the basis of preserving the social values, norms, and customs. During the negotiation, negotiators refer to these values as a way to pressure the other side. These values are maintained and preserved by the disputants in their social context. Even if a dispute is over scarce resources (such as money or debts or land), values such as "honor," "shame," "dignity," "social status," and "religious beliefs" are at stake.

Fourth, future relationships are very crucial elements in settling a dispute in this Middle Eastern context. The relationship between the disputants determines the intervention procedures, nature, size, and settlement. This dispute involved a powerful majority of Druze who, while they were heavily armed and closely united, recognized that their regional ethnic stability and balance could be jeopardized if the conflict was not contained. This recognition made them receptive to the intervention of a regional third party.

Fifth, conflict is negative, threatening, and disruptive to the normative order and needs to be settled quickly or avoided. The interveners' message focused on the damage and destruction that a conflict between two brothers, friends, or nations can bring.

Sixth, priority is given to people and relationships over task, structure, and tangible resources. In the intervention, there were no predetermined stages to complete; all the energies were concentrated on dealing with relationship and social status. The focus was on the nature of the relationship between the parties, rather than concrete, substantive compensations involved.

Seventh, in many cases, disputes are resolved without face-to-face bargaining or negotiation, which can be perceived by the parties as a further antagonistic step; in other cases it might be perceived as a humiliating act if taken by the victim's party. In this particular case, allowing the parties to present their story separately to the third party was the most crucial part of the negotiation process. This avoided the risk of elevating the level of antagonism between the parties or of humiliating either side, rather it was an opportunity to reflect the parties' social status and power, which was used as a bargaining tool by each party. During these sessions, story-telling was a primary tool used by parties and third party to present their positions and interests, and the conditions for a desired settlement.

NOTE

1. The Middle Eastern context is a term that refers to the traditional, rural, and nonindustrialized society. However, since Middle Eastern societies are different levels in the traditional-transitional-Industrial continuum, there are common norms, values, and other social characteristics among the adherents of the traditional society, and those who adhere to a transitional society.

Chapter 31

The Relevance of Culture for the Study of Political Psychology and Ethnic Conflict

Marc Howard Ross

Culture of Ethnic Conflict

The Cultural Context of Ethnic Politics

Ethnic groups are cultural units whose distinctiveness is marked by contextually defined features such as language, food, clothing, religion, and sense of identity and bolstered by an ideology of common descent which places emotional significance on real and fictive kin ties. The ethnic community, as Horowitz writes, is the family writ large; membership in the family separates insiders and outsiders. Some ethnic communities are formally organized as political units (such as states or autonomous regions in larger states) which make collective decisions and enforce ingroup rules on members. Often, however, in the contemporary world authority in ethnic communities is more informal but still can exert significant pressures over the behavior of group members, especially during periods of stress.

While the core of an ethnic group and consensus concerning who is part of the group is often high, a group's outer edges and the boundaries between one group and another are often fuzzy. In polities such as the former USSR, which require citizens to carry internal passports identifying one's nationality, there are frequently multiple criteria for classifying a person, allowing for a movement across boundaries which follows systematic patterns. Similarly, ethnic categories (and who is put in them) vary over time and context, reinforcing the importance of the subjective and changing character of ethnicity and possibilities for manipulating identity politically. In short, while cultural features distinguish one group from another, political dynamics are often central in deciding the relative importance of particular cultural features in any time and place. Political processes are crucial to shaping how and when cultural differences are emphasized. Culture, in this sense, does not cause conflict directly, but political groups and leaders use culture to mobilize followers in their pursuit of political goals.

From 18(2) *Political Psychology* 317–321 (1997). Blackwell.

Tightening the Boundaries and Defining Action

Perceived threat frequently leads to calls for tightening the boundaries between a group and all outsiders (not just stated enemies). Groups become more careful to monitor how members interact with outgroups and there is sometimes an increase in sanctioning of interpersonal interactions with outgroups, exchanges across boundaries, and even expressions of positive feeling for members of other groups. The most extreme form—unfortunately not uncommon—involves ethnic purification in which groups seek to remove any traces of connectedness or interaction with the enemy. This often takes symbolic forms such as removing foreign words from the language or books from libraries and bookstores or rewriting history to emphasize a lack of connectedness between two groups which have shared the same territory for long periods of time. Finally, ethnic cleansing and genocide involve the removal and killing of any members of the outgroup (as well as ingroup members about whom one has "doubts").

In escalating conflicts, groups frequently impose tests on their members requiring them to make public commitment to the group's cause, such as participation in group rituals which reaffirm the correctness of the group's position—taking an oath, wearing particular items of clothing, or giving up items of high value such as money or choice items of food. In such rituals, the group may focus particular emotional attention on individuals who in the past might have been critical of the group's position or even outsiders who support the group's cause as a way of emphasizing the righteousness of their cause.

Interpreting Events

Ethnicity is not equally important everywhere as a marker of social position, as a determiner of political rights and privileges, or as a line of political cleavage. Where it is significant, however, ethnicity provides a culturally based framework to explain the motives and actions of others, particularly in situations where the actions themselves are highly ambiguous. Ethnic (cultural) frameworks offer worldviews which interpret inherently complicated and potentially puzzling actions to make sense of them and to guide appropriate responses. The frameworks (or schemas) of particular interest here are those marked by relatively high ingroup homogeneity because they are learned within the ethnic community and socially reinforced through the relatively homogenous ethnic networks in which many people spend much of their lives. Sharing and reinforcing interpretations increases as stress increases in conflict situations, meaning that people have both less access to alternative interpretations and, more important, little social incentive to take seriously those they encounter.

At the core of psychocultural interpretations are the stories of the past and present which explain why an enemy behaves as it does and which justify a strong response from one's own group. Powerful metaphors help groups define the threats they face. Akenson, for example, offers a masterful account of how numbers of politically attuned Northern Irish Protestants, South African Afrikaners, and

Israeli Jews found great political meaning in the idea of the sacred covenant from the Biblical story of Exodus. The metaphor of the sacred covenant explains their vulnerable and precarious situation in the world but also provides a course of action which tightens ingroups' resolve in the face of widespread external opposition. Such worldviews, he argues, are highly defended and difficult to change.

A similar powerful metaphor is found in what Volkan calls a *chosen trauma*, "an event that causes a large group to feel helpless and victimized by another group." In his writing, Volkan gives many examples of such events, which clearly would include the Turkish slaughter of Armenians, the Nazi Holocaust, the experience of slavery and segregation for African-Americans, and the Serbian defeat at Kosovo by the Turks in 1389. If a group feels too humiliated, angry, or helpless to mourn the losses suffered in the trauma, he suggests that it then incorporates the emotional meaning of the traumatic event into its identity and passes on the emotional and symbolic meaning from generation to generation. The flip side is the *chosen glory*, in which a group perceives triumph over the enemy; this is seen clearly in the Northern Irish Protestant celebration of the Battle of the Boyne in 1689 every July 12. In escalating ethnic conflicts, the key metaphors, such as those in the chosen trauma or glory, serve both as a rallying point and as a way to make sense of events which evoke deep fears and threats to existence.

Cultural Mobilization

Culture offers contextually defined resources for political organization and mobilization in ethnic conflicts. Its ideology, for example, provides an explicit statement of what is often implicit in a group's worldview. While there is certainly great variability in the form and content of ideological statements, three politically critical themes which occur over and over in ethnic confrontation are the following: each side's feeling of relative *isolation*, "People don't know what it is like to be an X" and "We are alone in the world"; expression of *vulnerability*, "Unless we take extraordinary steps our existence is precarious"; and a sense that the group constitutes the *chosen people* who will survive and triumph.

The dynamics of increasing polarization involve mechanisms of selective emphasis on past events and selective perception of current ones, both of which are facilitated by the social and emotional separation between the group and others. In the creation of a politically acceptable past, the selective use of events is perhaps more important than outright distortions. It is not necessarily what groups get wrong that is as important as what they ignore. In fact, outside observers are often struck at how little groups in conflict (even those living in the same small place such as Protestants and Catholics in Northern Ireland) know about each other, and how strikingly different are the accounts of the conflict each side provides—not so much because of outright disagreements but because each highlights such different events.

Selective perception is maintained when each cultural group, emphasizing its status as a vulnerable minority, is unable to empathize with the other side's past losses and present fears. Ingroup accounts are selective but powerful, for they resonate with what people have experienced and the way they have come to understand the past. Old wounds don't heal when (small) slights continue to keep them festering. The construction of powerful metaphors to symbolize a group's plight, the development of rituals of unity, and the destruction of social ties between groups all inhibit efforts to bridge differences and make further onesided recounting of the conflict more likely.

Culture and Ethnic Peacemaking

If we take seriously the profoundly cultural nature of ethnic conflict, what are the prospects for peacemaking between two (or more) groups who have as basic a fear of and anger toward each other as the psychocultural dynamics described above suggest? Is it realistic to think that Protestants and Catholics in Northern Ireland or Tamils and Sinhalese in Sri Lanka can ever live together more peacefully than they have in the past twenty years?

The first point to make is that there are many examples of situations where once extremely hostile ethnic groups have come to live side by side in more peaceful ways. The once hostile peoples of France and Germany have developed a new culture of European cooperation since the Second World War, which has not ended all differences between the former adversaries, but created a much less threatening, nonviolent way of dealing with differences. Similarly, ethnic groups in Nigeria which fought a bitter civil war a generation ago have achieved significant reconciliation. Such examples make it irresponsible and factually irrelevant to write off ethnic conflict as inevitable and unmanageable.

Emphasizing the cultural dimensions of ethnic conflict is at odds with the hypothesis that a first step to resolving serious group difference lies in finding the right formula (i.e., constitution) to meet the core interests of each side. At best, such institutional arrangements might follow a much more complicated psychocultural process in which the groups come to believe that such arrangements are possible.[1] We have seen this at work in a number of recent examples of relatively successful ethnic conflict management, such as South Africa and the Middle East.

The theories of psychoanalysts like Volkan and cultural anthropologists like Geertz agree that a natural starting point is making sense of the stories parties in a conflict tell. Taking seriously a group's worldview does not mean agreeing with it but rather trying to understand why a group has come to see the world as it does, the consequences of the view it holds, and what would have to happen for it to change its current understanding. There is no doubt that third parties can be especially important in this process, but the key here is getting the parties themselves to approach each other's accounts in ways that permit them to conceptualize future arrangements which are potentially more satisfactory than past ones. Volkan argues that in the most intense conflicts, the inability to mourn past losses means that groups continue to fixate on the past. Cultural responses, such as building monuments, holding public rituals, and other events which help groups acknowledge past suffering and mourn real losses, are prerequisites to developing new relationships with old enemies.

NOTE

1. Kelman's list of prerequisites for an Israeli-Palestinian agreement is as useful a list of beliefs as I can imagine: (1) Each side must acquire some insight into the perspectives of the other. (2) Each side must be persuaded that there is someone to talk to on the other side and something to talk about. (3) Each side must be able to distinguish between the dreams and the operational programs of the other side. (4) Each side must be persuaded that mutual concessions will create a new situation, setting a process of change into motion. (5) Each side must be persuaded that structural changes, conducive to a stable peace, have taken place or will take place in the leadership of the other side. (6) Each side must sense a responsiveness to its human concerns and psychological needs on the part of the adversary.

Chapter 32

The Power of Not Understanding
The Meeting of Conflicting Identities

Z. D. Gurevitch

Dialogue begins with an other. When facing another person, a dialogic connection is made in two contradictory ways. The first is the way of the common, as Schutz and his followers have emphasized. According to this way, participants gear themselves toward forming a shared world of meanings through which they connect with one another and assume mutual existence in a common and immediately understood world. The second, "other side" of dialogue is the way of the stranger. This way focuses on setting the other at a distance as an other who stands at her or his own separate center and cannot be reduced to common understanding. Dialogue is the dialectical process combining these two ways, which are equally necessary. Without the common, there would be no other, and therefore no need for dialogue; if only strangeness prevailed, dialogue would not be possible. Dialogue requires understanding, but it never overcomes the strange. The strange remains a creative challenge, a source of possibility and vitality, and a seed of alienation, opposition, and war.

The Circle of Understanding

Our habitual experience in interpersonal dialogues is to take for granted that we understand each other, as Schutz's phenomenology shows. Rarely does anyone halt a conversation and point out that the other is not understood. People prefer to parry what others say and not confront others' statements by demanding that these be explained. Garfinkel demonstrates how people mutually agree to suppose (or, rather, to presuppose) that understanding takes place by constantly postponing the moment at which a full understanding of what has been said is expected. According to this view, we are creatures who live on taken-for-granted images in "our world," which is impossible to traverse.

Philosophically, this can lead us into a solipsistic deadlock, as Lawson demonstrates in his book on reflexivity. Experientially, however, this is not the case. We do indeed distinguish between states of understanding and nonunderstanding,

From 25(2) *Journal of Applied Behavioral Science* 161–166, 169–171 (1989).

even if we cannot validate this distinction philosophically. Understanding can be regarded as a movement from a state of *inability* to understand to a state of *ability* to understand. How does this happen? During the initial state of inability to understand, explanations, stories, information, and the like suffice. The basic assumption is the Schutzian one that a common world of understanding exists, and that if both sides speak to each other and convey themselves and their respective worlds, understanding will result. When the effort to conduct a dialogue is based on this assumption of a common world, it not only creates understanding regarding that which is common, it also indicates to the dialogic partners that their strangeness—that is, that which separates them from each other as others—cannot be noted and acknowledged in the dialogue, but instead must be glossed over according to the rules of understanding.

In such situations, however, the partners sooner or later lock themselves into what I call an *inability to not understand*. This is true in most close relationships, in which new understanding is often only a new version of old understanding, which cannot be opened to thought. Understanding, as well as not understanding, thus remains reactive rather than active because it is dominated by a supposition of understanding. In relationships ruled by opposition, this is even more emphatically the case. Both sides are locked into positions charged with interest, conviction, and belief, and no direct short cut to understanding exists. Further information and deeper acquaintance are interpreted only in terms of already formed conceptions thus strengthening the inability to not understand. To get out of this situation and open the way to understanding, a crucial point of passage is needed: *the ability to not understand.*

The ability to not understand is the ability to recognize and behold the other (or the self) as an other. In a moment of not understanding, what had been considered "understood" is relinquished as mere image. Elsewhere I have described this moment as a moment of "making strange." In contrast to the Schutzian moment of "growing old together," it highlights the other side of dialogue, the threatening yet exciting realm of strangeness, distance, and not understanding. When the other is perceived as strange, he or she is liberated from the image that one has projected onto the other's experience from the center of one's self. The other then emerges as an independent and "distant" phenomenon.

The full circle of understanding contains the four possibilities described above, and is depicted in Figure 32.1 as a logic (circular) square combining two negations: ability/inability and understanding/not understanding.

The figure illustrates that the ordinary conception of understanding is limited to the movement from *a* to *b*, through which one seeks information, explanations, and a perceptual gestalt. Often, however, when we think that we are in *b*, we are actually in *c*. In such situations, what we consider understanding is instead a case of taking the other (or ourselves) for granted. The introduction of posture *c* into the circle of understanding inevitably brings in posture *d*, in which the other is not unexplained, but is instead inexplicable and revealed as an other, which liberates the other from, and posits the other at, the outskirts of the interpreter's schemes of interpretation.

FIGURE 32.1
The Circle of Understanding

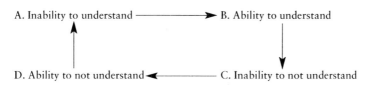

A. Inability to understand ⟶ B. Ability to understand

D. Ability to not understand ⟵ C. Inability to not understand

Instead of an oversimplified move from *a* to *b*, one realizes that reaching posture *b* may require a different type of ability and power, not that of additive knowledge (more information and explanations), but rather that of giving up information and explanation to make the already familiarized strange again. The way to point *b* calls for circular, arduous movement through the acknowledgment of *c* and the passage to *d*.

The ability to not understand has two major implications for the process of understanding in relationships. The first is clearer, and relates to the recognition and conception of the other in the eyes of the self. The second is that of seeing oneself in the eyes of the other. This, too, requires one to have the power of not understanding to activate the process of making strange. A shift must be made from the centered self to the perspective of the other, whereby one attains a separate and strange perceptive center of consciousness enabling one to view the self as other. Shifting the center from the self toward the other and taking the other's role allows one to gain not only a new understanding of the other, but also a new understanding of the self. This consequently alters the terms of the dialogue and revises and re-activates the understanding of both the self and the other.

Dialogue in Conflict

In a dialogue between conflicting identities, the inability to not understand is associated with a strong wish to place the opposite/other in the shadow as the negation of one's own justice, truth, and exclusiveness; to label the beliefs of the other as "misperceptions"; to ignore the real fear, anger, and pain of the other; and to ignore how one's own actions cause that fear, anger, and pain. Therefore, the effort invested in a dialogic project must oppose these projections and expose the parties' locked positions regarding each other. The real presence of the other, which has been concealed from the self by prejudiced projected images throughout the period of estrangement or animosity, must be newly revealed. For this purpose, one should not emphasize understanding the other, but rather should focus on *not understanding the other* so as to attain a necessary state of strangeness and opposition within the full circle of understanding.

This, however, is overlooked frequently. Often the initial situation is defined mistakenly as the inability to understand (rather than as the inability to not understand), leading one to assume that becoming more acquainted with the other and the other's life world will produce a state of understanding. People generally suppose that efforts should be directed toward common understanding. The "other side of dialogue" is disregarded, either because it is too threatening or because the model of dialogue employed emphasizes understanding and views not understanding as inability, rather than ability.

Kelman provides an example of this in his model of dialogue:

> Interactions in the context of a workshop enable each party to acquire some insight into the perspective of the other. They can gain a better understanding of the psychological environment and internal structure of the adversary's society. Thus, they become better able to take into account not only each other's actions, but also each other's purposes, perceptions, intentions, structural constraints, and particularly, each other's fundamental concerns.

These efforts directly focused on understanding are intended to circumvent one's encountering within dialogue the impossibility of understanding. This circumvention is not merely a moral issue. In studies of intergroup affairs, many have found that the assumption that mutual understanding and the reduction of prejudice will result from contact is incorrect and perhaps even self-defeating. Explanations offered to and for the other, exchanges of information, rituals of sharing, and manifestations of empathy are not necessarily conducive to real understanding and cannot resolve the core problem of the dialogue.

The real difficulty is how to debunk previous images of understanding—that is, to "de-explain" rather than explain, to "de-reason" rather than to reason, to restore strangeness into the active framework of the encounter. Thus, if efforts are made toward immediate understanding, they may very quickly reach a dead end, as I demonstrate further below in the description of actual dialogues. Moreover, the difficulty exists even before the actual dialogue begins, in one's very willingness to speak with the other, the opponent, the enemy, the demonic negation of the self. One's being prepared to sit with the other demonstrates the beginnings of an acknowledgment of the other as a respected self. Dialogue with the other as a legitimate other threatens to disintegrate a former self, which has been securely encrusted around some conviction, justification, identity, cause, or the like, which led to a packed, enclosed understanding of the issues at hand and of the self within them that denied the legitimacy of the other. Therefore, a long prenegotiation debate may occur over whether or not one should enter into the dialogue.

In agreeing to be "on speaking terms," the parties establish a minimal dialogical peace agreement, manifesting their willingness to listen to each other. Listening to the other means that power (of speaking, of asserting presence) is granted to the other. In cases of conflict, listening is more difficult than usual because when one listens to the other/opposite, one yields to a menacing opposition and thus goes against oneself. The face-to-face interaction thus becomes a confrontation of *face against face*. Thus, the problem associated with the dialogue is that of overcoming the tendency to not listen, which results from seeking to understand before listening and from imposing a complete set of meanings on the situation in an effort to define it as exclusive.

The difficulty of listening, which is ritually overcome when one initiates dialogue, is not necessarily deepened in the dialogue itself. On the contrary, every subject with any relevance to the core of the clash immediately arouses two conflicting "origins" of truth and justice. Some attempts will be made to push the heart of the dialogue—the conflict outside the actual encounter. That is, the parties will look for a milder, more remote topic of conversation, one they will find engaging, yet will not break the social encounter—and possibly cause an impasse leading them to resume their former state of affairs. Such denial cannot provide a long-term solution. Sooner or later, it leads to a new impasse, and each party will again regard itself as the sole authority on truth and justice.

How can we avoid the impasse of strangeness and opposition? The way of the common is used for this purpose. Yet because this way highlights understanding as a way out of the impasse threat, it avoids the whole dialogical issue. Alternatively, the way of not understanding treats the impasse as a necessary stage in which the parties encounter the blockage of communication, which creates a chance for a dialogic connection to happen. Whether this indeed occurs is a complicated matter and depends on the parties' motivation to gather the power to not understand, which is affected by both the pain induced by the strife and the moral considerations of the parties. First, the motivation to gather this power can exist if the distress and casualties caused by the conflict lead the parties to realize their need to relinquish previously held conceptions. Second, the power to not understand is based on the essential morality of dialogue and human relations, which is the obligation to recognize the other as an other. This is the foundation of honor and respect, without which we cannot imagine the civilized human relations of which dialogue is the prime exemplum.

Enemy Not Understood

An example of attempted dialogue involved two parties on opposite sides of the Israeli-Arab conflict. This group consisted of Jewish-Israeli and Arab-Palestinian teachers who convened to meet one another and attempt to create a dialogue concerning the two cultural and political "worlds" that exist within the same system (under the same ministry of education), yet oppose each other with respect to the Arab-Israeli conflict. The proclaimed reason for the meeting was to discuss possible educational programs focusing on meetings and conversation involving pupils from both sides. Everyone clearly saw, however, that the teachers themselves first had to experience such a meeting before they could commit their pupils to the prospective projects.

In the beginning, the conversation focused on the instances of "nonconflict" contact the participants had had previously with "the other." This ritual of commonality eased the dialogue and signaled a promise and commitment of benevolence. Furthermore, the immediate tendency in the opening rituals was imitation—that is, "taking the role of the other"—through demonstrating an acquaintance with the other side's food, behavior, accent, and figures of speech. The Israelis especially resorted to Arabic slang expressions (known to most Hebrew speakers in Israel), probably because the conversation was being conducted in Hebrew and they wanted to demonstrate equality.

The first state, characterized by ritualistic sharing and understanding—with an implicit promise of good intentions—was exhausted quickly, and signs of boredom, restlessness, and even anger started to appear. Although not explicitly stated, more and more evidence demonstrated that behind the superficial layer of kindness and understanding, nothing was actually happening in the discussion. Moments of silence occurred, combining the embarrassment of every new meeting with the parties' anxiousness to go beyond the ritual into the business of the conflict.

Finally, someone suggested that each person describe an event from her or his life involving relations with the opposite side. The first story was told by an Arab about the village where he was born, describing its location and life there. At this point, which seemed to evoke no difficulty in understanding, restlessness could be detected among the Israelis in the group. This seemed to be connected with a core problem of Arab-Israeli dialogue: feelings of belonging to the place, both on the political level (concerning to whom the land belongs) and the identity level (concerning who belongs to the land). Although they became conscious of this later, the Israelis were already unable to understand—let alone accept—that their land evokes the simple feeling of belonging in an other. Conversely, for the Arabs, the belonging myths of the Israelis seemed external and forced. Obviously, this issue was not a matter of gathering more information about that feeling, but rather one of an emotionally irreconcilable and irrefutable idea of belonging. This was the nucleus of the clash between identities of those forming the group.

The group persisted in denying and concealing the tension, continuing its effort toward gaining the ability to understand, and the establishment of a common world of meanings. The theme of belonging transformed itself on the surface into the commonality of the land, its landscapes, foods and weather, and the pedagogical problems of teachers who not only inhabit the land, but also educate the next generation. This shared topic supplied a sense of mutual understanding. Each side even was curious to hear how the other sees the same reality; for example, familiar landscapes were made strange when seen through the other's eyes. But this could not become the foundation of a dialogue. The ostensible sharing latently functioned as a tacit agreement of avoidance. As could be expected, after a while the ritualistic listening and ritualistic understanding became more of a burden. The undercurrents in the group accumulated and sought an outlet.

This became clear when one of the Arabs told about the 1948 Israeli invasion of his village that took place when he was a little boy, and his family's flight from his home. The Israelis found it unbearable to "understand" that situation. They interpreted the story not as a description of a person's life, but as a demand for identification, which immediately implied self-negation on their part—that is, that they see themselves as unjust aggressors. Understanding the other meant self-derogation, guilt, shame, and granting power to the enemy. Their response was rage in the form of a countering story told by an Israeli. An Israeli woman described growing up as the child of two survivors of the Nazi Holocaust. The central message the story delivered to the Arabs was this: "How can you say that I am an un-just aggressor if I am a survivor of horrors you cannot even imagine?" The story contrasted one form of suffering with another. The Arabs could not accept this, and dismissed the suffering of the Jews as irrelevant.

The two stories were followed by similar stories from other members of the group, which divided into two opposite camps that shot stories at each other. The respective claims for presence, empathy, and identification were resisted by coun-terclaims. This war in dialogue eventually reached the hard, impenetrable nucleus of the inability to not understand. Each side cloaked itself in its own sense of jus-tice. Mistaking the posture for one of inability to understand, rather than inability to not understand, the parties kept explaining to each other why they should be considered just, using historical, sociological, psychological, and biographical data to bolster their arguments. Yet any recognition of the other's otherness as standing at its own center, and thus having a different truth, was too threatening for each side to accept. Otherness was perceived as automatically implying the re-flexive enforcement of self-negation. To avoid this, the participants repeated their initial positions, with mounting rage.

The group soon reached an impasse, its members feeling that dialogue was im-possible. Accusations, guilt, and prejudices of the most extreme kind emerged. Each side presented itself as victimized by the other's aggression, reinforcing its statements with fantasies of destruction and despair. The conversation became a zero-sum game of identities. The forces acting toward dialogue (peace) were coun-teracted by forces acting toward overpowering the other (war). Only this double bind kept the conversation from exploding. This impasse lasted for hours. It be-came impossible for both parties not to understand what they were convinced they understood. This resulted in a prolonged process of a defensive (although seem-ingly aggressive) entrenchment. The overriding feeling was that of one closing in upon oneself and seeing that any further move inevitably would be no more than a sham, and would not move one forward.

After a few hours, the despair and fatigue resulting from the situation became more dominant than the rage. Explanations were exhausted. Silence took over, throwing the participants into their corners. Out of this impasse came a moment in which some uttered phrases about "the impossibility of talking to each other within the framework of existing understandings." Turning to a reflexive relation-ship marked a slow and difficult shift to a new dialogic strategy. The new strategy acknowledged that the Israelis and Arabs were locked in their own "blind" under-standing, and that even when exposing their blindness, they actually were unwill-ing to relinquish their former attitudes and listen to the other. Listening, which meant granting the power of speech and presence to the other, was not something they wanted to offer. In this they revealed their own hard selves.

The group's opening up to this experience was accompanied by a sense of "suf-focation." As one of the participants described it, they felt suffocated (locked) within their inability to not understand. The passage (in the circle of understand-ing) to the state of the ability to not understand was only hinted at in the group. Its main accomplishment was the mutual realization of each side's autocentric position. This realization bore in it the ability to not understand, because what became evident in the group process was the existence of more than one authoritative origin of meaning, truth, and justice. The depression of the group was a turning point from which new insights began to bloom.

In summarizing the group's work, the participants reported that the passage from ritual to automatic understanding—to the complexity involving reflexive distance—was their main insight. Readers must note that the participants developed no deep sense of understanding, empathy, or identification with the other, but rather a sense of having retreated a step from their former attitudes. Instead of making a real opening, this group came to a realization of one's own closure. The group also translated these insights into possible applications for educational programs for the classroom and for encounters between Israeli and Arab children.

Chapter 33

The Telltale Heart
Apology, Reparation, and Redress

Mari J. Matsuda and Charles R. Lawrence III

> I tremble for my country, when I reflect that God is just.
> —Thomas Jefferson

> They shall build up the ancient ruins, they shall raise
> up the former devastations; they shall repair the ruined
> cities, the devastations of many generations.
> —Isaiah 61:4

One sunny day, on the island of Yap, in part of the Pacific island group of Micronesia, I was running a course designed to teach the common law of torts to Micronesian judges. I posed a hypothetical designed to illustrate the master rule of fault-based liability in tort. "What if," I asked, "a little boy runs out from behind the high brush, into the road, and is hit by a car? The driver was driving carefully and could not have stopped in time to avoid the accident. The child is killed instantly."

This was the easy case, the first of a series of hypotheticals designed to show that once fault is unclear, liability becomes unclear. To the judges, however, it was not an easy case. It was a false case. No one could respond to it justly without more facts.

One of the judges, enjoying the Socratic method and intending to teach me a thing or two, asked for more facts. How many sons, he asked, in the family of the driver? How many sons in the family of the injured child? How did the family of the injured child learn of the injury? How soon, and from whom?

"Okay," I said, "I give up. You tell me how you would decide the case."

What the judges learned that day was the peculiar habit, in Western law, of limiting the relevant facts. All an American jurist would want to know is whether the driver was at fault in the accident; there would be no liability if the driver was exercising ordinary care.

From Charles R. Lawrence III and Mari J. Matsuda, *We Won't Go Back: Making the Case for Affirmative Action* (Boston: Houghton Mifflin, 1997), 231–233.

What I learned from the judges that day is that there is a universe of relevant questions to ask after an accident if one lives on a tiny, isolated island, and if it is an absolute imperative to live in peace.

Fault is irrelevant, the judges explained. If your driving hurts someone, you should make sure you go immediately to the family to tell of the tragedy and of your grief. They should not hear the news first from someone else. Your remorse must meet the test of sincerity. Your kin should come quickly with food and gifts to show their intent to make amends. If you are lucky, you will have a son to work the taro fields of the family who lost a son. Your son will work for them all of his days, as part of your apology, and the apology, sanctified by elders and sacred ritual, must find a gracious welcome in the wounded family. They allow their loss to overcome them, such that your sincere apology is received insincerely, they will lose status in the community.

This system of repairing great loss is not about account keeping. It is part of the sacred, in a culture that does not separate the sacred from the secular. The longstanding customs that govern reactions to the tragedy of an automobile accident guarantee the spiritual wholeness of all citizens. When either side—what we would call in Western law the plaintiff or the defendant—fails to comport itself according to custom, the well-being of the entire community is in jeopardy.

If the judges' system works in the idealized way they described, it achieves something the American legal system does not: both the plaintiff and the defendant walk away at peace.

In another part of the Pacific, Native Hawaiians speak matter-of-factly about the payback for human failings. Traditional Hawaiians place value in the concept of *pono*, the state of being that is peace, repose, goodness. Upsetting *pono*, disrupting the rhythms of the land and its people, is a wrong—not only to fellow human beings, but to the cosmology. The price is illness, misfortune, cataclysm. When the volcano erupts, taking out roads and villages, the Hawaiians look around for someone who acted against *pono*—perhaps the developer who bulldozed old burial grounds, or the politician who acted out of greed, or a family whose feud was left to fester.

In the Judeo-Christian tradition, the Lord says, "Vengeance is mine." There is a wisdom beyond human comprehension that determines what pain to exact for human transgression. Few cultures exist that do not have some notion of judgment. Actions have consequences. This is a law of physics we transmute to a law of our lives.

Those cultures which make active use of apology rituals are often the ones that acknowledge the importance of community cohesion. Apology rituals, within societies that depend on the clan or village to provide a social safety net, are essential for survival. A dispute resolution mechanism that results in one party's walking home happy and the other's walking away from the village forever is an utter failure. To make the community whole, to erase the bad feelings of the past, to come jointly once again to the table, is imperative. In the Jalé villages of New Guinea, for instance, elders require feuding clan members to come together to feast on pig, each tearing the best morsel from the bone to place in the mouth of the former foe. This is what makes the elders smile. An apology in such communities leads to a gain, not a loss, in status.

This approach contrasts with the modern Western view that an apology diminishes status. Typically, in American society, when someone confesses an error or wrongdoing, he is seen as weak and vanquished, disempowered and vulnerable. Ask an American lawyer what to do at the scene of an accident, whether a car crash or a nuclear meltdown, and the first rule is "Don't apologize."

In America we have no comparable clan, no network of kin and near kin with whom we must maintain peace, with whom we must ceremoniously share our food even when we don't want to. The failure to know that the globe is our village, that every act of disregard for the planet and its inhabitants sets in motion disruptions of the good, is the curse of modernism.

EDITOR'S NOTE

See also Deborah L. Levi, "The Role of Apology in Mediation," 72 *New York University Law Review* 1165 (1997).

Chapter 34

The Chinese Concepts of "Face"

Hsien Chin Hu

Investigations by anthropologists and psychologists have shown that while the desire for prestige exists in every human society, the value placed upon it and the means for attaining it vary considerably. In the analysis of a culture different in emphasis and basic attitudes from our own it is important to keep in mind that that society may have formed different conceptions of even the most universal aspects of human life. Very often this difference in conception is reflected in the vocabulary, but a careful investigation of the situations in which such concepts figure is required to interpret their full meaning for the bearers of the culture. The study of the concepts of "face" in China is particularly interesting because it reveals two sets of criteria by which prestige is gained and status secured or improved, and also how different attitudes can be reconciled within the framework of the same culture.

Verbally the two sets of criteria are distinguished by two words which on the physical level both mean "face." One of these, *mien-tzŭ*, stands for the kind of prestige that is emphasized in this country: a reputation achieved through getting on in life, through success and ostentation. This is prestige that is accumulated by means of personal effort or clever maneuvering. For this kind of recognition ego is dependent at all times on his external environment. The other kind of "face," *lien*, is also known to Americans without being accorded formal recognition. It is the respect of the group for a man with a good moral reputation: the man who will fulfill his obligations regardless of the hardships involved, who under all circumstances shows himself a decent human being. It represents the confidence of society in the integrity of ego's moral character, the loss of which makes it impossible for him to function properly within the community. *Lien* is both a social sanction for enforcing moral standards and an internalized sanction.

Of the two words for "face": *lien* and *mien*, the latter is by far the older, being found in ancient literature. *Mien* had acquired a figurative meaning referring to the relation between ego and society as early as the fourth century B.C. *Lien* is a more modern term, the earliest reference cited in the K'ang-hsi Dictionary dating from the Yuan Dynasty (1277–1367). This word seems to have originated some-

Reprinted by permission of the American Anthropological Association from *American Anthropologist* 46–50, 61–64 (1944). Not for further reproduction.

where in North China and gradually to have supplanted *mien* in the physical sense, and also to have acquired some of its figurative meaning. Meanwhile, *mien*, with the meaningless syllable *-tzŭ* attached, had developed different connotations. Both words are now current in North and Central China, though in Central China, that is the Yangtze provinces, *lien* is not used to the extent it is in the north. However, here the difference in the referents for *lien* and *mien* is understood, though it is not always consciously realized.

Lien

Tiu-lien—"to lose *lien*" is a condemnation by the group for immoral or socially disagreeable behavior. A serious infraction of the moral code of society, once come to the notice of the public, is a blemish on the character of the individual and excites a great deal of comment. A fraud detected, a crime exposed, meanness, poor judgment, lies told for one's own profit, unfaithfulness while in office, a broken promise, the cheating of a customer, a married man making love to a young girl, these are just some of the acts that incur the criticism of society, and are rated as "losing *lien*" for ego.

A simple case of *lien*-losing is afforded by the experience of an American traveler in the interior of China. In a little village she had made a deal with a peasant to use his donkey for transportation. On the day agreed upon the owner appeared only to declare that his donkey was not available, the lady would have to wait for one day. Yet he would not allow her to hire another animal, because she had consented to use his ass. They argued back and forth first in the inn, then in the courtyard; a crowd gathered around them, as each stated his point of view over and over again. No comment was made, but some of the older people shook their heads and muttered something, the peasant getting more and more excited all the time trying to prove his right. Finally he turned and left the place without any more arguments, and the American was free to hire another beast. The man had felt the disapproval of the group. The condemnation of his community of his attempt to take advantage of the plight of the traveler made him feel he had "lost *lien*."

A criminal case that occurred in Peiping in 1935 is a good example of the seriousness of "losing *lien*." A college student had come to be on very intimate terms with a girl-student. He had promised to marry her, but when she found herself pregnant, he denied his promise in a letter. Thereupon she went to see him in his dormitory. Not finding him in, she hanged herself then and there. The student was arrested at once and given a sentence of ten years. The feeling of the public against the irresponsibility of the young man which drove the young girl to despair ran high indeed. The suicide was the most severe accusation and caused many discussions of his bad character, making him "lose *lien*" completely. However, the judgment of the public does not always follow the grooves of the law. When a person commits a crime which is regarded as justified, though he be subject to punishment by justice, society will not think of him as one who flaunts moral standards for his own profit; he does not "lose *lien*."

In the above case the victim exposed the character of the culprit by her suicide. This may be effected by less serious means. A mistreated servant may turn on his master in exasperation and denounce him for his inhuman behavior. A student may show up his teacher for making a mistake. A customer who finds a business-man trying to get the better in a bargain can expose him by attracting a crowd and telling them what sort of a man the merchant is. As business-men are very careful of their reputation, they will often give in to a particularly quarrelsome customer, so as to avoid arousing unwelcome attention. The servant, the student, and the customer maintain their rights by making the other party "lose *lien*."

Because righteous indignation is a legitimate weapon in the hand of an inferior, or of a victim of fraud or injustice, a person of high status, such as a member of the gentry in a village, or the professional or scholar in the city has to be more circumspect in dealing with people of lower status. Such a person would be entitled to the respect of the younger and inferior, but this respect would be impaired if ego lost dignity by behavior very contrary to the expectation of society. Except for extreme cases, the higher the social standing of a person the more dignity he has to maintain, and the more vulnerable this *lien* becomes. While a poor man is justified in husbanding his resources, the wealthy man who shows himself stingy offends the code of decency and incurs public censure. For a person of education to be drawn into a violent argument with a rough country-fellow is much beneath his dignity. Education is regarded as training of character as much as the accumulation of knowledge, so "those who have drunk ink" should achieve greater self-control in social behavior than people who never had such a chance. Therefore an open quarrel with an illiterate person greatly damages the dignity of ego and causes him to "lose *lien*."

Status is graded within the family too. The father of the family occupies a higher standing and commands more respect than a younger brother attached to the household. A *faux pas* on his part in dealing with people of lesser status would cause much more comment and "loss of *lien*." Again, of two boys of the same age living in the same extended family, one may have achieved higher status through marriage. This confers the position of a responsible adult on him and he will have to refrain from childish behavior such as enjoying candy and firecrackers, which would be all right for his unmarried cousin.

It once happened to me to slap the face of a boy-servant for dishonesty. It is bad manners to hit anyone, for a young lady to administer physical punishment to a male servant is altogether beneath her dignity. For a long time I had to endure the reproaches of my family and in the eyes of the servants I had definitely "lost *lien*." No one had sympathy for me, but the boy went unreprimanded by the others.

To choose an example from international politics: The appeasement policy of Chamberlain up to the outbreak of the European War, in the face of Britain's treaty obligations to smaller nations, was felt as extremely "*lien*-losing" in China. To be unwilling to keep promises to weaker nations because of its own interests was compatible neither with its claim to status as the most powerful empire of the world, nor with the desire of the leaders of the nation to be termed gentlemen.

Thus, the "loss of *lien*" varies in intensity with the status of ego. Condoning factors in the life of the poor and downtrodden are taken into account when the public voices its opinion, while the misbehavior of the well-to-do is contrasted with their social eminence. A position of economic advantage has to be exploited without offending moral standards. Persons in subordinate positions can use the fact that their superiors must maintain their *lien* at a high level. Students at certain universities used to subject every new instructor to an intense questioning during his first lectures. Should he prove unable to answer, his incapability would be proven and his *lien* lost. The creditor, too, in a business transaction who cannot collect from a powerful debtor may press his debtor knowing that the latter will lose *lien* if he is called irresponsible and dishonest in public. The debtor for this reason often hides himself from his creditor, and by this act is regarded as having acknowledged his incapacity. The creditor is satisfied that the other is anxious to maintain his *lien* and will eventually pay his debt. He feels he has gained a moral advantage.

The consciousness that an amorphous public is so-to-say supervising the conduct of ego, relentlessly condemning every breach of morals and punishing with ridicule, has bred extreme sensitivity in some people. This is particularly obvious where the taking of the initiative may incur failure. The wooing situation provides a good example: Modern China does not believe in marriages arranged by parents. Yet a boy, though he knows a girl quite well, will often hesitate a long time before making up his mind to ask the decisive question, because he dreads a refusal and the consequent ridicule of his fellows. Similarly, boys are shy in approaching girls, fearing to make a clumsy impression and thus "losing *lien*." So they will ask friends to introduce them to the girl of their choice. A young person who fails to pass an examination will sometimes feel the shame so keenly as to commit suicide. To understand this aspect of *lien* we have to investigate a little further its relation to personality as conceived in this culture.

Western observers have often remarked that Chinese are excessively modest about their attainments and status; they sometimes go as far as accusing them of hypocrisy. The exaggerated modesty is not a sign of lack of self-confidence, as it appears to the objective observer at the first glance. The over-estimation of one's ability, the exaggeration of one's capacity, designed to elevate one above one's fellows, is frowned upon by society. As physical violence is discountenanced, so is every action that might call forth unpleasant feelings, such as envy and dislike, in other people. A person given to boasting will not have the sympathy of his group when he fails; rather will he incur ridicule. A person with such poor judgment of his powers is termed "light and floating" (*ch'ing-fou*) in character; a person serious in his endeavors but careful in reckoning his abilities and circumspect in his dealing with others is called "sinking and steady" (*ch'ên-chuo*) or "reliably heavy" (*wên-chung*). The former type of personality cannot be trusted, but the latter is a good citizen and trustworthy friend. Now it is not easy to gauge one's capacity exactly at every point nor is it possible to foresee the outcome of every venture, so it is wise to underestimate one's value. In this way one will always have the satisfaction of hearing friends deny this inferiority and thus gain greater conviction of the possibility of success. The fear of being considered "light and floating" is similar to that of being blamed for immoral behavior. So ego will depreciate his intelligence and capacity on every occasion, always confident that people will have an all the higher opinion of him.

This emphasis on modesty seems to be linked to the importance attributed to "self-training" (*hsiu-yang*). Since Confucius described the sequence of training through which ego has to pass to prepare for leadership in the state, scholars have often stressed the responsibility of the individual for the formation of his character. A person "without self-training" is one who shows no consideration for others or is given to boasting. Thus the failure of ego's venture demonstrates his immaturity and uncertainty, and so impairs the confidence of the community in his performance within his status.

This attitude also explains why a person's *lien* is lost if, after criticizing somebody, ego commits the same mistake. We have here identical behavior in A and B. On the part of B it may be unwitting or unintentional, or its import may not have been realized. By his reproof of B, A has shown himself superior in knowledge; at least, he has shown that he understands how unwise such conduct is. By committing the same mistake, he demonstrates either a weak will or an untrained character. The conception of human nature as inherently evil is absent in China;[1] the training of the personality should accompany the growing understanding of the mind. To be insincere in one's efforts to achieve a better character and at the same time to call attention to another's fault is like throwing stones when one lives in a glass house. The contempt of society is expressed in terms of "loss of *lien*."

We have seen that all infringements of the moral code, all acts contrary to behavior of a person of ego's status cause a depreciation of character. The loss of esteem is felt acutely and is symbolically expressed as "loss of *lien*." The fear of "losing *lien*" keeps up the consciousness of moral boundaries, maintains moral values, and expresses the force of social sanctions. Behavior that is usually not classed as immoral: the self-confidence of the opportunist, the criticism of another in the absence of control of one's own conduct, the failure of an undertaking through lack of judgment, also are punished by "loss of *lien*." "Loss of *lien*" is felt acutely, for it entails not only the condemnation of society, but the loss of its confidence in the integrity of ego's character. Much of the activity of Chinese life is operated on the basis of trust. As the confidence of society is essential to the functioning of the ego, the "loss of *lien*" has come to constitute a real dread affecting the nervous system of ego more strongly than physical fear.

Conclusion

Lien refers to the confidence of society in the moral character of ego. The concept of sin does not figure to any great extent in Chinese culture although it is not unknown. But the assumption of human nature as inherently good places on the individual the responsibility of training his character according to his own light and the demands of his status. A disregard for the standards of behavior causes the group to doubt the moral character of the individual and to question his ability to perform his roles. This "loss of *lien*" puts ego outside the society of decent human beings and threatens him with isolation and insecurity. *Lien* is not only an external sanction for behavior that violates moral standards, but constitutes an internal sanction as well. It will have been noticed that *lien* is conceived of as being maintained or lost as a whole; it forms an invisible entity as experienced by ego, though its loss may be felt more or less strongly. In extreme cases the realization that one's conduct has been damned by group standards drives an individual to suicide.

Mien-tzŭ differs greatly from *lien* in that it can be borrowed, struggled for, added to, padded—all terms indicating a gradual increase in volume. It is built up through initial high position, wealth, power, ability, through cleverly establishing social ties to a number of prominent people, as well as through avoidance of acts that would cause unfavorable comment. The value that society attaches to *mien-tzŭ* is ambivalent. On the one hand, it refers to well-earned popularity which is called *ming-yü*—"reputation" in its best sense; on the other, it implies a desire for self-aggrandizement. While moral criteria are basic in evaluating a person's worth to his group, self-maximation is allowed as a motive for greater exertion.

That *lien* and *mien-tzŭ* constitute separate concepts is well shown in the difference of reaction to the expressions "to have no *lien*" and "to have not *mien-tzŭ*." The former is the worst insult, casting doubt on the integrity of ego's moral character; the latter signifies merely the failure of ego to achieve a reputation through success in life. Again, "to want *mien-tzŭ*" is by no means the opposite of "not to want *lien*." As explained before, the latter means that society considers ego's action a deliberate flaunting of moral standards in order to obtain practical advantages. "To want *mien-tzŭ*" is to increase or maintain prestige beyond one's station in life. As soon as the motive behind ego's actions becomes apparent in this case, he is shamed by loss of *lien*. Ego's lack of ability to influence his fellow-men or to convince them that he is a valuable asset to the community may be regrettable from his point of view, but it does not provide a shock to his self-respect that the loss of the confidence of society in his character does.

As the basic prerequisite for the personality, *lien* is included among the conditions determining the amount of ego's *mien-tzŭ*. Once *lien* is lost, *mien-tzŭ* will be hard to maintain. Because of this interrelationship the concept of *lien* is bound to overlap with that of *mien-tzŭ*. Deliberately to make a person "lose *lien*" is termed non-consideration for so-and-so's *mien-tzŭ*. Very frequently what a sensitive person feels as "loss of *lien*" may be regarded as no more than "looking bad on his or her *mien-tzŭ*" by an outsider. Besides, the mores differing to some extent in different parts of the country, the line differentiating behavior leading to "loss of *lien*" or to a depreciation of *mien-tzŭ* varies considerably. Thus *lien* and *mien-tzŭ* are not two entirely independent concepts. Nevertheless, their referents clearly belong to two distinct sets of criteria for judging conduct.

The importance of *lien* and *mien-tzŭ* varies with the social circumstances of ego. All persons growing up in any community have the same claim to *lien*, an honest, decent "face"; but their *mien-tzŭ* will differ with the status of the family, personal ties, ego's ability to impress people, and so on. In a tightly-knit community the minimum requirements for the status of each person are well recognized. Anyone who does not fulfill the responsibilities associated with his roles will throw out of gear some part of the mechanism of well-ordered social life. For example, the head of a family who neglects his duties will place the burden for his dependents on the shoulders of his relatives or the village. Such irresponsible behavior in ego will arouse doubts as to his competence in maintaining his status. So society decrees that the "light-and-floating" character cannot be trusted, for such a person does not take his duties and obligations seriously; he does not have enough concern for *lien*. At the same time, the small farmer, the store-keeper, the laborer, and so forth know that the "heavy-steady" type can be trusted, for he prizes his *lien* above the riches of the world; they know that they themselves can always rely on the help of friends as long as they maintain their *lien* intact.

Thus *lien* operates within the community as a means for insuring the social-economic security of ego and for maintaining his self-respect. In order that the community may form an opinion of his moral character an individual necessarily has to live continually in the same locality. A change of residence will put him in a new environment, out of reach of the constant reminder of "loss of *lien*" when this has occurred. So the city with its many opportunities for work is the welcome refuge for many an individual who has lost the respect of his group through lack of virtue. But even in the city the criteria for *lien* operate when one seeks steady employment. A craftsman taking an apprentice will want to know more about his character and the character of his family; a firm hiring an accountant will demand that the good conduct of the candidate be endorsed by respectable people. Thus the custom has arisen that anyone who seeks employment, anyone who intends to conclude a deal with someone in a locality far from home brings a written guarantee from a shop with a good reputation in his own neighborhood. These people would know how much concern ego has shown for his *lien* when staying with his family.

To be able to count on the confidence of his fellow-men even the poorest peasant or laborer will be anxious to preserve his *lien*. He cannot achieve *mien-tzŭ*, the reward for success in life, but he can conduct his life so that no blemish can be cast on his character. This will assure him work when he is in need of it, sympathy in adversity, moral support in disputes, and recommendations to employers in other parts when it becomes necessary to leave home.

In the middle classes the individual has a good start in life and has many opportunities for rising higher, but he must also be on the guard not to slip down the social scale. Here *lien* is still very important. However, *mien-tzŭ* has become a serious concern for ego, for he knows that by the manipulation of all possibilities to increase his prestige he is certain of social advancement. To make use of the opportunities offered by society he has to exert his efforts to demonstrate his ability, enlarge his friendship circle and follow in detail the conventions regulating social intercourse. The higher he ascends the social ladder, the wider the circle of eyes fastened upon his career, the more he must try to impress people. "Loss of *lien*" must be avoided, of course; a question regarding the integrity of his moral character would cause him to sink low in the esteem of his group. But no politician, no lawyer, no doctor, no scholar will expect to rise in social standing without building up his *mien-tzŭ*.

Lien also figures in the business world, although *mien-tzŭ* is a prime consideration. Once the community has acknowledged that a person is honest in his dealings and lives up to his obligations, he has credit far beyond his perhaps very modest possessions. For his creditors know that concern for keeping the respect of the community will force him to the utmost effort in satisfying their claims. This is the reason that up to recent times Chinese business-men, though among the most prudent in the world, very often concluded deals without written contract. A person with a feeling for *lien* can be trusted implicitly, for *lien* is worth more than a fortune to those who value it. However, some merchants are unscrupulous. The fluidity of the city population has made it possible for these people to make profits in flagrant violation of the moral code. Much of the dislike for business men as a class is due to this emphasis on the profit motive. The feeling is that a person acting on such incentives cannot care for his moral character. Business thrives best where the mechanism of supply-and-demand is trusted to keep all parties satisfied. In Chinese society it had to accommodate itself to the insistence on *lien* as part of one's reputation; in those instances, for example, when business deals were at the expense of the seller or borrower, the business-man was assailed by all classes.

Lien is prized even by people living outside the pale of organized society. Banditry is often the result of famines and depressions. Even though defying the law, some outlaws do not lose their sense of decency, and will confine themselves to looting those who have too much, while on occasion helping the poor. In recent years before the war a thief in Peiping had achieved a good deal of popularity by stealing from the rich and handing a good deal of his wealth to the indigent. Such individuals naturally have not the slightest *mien-tzŭ*, but their actions show a respect for virtue which indicates that they were compelled by circumstances to become outlaws. They are not people who "do not want *lien*."

We have seen how important the idea of *lien* is for judging the personality: how *mien-tzŭ* confers on a person social standing far above one's fellows; how the middle classes have to struggle to maintain *lien* and increase their prestige. As the upper class is recruited largely from a middle class base, the highest executives in the government have always striven for both. Many a minister has ended his life by his own hands because he felt that on account of his inefficiency he had "no *lien* to see his emperor." Yet among the people who rise on top, particularly in times of stress and strain, there are those who care for *mien-tzŭ* far more than for *lien*. Opportunists often build up their reputation by all possible means, avoiding social censure for a time. Then, once wealth is acquired, power attained, and position consolidated, they trust their *mien-tzŭ* to be strong enough to hush talk about their moral character. The warlords during the early part of the Republic are a good example. Each of them maintained his power by military force, perpetrating many crimes for the sake of money, but not allowing these to become public, meanwhile attracting to them politicians to help them devise taxing systems. They found the troubled conditions an easy opportunity to achieve success and sought to do so without regard to the moral standards of society, so that their liquidation was treated with rejoicing by all classes. They believed that they could maintain their position and prestige by means of money and military force, but their disregard for lies earned for them the contempt of their nation.

NOTE

1. We are speaking here of the society as a whole. Individual thinkers have discussed the probability of man's nature being inherently evil and needing training to fit it for a well-ordered social life. Foremost among these was Hsün-tzu, a disciple of Confucius. But in the long run, his philosophy could not prevail against that of Mencius, also a disciple of Confucius, who maintained the inborn tendency to goodness in man. Through the centuries Mencius has been read by every schoolboy, Hsün-tzu only by a few philosophers.

Chapter 35

Pirates, Dragons, and U.S. Intellectual Property Rights in China
Problems and Prospects of Chinese Enforcement

Glenn R. Butterton

Chinese Culture : Confucianism and Legalism

In its purest form, the thesis that China is fundamentally at odds with the Western Rule of Law tradition argues that Chinese society is not and essentially never has been devoted to or guided by the concept of law as it is known in the West. In place of Western-style law, the Chinese rely on a notion of personal relationship associated with the concept of li. The concept, though it is widely identified with the teachings of Confucius (551–479 B.C.), antedated him and appears to have been established in Chinese bureaucratic thought and the larger culture during the Western Zhou Period (1122–771 B.C.), if not before. What I will call the "Confucian" perspective turns on the concept of li, particularly as it stands in opposition to the concept of fa. But where the concept of li is identified with Confucius' work, the concept of fa is associated with the work of the Chinese Legalist philosophers and the harsh rule of the Qin dynasty in the third century B.C. Put in concise, if misleadingly simple, terms, li is associated with propriety and moral force, while fa is associated with physical force and law, though the concept of law here invoked includes only a limited subset of the meanings of the word "law" in English.

The Concept of Li

The concept of li, when narrowly construed, refers to proper conduct, or politeness or etiquette; more broadly construed, it refers to the whole range of political, social, and familial relationships that are the underpinnings of a harmonious Confucian society.[1] Those who are guided by li stand ready to adjust their views and demands in order to accommodate the needs and desires of others, and they demonstrate this by yielding to others for the sake of harmony when confrontation and conflict arise. When all parties to a dispute endeavor to make concessions, the necessity for litigation and the promotion of individual rights

From 38 *Arizona Law Review* 1081, 1108–1113 (1996). Copyright © 1996 by the Arizona Board of Regents. Reprinted by permission.

are both avoided. Individual interests are subordinated to the interests of the group such that one who, to the contrary, insists on individual rights is very much at odds with li and with the group as well. "The proper disposition with regard to one's interests," writes Benjamin Schwartz, "is the predisposition to yield rather than the predisposition to insist." Li thus tends to lead naturally to compromise and mediation framed not in terms of a legal proposition or requirement but in terms of the circumstances of the participants. As Alice Tay puts it, "Chinese tradition personalizes all claims, seeing them in the context of social human relationships."

Social Roles and the Five Relations

The "relationships" of Confucian society consist of connections between various types of political, social, and familial roles. The roles are also normative, embodying prescriptions that tell those who play the roles how they ought to act when playing them. Thus, the role of father embodies a norm of proper fatherly behavior; the role of friend embodies a norm of friendship; and similarly, other norms are expressed for the other fundamental roles of wife, child, ruler, subject, elder brother, and younger brother. Eventually, Confucianism reduced all relationships to a finite set of fundamental relationships that were presumed to be exhaustive, the so-called Five Relations which obtained between father and child, husband and wife, elder and younger brother, ruler and subject, and friend and friend.[2] The li expressed the rules of conduct involved in all of these basic relationships, and, at bottom, the li were about the obligations between parties to relationships. Writes William Alford:

> The li in their most rigid pre-Confucian form clearly envisioned a hierarchical world, not only along class lines . . . but also along those of gender and age. They also, however, clearly provided that the person who enjoyed the loyalty or support of others by virtue of holding a superior position—be it socially, politically or in the family— owed a commensurate obligation to those providing that loyalty or support.

Fa and the Rule of Law

It is typically assumed that when government leans heavily on fa to reinforce its authority, it does so because it has no effective ability to rule by li. Fa, in contrast to li, is a penal concept; it is associated with punishment, serving to maintain public order through the threat of force and physical violence. The intellectual roots of fa are in the Legalist movement—a group of political philosophers primarily active in the China of the fourth and third centuries B.C., who held that social order could only be maintained by the use of law as a tool for manipulating society. The Qin dynasty adopted the Legalist philosophy and effectively integrated and centralized the whole of the Chinese Empire in the third century B.C. (221–209 B.C.). The Qin ruled with the aid of a harsh penal law and brutal tactics, and developed a vast administrative law bureaucracy to manage the empire they had created. They thus shaped an image of the "rule of law" as brutal and rigid, and that image

endured throughout the greatest period of Confucian influence from the first century A.D. to the development of civil-law criminal codes during the late nineteenth-century portion of the Qing dynasty (1644–1912 A.D.) and the beginning
of the Republican period following the 1912 revolution, when the last incarnation
of those codes was enacted. As for comparing fa to li, the Confucius of the
Analects said, "Govern the people by regulations, keep order among them by
chastisements, and they will flee from you, and lose all self-respect. Govern them
by moral force, keep order among them by ritual and they will keep their self-respect and come to you of their own accord."

Magistrates, the Legal Profession, and Extra-Legal Procedures

The penal character of Chinese law led to a general neglect, or at best a limited
interest in, such civil-law matters as contract, marriage, inheritance, and property
rights. By contrast, acts of impropriety or criminal violence tended to upset social
harmony which had to be restored through the punishment of the perpetrator.
Generally, the law operated not between two individuals with the state acting as
an intermediary, but rather between an individual and the state. Persons who had
suffered injury brought complaints to the state which would then determine
whether to act against the offending party; injured individuals never brought
claims directly against offending parties nor could they secure legal assistance or
expertise from lawyers since there was no formal legal profession that could aid
individuals. Typically, an injured party brought a complaint to a magistrate at the
district or county level who had wide ranging administrative responsibilities, including according to William P. Alford "the collection of taxes, the maintenance
of public order, and the investigation, prosecution and adjudication of criminal
matters." The magistrate, acting as judge and prosecutor, typically had no legal
training, but was assisted by an unofficial secretary who was often familiar with
the relevant laws and rules and was able to organize trials, propose sentences, and
write case reports.

The magistrate structure was the device through which the formal system of law
figured into the life of the average Chinese, but it was quite distinct from the web of
social relationships that gave expression to li and effectively shaped behavior in Confucian China. Those relationships included one's extended family and lineage; one's
non-blood relatives or extended "family" acquired through friendship; the trade association, guild, or crafts group to which one might belong; and the collection of
sages in one's community or within one's social circles. The advice, opinions, criticism, mediation efforts, and general normative influence of persons in those relationships tended to be the anchor of local society. If conflicts or controversies arose,
they were resolved not by the meager formal legal apparatus provided by the Emperor, but by elements of the social court of Confucian society, through the functioning of what are sometimes called "extra-legal procedures." This orientation toward community norms rather than formal law also betrays a deep skepticism toward formal law, its methods of dispute settlement, and especially its outcomes. The
extra-legal system, by contrast, had the pragmatic virtue of promising and delivering

results since it had the respect of the participants and was built on a deep, local knowledge of the issues and disputants, as well as a powerful drive to restore and maintain community harmony.[3]

Lingering Confucian Influences

Since Confucius has been alternately reviled and embraced in China under the Communists, it is perhaps not surprising that many Confucian habits have not only survived but prospered in the post-1979 China of Deng's reforms. The personal relationship or connection, what the Chinese call guanxi, remains central in interpersonal, bureaucratic, and commercial dealings in China today. The Chinese do not necessarily care to be bound by the fetters of law as they appear, for example, in the written language of contract, or in precise codifications of terms or individual rights and responsibilities. They prefer instead to remain flexible, free to adjust their views from time to time as befits unfolding circumstances in light of the needs of their ongoing personal relationships. To many, the shifting sands of "flexibility" and ad hoc adjustments are synonymous with a host of corrupt business practices, and the opportunism, rent-seeking, and shirking that are endemic in the state industries and administrative bureaucracies of Communist China. To the extent that the rule of law is antithetical to such practices, fa remains in low esteem, and the concept of li, as regards the centrality of personal relationships, endures as a guiding principle of Chinese social and economic life.

NOTES

1. In its narrowest construction, li is associated with the proper performance of ancestral sacrifices and other religious rituals. In fact, sinologists believe that li developed in conjunction with rituals that accompanied religious observances and sacrifices; the rituals were conducted by an elite class, so li regulated the behavior of members of the class, and eventually regulated behavior in the general population. Thus, beyond rituals, li embraces every kind of ceremonial and polite behavior, religious and secular, and embodies rules for relationships as diverse as getting married and entering into battle. See Benjamin Schwartz, *The World of Thought in Ancient China* (1985), 67–75, 151–56. See also Derk Bodde and Clarence Morris, *Law in Imperial China* (1967), 19.

2. *Editor's note:* It would appear that these gender-specific labels are intentional and that mothers and sisters, for instance, did not receive the same status and recognition as fathers and brothers. Presumably, however, mothers and sisters were still subject to "less fundamental" status and relationship rules. For example, a daughter-in-law was obligated and deferred to her mother-in-law in very specific ways.

3. For some economic accounts of Japanese actions that are typically characterized in cultural terms, see J. Mark Ramseyer, "Legal Rules in Repeated Deals: Banking in the Shadow of Defection in Japan," 20 *Journal of Legal Studies* 91 (1991); and Mark West, "The Pricing of Shareholder Derivative Actions in Japan and the United States," 88 *Northwestern University Law Review* 1436 (1994). William Alford sounds a wise cautionary note to those engaged in the theoretical analysis of Chinese and other foreign cultures:

[I]t is incumbent upon all of us in the field of comparative law—and particularly those of us who focus upon non-Western legal systems—to resist the pressure, often emanating from well-meaning colleagues, to approach distant cultures armed with or in search of "grand theory."

See William P. Alford, "On the Limits of 'Grand Theory' in Comparative Law," 61 *Washington Law Review* 945, 946 (1986). Alford does not suggest that "we should avoid bringing our own values to bear in evaluating foreign legal systems, even if we could do so," but rather is concerned that our efforts at engaging in broad theoretical work may unwittingly lead us to believe that we are considering foreign legal cultures in universal or value-free terms when, in fact, we are examining them through conceptual frameworks that are products of our own values and traditions, and that are often applied merely to see what foreign societies have to tell us about ourselves. In this regard, I should make clear that my focus in the present work is strictly on explanation and prediction. I make no claim that this discussion considers China in universal or value-free terms, only that it may enhance our ability to explain Chinese decision making.

Chapter 36

Autonomous Lawmaking
The Case of the "Gypsies"

Walter Otto Weyrauch and Maureen Anne Bell

Historical Origins and Ethnic Setting

There are anywhere from three to fifteen million Gypsies living in forty countries today. Although research in linguistics suggests a common Indian source, the origins of the Gypsy people remain unclear because their history is largely unrecorded. Some social scientists attribute this lack of recorded history to the high rate of illiteracy among the Gypsies. Interestingly, Gypsy illiteracy may have been purposeful. Gypsies share a fervent belief in their own uniqueness, and ethnocentricity has kept them from violating their prohibition against cultural integration. Likewise, myths surrounding the Gypsies and their origins might have been a matter of faith, or perhaps were devised to mislead non-Gypsies, and thus to support their own cultural insularity. A history of persecution has further reinforced this isolationism. As a result of suspicion and hostility, countries in western and central Europe have tried for centuries to rid themselves of the Roma. State-sponsored discriminatory measures have included forced assimilation and slavery, as well as the systematic murder of Gypsies in Nazi concentration camps. In spite of this persecution, or perhaps because of it, Gypsies have succeeded remarkably in retaining their cultural identity, often by engaging in the migratory behavior characteristic of the nomads of Asia.

The precise reasons why the Roma left their homeland remain uncertain. Current research suggests that the Roma are descendants of the Dravidians who inhabited India before the arrival of Indo-European populations. They appear to have left northern India between A.D. 1000 and 1025 during a period of frequent invasions of the Sind and Punjab regions by Islamic forces. Although the ethnic and caste origins of the Roma may have been mixed, prolonged separation from the Punjab weakened their identification with the subcontinent and eventually resulted in a culturally distinct population. Linguistic evidence supports this theory, but a more detailed historical foundation is still lacking.

No reliable sources document the arrival of the Gypsies in the United States or

Reprinted by permission of The Yale Law Journal Company and Fred B. Rothman & Company from *The Yale Law Journal*, vol. 103, pages 232–399.

their departure from other countries. An initial handful may have come with Columbus, and later England deported others. A significant number of Gypsies arrived in the United States with the immigration waves of the nineteenth and early twentieth centuries. In the United States, the Gypsies were not identified as such for quite some time, for several reasons. First, the United States, with its vast size and mobile population, offered a favorable environment for a population that often does not adhere to a sedentary life. Second, Gypsies commonly do not identify themselves as Gypsies, but merely indicate their last host home as their nationality. Finally, the presence of other non-white population groups helped the Roma to blend in unnoticed.

Functions of Concepts of Impurity (Marime)

The Gypsies' determination not to assimilate into the dominant society has been crucial to their survival as a separate population. This drive stems in part from the Roma's belief that non-Gypsies are in a state of defilement because of their ignorance about rules on purity and impurity. Gypsy society relies heavily on distinctions between behavior that is pure (*vujo*) and polluted (*marime*). The *marime* concept has powerful significance for Gypsies. *Marime* has a dual meaning: it refers both to a state of pollution and to the sentence of expulsion imposed for violation of purity rules or any behavior disruptive to the Gypsy community. Pollution and rejection are thus closely associated with one another. The *marime* rules minimize and regulate association between Gypsy and non-Gypsy. Although the notion of *marime* supports the Roma's desire for autonomy, Gypsy pollution taboos evolved in part to prevent dissension and disease among people living in deprived and unstable conditions.

According to *romaniya*, or Gypsy law, the human body is both pure and impure. The waist is the equator, or dividing line. The lower body is *marime* because the genital areas and the feet and legs may cause pollution and defilement. The upper body is fundamentally pure and clean. Any unguarded contact between the lower and upper bodies is *marime*. Rituals of purification preserve the power attributed to the upper half of the body and the health of the Gypsy concerned. Only the hands may transgress the boundary line between the upper and lower parts of the body.

Notions of purity and impurity follow the life cycle. Gypsies consider children *marime* for six weeks after birth because the birth canal is a polluting site. After this six-week period, children enjoy a privileged status in society until puberty, when they become subject to *marime* taboos. Following the onset of puberty, women remain in a latent stage of impurity until they reach menopause. In old age, Gypsies believe that one regains some of the innocence of childhood. As Carol J. Miller has noted, Gypsies consider elders "close to the gods and the ancestors." Postmenopausal women do not have the power to pollute by tossing their skirts (as they can before they reach menopause), because they no longer menstruate or bear children.

Pollution taboos vary from group to group and often among smaller Romani units. Nevertheless, Gypsies define themselves in part by their adherence to these cleanliness rituals. There may be class distinctions among some Roma, based on how strictly individuals or families maintain distinctions between purity and impurity. All these taboos involve rules that are aspirational. The actual behavior of the Gypsy people is likely to fall short of the communal expectations expressed in the taboos.

According to Elwood Trigg, the *marime* rules fall into four overlapping categories: (1) taboos directly or indirectly related to the fear of being contaminated by women; (2) sexual taboos; (3) things considered to be dirty or unhygienic; and (4) disdain of socially disruptive behavior. Adherence to these ritual purity laws is central in setting Gypsies apart from their host cultures.

Contamination by Women

Women may contaminate men in a number of ways.[1] Because of menstruation and childbirth, the Gypsies consider the female genitalia impure. A severe state of *marime* befalls any man if a woman lifts her skirt and exposes her genitals to him ("skirt-tossing"). A woman must never walk by a seated man because her genitals would be at the same height as his face. A man may not walk under a clothesline where women's clothes are hanging. Women cover their legs when they sit down and, in mixed company, single women keep their legs together when seated. These stringent rules may explain the traditionally long and wide skirts worn by Gypsy women. Especially in the United States, clothing has changed among Gypsy women, but skirts typically are still long. Slacks have also become acceptable apparel for women.

Historically, *marime* taboos were quite strict. For example, if a woman stepped into a stream, no one could drink from it for several hours because the water had been exposed to her genitals. The same taboo extended to food and dishes, all of which were thrown out if a woman stepped over them. Even today, some Roma will not rent a lower floor apartment for fear that a woman living upstairs will at some point pollute them by walking overhead. Similarly, a woman may get out of the car if her husband has to look under it because of mechanical trouble.

When a Gypsy woman goes to the toilet, special precautions must be taken to prevent any man from entering. Even a married couple will not share the bathroom at the same time. A man can become *marime* by using a toilet seat that a woman has sat on. To avoid this problem, Gypsies prefer to rent or buy residences that have two bathrooms. Among some groups, a woman cannot comb her hair or let it down in the presence of a man. A wife must undress with her back to her husband and get into bed before him. She must also rise in the morning before he does.

During her menstrual cycle, a woman is *marime* and must avoid contact with others. Among some groups, a menstruating woman must eat alone and cannot prepare food that will be eaten by a man. In addition, she must not sleep with her husband, or he will become polluted. With the onset of menstruation at puberty, a girl's clothing cannot be washed with men's, boys', or premenstrual girls' clothing.

Some researchers have indicated that much of the Gypsies' fixation with menstruation originates in India.

Pregnancy also signals danger of pollution for others. A pregnant woman may not prepare food for other Gypsies. She is expected to eat by herself and her food must be cooked in her own pots and pans. She cannot share a bed with her husband. Even after birth, there is still a period of time, up to six weeks, during which a woman is unclean. In former times, a pregnant woman's clothing, bedding, utensils, and even her tent were burned. Today, Gypsies view childbirth in hospitals as a convenience because the *gaje* [non-Gypsies] dispose of the polluted items. In public, couples strictly observe *marime* taboos, but privately husbands and wives may relax the standards somewhat.

Sexual Taboos

Sexual taboos have great importance in Gypsy law. The potential for defilement is greatly heightened at marriage because Gypsies perceive it as the end of a woman's innocence. Traditionally, marriage for Gypsies has occurred early, after age nine but usually before age fourteen. *Gajikano* influence may have undermined this tradition.

Sexual mores are rigorously enforced and a wife's complaint of "shameful practices" is ground for annulment as well as a sentence of *marime* and banishment of the husband. Gypsy law considers oral sex, sodomy, and homosexuality crimes against nature and prohibits them, although these acts may occur in secrecy. Moreover, even "appropriate" sexual activity between husband and wife may be "tinged with shame." Merely making implicit references to genitals, defecation, or sexual intercourse brings shame, especially when both sexes are present. In addition, Gypsies consider yawning or looking sleepy shameful, because they suggest that one is thinking about going to bed.

In spite of myths of Gypsy immorality, most Roma follow strict rules of sexual behavior. Prostitution and infidelity are unusual. *Marime* rules are particularly harsh on women. For example, if a Gypsy male marries a *gaji* (non-Gypsy female), his community will eventually accept her, provided that she adopts the Gypsy way of life. But it is a worse violation of the *marime* code for a Gypsy female to marry a *gajo* (non-Gypsy male), because Gypsy women are the guarantors for the survival of the population. Gypsies expect females to be virgins when they marry and to remain faithful to their husbands until death. Infidelity in marriage historically has had serious consequences for the wife, including mutilation or a sentence of *marime*.

Hygienic Matters

Complex rules also govern tangible items considered dirty or unhygienic. In Romani society, food preparation is replete with ritual. A woman must serve a man from behind and guard against reaching across or in front of him. Gypsies use the dining table exclusively for eating and keep it immaculately clean. In the past, women wore full white aprons when preparing meals or mending men's clothing in order to protect the food or clothing from the "dirt" of their dresses. Gypsies guard their dishes and utensils closely and generally do not share them with their *gajikane* guests. Visitors have to provide their own. If necessary, their hosts provide them with a set which traditionally must be destroyed afterwards or saved for other non-Gypsy visitors. Today, Gypsies use paper or plastic plates and tableware for this purpose. Silverware may regain purity after being soaked in bleach. Food in which a hair has been found must be discarded. Blowing one's nose or sneezing would pollute the food and make the offender *marime*, as would neglecting to wash one's hands before eating. A man who touches a woman's skirt should not handle food without washing his hands first. Even a shadow can pollute food.

A kitchen sink cannot be used for washing hands or clothes, only for cleaning dishes and silverware. A Rom who accidentally washes his hand in a basin for washing dishes is *marime*. Dishes that are mistakenly washed in a "polluted" place, regardless of their apparent cleanliness, must be destroyed or soaked in bleach. Gypsies divide their living quarters into *marime* and *vujo* areas. The front of the house could be *marime* unless protective measures are taken, since this is where the *gaje* may enter. Gypsies often reserve one chair for *gajikane* visitors. A Rom must never sit in this chair, for if he does, he will be deemed *marime*. Today, other furniture is protected from pollution with plastic covers. Gypsies never permit *gaje* in the back of the house.

The division between pure and impure extends to bodily by-products. Gypsies consider tears, spit, and even vomit clean because they emanate from the top half of the body, whereas emissions from the lower half of the body are polluting. Gypsies will take extreme measures to conceal the fact that they need to urinate.

Marime taboos extend to animals as well, from the edibility of certain types of meat to pet ownership. For example, dogs and cats, as opposed to horses, are considered polluted because of their unclean living habits. Gypsies consider cats particularly unclean because they lick their paws after burying their feces. The critical concern (as with dogs licking themselves) is that the uncleanliness of the external world may defile the purity of the inner self if it is permitted to enter the body through the mouth. Cats are also a sign of impending death. If a cat sets foot in a Gypsy's house, trailer, or automobile, a purification ceremony is required. Dogs are also unclean, but to a lesser extent. Dogs are tolerated outside the house because of their value as watchdogs.

Social Transgressions

Socially disruptive behavior may result in legal sanctions, including a sentence of *marime*. In addition to strong taboos against exploiting or stealing from a fellow member of the Gypsy community, Gypsies consider crimes of violence and noncommercial association with *gaje* as crimes against Romani society as a whole and therefore *marime*. A *marime* label can be removed by the forgiveness of the offended party, the passage of time, or a Gypsy legal proceeding called *kris Ro-*

mani. Readmission to Gypsy society following a sentence of *marime* is cause for celebration.

In all cases of *marime*, enforcement depends primarily on a superstitious fear of the consequences of violating the *marime* rules. The individual who violates a *marime* prohibition has succumbed to powers of evil and destruction that are so frightening that even his own family shuns him for fear of contamination. Such an individual becomes tainted and can be redeemed only by making the prescribed amends.

Administration of Justice

Because of the general lack of territorial boundaries, each Gypsy group can determine its own form of adjudication. Although there are many words for "group" in the Gypsy language, four primary associations can be identified: *natsia*, meaning nation; *kumpania*, an alliance of households not necessarily of the same *natsia* but of the same geographic area bound together for socioeconomic reasons; *vitsa*, or clan; and *familia*, which consists of the individual extended family. Each associational unit is involved administration of justice, beginning with the smallest, the *familia*, which informally settles minor disputes, and extending to the larger unit with increasing formality.

Role of Chiefs

Gypsies have no kings in the traditional meaning of the term. Every *vitsa* has *a rom baro*, literally meaning "Big Man," commonly referred to as the chief. The chief is elected for life, and the position is not inheritable. If a chief dies or falls into disgrace, another chief is chosen to replace him. The main criteria for chiefdom are intelligence and a sense of fairness. Wealth and large physical stature are not required, although they help. Most chiefs are literate. Elders are considered particularly suited to this role because they have greater knowledge of *romaniya* and are believed to be less susceptible to the temptations of violating the *marime* code. The chief chairs the council of elders, generally the patriarchs of the extended families. He is held accountable if he himself violates Gypsy law or ignores the other chiefs. All chiefs have equal authority and decide jointly about when the larger group should migrate.

There is a female counterpart to the chief. Her power is unofficial but substantial. The Vlax [a Gypsy group from Wallachia, Rumania] call her *mami*, *daki-dei*, or *dadeski-dei*. Other Gypsy groups use the term *phuri-dae* (old mother). She is the guardian of the moral code and helps decide matters involving women and children. In important affairs involving the entire *kumpania*, she is the spokeswoman for Gypsy women.

The tribal chiefs are not necessarily aware of all the laws; not only are the laws too numerous, but many laws have been lost because they have never been written down. The Gypsies interpret laws according to contemporary custom. Former rationales and interpretations of laws gradually may be revised as the needs of the community evolve. The exclusive reliance on oral transmission has led to a high degree of flexibility. Nevertheless, there is a shared, though not necessarily realistic, feeling that the law is clearly defined. Few ever challenge this notion. This strict adherence to the law in part accounts for the continued cohesion of the Gypsies in spite of their persecution and forced migration. Secrecy surrounds Gypsy law; unauthorized disclosure to the *gaje* may lead to sanctions.

Each chief handles all day-to-day conflicts within his population. When conflict emerges between Gypsies of different *vitsi* or *kumpaniyi* (singular *kumpania*), a *divano* may assemble. A *divano* is an informal proceeding where the chiefs of the various clans try to mediate a dispute. The parties themselves are not required to attend—and they are not technically bound by the chiefs' suggestions. But the contestants sometimes do bow to peer pressure and settle the case. Blatant disregard for the chiefs' recommendations could cost them the respect of the community.

Role of Courts *(Kris)*

When the Roma cannot settle a controversy amicably in a *divano*, a *kris* may become necessary. In former times, the *kris* usually adjudicated three kinds of cases: property losses, matters of honor, and moral or religious issues, including nonobservance of *marime* taboos. Brawls, demands by parents for return of their married daughters, defaults in payments of debts, *marime* violations, and personal retribution all required the attention of the *kris*. In the United States today, the *kris* calendar is largely occupied by divorce cases and economic disputes.

Divorce cases are complex. Even today, most Gypsy marriages which may not be legal marriages according to *gajikano* law are arranged, and the groom's family pays a bride price. If the marriage ends in divorce, a *kris* may be called to determine how much, if any, of the bride price should be returned to the groom's family.

Economic cases, on the other hand, cover such issues as who has the right to engage in fortune-telling in a specific territory. Gypsies believe that every Gypsy has the right to work. Accordingly, groups divide territory into economic units. Controversies may result when some Gypsies poach on others' turf, and then a *kris* is called. A first-time offender may receive a warning by the *kris*. Repeated violations result in a sentence of *marime*.

In all cases, it is the aggrieved party who must request the *kris*, which is then held at a neutral *kumpania*. If the alleged victim is old, sick, or very young, the victim's nearest male relative brings the case to the *kris*. If the welfare of the community demands joint action, the entire clan may be a plaintiff.

The elders of the tribes then hold a meeting and select one or more men to act as the *krisnitorya* (singular *krisnitori*), or judges. The plaintiff is allowed to choose the judge who will preside over his case, but the defendant has a right to veto that choice. Among the Roma in the United States it is not unusual for more than one judge to preside. The senior judge is surrounded by the members of the *kris* council, who act as associate judges. Generally, five or more men from both sides, usually the elders, form the council. In the United States, the council may have as many as twenty-five members.

The audience of a *kris* was once largely male. Women and unmarried or childless men were allowed to attend only if they were needed as witnesses. It is now acceptable, if unusual, to have the entire family present for support. Witnesses may speak freely about the case, for the Gypsies believe there can be no justice without hearing the matter out to its fullest. Exaggerated claims and ornate stories referring to folktales and mythology are common. When members of the audience think the witness is not being truthful or responsive, they hiss or make jokes. In some delicate matters, such as adultery, the public and witnesses can be excluded. At a *kris* only Romani may be spoken, and participants discourage lapses into English by shouting and hissing. Furthermore, arguments are often presented in a special oratory that differs grammatically from ordinary Romani and resembles a legal jargon. When the accused testify on their own behalf they are expected to be truthful. The *kris* can further ensure their honesty by invoking the magic power of the dead with an oath. If the witnesses must swear an oath, an altar of justice consisting of icons of the clans present is erected. In complex situations, the judge may ask for expert opinions from tribal chiefs or the elders. Nonetheless, only the judge decides guilt and punishment.

The judge declares the verdict in public to those who are present. In former times, if the accused Rom was found guilty, a married Gypsy woman was symbolically called on to tear a piece of cloth from her dress and throw it at the Rom, but this ritual is no longer practiced. If the accused is found innocent, there is a celebration and an oath of peace is sworn. The decision of the *kris* is final and binding. Even in countries such as Spain and the United States, where the Roma are considered by some *gajikane* scholars to be semi-assimilated, the verdict of an official state trial is not final: a *kris* will still be held. Beyond its judicial function, the *kris* plays an important role in maintaining the customs of the Gypsy people.

Legal Sanctions

The *kris* imposes punishment according to the seriousness of the offense. The death penalty, once an acceptable option, is now virtually unknown—possibly because of the Gypsies' fear of spirits and belief that the angry ghost of the deceased will take revenge upon the executioner. In times when the death penalty was still employed, the entire community would participate in the execution to prevent revenge by the spirit. The Roma seemed to feel a joint undertaking was safer, although today they rarely test this belief. Nowadays, the *kris* relies primarily on such sanctions as fines, corporal punishment, and banishment. The responsibility to pay a *kris*-imposed fine, called *glaba*, falls collectively on the wrongdoer's lineage. Corporal punishment, rarely employed today, is typically used only in cases of a wife's infidelity.

A sentence of *marime*, or banishment, is today considered the most severe punishment. *Marime* stigmatizes all wrongdoers as polluted and justifies their expulsion from the community. No one will eat with them. If they touch an object it must be destroyed, no matter what the value. Nobody will even attempt to kill them, for fear of contamination. When they die, no one will bury them, and they will not have a funeral. They will soon be forgotten. No marriages are arranged for those stigmatized as *marime*, and without marriage in Gypsy society one's economic and social life is over. In other words, permanent banishment is the equivalent of social death. Such punishment is rare and used only for serious crimes such as murder. An escape into *gajikano* society is not an alternative for the banished wrongdoer, however. Disdain for the non-Gypsy world, acquired in early infancy, maintains its hold over most Roma even after their expulsion from the community.

A temporary *marime* sentence may be imposed for less serious crimes. If a Gypsy steals from another Gypsy, for example, the thief is publicly shamed and banished from the community until he or she has repaid the victim. The *kris* may impose a form of "community service" and require the *marime* Rom to work for an indefinite time without pay in order to compensate Gypsy society for violating the taboo of stealing from another Gypsy. Temporary sentences of *marime* are also imposed for offenses such as familiarity with the *gaje* or failure to pay a debt on time.

The entire Gypsy community is responsible for enforcing sanctions. Gypsies have no police or prisons; they have no "law enforcement" in the *gajikano* sense. Peer pressure fanned by gossip and communal knowledge of the verdict tend to ensure the wrongdoer's compliance. The Gypsy community may place a curse on the guilty party to ensure that he or she accepts the chosen punishment, and it appears that this practice is still effective. Only in rare cases, when the Roma have difficulty enforcing a judgment by the *kris*, do they turn to the *gajikano* penal system. The *kris* may ask the *gajikane* authorities to arrest the renegade, and if necessary will employ false charges as a basis for the arrest. At this point the wrongdoer will usually accept the punishment and the charges will be dropped. Should the wrongdoer persist, however, he or she might be forced to endure a *gajikano* court trial.

NOTE

1. It should be noted that many of the elements of Gypsy law described in this article have come to light only recently, significantly through the efforts of female scholars. The guardians of *romaniya* are primarily Gypsy women who orally transmit knowledge to their children. *Gajikane* [non-Gypsy] males could not have obtained this confidential information, because Gypsy women would never reveal many important aspects of Gypsy law, including those which relate to sexual taboos and other highly intimate matters, to a non-Gypsy man. Women scholars have also noted the problems of scientific ethics connected with gathering intimate and confidential information. Rena C. Gropper, *Gypsies in the City: Culture Patterns and Survival* (1975), ix (noting promises made to Gypsy informants and invasion of privacy). The same concerns apply to this article, which disseminates confidential information to a wider public.

Problems similar to those posed by Gypsy law find parallels in other areas of religious law. Female legal scholars have been concerned with reexamining ancient notions of purity and pollution as contained in Jewish and Christian tradition from a feminist perspective.

See, e.g., Mary E. Becker, "The Politics of Women's Wrongs and the Bill of 'Rights': A Bicentennial Perspective," 59 *University of Chicago Law Review* 453, 466–467 (1992); Jeanne L. Schroeder, "Feminism Historicized: Medieval Misogynist Stereotypes in Contemporary Feminist Jurisprudence," 75 *Iowa Law Review* 1135, 1190–1195 (1990).

Institutional Non-Marriage in the Finnish Roma Community and Its Relationship to Rom Traditional Law

Martti Gronfors

Culture and Social Organization of Finnish Roma

The culture and social organization of the Finnish Roma seem to be a mixture of the culture and organization of various Roma groups found all over the world. Unlike most other Roma groups, the Finnish Roma lack any central organ for decision-making in important matters. Even the geographically closest Roma group to the Finnish Roma, the traditional Swedish "tattare," had a general judicial organ called "Kris" for issues comparable to civil and criminal law. No present-day Finnish Roma can remember a Kris ever having operated among the Roma in Finland, and no documentary evidence about it exists. The absence of this form of authority could be speculated to be due to the fact that the Roma of different tribal backgrounds and different arrival times could not agree on the establishment of such an organ, and the main "judicial" power was claimed by the kin groups themselves, who acted as relatively autonomous legal units.

Blood Feuding as an Instrument of Law

Blood feuding, as the ultimate internal organ of social control among the Finnish Roma, was the main institution of internal justice, more specifically an alternative system of justice to that of the state justice. Lasswell has defined feuding as "relations of mutual animosity among intimate groups in which a resort to violence is anticipated on both sides." Blood feuding assumes that the relevant groups are composed of kin—"blood-relatives." In my view feuding is a condition, an atmosphere of mutual hostility from which an action may or may not follow. Intergroup killing is sufficient to create such an atmosphere, sometimes even serious intentional bodily harm. The feuding is evident in the hostile relations that the parties have and that may never lead to a counter-killing. It is cru-

From 45 *American Journal Comparative Law* 305, 309, 311–318, 321–323, 326–327 (1997).

cial to understanding the nature of blood-feuding that it could lead to violence and other killings.

The feuding of the Rom was governed by conventions accepted by parties and by the fact that the offense was against the whole group and not only against the individual member. From a comparative analysis of societies practicing blood feuding, it is clear that it is only practiced between people who are in a reciprocal relationship to each other, and thus fall under the same "jurisdiction." Blood feuding is a very drastic way of handling internal disputes and therefore, as Max Gluckman argues, it is necessary to resort to drastic measures in cases of serious breaches between people who are mutually dependent on each other. Such sanctions are not necessary against people with whom the group does not maintain intimate relationships and on whom it does not depend for its survival. In Finnish Roma feuding, the responsibility for revenge for the killed or wounded relative rested upon the kin. Outsiders could not participate in the feuding activities. The revenge could ideally be directed at any kin member. However, in practice the risk was reduced in the cases of the more distant relatives, women, children, and old people. A revenge act could be launched ideally by anyone in the offended group, but in practice similar qualifications applied.

While dueling was a highly stylized form of settling disputes, the same could not have been said about the Roma blood feuding. In principle anything was allowed in blood feuding. Unlike in many other feuding societies, successful revenge did not stop hostilities; only the roles of the revenger and the revenged changed. Also in the Finnish Roma society there was no way in which the blood feuding could be brought to a halt by negotiation or compensatory action. The fact that "anything goes" in revenge fights could have been taken as an indication that feuding was an extralegal measure, indicative of social disorder rather than order. To view feuding this way, however, would be misunderstanding its nature. Together with the attitude that "anything goes" was a concurrent inhibitive regulative force of avoidance behavior. So while the whole offended group acted ritually in the manner that imminent revenge was to follow, at the same time they followed the cultural norm of refraining from it by practicing substitutive avoidance of the other group and its individual members. Similarly the group who was the target of a blood feuding action was required to observe strict avoidance. The hostilities were continued at the level of ill-talk and other non-direct action, but the two groups remained enemies.[1] Through feuding, the offended group had a chance to show its willingness to defend its members against other groups; or even more strongly, through feuding the idea of collectivity, solidarity, and kin-based loyalty was strengthened, as well as the concept of kin-based political autonomy. It is this aspect which makes blood feuding an instrument of order rather than disorder.

As the Finnish Roma did not have any intergroup political unit or organ, much depended on the kin-based group. In addition to any economic, social, and emotional security, the kin-based group also was the sole guarantor of physical safety for its members. It is against this light that the institution of Finnish Roma's non-marriage should be examined.

Marriage as a Global Institution

In anthropological literature, marriage in its variety of forms is considered an institution that is truly global. The fact that the Finnish Roma do not seem to have that institution in its usual form does not necessarily counteract that claim. To the contrary, the various arrangements, prohibitions, and taboos which surrounded the Finnish Roma sexuality, forming liaisons, reproduction, and other such matters could also be taken as an acknowledgment of marriage as an institution, but at the same time should be given no place in the Finnish Roma society. Its potential for making connections between kin-groups, of loyalties and conflicting loyalties, and of danger for the kin-based solidarity can also be said to acknowledge the institution but disregard it nevertheless.

When [Finnish Roma] youngsters fell in love they could not show it in any way lest the movements of the girl were going to be watched even more tightly. The only way in which the young could get together was elopement. The usual case for them was to agree to the time and place where they could meet, and after meeting they attempted to go as far as they could, often hundreds of kilometers away, without anybody's knowledge. Once their escape was discovered a search was on, often by brothers and male cousins, and if they were discovered she was brought home. Traditionally the young tried to remain in hiding for at least two years, by which time a child would be conceived and about one year old before reunification with the families was attempted. Unlike other societies which practice elopement, the suspicion of defilement was not adequate grounds for allowing them to be together. As there was no accepted way of getting married, virginity as such was not something to be guarded in these situations. It was her becoming a "wife" that mattered, with the implication that they slept together. And as there was no accepted way of forming liaisons, her chances of finding another partner were not lessened by the event. Only repeated abscondings with the same man could convince the family that it was useless to try to keep them separate, and a slow process of acceptance of the liaison would start. Although they were eventually admitted into the families again, the rules of decency demanded that they should not "advertise" their union. However, even then, the only acceptable partner was a person from another kin-group. No matter how distantly related the parties were, liaisons within the kin group would have been considered incestuous. In that way the Finnish Roma can be said to be exogamous.

Pregnancy, Childbirth, and Being a Mother

When a Rom woman became pregnant, the event received no public attention. No special arrangements or taboos were connected to pregnancy. In fact, since the entire matter was not acknowledged, special taboos would have drawn attention to an event not acknowledged institutionally. The abundant female clothing offered good protection for much of the pregnancy. In former times, when the Roma were still a traveling folk, it was common for a pregnant woman to leave her group before her time was due, together with the father of the child. When her time came, an attempt was made to secure a Finnish farmer's sauna (bathhouse) or some other neutral place for the delivery.

When maternity hospitals became more common and within reach of poor people, they were quickly used by the Roma women, although they usually did their utmost not to place themselves in hospitals or other institutions where they would be entirely at the mercy of non-Roma. The maternity hospital effectively removed the Roma women from their community for the birth. At maternity hospitals, only women younger than the mother herself were allowed to visit her. Even an older sister could not see her there. Men, including the father of the child, could never have visited her. Childbirth was attempted to be kept as much a non-event as possible, and all overt references to pregnancy and childbirth were forbidden. When references could not be avoided, for example, for practical reasons, it was done in whispers and with considerable shame. Euphemisms were also employed to avoid the mentioning of these [implicitly] tabooed topics.

The ignoring of the child and its relationship to the mother continued at least until the child was able to walk. Then the child was no longer an infant, but a person with whom people were able to communicate directly without the intermediary of the mother and who no longer needed breast feeding. If it was possible, the mother and the father set off on their own to travel the countryside, avoiding other traveling Roma at least for a year after the birth of their child. When the child was a toddler, a slow and gradual return to the Roma community was made.[2]

Special Taboos Relating to Sexuality and Marriage

If a non-Rom asked a Rom woman about the number of children she might have, the answer "none" could contradict other evidence. Only an outsider would address the Finnish Roma with such a question; the Roma themselves would know the inappropriateness of the inquiry. As there was no arena for legitimate sexual relationships within the Finnish Roma society, anything that referred to sex became taboo. To have children was breaking the taboo, and therefore it was good behavior not to draw attention to them or to attach them to particular parents.

Similarly, to inquire about the age of a child was not appropriate, because an answer would have referred to an event not legitimate in the Finnish Roma society. As the age is determined from the birth, and as the birth is something against the norms of Roma society, giving the age would acknowledge the breach of these norms. This law was particularly strong in regard to the child's natural parents, who would have been implicated as the "culprits" of such a breach. Thus, birthdays of children were not traditionally celebrated. Only when the person grew older and when the "distasteful" event was far enough in the past could the Roma celebrate birthdays. The fortieth birthday was usually the first one which was celebrated in the Finnish Roma society.

The norms regulating the public behavior of the couple were strict, and all were aimed at publicly telling people that the two concerned persons in no way belonged to each other. A couple could not sit publicly side by side, nor appear in photographs together. There could be no inference that they were actually sleeping together which meant that, if there was no room in the house for the exclusive use of the couple, the woman had to stay up until everybody else in the room had gone to sleep. Only then could she join her man in bed under the cover of darkness. In the morning, she had to make sure to be up before anybody else and be fully dressed before the others woke up. The couple could not touch in public or show affection in any way in front of other people, especially in the presence of the older generation. In brief, the norms of the Finnish Roma society demanded the couple to act in an exaggerated way to demonstrate that they had no intimate relationship between them.[3]

Status of a "Spouse"

As the legitimacy of marriage was not acknowledged, both parties in a liaison remained members of their own kin groups. There was no way in which the Finnish Roma society could acknowledge affinal relationships. This could make the life of a "spouse" difficult on occasion. If a woman was living with her man's kin, she had nobody readily at hand in crisis situations, for example, when her man mistreated her. In the household of her man she was usually the only non-kin female, which could have meant that she was also under the control of his female relations, who could order her about a great deal.

The man who was living with the woman's relatives could find himself in a vulnerable situation also. He had to watch his step as far as his woman was concerned, because she could always call upon her male relatives for support. He also had to make sure that he got along well with her male relatives, who could view him as a threat to the internal cohesion of the family and as a "seducer" of one of the women in the family. There seemed to be no particular prerequisite in terms of patrilocality or matrilocality, although it was natural that a man would prefer to have his woman living with his family. It was not uncommon, though, to find a man living with her family.

In a situation of blood feuding the responsibility under the feuding system was not extended to people other than the consanguine kin (the so-called blood-relatives). This could have meant, for example, that, although the man may have had to be on his guard in terms of a blood feuding relationship that his family had with another family, his woman did not have to face this kind of threat at all. She could even continue to associate with her man's enemies in a blood feuding situation. Similarly, if she had a blood feuding relationship with another family, her man was unaffected by this relationship. Should it have happened that the couple's respective families got into a blood feuding relationship with each other, then the Finnish Roma norms required the couple to separate immediately. The behavior expected in blood feuding was such that there was no way in which the couple could have continued to live together under such circumstances, no matter how they felt toward each other privately. Liaisons between men and women could never have been acceptable if there was an existing blood feuding relationship between their respective families.

At the everyday level, emotional and social responsibilities between the couple and between the couple and others were similar to responsibilities of people of their age and gender. The woman accorded deference to her man, and he had authority over her in a similar fashion to the authority he had over equivalent age female kin, plus—naturally—the publicly ignored sexual rights. In situations of severe crisis, his sisters assumed the prime responsibility. In economic respects the woman was expected to carry the main responsibility, and the care of the children's emotional and material needs was almost exclusively a female responsibility.

Discussion

Blood feuding is the way in which the Finnish Roma deal with—not settle—the most serious offending that may occur in that community, the killing or sometimes grievous bodily injury caused by the intent to kill. Killings and injuries form the only matters which could be called "public" issues concerning the entire community. The aim of blood feuding is not to bring peace, as is the case in many other blood feuding societies, but it is more a show of strength by the kin group. It attempts to declare publicly that, although the group had suffered a loss, it can still defend its members. Blood feuding is also connected to the honor and shame of the kin groups. Showing readiness for feuding is honorable, and to shy away from it is dishonorable and could be a fatal show of weakness. As said earlier, blood feuding is kin-based in such a way that it concerns only consanguine kin. As blood feuding is a truly serious matter in the Finnish Roma community, a calamity of huge proportions, to survive it intact requires an absolute loyalty from the kin members.

It is here, where the possible explanation for the absence of marriage as an institution rests. In the Finnish Roma community so much is laid on the shoulders of the kin-based group that it cannot afford any competing or conflicting loyalties. As the finally accepted partner in a couple-relationship has to come from another kin group, there is a danger that in a crisis situation the demands of the kin group and those of the person who comes from another kin group might conflict. By giving no status to such relationships, there is a clear message that first and foremost the loyalties must lie with one's own kin group. By not giving any place for marriage or any affinal relationships which might result from marriage relationships, the lines of loyalty are always well-drawn.[4]

NOTES

1. This state of affairs continued as long as the descendants of the two parties could remember the circumstances and the participants and as long as the two groups remained distinct entities. In the bilineal Finnish Roma society the liaisons formed between the groups

over time meant that there was mixing and merging of kin-based groups. This happened even though the members of the feuding groups were not supposed to form marriage-like liaisons. Over the generations, the borders of groups were sufficiently blurred at the edges that it became unclear who was on which side of the feuding. But it usually took several generations of Roma and decades for this to happen.

2. The Finnish Roma have an institutional way of showing appropriate shame. If they are in the company of people to whom the taboos apply, any reference to a taboo topic sends the younger generation out of the room, women cover their heads with aprons, and men put hands over their eyes. This is sometimes used to reinforce normative behavior when the older people teasingly and purposefully refer to taboo topics and, at the same time, expect the younger ones to show the appropriate shame. In this way, younger people let the older generations know that they know the culture and appropriate behavior.

3. An anecdote from my field work illustrates the strictness of these rules. I was in the field together with my wife, staying at a Rom house. I got up before my wife and came to the kitchen for breakfast. In the kitchen was a Rom woman, with whom I was chatting while I was having my breakfast. She was sitting by the wall on a chair, while I was sitting alone on a long bench by the table. My wife came into the kitchen to have her breakfast and, as soon as she appeared in the room, the Rom woman stood up from her chair and hastily came to sit next to me. What she was doing was acting out her role as a Rom woman. One of her main tasks was to prevent any social disgrace by resorting to diversionary tactics, and do this without anybody really noticing that such action took place. By moving next to me at the table, she effectively prevented my wife from committing a social disgrace. She thought, probably with some validity, that my non-Rom wife probably would not know about the prohibition that prevented couples sitting together. Rather than finding out if my wife knew about such custom or not, she shortcircuited a potential embarrassment by moving to sit next to me.

4. One notable exception is the children born out of this relationship. In the bilineal society of the Finnish Roma the children are members of both kin groups, mother's and father's. Should the parents get into opposite sides of a blood feuding, the children's position is unclear as they are related to both warring parties. The blood feuding relationship therefore does not extend to them, as they are at the same time friends and enemies in the same person. When they grow older, the children may choose on whose side their loyalties lie, as especially the men in such situations frequently did, but still they avoid getting into open conflicts with either side.

Chapter 38

Values in Tension
Ethics Away from Home

Thomas Donaldson

When we leave home and cross our nation's boundaries, moral clarity often blurs. Without a backdrop of shared attitudes, and without familiar laws and judicial procedures that define standards of ethical conduct, certainty is elusive. Should a company invest in a foreign country where civil and political rights are violated? Should a company go along with a host country's discriminatory employment practices? If companies in developed countries shift facilities to developing nations that lack strict environmental and health regulations, or if those companies choose to fill management and other top-level positions in a host nation with people from the home country, whose standards should prevail?

Even the best-informed, best-intentioned executives must rethink their assumptions about business practice in foreign settings. What works in a company's home country can fail in a country with different standards of ethical conduct. Such difficulties are unavoidable for businesspeople who live and work abroad.

But how can managers resolve the problems? What are the principles that can help them work through the maze of cultural differences and establish codes of conduct for globally ethical business practice? How can companies answer the toughest question in global business ethics: What happens when a host country's ethical standards seem lower than the home country's?

Competing Answers

One answer is as old as philosophical discourse. According to cultural relativism, no culture's ethics are better than any other's; therefore there are no international rights and wrongs. If the people of Indonesia tolerate the bribery of their public officials, so what? Their attitude is no better or worse than that of people in Denmark or Singapore who refuse to offer or accept bribes. Likewise, if Belgians fail to find insider trading morally repugnant, who cares? Not enforcing insider-trading laws is no more or less ethical than enforcing such laws.

The cultural relativist's creed—When in Rome, do as the Romans do—is tempting, especially when failing to do as the locals do means forfeiting business opportunities. The inadequacy of cultural relativism, however, becomes apparent when the practices in question are more damaging than petty bribery or insider trading.

In the late 1980s, some European tanneries and pharmaceutical companies were looking for cheap waste-dumping sites. They approached virtually every country on Africa's west coast, from Morocco to the Congo. Nigeria agreed to take highly toxic polychlorinated biphenyls. Unprotected local workers, wearing thongs and shorts, unloaded barrels of PCBs and placed them near a residential area. Neither the residents nor the workers knew that the barrels contained toxic waste.

We may denounce governments that permit such abuses, but many countries are unable to police transnational corporations adequately even if they want to. And in many countries, the combination of ineffective enforcement and inadequate regulations leads to behavior by unscrupulous companies that is clearly wrong. A few years ago, for example, a group of investors became interested in restoring the SS *United States*, once a luxurious ocean liner. Before the actual restoration could begin, the ship had to be stripped of its asbestos lining. A bid from a U.S. company, based on U.S. standards for asbestos removal, priced the job at more than $100 million. A company in the Ukranian city of Sevastopol offered to do the work for less than $2 million. In October 1993, the ship was towed to Sevastopol.

A cultural relativist would have no problem with that outcome, but I do. A country has the right to establish its own health and safety regulations, but in the case described above, the standards and the terms of the contract could not possibly have protected workers in Sevastopol from known health risks. Even if the contract met Ukranian standards, ethical businesspeople must object. Cultural relativism is morally blind. There are fundamental values that cross cultures, and companies must uphold them.

At the other end of the spectrum from cultural relativism is ethical imperialism, which directs people to do everywhere exactly as they do at home. Again, an understandably appealing approach but one that is clearly inadequate. Consider the large U.S. computer-products company that in 1993 introduced a course on sexual harassment in its Saudi Arabian facility. Under the banner of global consistency, instructors used the same approach to train Saudi Arabian managers that they had used with U.S. managers: the participants were asked to discuss a case in which a manager makes sexually explicit remarks to a new female employee over drinks in a bar. The instructors failed to consider how the exercise would work in a culture with strict conventions governing relationships between men and women. As a result, the training sessions were ludicrous. They baffled and offended the Saudi participants, and the message to avoid coercion and sexual discrimination was lost.

The theory behind ethical imperialism is absolutism, which is based on three problematic principles. Absolutists believe that there is a single list of truths, that they can be expressed only with one set of concepts, and that they call for exactly the same behavior around the world.

The first claim clashes with many people's belief that different cultural traditions must be respected. In some cultures, loyalty to a community—family, organization, or society—is the foundation of all ethical behavior. The Japanese, for example, define business ethics in terms of loyalty to their companies, their business networks, and their nation. Americans place a higher value on liberty than on loyalty; the U.S. tradition of rights emphasizes equality, fairness, and individual freedom. It is hard to conclude that truth lies on one side or the other, but an absolutist would have us select just one.

The second problem with absolutism is the presumption that people must express moral truth using only one set of concepts. For instance, some absolutists insist that the language of basic rights provide the framework for any discussion of ethics. That means, though, that entire cultural traditions must be ignored. The notion of a right evolved with the rise of democracy in post-Renaissance Europe and the United States, but the term is not found in either Confucian or Buddhist traditions. We all learn ethics in the context of our particular cultures, and the power in the principles is deeply tied to the way in which they are expressed. Internationally accepted lists of moral principles, such as the United Nations' Universal Declaration of Human Rights, draw on many cultural and religious traditions. As philosopher Michael Walzer has noted, "There is no Esperanto of global ethics."

The third problem with absolutism is the belief in a global standard of ethical behavior. Context must shape ethical practice. Very low wages, for example, may be considered unethical in rich, advanced countries, but developing nations may be acting ethically if they encourage investment and improve living standards by accepting low wages. Likewise, when people are malnourished or starving, a government may be wise to use more fertilizer in order to improve crop yields, even though that means settling for relatively high levels of thermal water pollution.

When cultures have different standards of ethical behavior—and different ways of handling unethical behavior—a company that takes an absolutist approach may find itself making a disastrous mistake. When a manager at a large U.S. specialty-products company in China caught an employee stealing, she followed the company's practice and turned the employee over to the provincial authorities, who executed him. Managers cannot operate in another culture without being aware of that culture's attitudes toward ethics.

If companies can neither adopt a host country's ethics nor extend the home country's standards, what is the answer? Even the traditional litmus test—What would people think of your actions if they were written up on the front page of the newspaper?—is an unreliable guide, for there is no international consensus on standards of business conduct.

Balancing the Extremes: Three Guiding Principles

Companies must help managers distinguish between practices that are merely different and those that are wrong. For relativists, nothing is sacred and nothing is wrong. For absolutists, many things that are different are wrong. Neither extreme illuminates the real world of business decision making. The answer lies somewhere in between.

When it comes to shaping ethical behavior, companies must be guided by three principles:

- Respect for core human values, which determine the absolute moral threshold for all business activities.
- Respect for local traditions.
- The belief that context matters when deciding what is right and what is wrong.

Consider those principles in action. In Japan, people doing business together often exchange gifts—sometimes expensive ones—in keeping with long-standing Japanese tradition. When U.S. and European companies started doing a lot of business in Japan, many Western businesspeople thought that the practice of gift giving might be wrong rather than simply different. To them, accepting a gift felt like accepting a bribe. As Western companies have become more familiar with Japanese traditions, however, most have come to tolerate the practice and to set different limits on gift giving in Japan than they do elsewhere.

Respecting differences is a crucial ethical practice. Research shows that management ethics differ among cultures; respecting those differences means recognizing that some cultures have obvious weaknesses—as well as hidden strengths. Managers in Hong Kong, for example, have a higher tolerance for some forms of bribery than their Western counterparts, but they have a much lower tolerance for the failure to acknowledge a subordinate's work. In some parts of the Far East, stealing credit from a subordinate is nearly an unpardonable sin.

People often equate respect for local traditions with cultural relativism. That is incorrect. Some practices are clearly wrong. Union Carbide's tragic experience in Bhopal, India, provides one example. The company's executives seriously underestimated how much on-site management involvement was needed at the Bhopal plant to compensate for the country's poor infrastructure and regulatory capabilities. In the aftermath of the disastrous gas leak, the lesson is clear: companies using sophisticated technology in a developing country must evaluate that country's ability to oversee its safe use. Since the incident at Bhopal, Union Carbide has become a leader in advising companies on using hazardous technologies safely in developing countries.

Some activities are wrong no matter where they take place. But some practices that are unethical in one setting may be acceptable in another. For instance, the chemical EDB, a soil fungicide, is banned for use in the United States. In hot climates, however, it quickly becomes harmless through exposure to intense solar radiation and high soil temperatures. As long as the chemical is monitored, companies may be able to use EDB ethically in certain parts of the world.

Defining the Ethical Threshold: Core Values

Few ethical questions are easy for managers to answer. But there are some hard truths that must guide managers' actions, a set of what I call *core human values,*

TABLE 38.1
What Do These Values Have in Common?

Non-Western	Western
Kyosei (Japanese): Living and working together for the common good	Individual liberty
Dharma (Hindu): The fulfillment of inherited duty	Egalitarianism
Santutthi (Buddhist): The importance of limited desires	Political participation
Zakat (Muslim): The duty to give alms to the Muslim poor	Human rights

which define minimum ethical standards for all companies. The right to good health and the right to economic advancement and an improved standard of living are two core human values. Another is what Westerners call the Golden Rule, which is recognizable in every major religious and ethical tradition around the world. In Book 15 of his *Analects*, for instance, Confucius counsels people to maintain reciprocity, or not to do to others what they do not want done to themselves.

Although no single list would satisfy every scholar, I believe it is possible to articulate three core values that incorporate the work of scores of theologians and philosophers around the world. To be broadly relevant, these values must include elements found in both Western and non-Western cultural and religious traditions. Consider the examples of values in Table 38.1, "What Do These Values Have in Common?"

At first glance, the values expressed in the two lists seem quite different. Nonetheless, in the spirit of what philosopher John Rawls calls *overlapping consensus*, one can see that the seemingly divergent values converge at key points. Despite important differences between Western and non-Western cultural and religious traditions, both express shared attitudes about what it means to be human. First, individuals must not treat others simply as tools; in other words, they must recognize a person's value as a human being. Next, individuals and communities must treat people in ways that respect people's basic rights. Finally, members of a community must work together to support and improve the institutions on which the community depends. I call those three values *respect for human dignity, respect for basic rights*, and *good citizenship*.

Those values must be the starting point for all companies as they formulate and evaluate standards of ethical conduct at home and abroad. But they are only a starting point. Companies need much more specific guidelines, and the first step to developing those is to translate the core human values into core values for business. What does it mean, for example, for a company to respect human dignity? How can a company be a good citizen?

I believe that companies can respect human dignity by creating and sustaining a corporate culture in which employees, customers, and suppliers are treated not as means to an end but as people whose intrinsic value must be acknowledged, and by producing safe products and services in a safe workplace. Companies can respect basic rights by acting in ways that support and protect the individual rights of employees, customers, and surrounding communities, and by avoiding relationships that violate human beings' rights to health, education, safety, and an adequate standard of living. And companies can be good citizens by supporting essential social institutions, such as the economic system and the education system, and by working with host governments and other organizations to protect the environment.

The core values establish a moral compass for business practice. They can help companies identify practices that are acceptable and those that are intolerable—even if the practices are compatible with a host country's norms and laws. Dumping pollutants near people's homes and accepting inadequate standards for handling hazardous materials are two examples of actions that violate core values.

Similarly, if employing children prevents them from receiving a basic education, the practice is intolerable. Lying about product specifications in the act of selling may not affect human lives directly, but it too is intolerable because it violates the trust that is needed to sustain a corporate culture in which customers are respected.

Sometimes it is not a company's actions but those of a supplier or customer that pose problems. Take the case of the Tan family, a large supplier for Levi Strauss. The Tans were allegedly forcing twelve hundred Chinese and Filipino women to work seventy-four hours per week in guarded compounds on the Mariana Islands. In 1992, after repeated warnings to the Tans, Levi Strauss broke off business relations with them.

Creating an Ethical Corporate Culture

The core values for business that I have enumerated can help companies begin to exercise ethical judgment and think about how to operate ethically in foreign cultures, but they are not specific enough to guide managers through actual ethical dilemmas. Levi Strauss relied on a written code of conduct when figuring out how to deal with the Tan family. The company's Global Sourcing and Operating Guidelines, formerly called the Business Partner Terms of Engagement, state that Levi Strauss will "seek to identify and utilize business partners who aspire as individuals and in the conduct of all their businesses to a set of ethical standards not incompatible with our own." Whenever intolerable business situations arise, managers should be guided by precise statements that spell out the behavior and operating practices that the company demands.

Ninety percent of all *Fortune* 500 companies have codes of conduct, and 70 percent have statements of vision and values. In Europe and the Far East, the percentages are lower but are increasing rapidly. Does that mean that most companies have what they need? Hardly. Even though most large U.S. companies have both statements of values and codes of conduct, many might be better off if they didn't. Too many companies don't do anything with the documents; they simply paste them on the wall to impress employees, customers, suppliers, and the public.

As a result, the senior managers who drafted the statements lose credibility by proclaiming values and not living up to them. Companies such as Johnson & Johnson, Levi Strauss, Motorola, Texas Instruments, and Lockheed Martin, however, do a great deal to make the words meaningful. Johnson & Johnson, for example, has become well known for its Credo Challenge sessions, in which managers discuss ethics in the context of their current business problems and are invited to criticize the company's credo and make suggestions for changes. The participants' ideas are passed on to the company's senior managers. Lockheed Martin has created an innovative site on the World Wide Web and on its local network that gives employees, customers, and suppliers access to the company's ethical code and the chance to voice complaints.

Codes of conduct must provide clear direction about ethical behavior when the temptation to behave unethically is strongest. The pronouncement in a code of conduct that bribery is unacceptable is useless unless accompanied by guidelines for gift giving, payments to get goods through customs, and "requests" from intermediaries who are hired to ask for bribes.

Motorola's values are stated very simply as "How we will always act: [with] constant respect for people [and] uncompromising integrity." The company's code of conduct, however, is explicit about actual business practice. With respect to bribery, for example, the code states that the "funds and assets of Motorola shall not be used, directly or indirectly, for illegal payments of any kind." It is unambiguous about what sort of payment is illegal: "the payment of a bribe to a public official or the kickback of funds to an employee of a customer." The code goes on to prescribe specific procedures for handling commissions to intermediaries, issuing sales invoices, and disclosing confidential information in a sales transaction—all situations in which employees might have an opportunity to accept or offer bribes.

Codes of conduct must be explicit to be useful, but they must also leave room for a manager to use his or her judgment in situations requiring cultural sensitivity. Host-country employees shouldn't be forced to adopt all home-country values and renounce their own. Again, Motorola's code is exemplary. First, it gives clear direction: "Employees of Motorola will respect the laws, customs, and traditions of each country in which they operate, but will, at the same time, engage in no course of conduct which, even if legal, customary, and accepted in any such country, could be deemed to be in violation of the accepted business ethics of Motorola or the laws of the United States relating to business ethics." After laying down such absolutes, Motorola's code then makes clear when individual judgment will be necessary. For example, employees may sometimes accept certain kinds of small gifts "in rare circumstances, where the refusal to accept a gift" would injure Motorola's "legitimate business interests." Under certain circumstances, such gifts "may be accepted so long as the gift inures to the benefit of Motorola" and not "to the benefit of the Motorola employee."

Striking the appropriate balance between providing clear direction and leaving room for individual judgment makes crafting corporate values statements and ethics codes one of the hardest tasks that executives confront. The words are only a start. A company's leaders need to refer often to their organization's credo and code and must themselves be credible, committed, and consistent. If senior managers act as though ethics don't matter, the rest of the company's employees won't think they do, either.

Conflicts of Development and Conflicts of Tradition

Managers living and working abroad who are not prepared to grapple with moral ambiguity and tension should pack their bags and come home. The view that all business practices can be categorized as either ethical or unethical is too simple. As Einstein is reported to have said, "Things should be as simple as possible—but no simpler." Many business practices that are considered unethical in one setting may be ethical in another. Such activities are neither black nor white but exist in what Thomas Dunfee and I have called *moral free space*. In this gray zone, there are no tight prescriptions for a company's behavior. Managers must chart their own courses—as long as they do not violate core human values.

Consider the following example. Some successful Indian companies offer employees the opportunity for one of their children to gain a job with the company once the child has completed a certain level in school. The companies honor this commitment even when other applicants are more qualified than an employee's child. The perk is extremely valuable in a country where jobs are hard to find, and it reflects the Indian culture's belief that the West has gone too far in allowing economic opportunities to break up families. Not surprisingly, the perk is among the most cherished by employees, but in most Western countries, it would be branded unacceptable nepotism. In the United States, for example, the ethical principle of equal opportunity holds that jobs should go to the applicants with the best qualifications. If a U.S. company made such promises to its employees, it would violate regulations established by the Equal Employment Opportunity Commission. Given this difference in ethical attitudes, how should U.S. managers react to Indian nepotism? Should they condemn the Indian companies, refusing to accept them as partners or suppliers until they agree to clean up their act?

Despite the obvious tension between nepotism and principles of equal opportunity, I cannot condemn the practice for Indians. In a country, such as India, that emphasizes clan and family relationships and has catastrophic levels of unemployment, the practice must be viewed in moral free space. The decision to allow a special perk for employees and their children is not necessarily wrong—at least for members of that country.

How can managers discover the limits of moral free space? That is, how can they learn to distinguish a value in tension with their own from one that is intolerable? Helping managers develop good ethical judgment requires companies to be clear about their core values and codes of conduct. But even the most explicit set of guidelines cannot always provide answers. That is especially true in the thorniest ethical dilemmas, in which the host country's ethical standards not only are different but also seem lower than the home country's. Managers must recognize that when countries have different ethical standards, there are two types of conflict that commonly arise. Each type requires its own line of reasoning.

In the first type of conflict, which I call a *conflict of relative development*, ethical standards conflict because of the countries' different levels of economic development. As mentioned before, developing countries may accept wage rates that seem inhumane to more advanced countries in order to attract investment. As economic conditions in a developing country improve, the incidence of that sort of conflict usually decreases. The second type of conflict is a *conflict of cultural tradition*. For example, Saudi Arabia, unlike most other countries, does not allow women to serve as corporate managers. Instead, women may work in only a few professions, such as education and health care. The prohibition stems from strongly held religious and cultural beliefs; any increase in the country's level of economic development, which is already quite high, is not likely to change the rules.

To resolve a conflict of relative development, a manager must ask the following question: Would the practice be acceptable at home if my country were in a similar stage of economic development? Consider the difference between wage and safety standards in the United States and in Angola, where citizens accept lower standards on both counts. If a U.S. oil company is hiring Angolans to work on an offshore Angolan oil rig, can the company pay them lower wages than it pays U.S. workers in the Gulf of Mexico? Reasonable people have to answer yes if the alternative for Angola is the loss of both the foreign investment and the jobs.

Consider, too, differences in regulatory environments. In the 1980s, the government of India fought hard to be able to import Ciba-Geigy's Entero Vioform, a drug known to be enormously effective in fighting dysentery but one that had been banned in the United States because some users experienced side effects. Although dysentery was not a big problem in the United States, in India, poor public sanitation was contributing to epidemic levels of the disease. Was it unethical to make the drug available in India after it had been banned in the United States? On the contrary, rational people should consider it unethical not to do so. Apply our test: Would the United States, at an earlier stage of development, have used this drug despite its side effects? The answer is clearly yes.

But there are many instances when the answer to similar questions is no. Sometimes a host country's standards are inadequate at any level of economic development. If a country's pollution standards are so low that working on an oil rig would considerably increase a person's risk of developing cancer, foreign oil companies must refuse to do business there. Likewise, if the dangerous side effects of a drug treatment outweigh its benefits, managers should not accept health standards that ignore the risks.

When relative economic conditions do not drive tensions, there is a more objective test for resolving ethical problems. Managers should deem a practice permissible only if they can answer no to both of the following questions: Is it possible to conduct business successfully in the host country without undertaking the practice? and Is the practice a violation of a core human value? Japanese gift giving is a perfect example of a conflict of cultural tradition. Most experienced businesspeople, Japanese and non-Japanese alike, would agree that doing business in Japan would be virtually impossible without adopting the practice. Does gift giving violate a core human value? I cannot identify one that it violates. As a result, gift giving may be permissible for foreign companies in Japan even if it conflicts with ethical attitudes at home. In fact, that conclusion is widely accepted, even by companies such as Texas Instruments and IBM, which are outspoken against bribery.

Does it follow that all nonmonetary gifts are acceptable or that bribes are generally acceptable in countries where they are common? Not at all. What makes the routine practice of gift giving acceptable in Japan are the limits in its scope and intention. When gift giving moves outside those limits, it soon collides with core human values. For example, when Carl Kotchian, president of Lockheed in the 1970s, carried suitcases full of cash to Japanese politicians, he went beyond the norms established by Japanese tradition. That incident galvanized opinion in the United States Congress and helped lead to passage of the Foreign Corrupt Practices Act. Likewise, Roh Tae Woo went beyond the norms established by Korean cultural tradition when he accepted $635.4 million in bribes as president of the Republic of Korea between 1988 and 1993.

Guidelines for Ethical Leadership

Learning to spot intolerable practices and to exercise good judgment when ethical conflicts arise requires practice. Creating a company culture that rewards ethical behavior is essential. The following guidelines for developing a global ethical perspective among managers can help.

Treat corporate values and formal standards of conduct as absolutes. Whatever ethical standards a company chooses, it cannot waver on its principles either at home or abroad. Consider what has become part of company lore at Motorola. Around 1950, a senior executive was negotiating with officials of a South American government on a $10 million sale that would have increased the company's annual net profits by nearly 25 percent. As the negotiations neared completion, however, the executive walked away from the deal because the officials were asking for $1 million for "fees." CEO Robert Galvin not only supported the executive's decision but also made it clear that Motorola would neither accept the sale on any terms nor do business with those government officials again. Retold over the decades, this story demonstrating Galvin's resolve has helped cement a culture of ethics for thousands of employees at Motorola.

Design and implement conditions of engagement for suppliers and customers. Will your company do business with any customer or supplier? What if a customer or supplier uses child labor? What if it has strong links with organized crime? What if it pressures your company to break a host country's laws? Such issues are best not left for spur-of-the-moment decisions. Some companies have realized that. Sears, for instance, has developed a policy of not contracting production to companies that use prison labor or infringe on workers' rights to health and safety. And BankAmerica has specified as a condition for many of its loans to developing countries that environmental standards and human rights must be observed.

Allow foreign business units to help formulate ethical standards and interpret ethical issues. The French pharmaceutical company Rhône-Poulenc Rorer has allowed foreign subsidiaries to augment lists of corporate ethical principles with their own suggestions. Texas Instruments has paid special attention to issues of international business ethics by creating the Global Business Practices Council, which is made up of managers from countries in which the company operates. With the overarching intent to create a "global ethics strategy, locally deployed," the council's mandate is to provide ethics education and create local processes that will help managers in the company's foreign business units resolve ethical conflicts.

In host countries, support efforts to decrease institutional corruption. Individual managers will not be able to wipe out corruption in a host country, no matter how many bribes they turn down. When a host country's tax system, import and export procedures, and procurement practices favor unethical players, companies must take action.

Many companies have begun to participate in reforming host-country institutions. General Electric, for example, has taken a strong stand in India, using the media to make repeated condemnations of bribery in business and government. General Electric and others have found, however, that a single company usually cannot drive out entrenched corruption. Transparency International, an organization based in Germany, has been effective in helping coalitions of companies, government officials, and others work to reform bribery-ridden bureaucracies in Russia, Bangladesh, and elsewhere.

Exercise moral imagination. Using moral imagination means resolving tensions responsibly and creatively. Coca-Cola, for instance, has consistently turned down requests for bribes from Egyptian officials but has managed to gain political support and public trust by sponsoring a project to plant fruit trees. And take the example of Levi Strauss, which discovered in the early 1990s that two of its suppliers in Bangladesh were employing children under the age of fourteen—a practice that violated the company's principles but was tolerated in Bangladesh. Forcing the suppliers to fire the children would not have ensured that the children received an education, and it would have caused serious hardship for the families depending on the children's wages. In a creative arrangement, the suppliers agreed to pay the children's regular wages while they attended school and to offer each child a job at age fourteen. Levi Strauss, in turn, agreed to pay the children's tuition and provide books and uniforms. That arrangement allowed Levi Strauss to uphold its principles and provide long-term benefits to its host country.

Many people think of values as soft; to some they are usually unspoken. A South Seas island society uses the word *mokita*, which means, "the truth that everybody knows but nobody speaks." However difficult they are to articulate, values affect how we all behave. In a global business environment, values in tension are the rule rather than the exception. Without a company's commitment, statements of values and codes of ethics end up as empty platitudes that provide managers with no foundation for behaving ethically. Employees need and deserve more, and responsible members of the global business community can set examples for others to follow. The dark consequences of incidents such as Union Carbide's disaster in Bhopal remind us how high the stakes can be.

Chapter 39

Nisa

The Life and Words of a !Kung Woman

Marjorie Shostak

This story was told to me in the !Kung language by Nisa, an African woman of about fifty years of age, living in a remote corner of Botswana, on the northern fringe of the Kalahari desert. It was March 1971, the last month of my twenty-month field stay among the !Kung San. Nisa is a member of one of the last remaining traditional gatherer-hunter societies, a group calling themselves the Zhuntwasi, "the real people," who currently live in isolated areas of Botswana, Angola, and Namibia.

Besa and I eventually moved back East again. But after we had lived together for a long time, we no longer were getting along. One day I asked, "Besa, won't you take me back to my family's village so I can live there?" He said, "I'm no longer interested in you." I said, "What's wrong? Why do you feel that way?" But then I said, "Eh, if that's how it is, it doesn't matter."

I was working for a European woman at the time, and when I told her what Besa was saying to me, she told him, "Listen to me. You're going to chase your wife away. If you continue to speak to her like this, she'll be gone. Today, I'm pregnant. Why don't you just let her be and have her sit beside you. When I give birth, she will work for me and help me with the baby."

That's what we did. We continued to live together until she gave birth. After, I helped wash the baby's clothes and helped with other chores. I worked for her for a long time.

One day, Besa broke into a little box I had and stole the money she had paid me with. He took it and went to drink beer. I went to the European woman and told her Besa had taken five Rand from me and had left with it. I asked her to help me get it back. We went to the Tswana hut where everyone was drinking and went to the door. The European woman walked in, kicked over a bucket, and the beer spilled out. She kicked over another and another and the beer was spilling everywhere. The Tswanas left. She turned to Besa and said, "Why are you treating this young Zhun/twa woman like this? Stop treating her this way." She told him to give her the money and when he gave it to her, she gave it to me. I went and put the money in the box, then took it and left it in her kitchen where it stayed.

Later Besa said, "Why did you tell on me? I'm going to beat you." I said, "Go ahead. Hit me. I don't care. I won't stop you."

Soon after that, I became pregnant with Besa's child. But when it was still very tiny, when I was still carrying it way inside, he left me. I don't know what it was that made him want to leave. Did he have a lover? I don't know. He said he was afraid of a sore I had on my face where a bug had bitten me. It had become swollen, and eventually the Europeans helped to heal it. Whatever it was, his heart had changed toward me and although my heart still liked him, he only liked me a very little then. That's why he left.

It happened the day he finished working for the Europeans. He came back when the sun was low in the sky and said, "Tomorrow, I'm going to visit my younger brother. I have finished my work and have been paid. I'm going, but you'll stay here. Later, Old Debe and his wife can take you back to your brothers' village." I said, "If you are leaving, won't I go with you?" He said, "No, you won't go with me." I said, "Why are you saying you'll go without me? If I go with you and give birth there, it will be good. Don't leave me here. Let me go with you and give birth in your brother's village." But he said, "No, Old Debe will bring you back to your family."

When I saw Old Debe, he asked me what was wrong. I said, "What is Besa doing to me? If he doesn't want me, why doesn't he just end it completely? I've seen for a long time that he doesn't want me." I thought, "Besa . . . he took me to this faraway village, got me pregnant, and now, is he just going to drop me in this foreign place where none of my people live?"

Later, I said to Besa, "Why did you take me from my people? My brothers are still alive, yet you won't take me to them. You say someone else will. But, why should someone else, a near stranger, take me to my family after you've given me this stomach. I say you should take me to them, take me there and say, 'Here is your sister. Today I am separating from her.' Instead, you're saying you'll just leave me here, with these strangers? I followed you here, to where you were working, because you wanted me to. Now you're just going to leave me? Why are you doing this? Can there be any good in it?"

I continued, "You're the one who came here to work. Yet, you have no money and have no blankets. But when you had no more work and no more money, I worked. I alone, a woman. I entered the work of the European and I alone bought us blankets and a trunk. I alone bought all those things and you covered yourself with my blankets. When you weren't working, you asked people to give you things. How can you leave me here in this foreign place after all that?" He answered, "What work could I have done when there wasn't any to be had?"

I said, "It doesn't matter, because I can see that you will only be here for a few more nights, then you will go. I know that now. But, if you leave me like this today, then tomorrow, after you have gone and have lived with your brother, if you ever decide to come to where I am living, I will refuse you and will no longer be your wife. Because you are leaving me when I am pregnant."

The next morning, early, he tied up his things and left. He packed everything from inside the hut, including all our blankets, and went to his brother's village to live. I thought, "Eh, it doesn't matter, after all. I'll just sit here and let him go." He left me with nothing; the people in the village had to give me blankets to sleep with.

Besa, that man is very bad. He left me hanging like that.

Then one day, just as my heart had said, my body felt like fire and my stomach was in great pain. I told Old Debe's wife, "Eh-hey, today I'm sick." She asked, "Where does it hurt? Do you want some water? Where is the sickness hurting you." I said, "My whole body hurts, it isn't just my stomach." I lay there and felt the pains, rising again and again and again. I thought, "That man certainly has made me feel bad; even today, I'm lying here in great pain."

She looked at my stomach and saw how it was standing out. She said, "Oh, my child. Are you going to drop your pregnancy? What is going to happen? Will you be able to give birth to this child or will it be a miscarriage? Here, there are just the two of us; I don't see anyone who will bring more help to you. If you miscarry, it will be only us two." I said, "Yes, that's fine. If I drop this pregnancy, it will be good. I want to drop it, then I can leave. Because my husband certainly doesn't want it."

We stayed together all day. When the sun was late in the sky, I told her it was time and we went together to the bush. I sat down and soon the baby was born. It was already big, with a head and arms and a little penis; but it was born dead. Perhaps my heart had ruined my pregnancy. I cried, "This man almost ruined me, did he not?" Debe's wife said, "Yes, he destroyed this baby, this baby which came from God. But if God hadn't been here helping you, you also would have died. Because when a child dies in a woman's stomach, it can kill the woman. But God . . . God gave you something beautiful in giving you this baby and although it had death in it, you yourself are alive." We left and walked back to the village. Then I lay down.

After that, I just continued to live there. One day I saw people visiting from Besa's village. I told them to tell him that our marriage had ended. I said, "Tell him that he shouldn't think, even with a part of his heart, that he still has a wife here or that when we meet another time in my village that he might still want me." That's what I said and that's what I thought.

Because he left me there to die.

Soon after, a man named Twi saw me and said, "Did your husband leave you?" I said, "Yes, he left me long ago." He asked, "Then won't you stay with me?" I refused the first time he asked as well as the second and the third. But when he asked the next time, I agreed and we started to live together. I continued to work for the European woman until my work was finished and she told me I could go home. She gave us food for our trip and then all of us—Old Debe, his wife, Twi, and me—traveled the long distance back to where my family was living.

Twi and I lived together in my brothers' village for a long time. Then, one day, Besa came from wherever he had been and said, "Nisa, I've come to take you back with me." I said, "What? What am I like today? Did I suddenly become beautiful? The way I used to be is the way I am now; the way I used to be is what you left behind when you dropped me. So what are you saying? First you drop me in the heart of where the white people live, then you come back and say I should once again be with you?" He said, "Yes, we will pick up our marriage again."

I was stunned! I said, "What are you talking about? This man, Twi, helped bring me back. He's the man who will marry me. You're the one who left me." We talked until he could say nothing more; he was humbled. Finally he said, "You're shit! That's what you are." I said, "I'm shit you say? That's what you thought about me long ago, and I knew it. That's why I told you while we were still living in the East that I wanted you to take me back to my family so we could end our marriage here. But today, I came here myself and you only came afterward. Now I refuse to have anything more to do with you."

That's when Besa brought us to the Tswana headman to ask for a tribal hearing. Once it started, the headman looked at everything. He asked me, "Among all the women who live here, among all those you see sitting around, do you see one who lives with two men?" I said, "No, the women who sit here . . . not one lives with two men; not one among them would I be able to find. I alone, have two. But it was because this man, Besa, mistreated and hurt me. That's why I took this other man, Twi, who treats me well, who does things for me and gives me things to eat." Then I said, "He is also the man I want to marry; I want to drop the other one. Because Besa has no sense. He left me while I was pregnant and the pregnancy almost killed me. This other one is the one I want to marry."

We talked a long time. Finally, the headman told Besa, "I have questioned Nisa about what happened and she has tied you up with her talk; her talk has defeated you, without doubt. Because what she has said about her pregnancy is serious. Therefore, today she and Twi will continue to stay together. After more time passes, I will ask all of you to come back again." Later, Twi and I left and went back to my brothers' village to sleep.

Twi and I continued to live together after that. But later we separated. My older brother caused it, because he wanted Besa to be with me again. He liked him and didn't like Twi. That's why he forced Twi to leave. When Twi saw how much anger both Dau and Besa felt toward him, he became afraid, and finally he left.

I saw what my brother had done and was miserable; I had really liked Twi. I said, "So, this is what you wanted? Fine, but now that you have chased Twi away, I'll have nothing at all to do with Besa." That's when I began to refuse Besa completely. Besa went to the headman and said, "Nisa refuses to be with me." The headman said, "Nisa's been refusing you for a long time. What legal grounds could I possibly find for you now?"

After years of living and having everything that happened to me happen, that's when I started with Bo, the next important man in my life and the one I am married to today.

Besa and I lived separately, but he still wanted me and stayed near me. That man, he didn't hear; he didn't understand. He was without ears, because he still said, "This woman here, Nisa, I won't be finished with her."

People told Bo, "You're going to die. This man, Besa, he's going to kill you. Now, leave Nisa." But Bo refused, "Me . . . I won't go to another hut. I'll just stay with Nisa and even if Besa tries to kill me, I'll still be here and won't leave."

At first, Bo and I sneaked off together, but Besa suspected us; he was very jealous. He accused me all the time. Even when I just went to urinate, he'd say that I had been with Bo. Or when I went for water, he'd say, "Did you just meet your lover?" But I'd say, "What makes you think you can talk to me like that?" He'd say, "Nisa, are you not still my wife? Why aren't we living together? What are you doing?" I'd say, "Don't you have other women or are they refusing you, too? You have others so why are you asking me about what I'm doing?"

One night, Bo and I were lying down inside my hut and as I looked out through the latched-branch door, I saw someone moving about. It was Besa; I was able to see his face. He wanted to catch us, hoping I would feel some remorse and perhaps return to him.

I said, "What? Besa's here! Bo . . . Bo . . . Besa's standing out there." Bo got up; Besa came and stood by the door. I got up and that's when Besa came in and grabbed me. He held onto me and threatened to throw me into the fire. I cursed him as he held me, "Besa-Big-Testicles! Long-Penis! First you left me and drank of women's genitals elsewhere. Now you come back, see me, and say I am your wife?" He pushed me toward the fire, but I twisted my body so I didn't land in it. Then he went after Bo. Bo is weaker and older than Besa, so Besa was able to grab him, pull him outside the hut, and throw him down. He bit him on the shoulder. Bo yelled out in pain.

My younger brother woke and ran to us, yelling, "Curses to your genitals!" He grabbed them and separated them. Bo cursed Besa. Besa cursed Bo, "Curses on your penis!" He yelled, "I'm going to kill you Bo, then Nisa will suffer! If I don't kill you, then maybe I'll kill her so that you will feel pain! Because what you have that is so full of pleasure, I also have. So why does her heart want you and refuse me?"

I yelled at him, "That's not it! It's you! It's who you are and the way you think! This one, Bo, his ways are good and his thoughts are good. But you, your ways are foul. Look, you just bit Bo; that, too, is part of your ways. You also left me to die. And death, that's something I'm afraid of. That's why you no longer have a hold over me. Today I have another who will take care of me well. I'm no longer married to you, Besa. I want my husband to be Bo."

Besa kept bothering me and hanging around me. He'd ask, "Why won't you come to me? Come to me, I'm a man. Why are you afraid of me?" I wouldn't answer. Once Bo answered, "I don't understand why, if you are a man, you keep pestering this woman? Is what you're doing going to do any good? Because I won't leave her. And even though you bit me and your marks are on me, you're the one who is going to move out of the way, not me. I intend to marry her."

Another time I told Bo, "Don't be afraid of Besa. You and I will marry; I'm not going to stay married to him. Don't let him frighten you. Because even if he comes here with arrows, he won't do anything with them." Bo said, "Even if he did, what good would that do? I am also a man and am a master of arrows. The two of us would just strike each other. That's why I keep telling him to let you go; I am the man you are with now."

The next time, Besa came with his quiver full of arrows, saying, "I'm going to get Nisa and bring her back with me." He left with another man and came to me at my village. When he arrived, the sun was high in the sky. I was resting. He said, "Nisa, come, let's go." I said, "What? Is your penis not well? Is it horny?"

People heard us fighting and soon everyone was there, my younger and older brothers as well. Besa and I kept arguing and fighting until, in a rage, I screamed, "All right! Today I'm no longer afraid!" and I pulled off all the skins that were covering me—first one, then another, and finally the leather apron that covered my genitals. I pulled them all off and laid them down on the ground. I cried, "There! There's my vagina! Look, Besa, look at me! This is what you want!"

The man he had come with said, "This woman, her heart is truly far from you. Besa, look. Nisa refuses you totally, with all her heart. She refuses to have sex with you. Your relationship with her is finished. See. She took off her clothes, put them down, and with her genitals is showing everyone how she feels about you. She doesn't want you, Besa. If I were you, I'd finish with her today." Besa finally said, "Eh, you're right. Now I am finished with her."

The two of them left. I took my leather apron, put it on, took the rest of my things and put them on.

Mother! That was just what I did.

Besa tried one last time. He went to the headman again, and when he came back he told me, "The headman wants to see you." I thought, "If he wants to see me, I won't refuse."

When I arrived, the headman said, "Besa says he still wants to continue your marriage." I said, "Continue our marriage? Why? Am I so stupid that I don't know my name? Would I stay in a marriage with a man who left me hanging in a foreign place? If Old Debe and his wife hadn't been there, I would have truly lost my way. Me, stay married to Besa? I can't make myself think of it."

I turned to Besa, "Isn't that what I told you when we were still in the East?" Besa said, "Mm, that's what you said." I said, "And, when you left, didn't I tell you that you were leaving me pregnant with your baby. Didn't I also tell you that?" He said, "Yes, that's what you said." I said, "And didn't I say that I wanted to go with you, that I wanted you to help make our pregnancy grow strong? Didn't I say that and didn't you refuse?" He said, "Yes, you said that." Then I said, "Mm. Therefore, that marriage you say today, in the lap of the headman, should be continued, that marriage no longer exists. Because I am Nisa and today, when I look at you, all I want to do is to throw up. Vomit is the only thing left in my heart for you now. As we sit together here and I see your face, that is all that rises within and grabs me."

The headman laughed, shook his head and said, "Nisa is impossible!" Then he said, "Besa, you had better listen to her. Do you hear what she is saying? She says that you left her while she was pregnant, that she miscarried and was miserable. Today she will no longer take you for her husband." Besa said, "That's because she's with Bo now and doesn't want to leave him. But I still want her and want to continue our marriage."

I said, "What? Besa, can't you see me? Can't you see that I have really found another man? Did you think, perhaps, that I was too old and wouldn't find someone else?" The headman laughed again. "Yes, I am a woman. And that which you have, a penis, I also have something of equal worth. Like the penis of a chief . . . yes, something of a chief is what I have. And its worth is like money. Therefore, the person who drinks from it . . . it's like he's getting money from me. But not you, because when you had it, you just left it to ruin."

The headman said, "Nisa is crazy; her talk is truly crazy now." Then he said, "The two of you sleep tonight and give your thoughts over to this. Nisa, think about all of it again. Tomorrow, I want both of you to come back."

Besa went and lay down. I went and lay down and thought about everything. In the morning, I went to the headman. I felt ashamed by my talk of the night before. I sat there quietly. The headman said, "Nisa, Besa says you should stay married to him." I answered, "Why should he stay married to me when yesterday I held his baby in my stomach and he dropped me. Even God doesn't want me to marry a man who leaves me, a man who takes my blankets when I have small children beside me, a man who forces other people to give me blankets to cover my children with. Tell him to find another woman to marry."

The headman turned to Besa, "Nisa has explained herself. There's nothing more I can see to say. Even you, you can hear that she has defeated you. So, leave Nisa and as I am headman, today your marriage to her is ended. She can now marry Bo."

Besa went to the headman one more time. When he tried to discuss it again, saying, "Please, help me. Give Nisa back to me," the headman said, "Haven't you already talked to me about this? You talked and talked, and the words entered my ears. Are you saying that I have not already decided on this? That I am not an important person? That I am a worthless thing that you do not have to listen to? There is no reason to give Nisa back to you."

I was so thankful when I heard his words. My heart filled with happiness.

Chapter 40

How War Was Ended

Heather Forest

Five hundred years before the first outsiders came to central Alaska, there lived a powerful Yup'ik warrior named Apanugpak. He was renowned by the Yup'ik people for his skill with the harpoon and bow and arrow.

It was a time of great madness and terror among the Yup'ik. Warring groups attacked each other across the tundra. People lived in fear within their subterranean sod houses, unable to safely light fires or to cook food. Each band of warriors had a "smeller" who traveled with them. The "smellers" had such keen noses they could sense even one particle of smoke in the pristine air of the cold tundra and direct the warriors to the source of the fire. People were cold, hungry, and afraid.

It came to pass that one day Apanugpak had a vision. In the vision he saw houses in villages everywhere vanishing into the sky as curling wisps of black smoke. He saw a crimson lake of blood, made from the dripping wounds of slain warriors. As he gazed at these strange sights, Apanugpak, the bravest of warriors, was struck with terror. He trembled as he watched the ghosts of dead warriors slowly rise up to do battle with the living.

At that moment, Apanugpak knew that war was futile. No side could win, for as warriors killed more and more people, the vast army of ghosts would continue to increase. Like memories of horror driving people to revenge, the ghosts of war would vanquish the living and cause great suffering to continue endlessly. Apanugpak knew then that war must end.

He was the most respected of all the fierce warriors. People were surprised when he held up his harpoon and his bow and arrows and said, "These things were created to help us hunt for food, not to cause death to each other. I will not use these tools to fight people any longer." When Apanugpak, the greatest warrior, put down his weapons, all the others followed. The time of madness was over. The killing was finished.

Discord between people found a different expression. People created new kinds of contests. Instead of killing each other in battle, warring bands began to compete energetically with each other in singing contests, dancing contests, and insulting contests. Colorful gatherings rich in music, movement, and pointed, clever ›rds settled disputes.

m Heather Forest, *Wisdom Tales from Around the World* (August House 1996), 125–126.

Peace prevailed and people were able to light their hearth fires again. The sweet smell of savory food, cooking in subterranean homes, signaled the return of sanity to the land of ice and cold.

       —A Tale from North American Arctic–Central Yup'ik Eskimo

Further Comments

1. Throughout Part 4, we ask how the attitudes and assumptions of non-U.S. cultures differs from ours—and what the consequences of these differences are. For instance, if the United States were to implement the belief system described by Bonta in his article on peaceful societies, how would the United States have to change? Certainly there would have to be attitudinal changes, but would there be institutional changes as well? In what ways are the premises of our legal and governing systems in conflict with the worldview that Bonta describes? As Parts 2 and 3 illustrate, U.S. culture encompasses many subcultures. In what ways are the belief systems of these ethnic, racial, religious subcultures more like or less like the belief systems of these peaceful societies?

2. The Salem, Abu-Nimer, and Gurevitch pieces offer interesting juxtapositions of differing cultural assumptions—Arab to Western, Jewish to Christian, Jewish to Arab—all played out in a Middle Eastern context. Salem's essay reminds us of one of the messages from Nader and Cobb and Rifkin in Part 1, that one's attitudes about conflict can in part be shaped by political purposes and orientation. It also might be interesting to revisit the constructs described in Part 1, such as individualism versus collectivism or high context versus low context, to see if they can be helpful in explaining these differing cultural assumptions about conflict.

Marc Howard Ross and others have written extensively about ethnic conflict.[1] The piece here illustrates Ross's interest in trying to explain its causes, which, given the various tragic ethnic conflicts around the world, continues to be an important and urgent pursuit. Louk Hagendoorn has discussed three explanations for negative ethnic attitudes: (1) the anthropologically oriented explanation is that negative attitudes between ethnic groups are the result of cultural misunderstandings; (2) the sociologically oriented explanation is that negative attitudes between ethnic groups reflect a struggle for power; and (3) the social-psychological explanation, illustrated by Ross's writing, is that ethnocentricism is the inevitable consequence of the fact that people evaluate their own and other groups in order to define their identity.[2]

Others have focused on how to resolve these disputes and move toward peace. Louise Diamond's work is applicable. She describes a five-step process for what she calls the "heroic journey for conflict transformation": (1) the Source—identifying the inner source of our motivations, ideals, values, and inspirations; (2) the Quest—to begin to actualize our ideal by making transparent our intention for the journey in relation to our vision for the future; (3) the Test—meeting the immediate challenges from forces opposed to any changes in the status quo, including confronting the root cause, system dynamics, the pain and anger, the history, and the differences between our and others' perceptions; (4) the Shift—moving away from a cycle of mutual blaming and introducing responsibility sharing, letting go, and reconciliation; and (5) the Renewal—reframing, re-envisioning, creative problem solving, action, and commitment.[3]

3. Considerable research has been directed at the concept of "face," as summarized by both Stella Ting-Toomey[4] and Steven Wilson.[5] In discussing its role in negotiation (and referring to Erving Goffman's work), Wilson describes face as "the positive value that individuals attach to their situated identities" and "facework" as individuals' actions to make whatever they are doing consistent with face. Scholars have studied tactics that threaten face, situational features that increase concern about face, and effects of face-saving concerns on negotiation outcomes. Some have considered whether there are gender differences involved in "face."[6] Some argue that concepts of face are universal, while others question that conclusion. David Augsburger also has related face to concepts of shame and guilt, honor and apology—and has offered numerous cross-cultural examples and stories.[7]

4. John Kohls and Paul Buller explore a model for resolving ethical dilemmas in cross-cultural business decision making.[8] They propose the following factors as relevant:

> (i) Centrality: Are the values implicated central to the manager's culture or central to the manager's understanding of what is really important in life (core values) or at the other end are the values are important, but much less so because they are less central (peripheral values)?
>
> (ii) Social Consensus: Are the values universally shared in the foreign country or on the other end are they rarely valued in the culture?
>
> (iii) Manager/Corporate Influence: Does the manager or company have complete control over the situation or do they have no ability to change the situation?
>
> (iv) Urgency: How quickly or how slowly must something be done in the situation? If urgent, strategies of avoidance, force, or accommodation may be required. If there is more time, education, negotiation, or collaboration are more viable strategies.

5. The business and employment laws of a particular country also reflect its cultural values. Anita Bernstein, for instance, has written about how sexual harassment laws in the United States and in European countries differ.[9]

Teaching Ideas

1. The film *The Story of Qiu Ju* (1993) depicts a modern-day dispute in a Chinese village involving a village family who believe they were unfairly harmed by the "chief" of the village. The story describes the dispute resolution processes (both informal and formal) that ultimately prove inadequate for satisfying the parties' real needs. It also provides the opportunity to discuss the role of face and the traditional concepts of Chinese law explained in your readings.

After viewing the film, consider these questions:

- How would each party describe the dispute? What interests are at stake? Who or what would be affected by how the dispute was treated and resolved?
- In what ways were the key characters susceptible to "losing face" or "gaining face"? Were the different types of "face" relevant here?
- In what ways did the cultural context shape the conflict or its resolution?
- In what way was the formal dispute resolution system effective or ineffective? What were the system's goals, and how did they complement or conflict with the parties' goals?
- If the dispute were analyzed and resolved in a way that was consistent with the traditional Chinese conceptions of law described in your reading, what would be the analysis and resolution?
- What parallels do you see between the Chinese system depicted in the film and the American system?

2. Nisa's narrative can be used for case analysis and the basis for reflecting on many of the issues raised in this reader. From Part 1, for instance, consider how you would use the constructs individualism and collectivism to explain what occurs. How would Cobb and Rifkin analyze the narrative in terms of neutrality, power, and dominance? From Parts 2 and 3, in what ways might Gilligan, Grillo, and Ward predict how Nisa and Besa might interpret their relationship, their dispute, and its resolution differently? Drawing from the readings on cultural relativism by Higgins, Coleman, and Donaldson in Parts 2, 3, and 4, how would different cultures (for instance, mainstream U.S. or Gypsy culture) evaluate Nisa and Besa's conduct, levels of social impropriety, and viable solutions?

3. Finally, a range of resources is available for simulations and other exercises, as well as self-assessment instruments relevant to cross-cultural dispute resolution. For example, consider Kenneth Cushner and Richard Brislin's book *Improving Intercultural Interactions: Modules for Cross-Cultural Training Programs*, volume 2.[10] The Intercultural Press also offers various relevant books and resource materi-

als,[11] and the Institute for Intercultural Communication offers relevant summer conferences.

NOTES

1. E.g., Marc Howard Ross, *The Culture of Conflict: Interpretations and Interests in Comparative Perspective* (New Haven: Yale University Press, 1993); Mohamed Rabie, *Conflict Resolution and Ethnicity* (Westport, Conn.: Praeger, 1994); Walter Morris-Hale, *Conflict and Harmony in Multi-Ethnic Societies: An International Perspective* (New York: P. Lang, 1996); Joseph V. Montville, ed., *Conflict and Peacemaking in Multiethnic Societies* (Lexington, Mass: Lexington Books, 1990); Rodolfo Stavenhagen, *The Ethnic Question: Conflicts, Development, and Human Rights* (Tokyo, Japan: United Nations University Press, 1990).

2. Louk Hagendoorn, "Ethnic Categorization and Out Group Exclusion: Cultural Values and Social Stereotypes in the Construction of Ethnic Hierarchies," 16(1) *Ethnic and Racial Studies* 26–51 (1993).

3. Louise Diamond, *Beyond Win/Win: The Heroic Journey of Conflict Transformation*, Occasional Paper No. 4, rev. ed. Institute for Multi-Track Diplomacy (January 1996).

4. Stella Ting-Toomey and Beth-Ann Cocroft, "Face and Facework: Theoretical and Research Issues," in Stella Ting-Toomey, ed., *The Challenge of Facework: Cross-Cultural and Interpersonal Issues* (Albany: State University of New York Press, 1994), 307–342.

5. Steven R. Wilson, "Face and Facework in Negotiation," in Linda L. Putnam and Michael E. Roloff, eds., *Communication and Negotiation* (Newbury Park, CA: Sage, 1992), 176–201.

6. Susan B. Shimanoff, "Gender Perspectives on Facework: Simplistic Stereotypes vs. Complex Realities," in Stella Ting-Toomey, ed., *The Challenge of Facework: Cross-Cultural and Interpersonal Issues.* (Albany: State University of New York Press, 1994).

7. In David W. Augsburger, *Conflict Mediation across Cultures: Pathways and Patterns* (Louisville: Westminster/John Knox Press, 1992), 73–112.

8. John Kohls and Paul Buller, "Resolving Cross-Cultural Ethical Conflict: Exploring Alternative Strategies," 13 *Journal of Business Ethics* 31–37 (1994).

9. Anita Bernstein, "Law, Culture, and Harassment," 142 *University of Pennsylvania Law Review* 1227 (1994). Corporate goverance rules also differ: see, e.g., Robert W. Lightfoot, "Note on Corporate Governance Systems: The United States, Japan, and Germany," Note No. 9-292-012, Harvard Business School (1992).

10. Kenneth Cushner and Richard Brislin, *Improving Intercultural Interactions: Modules for Cross-Cultural Training*, vol. 2 (Newbury Park, CA: Sage, 1997).

11. P.O. Box 700, Yarmouth, Maine 04096; 800-370-2665.

Index

Abu-Nimer, Mohammed, 203, 230
Ackerman, Douglas, 195
Africa, 38, 205, 295
African Americans, 88, 120, 152, 163, 191
Alaska, 302
Alford, William, 264
alternative dispute resolution (ADR), as coercive, 42
Akutagawa, Ryunosuke, 3, 31
Amish, 212, 214, 216
Anabaptist peoples (Mennonites, Amish), 214
anti-essentialism, 109, 113
apology, different views toward, 249
Arab (*see also* Middle East), 230, 245; view of conflict resolution, 220
Asian Americans, 88, 152, 163, 182, 192
Auerbach, Jerold S., 41, 194
Avruch, Kevin, 3, 7
Azuma, Eiichiro, 194

Banks, Taunya Lovell, 129, 163
Bartlett, Katharine, 124
Bell, Derrick, 192
Bell, Maureen Anne, 205, 266
Bem, Sandra, 66
Bernstein, Anita, 305
biblical verses, 207, 249
Black, Peter W., 3, 7
Bonta, Bruce D., 203, 207
Brislin, Richard, 306
Buller, Paul, 305
Burma, 167
Butterton, Glenn R., 204, 261

care. *See* ethic of care
Carleton, Jennifer Nutt, 195
Carroll, Raymonde, 9
Central America, applying elicitive approach, 20
Chamallas, Martha, 64, 93
Chanock, Martin, 39
Chew, Pat K., 45, 313
Chicago, 169
Chicano perspective, regarding tort law, 94
China, 306; concepts of fa and the "rule of law," 262; Confucian influences, 264; "face," 204;

li, 261; proverb from, 5; traditional concepts, 252
Christianity, 38, 141; as coercive, 41
circle of "understanding" and "not understanding," 241
coalition-building, 163, 193
Cobb, Sara, 3, 24, 304
coercion, use of, 38, 80, 115
Coleman, Doriane Lambelet, 130, 182
collectivism and individualism, 52
conflict: as normal, 211; assuming responsibility for, 167; struggle as part of conflict resolution, 221; world view of, 216
conflict and culture, 56; introduction to, 3; pioneers in the field, 56; research trends, 56
conflict resolution strategies: "heroic journey for conflict transformation," 304; in ethnic disputes, 193; in Middle East, 234; in peaceful societies, 209; political structures, 215; power of not understanding, 241; punishment, 212; use of armies, 213
core values, 286
corporate ethics and codes of conduct, 288
cultural analysis, 8; as applied to everyday disputes, 58; balancing, 185; core values, 286; elicitive approach, 18; high context versus low context, 46; prescriptive model, 18; universalism versus cultural relativism, 110
cultural defense, 182; domestic violence among ethnic groups, 196
"cultural map," 58
cultural relativism, 121, 196, 205; business disputes, 205; cultural defense, 182; guiding principles, 285; human rights, 109; international business, 283
culture: constructs for comparison, 46, 52, 57, 58; meaning of, 7, 56; of peacefulness, 207
Cushner, Kenneth, 306

Delgado, Richard, 121
Diamond, Louise, 304
Donaldson, Thomas, 205, 283
dress as issue: in Gypsy culture, 268; in religious dispute, 100
Druze, 230
Duffy, Karen G., 88

economic development, as factor in conflict resolution, 224, 290

elicitive approach, in cultural analysis, 18

Ellickson, Robert, 56

Erdmans, Mary Patrice, 129, 169, 194

ethical dilemmas, resolving, 285, 305

ethic of care, 81; and African Americans, 120, 147; consequences of, 82; gender differences, 74

ethnic and racial conflict, 141, 192, 204, 236; Black and Asian, 163; Black and Brown, 192; Black-Korean conflict, 152; coalition-building, 163, 193; group insularity, 164; toward resolutions, 193; varying constructions, 159; within an ethnic group, 169, 194

ethnicity: as factor in conflict, 237; differences in outcomes and satisfaction with dispute resolution processes, 91; differences in types of mediated conflicts, 88

ethnicity and conflict: challenges of multicultural society, 191; culture of racism, 133; further commentary, 191; images in picture books, 192; in film, 163, 198; introduction to, 129

ethnic politics, 236

fables and proverbs, 5, 45, 131, 163, 167, 302

"face," 204, 252, 305

feminist politics, global politics and the appeal of essentialism, 112

feminist theory, 64, 111, 120, 122

films, used to analyze conflict and culture, 163, 198, 306

Finnish Roma, 276

force, in conflict resolution, 213

Forest, Heather, 302

Fung, Margaret, 183

Gadlin, Howard, 129, 133

gender: dangers of generalizing differences, 120; differences in law school experience, 124; differences in moral reasoning, 74; differences in outcomes and satisfaction with dispute resolution processes, 91; differences in tort law, 93; differences in types of mediated conflicts, 88; *gender* and *sex* as terms, 68; gendering dispute resolution processes, 120, 124; Gypsy view of role of women, 268, 278; issues in cultural relativism, 109, 182; political processes and dominant stories, 24; process dangers for women, 80; regulation in religion, 97; as social construction, 67

gender and conflict: introduction to, 63; the necessity of studying relationship, 65; power imbalances, 122; role of power, 70; psychological research, 95

Gentile, Mary, 56, 121, 198

Gilligan, Carol, 63, 74, 81, 120, 124

global perspectives, introduction to, 203

Golden Rule, 287

Greece, 23

Grillo, Trina, 63, 80

Gronfors, Martti, 205, 276

Grosch, James W., 64, 88

Gunning, Isabelle, 121, 191

Gurevitch, Z. D., 204, 241

Gwartney-Gibbs, Patricia, 121

Gypsies (Roma), 204, 266, 276; blood feuding, 276; Finish Roma, 272; impurity (*marime*), 267; justice system, 272; role of mother, 278; sexual taboos, 279

Hagendoorn, Louk, 304

Hall, Edward, 14, 48

Hammer, Mitchell, 56

Harlins-Du case, 152

harmony and peace, views toward, 221

harmony models and ideology, as tools of control, 38

Hawaiians, 176

Hermann, Michele, 64, 91

Higgins, Tracy E., 64, 109, 122

high-context versus low-context cultures, 46

Hispanics, 88, 94, 192

Hofstede, Geert, 57

Ho'oponopono, 176; as compared to mediation, 180

Hsien Chin Hu, 204, 252

Huber, Marg, 195

Hui, C. Harry, 52

human rights, 109

immigrants, 194; cultural defense, 182; Polish Americans, 169

individualism and collectivism, 52; antecedents and consequences, 54

intellectual property rights in China, 261

intercultural encounters, 11

Israel, 230, 245

Israeli-Arab conflict (*see also* Middle East), 245

James, Teresa, 195

Janoff, Sandra, 124

Japan: alternative perspectives of narrative, 31; as high-context culture, 50

Jewish-Arab conflict, 204, 245

Jewish congregation, dispute over gender issues, 97

justice: African Americans, 142; Gypsies, 271; in moral reasoning, 74

Keashly, Loraleigh, 64, 95

Kluckhorn, Florence, 57

Kochman, Thomas, 14, 135, 191

Kohlberg, Lawrence, 75

Kohls, John, 305

Kolb, Deborah, 120
Korean Americans, 152, 191; culture of, 157
kris, 272
!Kung, 211, 295
Kwan, Leonard Ke'ala, 180

Lach, Denise, 121
Ladakh, 213
Lawrence, Charles R., III, 138, 249
Le Baron, Michelle, 56, 195
Lederach, John Paul, 3, 17, 203
LeResche, Diane, 191
Levi, Deborah L., 251
li, 261
lien, 253
Locke, John, 228
Los Angeles, 152
low-context versus high-context cultures, 46

Mabry, Cynthia, 191
MacDonald, Margaret Read, 167
MacKinnon, Catharine, 83
Malay Peninsula, 207
marime, 268
marital dispute, 295
Matsuda, Mari J., 204, 249
McCusker, Christopher, 52
McIntosh, Peggy, 139
mediation, 24, 88, 91; and ho'oponopono, 180; as political process, 24; risks for women, 80; structure as political process, 26; vocabulary as political process, 28
mediator, as political participant, 25
mehitzah dispute, 102–5
Menkel-Meadow, Carrie, 82, 191
Merry, Sally Engle, 84
Mexican American proverb, 131
Meyer, Manu Aluli, 130, 176
Micronesia, 249
Middle East, 203, 230, 245; view of conflict, 234
Miller, Judi Beinstein, 63, 65
Mississippi Masala, 163
moral reasoning: African Americans, 141; cognitive obstacles, 198; gender differences, 74

Nader, Laura, 3, 38, 304
Narayan, Uma, 121
narrative processes, dominant stories, 24
narratives: African Americans, 141; alternative perspectives, 31
Native Americans, 88, 194, 195; Hawaiian peacemaking, 195; Navajo peacemaking, 194
Native Canadians, 195
Navajo, 194
New Mexico, 91
Nisa's narrative, 295, 306
North America, as low-context culture, 47

Northrup, Terrell, 122
Nunn, Kenneth B., 44

Olczak, Paul V., 88

Park, Kyeyoung, 129, 152
peaceful societies, 207; strategies of conflict resolution, 209
Pescosolido, Bernice, 192
Piatt, Bill, 192
Polish Americans, 169
political processes, in mediation, 24
political structures, in conflict resolution, 215
Porter, Robert, 195
postmodernism: and conflict, 225; as reflected in literature research, 56
Potts, Jim, 195
power: in mediation process as political tool, 30; role of power in gender and conflict issues, 70, 122
prescriptive model, in cultural analysis, 18
punishment and ostracism, in conflict resolution, 212
Putnam, Linda, 120

Qiu Ju, The Story of, 306

race and conflict, introduction to, 129
race and ethnicity, construction by Korean immigrants, 155
race in contrast to culture, 136
racial conflict. *See* ethnic and racial conflict
racism, 137, 192; alternative perspectives, 139; rituals of racism, 133
relativism. *See* cultural relativism
religion: a factor in conflict, 38, 172; conflict within, 97
responsibility: for conflict, 167; for conflict resolution, 302
review of literature, 56
Rifkin, Janet, 3, 24, 304
Rimonte, Nilda, 187, 189
Roscoe Pound Conference, 42
Rose, Carol, 120
Ross, Marc Howard, 204, 217, 236, 304
Rubin, Jeffrey Z., 3, 15

Salem, Paul E., 203, 220
Sander, Frank E. A., 3, 15
Savage, Cynthia, 57
Schneider, Elizabeth, 120
Schuck, Peter, 56
Semai, 207, 218
Sered, Susan, 98
sex as distinguished from *gender*, 67–68
Shook, Victoria, 180
Shostak, Marjorie, 205, 295

shunning and ostracism, 189
Silbey, Susan S., 84
Somali immigrant, 182
Stack, Carol, 120
Steele, Claude, 139
stereotyping, 197; benefits and risks, 15
Summerfield, Ellen, 198
Swaziland, 40

Taylor, Anita, 63, 65
teaching ideas, 58, 124, 197, 306
Thailand, 167
Ting-Toomey, Stella, 4, 46, 305
tort law, gender bias in, 93
Triandis, Harry C., 4, 52
Tzu, Lao, 5

universalism, 110
utilitarianism, Western and Arab views toward, 223

Valdes, Franciso, 193
Villarreal, Carlos, 94

vocabulary and dialogue: becoming issue in religious dispute, 99; obscuring political processes, 28; on not understanding, 243
Volpp, Leti, 56

Ward, Janie Victoria, 129, 141
Washington, 98
Weaver, Gary, 56
Western values, in contrast to others, 287
Western view of conflict, 208; and suffering, 223; in comparison with others, 203; in contrast to Arab view, 220; in contrast to Middle Eastern views, 230

Weyrauch, Walter Otto, 205, 266
Whites, role of, in ethnic conflict, 156, 164
Wilson, Steven, 305

Yamamoto, Eric, 192, 193
Yazzie, Robert, 194
Young, Iris, 122

Zuckerman, Phil, 64, 97

About the Editor

Pat K. Chew is a professor at the University of Pittsburgh School of Law. She teaches dispute resolution in various cultural contexts, corporate law, employment law, and international law particularly dealing with China. She also recently taught on the Semester-at-Sea program, a university that sails around the world while studying and visiting countries in South America, Africa, and Asia.

Raised in the multi-cultural border city of El Paso, Texas, she went on to complete her undergraduate psychology and communications degree at Stanford University. At the University of Texas at Austin, she received graduate degrees in law and in education psychology, and did graduate work in business.

Professor Chew is the author of several books in business law and has written numerous articles on dispute resolution in international contexts, ethnicity and race issues, and business and employment law topics. She has made presentations both in the United States and abroad. Most recently, she has spoken about diversity issues in the dispute resolution process.